Communion with the Triune God

Princeton Theological Monograph Series

K. C. Hanson, Charles M. Collier, D. Christopher Spinks,
and Robin A. Parry, Series Editors

Recent volumes in the series:

Koo Dong Yun
*The Holy Spirit and Ch'i (Qi):
A Chiological Approach to Pneumatology*

Stanley S. MacLean
*Resurrection, Apocalypse, and the Kingdom of Christ:
The Eschatology of Thomas F. Torrance*

Brian Neil Peterson
*Ezekiel in Context: Ezekiel's Message Understood in Its Historical
Setting of Covenant Curses and Ancient Near
Eastern Mythological Motifs*

Amy E. Richter
Enoch and the Gospel of Matthew

Maeve Louise Heaney
Music as Theology: What Music Says about the Word

Eric M. Vail
Creation and Chaos Talk: Charting a Way Forward

David L. Reinhart
*Prayer as Memory: Toward the Comparative Study of Prayer
as Apocalyptic Language and Thought*

Peter D. Neumann
Pentecostal Experience: An Ecumenical Encounter

Ashish J. Naidu
*Transformed in Christ:
Christology and the Christian Life in John Chrysostom*

Communion with the Triune God

The Trinitarian Soteriology of T. F. Torrance

DICK O. EUGENIO

◈PICKWICK *Publications* · Eugene, Oregon

COMMUNION WITH THE TRIUNE GOD
The Trinitarian Soteriology of T. F. Torrance

Princeton Theological Monograph Series 204

Copyright © 2014 Dick O. Eugenio. All rights reserved. Except for brief quotations in critical publications or reviews, no part of this book may be reproduced in any manner without prior written permission from the publisher. Write: Permissions, Wipf and Stock Publishers, 199 W. 8th Ave., Suite 3, Eugene, OR 97401.

Pickwick Publications
An Imprint of Wipf and Stock Publishers
199 W. 8th Ave., Suite 3
Eugene, OR 97401

www.wipfandstock.com

ISBN 13: 978-1-62564-036-9

Cataloguing-in-Publication data:

Eugenio, Dick O.

    Communion with the Triune God : the trinitarian soteriology of T. F. Torrance / Dick O. Eugenio.

    xxii + 242 pp. ; 23 cm. Includes bibliographical references and index.

    Princeton Theological Monograph Series 204

    ISBN 13: 978-1-62564-036-9

    1. Torrance, Thomas F. (Thomas Forsyth), 1913–2007. 2. Salvation—Christianity. 3. Trinity. I. Series. II. Title.

BT220 E943 2014

Manufactured in the U.S.A.

All biblical quotations, unless otherwise indicated, are from the New Revised Standard Version of the Bible, copyright © 1989, the Division of Christian Education of the National Council of the Churches of Christ in the United States of America. Used by permission. All rights reserved.

To *Mary Ann* and *Heloise*,
the two ladies of my life

Contents

Foreword ix

Preface xiii

Abbreviations xvii

Introduction xix

1 Scientific, Evangelical, and Trinitarian Soteriology 1

2 The Grace of Our Lord Jesus Christ 30

3 The Love of God the Father 83

4 The Communion of the Holy Spirit 115

5 Communion with the Triune God 156

Summary and Conclusions 205

Bibliography 215

Index 239

Foreword

It is commonly said that the last seventy years or so have seen a Trinitarian revival and the credit for initiating this usually goes to Karl Barth and Karl Rahner. It is certainly true that the doctrine of the Trinity suffered an eclipse during the high point of Enlightenment modernity. "Religion" was reduced to the cardinal points that would be accepted universally by all "reasonable" people irrespective of culture, tradition, and background: that there was one God, the designer of the universe, that he was the source and guarantee of the physical and moral order, and that he would reward the good and punish the wicked in the hereafter. All the great religions of the world, including Christianity, could be boiled down to this one central affirmation now being set forth as the world was finally and joyfully "enlightened" by this oh-so-reasonable creed of Deism. That God was a Trinity, that one of the persons of the Trinity became incarnate in Jesus Christ, and that Christ died to make atonement for the sins of the world—these assertions peculiar to the Christian tradition could be set aside. At best they were marginalized in the deistic faith of many who still thought of themselves as part of the church. The atonement was a piece of primitive superstition, the incarnation was some kind of myth, and the doctrine of the Trinity was a self-contradictory conundrum.

In the nineteenth century, as deism collapsed into atheism, Hegel seemed to offer a revived Trinitarianism. But, of course, the doctrines of the Incarnation and the Trinity were merely illustrative of the way in which the Absolute Spirit had realized itself in creating its opposite, creation, and then in realizing itself in entering into a new synthesis with creation through the process of world history. Such a confusion of the generation of the Son with the creation of the world had not been seriously mooted in Christian thought since before Nicaea. Meanwhile traditional Catholics and Protestants continued to affirm their belief in the Trinity, but the doctrine seemed to be rather esoteric, abstract, confusing, and irrelevant to the life and mission of the church.

Given then that Hegel was reinterpreting the doctrine of the Trinity as an illustration of his own philosophy, and that orthodox Christians clung to it merely as a badge of orthodoxy, it appears to be true that the real revival of the *church* doctrine of the Trinity did not come till the mid-twentieth century. Barth re-formulated it in terms of the concept so central to the church's response to the epistemological challenges of the Enlightenment—revelation. "God reveals himself as Lord." And so this one God is the Revealed, the Revealer, and the resulting Revelation. Rahner tackled the problem that the doctrine of the Trinity seemed to be irrelevant by questioning the divorce in Christian theology between the "Immanent Trinity" and the "Economic Trinity." Rahner's "rule" (as it was called) insisted that the Immanent Trinity *is* the Economic Trinity and the Economic Trinity *is* the Immanent Trinity. But that was rather ambiguous. Did this mean that God did not exist as Immanent Trinity apart from the world? Another Catholic theologian, Catherine Mowry LaCugna, did not hesitate to affirm that that was what we had to say to end the irrelevancy of the doctrine of the Trinity. But the ghost of Hegel seemed to be hanging around.

There was another line of development. Rahner criticized the tendency to make the unity of God more fundamental than God's being as the Trinity. But this line was taken further by a reaction against what was seen to be the "single subject" God of Barth or Rahner. Was this not still influenced by Augustine in its overemphasis on the *one* God? They were not then Trinitarian enough! The development of the "social analogy" for the Trinity has therefore been presented as a correction to the whole Augustinian tradition of the West in which (it has been said) Augustine's "psychological analogy" has been too dominant. The resulting strong emphasis on the unity was said to be characteristic of the Latin West (according to the de Régnon thesis), while the Greek East began instead from the three.

The "social analogy," which has been seen as the counter to this Augustinian "psychological analogy" and the strong Western bias to unity, was actually introduced at the same time as Barth's revival of the Trinity, by some rather forgotten Anglicans, Leonard Hodgson and Charles Lowry. Hodgson speaks of God as a "divine society" and Lowry goes so far as to refer to the three persons as "three centres of consciousness." But the so-called "social analogy" only came to the centre of discussion as similar perspectives on the doctrine of the Trinity were put forward by Jürgen Moltmann and John Zizioulas. Moltmann's Trinitarian theology began in truly Lutheran fashion as a *theologia crucis*. If Moltmann's Trinitarian theology makes the Trinity relevant by portraying the God who suffers with us, Zizioulas makes the doctrine relevant by his account of how the Cappadocian theologians were the source of a new ontology of personhood. Our understanding of personal relationships can be seen to be grounded in Trinitarian theology. The unity of the Three Persons is not to be understood by some Greek metaphysical idea of impersonal substance (*ousia*), but their unity as the one God consists in their inter-personal communion (*koinonia*). But Zizioulas's doctrine contrasts strongly with Moltmann in that, while they both accentuate the distinctions among the persons, Moltmann moved increasingly under the influence of his political and social egalitarianism to emphasize the equality of the Three and to reject any kind of precedence or order.

But more recently, the various differing understandings of the "social analogy" have come under fire. While philosophical theologians such as Cornelius Plantinga and Richard Swinburne are sympathetic, others such as Michael Rae and Brian Leftow have been critical. Among other leading theologians, Colin Gunton (sympathetic to Zizioulas but not to Moltmann) wrestled with the relation of Trinitarian doctrine to the doctrine of creation, and Robert Jenson has wrestled with the relation of the Triune God to time. But Stephen Holmes has argued that the contemporary "revival" of Trinitarian theology has not been a "revival" at all, but is in fact quite at variance with the Trinitarian theology of the Fathers.

In this context, the Trinitarian Theology of Thomas F. Torrance deserves the attention of the church. Far from devising a doctrine of the Trinity crafted to speak to contemporary debates (reason and revelation, relevance to the life of the church, God and suffering, human personhood), Torrance's theology begins with a deep understanding of the Fathers. It is not that he simply recovers their thought in the supposedly detached and neutral way of the historian, but neither does he begin from contemporary issues. He begins with the Trinitarian thought of the Fathers, not read superficially in order to find support for contemporary causes, but read *theologically* in order to discern their deep structure and inner logic. This Trinitarian theology is then seen to speak powerfully to the church in every age, and particularly the contemporary church.

A number of major accounts of Torrance's theology have now been published by Alister McGrath, Elmer Colyer, Paul Molnar, and others, and an increasing stream of doctoral theses is examining different aspects of his thought. This book is based on a first-class thesis in which Dick Osita Eugenio shows the profound coherence and integration between Torrance's doctrine of the Trinity and his doctrine of salvation. These two

Foreword

areas of Christian theology are often held apart, but Torrance has a deeply soteriological doctrine of the Trinity and a deeply Trinitarian soteriology. While Trinitarian theology no doubt has much to say to concerns about reason and revelation, the mission of the church, human personhood and personal relations, God's relation to the creation, and the suffering of the world, Torrance's exposition of the doctrine relates it primarily and profoundly to the gospel. This book makes a significant contribution not only to our understanding of Torrance's thought but to the contemporary need of the church to grasp at a deeper level how the salvation of the world is being accomplished by the Triune God, and to live in alignment with the mission of the One who is eternally Father, Son, and Holy Spirit.

T. A. Noble
Professor of Theology,
Nazarene Theological Seminary, Kansas City;
Senior Research Fellow in Theology,
Nazarene Theological College, Manchester

Preface

SOTERIOLOGY HAS ALWAYS FASCINATED ME. I RECALL THAT EVEN AS AN undergraduate student, my most interesting conversations and debates with others revolved around this theme. As one who has received his theological education from Wesleyan institutions, discussions about and around the *ordo salutis* were an anticipated part of classroom interactions and informal conversations. And although the Calvinism-Wesleyanism soteriological division has degenerated to a cliché a long time ago in my theological and ministerial life, I am not surprised that it is still receiving increasing scholarly attention. There will always be new nuances that will be discovered, which in turn will open up new discussions. This immense assiduity to soteriology is bound to continue, so long as the gospel is directed to humanity and so long as theologizing desires to be relevant in the life of the church. History reveals that the greatest theological revolutions that transpired within the two millennia of Christianity—such as the formation of the creeds during the patristic era and the Reformation of the sixteenth century—were about the doctrine of salvation. Soteriological formulation will always remain central in both the reflective and practical dimensions of the life of the church.

My enduring enthrallment with soteriology received even greater impetus after attending a class at Nazarene Theological College, Manchester in 2007 that sketched the doctrine of holiness in light of the being and work of the Triune God. To me, such a procedure generates important biblical and theological implications that provide answers to the gaps created by merely pragmatic and experience-based formulation of the doctrine. Immediately, this exhilarating discovery planted doubts in my heart whether pursuing what I originally planned to write for my doctoral thesis—i.e., a comparison of John Wesley and Karl Rahner on their theologies of grace—remained the best way forward. I am now very pleased that I followed the dictates of my heart, for my interaction with Thomas F. Torrance's Trinitarian soteriology, as I anticipated, provided exhilarating new insights into what it means to be saved.

Preface

This project would never have materialized without those who sponsored my post-graduate studies, including the Church of the Nazarene—Asia-Pacific Region, Asia-Pacific Nazarene Theological Seminary, Nazarene Theological College (Manchester), and all other institutions and personalities (some even unknown to me). My special thanks to Dr. Floyd Cunningham, a wonderful *ninong* and friend, for the confidence he has in me. Also, Brooklands Church of the Nazarene has been my church while in Manchester. That I served there as the youth minister while doing my studies also deepens the love I have for the church, its ministries, and its people. I thank the minister, Rev. Karl Stanfield and his family who were always welcoming, and members of the church who were very supportive and caring.

I was blessed to have been under the supervision of Dr. Thomas A. Noble, who, in the midst of his busy-ness, was always prompt in responding to my inquiries and returning my work. He has been extremely helpful from the beginning of my thesis. When finally I submitted my whole draft to him and he said "I will be looking for chaotic features in here," I laughed, but I knew that that was what he was going to do. Also, because he has been a student of Thomas F. Torrance himself, a mystical bond, if I were permitted to say so, mediated through him, between me and the theologian I am writing about is certainly a source of joy. I always jokingly mention at every available opportunity (and will most probably continue to do so) of the "historical succession" that runs from Barth to Torrance to my supervisor to me. All the faculty, staff, and co-students at NTC were also supportive and generous since I came to the UK. The familial bond shared within the community is very special. The faculty were very helpful to me as an international student. And of course to my fellow PhD students and friends who gave me inspiration and companionship, thanks. In the preparation for publication of this monograph, Marie Joy Pring, my student at APNTS, also helped in formatting the final manuscript.

I also thank God for giving me a most understanding wife, companion, ministry partner, encourager, friend, and sponsor, Mary Ann. Her support, patience, and companionship made this journey certainly lighter and more enjoyable. The love, happiness, joy, and laughter we share are antidotes to doubts and discouragements along the way. Our daughter, Heloise, is another angel to me. She is, and will always be, dearly loved. She is the creaturely *vinculum amoris* of my happy family. And most importantly,

Preface

Praise God from whom all blessings flow
Praise Him I, a creature here below
Praise Him above, joining the heavenly hosts
Praise Father, Son, and Holy Ghost. Amen.[1]

---

1. Personalized and revised version of The Doxology, written by Thomas Ken (1637–1711).

Abbreviations

Adel.   Athanasius, *Ad Adelphium*

ANF   *Ante-Nicene Fathers: The Writings of the Fathers down to A.D. 325.* Reprint. Edited by Alexander Robertson and James Dolandson. Peabody, MA: Hendrickson, 2004.

CD   *Church Dogmatics.* Karl Barth. Edited by G. W. Bromiley and T. F. Torrance. Edinburgh: T. & T. Clark, 1956–75.

C. Ar.   Athanasius, *Orationes contra Arianos* (*Orations against the Arians*)

C. Cel.   Origen, *Contra Celcius* (*Against Celcius*)

Cat.   Cyril of Jerusalem, *Catechetical Lectures*

Dec.   Athanasius, *De Decretis* (*Defence of the Nicene Council*)

Haer.   Irenaeus, *Adversus haereses* (*Against Heresies*)

In Ill. Om.   Athanasius, *In Illud Omnia*

Institutes   *Institutes of the Christian Religion.* John Calvin. Edited by John T. McNeill. Translated by Ford Lewis Battles. Louisville: Westminster John Knox, 1960.

NPNF[1]   *Nicene and Post-Nicene Fathers of the Christian Church.* First Series. Edited by Philip Schaff. Reprint. Grand Rapids: Eerdmans, 1980.

NPNF[2]   *Nicene and Post-Nicene Fathers of the Christian Church.* Second Series. Edited by Philip Schaff and Henry Wace. Reprint. Grand Rapids: Eerdmans, 1980.

Ser.   Athanasius, *Ad Serapionem*

Abbreviations

Sp. Sanc.	Basil, *De Spiritu Sancto* (On the Holy Spirit)
Strom.	Clement of Alexandria, *Stromata*
Syn.	Athanasius, *De synodis* (On the Councils of Ariminum and Seleucia)
Trin.	Augustine, *De Trinitate* (On the Holy Trinity)
Ver. rel.	Augustine, *De Vera Religione*

Introduction

ELMER COLYER AND ALISTER MCGRATH EXTOL THOMAS FORSYTH Torrance as one of the premier theologians of the twentieth century, particularly in the light of his voluminous works and contributions on the relationship between science and theology, ecumenism, and trinitarian theology.[2] Torrance was born in West China on August 30, 1913 to missionary parents, which explains his heart for evangelism and evangelizing theology. In 1927, around the time recession hit the world, the family returned to Scotland and Torrance pursued his education in Scotland. At New College, Edinburgh, while doing his Bachelor of Divinity, he studied under Hugh Ross Mackintosh, who introduced him to Karl Barth's theology. In 1937 he won a scholarship that provided him the opportunity to be under Barth's supervision while writing his thesis, later published as *The Doctrine of Grace in the Apostolic Fathers* (1946). It is not an exaggeration to conclude that the lifelong and prominent themes of Torrance's theological *oeuvre*, namely: Trinitarian theology, engagement with science and emphasis on scientific theology, and commitment to patristic theology, were fuelled by his engagement with Barth. In some areas, however, Torrance has surpassed Barth, such as his engagement with the natural sciences, which won him the Templeton Prize for the Progress in Religion in 1978. Torrance died on December 2, 2007, eighteen years after his retirement from New College as the Professor of Christian Dogmatics.[3]

Among Torrance's accomplishments as theologian, philosopher of science, and churchman is his consistent trinitarian theology. As such, he deserves Paul Molnar's assessment of him as a "theologian of the Trinity."[4] The doctrine of the Trinity not only permeates Torrance's large theological

---

2. Colyer, *How To Read*, 11; McGrath, *An Intellectual Biography*, xi.

3. For Torrance's biography and introduction, see McGrath, *An Intellectual Biography*; Hesselink, "A Pilgrimage in the School of Christ," 49–64; and Noble, "Thomas Forsyth Torrance," 823–24. See also the several eulogies and recollections in *Participatio* 1 (2009) 6–48.

4. Molnar, *Theologian of the Trinity* (2009).

Introduction

corpus, but is the consistent "ground and grammar" of his theology.[5] Even his ecumenical engagement with other theological traditions is fuelled by this biblical and patristic doctrine, particularly evident in the two volumes of the *Theological Dialogue between Orthodox and Reformed Churches*. It is not an exaggeration to say that as a *Christian theologian,* the doctrine of the Trinity is the *canon* by which Torrance engages theological traditions (including his own), and approaches and formulates his whole theological program. As Eric Flett writes, "no particular feature of Torrance's theological project can be understood apart from a deep appreciation of [the truth of the Trinity]."[6] Consequently, presentation of any aspect of Torrance's theology should be evaluated through Torrance's own hermeneutical dictum that the Trinity is "the ground and grammar of theology."

The primary interest of this book is Torrance's soteriology, but it could not but be a trinitarian soteriology. For Torrance, the doctrine of the Trinity is always soteriological and soteriology is always trinitarian. To isolate one from the other means to separate the being of God from his act, and *vice versa*. Elmer Colyer's *How to Read T. F. Torrance* and Paul Molnar's *Theologian of the Trinity* are excellent publications offering a comprehensive presentation of Torrance's doctrine of the Trinity.[7] But although there are sections in these books where soteriology is discussed, there is a discernible lack of *explicit* connection between Torrance's doctrines of the Trinity and salvation that Torrance himself asserts. The distinct contribution of this book, therefore, is that, building on Colyer's and Molnar's fine works, it consciously presents Torrance's soteriological Trinity and trinitarian soteriology at the same time. In this book, *soteriological Trinity* refers to the fact that Torrance's doctrine of the Triune God is always a God *with* and *for* us. The being of God is inseparable from his acts. As such, even presentations of each of the Persons of the Triune God require a soteriological outlook: there is no Christology which is not soteriological Christology, there is no Pateriology which is not a soteriological Pateriology, and there is no Pneumatology which is not soteriological Pneumatology. Reciprocally, *trinitarian soteriology* here means that (1) salvation is the work of the Persons of the Triune God, and that (2) because, in addition to (1), salvation is grounded in the being of the Triune God, (3) the ultimate *telos* of salvation is relationship with the Triune God. Chapters 2, 3, and 4 present the works of each of the Triune Persons, arguing

---

5. Torrance, *Ground and Grammar of Theology* (1980).
6. Flett, "Persons, Powers and Pluralities," 220.
7. Colyer, *How to Read* (2001); and Molnar, *Theologian of the Trinity* (2009).

Introduction

that all three Persons are soteriologically involved in the mediation of reconciliation. In these chapters, it will be argued that Torrance employs a *kath hypostasin* trinitarian soteriology, or that the Persons of the Trinity fulfil distinct agencies in the salvific economy in strict accordance with their hypostases as Father, Son, and Holy Spirit. It will also be argued that the distinct works of the three Persons are the works of the whole Triune God, and thus the *telos* of their specific salvific agencies find culmination in humanity's participation in the life and love of God's communion. Secondly, chapter 5 presents the being and work of the communion of love that God is, and it will be argued that Torrance employs a *kat' ousian* trinitarian soteriology, or that the origin and *telos* of salvation are in strict accordance with the being of God as personal communion.

Inasmuch as Torrance's doctrine of the Trinity is soteriological, this work also argues that his soteriology is a *Trinitarian soteriology* and nothing else. As such, presentations of Torrance's soteriology that fail to be fully trinitarian should be revised and reformulated in order to do adequate justice to Torrance. Most of the studies of Torrance's soteriology focus on Christ, and to a certain degree, these works faithfully depict Torrance's christocentric theology. It is beyond doubt that one of the many contributions of Torrance to contemporary theology is the recovery of the Irenaeus-Athanasius axis of incarnational redemption. Kye Won Lee's *Living in Union with Christ* and Peter Cass's *Christ Condemned in the Flesh* are examples of the fascination with this significant Torrance soteriological distinctive.[8] The question, however, is whether or not these studies do sufficient justice to Torrance's more holistic and trinitarian orientation. The danger that lurks in this microscopic analysis, especially owing to Torrance's integrative approach, is that it can lead to serious misinterpretations. Man Kei Ho's *A Critical Study on Torrance's Theology of Incarnation*, for instance, is an unfortunate cornucopia of awkward theological critiques because it only looks at one aspect of Torrance's thought while evaluating it from many sides.[9] If Ho had approached the incarnation primarily in the light of Torrance's trinitarian soteriology, his conclusions would have been different. The study closest to Torrance's trinitarian soteriology is Myk Habets's *Theosis in the Theology of Thomas F. Torrance*.[10] Habets rightly discerns that the origin and *telos* of salvation is participation in the life and love of the Triune God. He also takes on board the works of the incarnate

---

8. Lee, *Living in Union* (2003); and Cass, *Christ Condemned Sin in the Flesh* (2009).
9. Ho, *A Critical Study* (2008).
10. Habets, *Theosis in the Theology of Thomas Torrance* (2009).

Introduction

Son and the Holy Spirit in the economy of salvation. In terms of a robust trinitarian soteriology, however, its weakness lies in the absence of a fuller treatment of the Person and work of the Father, which this book provides. Ultimately, this book is a contribution to the increasing number of interpretations of Torrance's soteriology. It is not intended to stand on its own, and because it seeks to address certain elements which I deem neglected in other writings, it has its specific foci—foci which the author hopes to have important bearings in Torrance scholarship.

Torrance's trinitarian soteriology could be explored and elaborated from various angles. This book, however, is concerned mainly with two things, namely (1) the specific works of the Persons of the Triune God in Torrance's trinitarian soteriology, and (2) the *telos* of being saved by the Triune God, respectively. On the first, Torrance's trinitarian soteriology is informed by his insistence on a *kataphysic* and Gospel/revelation-founded theology. This book insists that Torrance's theological methodology could not but affect his soteriological formulation. Chapter 1 thus discusses the interrelation of Torrance's scientific theology, evangelical theology, and trinitarian soteriology. Then, following Torrance's gospel-oriented starting point, chapter 2 begins to explore the Person and work of Christ in the economy of salvation, followed by two chapters on the Persons and works of the Father and the Holy Spirit, respectively. This sketch follows the Pauline benediction formula "the grace of the Lord Jesus Christ, the love of God and the communion of the Holy Spirit" (2 Cor 13:14), which for Torrance "constitute[s] the Trinitarian structure of all Christian faith and life."[11] This is what makes Torrance's theology *evangelical*: it considers the whole Triune God revealed in the salvific economy and follows the revealed trinitarian *taxis* of the salvific economy. Finally, chapter 5 articulates the nature and shape of our salvation in light of the being of God as communion mediating reconciliation in the world. It will be argued that just as the origin of salvation is a communion of love, so the *telos* of salvation is participation in the life and love of the Triune God.

---

11. Torrance, "Crisis in the Kirk," 21–22; and *School of Faith*, xxi.

1

Scientific, Evangelical, and Trinitarian Soteriology

> Almighty God, who hast given us thine only begotten Son to take our nature upon him, and as at this time to be born of a pure Virgin: Grant that we being regenerate, and made thy children by adoption and grace, may daily be renewed by thy Holy Spirit; through the same our Lord Jesus Christ, who is alive and reigns with thee and the same Spirit ever one God, world without end.[1]

IN DANIEL HARDY'S EVALUATION, IN RESPECT TO CONTENT AND FORM, Torrance's theology is both *declarative* and *relational*. First, it is declarative because it determines and demonstrates core Christian doctrines as they developed through the history of the church, particularly in relation to the patristic conciliar declarations on the doctrine of the Trinity. Evidence is found in his conspicuous preoccupation with the doctrinal formulations of Athanasius and the Reformation in his writings. In this sense, Torrance's theology is more analytic than constructive, but it is false to assume that Torrance possesses no originality.[2] His recurrent recourse to historical theology is apologetic, in that he seeks to show that his theology is grounded upon and is an exposition of creedal beliefs. Furthermore, as T. A. Noble writes, Torrance approaches classical theologians "as a 'historical theologian' interested in the profound convergence of thought, rather than as a 'theological historian' concerned with cultural relativities."[3] Secondly, his theology is relational because it is not only integrative, but also unique.[4] A theological glue holds together Torrance's over six hundred

---

1. B43 Untitled sermon on Matthew 1:18–25, 3.

2. John Webster thinks of Torrance as a performer, not a composer, and refers to him as "the British *resourcement* theologian," in "Editorial: T. F. Torrance," 370.

3. Noble, "Thomas Forsyth Torrance," 824.

4. Hardy, "T. F. Torrance," 165–67.

published materials, and makes the several interrelated themes and aspects within them consistent and coherent. This is why an introductory presentation of other aspects of his thought is necessary for us to understand his trinitarian soteriology. There are two important aspects in particular: (1) scientific theology, and (2) evangelical theology. Torrance admits that the nature of trinitarian theology requires a circular procedure in presentation, but adds that this does not imply "operating with a vicious cycle, begging the question, or falling into the fallacy of a *petitio principii*."[5] Rather, this procedure actually prevents theologizing from moving outside of its own theo-logic, or arguing from some starting point of our own choosing through which theological truths may be judged or validated.

Scientific Theology and the Trinity

Torrance ranks among a few recent theologians whose interest in science overlaps and influences their theology. In Torrance's case, the awareness came early. Upon Hugh Ross Mackintosh's introduction of the theology of Barth to him in 1935, and his consequent reading of Barth's *Church Dogmatics* I/1, Torrance was "immensely exhilarated by the insight of Barth . . . and by his presentation of dogmatics as a science."[6] Equally enlightening to him was Barth's scientific-trinitarian theology, as also manifest in the creeds. Torrance was immediately convinced that any serious scientific attempt at knowledge should be governed by the given data. In the case of theology, therefore, theologizing should be governed by the self-revelation of God as recorded in the Scriptures, and particularly by the self-manifestation of God in history in the incarnate Son and the Holy Spirit. As will be seen later, this has profound consequences in Torrance's trinitarian soteriology.

General Relationship between Science and Theology

Torrance acknowledges the animosity between the church and the sciences, and his attempt to reconcile these two often bifurcated fields is

---

5. Torrance, *Christian Doctrine of God*, 27. In a circular manner, Torrance employs Claude Welch's two approaches to the doctrine of the Trinity, *synthetic* and *basic*, or summative and starting point. See *In This Name*, 47–48.

6. Torrance, *Karl Barth*, 121. Stephen D. Wigley argues that Torrance's concern for theological science has its origin in an Anselmian epistemology, and also through Barth's influence, in "Karl Barth on St. Anselm," 79–97.

primarily apologetic.[7] Firstly, he shows scientists that theology is a science in its own right; and secondly, which comprises the larger part, he enlightens the church that science and theology inform one another, and that science is not inherently an enemy of the Christian truth. Torrance even asserts that thinking about the interrelation of theological and natural sciences is a part of the calling of both Christians and scientists.[8] The church's hostile disposition against science and its agenda, Torrance states, is grounded upon false and obsolete presuppositions. The idea that science is an enemy of the Christian faith, he optimistically proclaims, is no longer true. Modern science's arrogant superiority complex has already been abandoned by contemporary science. Forced by the very advances of science itself, scientists are beginning to realize the boundaries of natural investigation and the futility of the modern agenda for a methodological secularization. Since natural science is concerned not simply with the convenient arrangements of observational data which can be generalized into universal explanatory forms, but with the intrinsic structures of the universe, the relation of the universe to God seems to be steadily forced on scientists by their own limitations to explain certain events and principles. This is encapsulated by Albert Einstein's redefinition of physics: "a finite but unbounded universe with open, dynamic structures grounded in a depth of objectivity and intelligibility which commands and transcends our comprehension."[9]

Secondly, the church is appropriating an outdated science. Torrance asserts that science has already moved on, but the church has failed to recognize it. This unawareness on the part of the church portrays her inability to take on the challenge of keeping up-to-date with new discoveries and trends. Torrance's favorite example is the obsolete dualist frame of thought that still pervades theology today. Augustinian and Thomist dualism should now be replaced by a holistic framework, just as Newton's dualistic and mechanistic concept of the universe has already been discarded by science in favor of Einstein's unitary and integrative outlook. Indeed, as Torrance desires, the church should undergo a "conceptual surgery,"

---

7. Langford, "T. F. Torrance's *Theological Science*," 157. See also Pannenberg, "Problems between Science and Theology," 105–12. Pannenberg argues that it is misleading to speak of warfare between science and Christian theology as if it was on a grand scale.

8. Torrance, *Ground and Grammar of Theology*, 7. In particular, Torrance comments: "Theology cannot operate on its proper ground in complete detachment from cosmology," in *Divine and Contingent Order*, 63–65.

9. Quoted in Torrance, *Divine and Contingent Order*, 11.

where old patterns of thought should be changed.[10] When this happens, one great benefit will be "a profounder grasp of the created or contingent order within which both natural and theological science have to operate and to cooperate in fidelity to the nature of the universe that God has made."[11]

Scientific Methodology and Theology

Torrance's interest in the dialogue between science and theology goes beyond his desire to appropriate scientific discoveries for theological formulations. Although he exploits the *contents* of scientific investigation, his greatest aspiration is for theology to learn from the *methods* of scientific inquiry, although not in the sense that theology should borrow something new from modern science, but that it should return to the biblical and patristic theological approach. In fact, Torrance laments the divergences of modern theology from the gospel presentation of Christ in both the *method* of how a concept was conceived and the *content* of the same conceived concept. He puts the stronger blame, however, on the erroneous procedure that led to wrong conclusions.[12] That *scientific methodology* constitutes Torrance's main focus is important to note. Frank Schubert argues that Torrance's theological science fails to solve the historically restrained relationship between science and religion, but this reflects his misunderstanding of Torrance, because nowhere does Torrance say that his intention is to resolve fully the tension between the two.[13] In fact, Torrance argues that similarity and distinction between science and theology should be maintained. The similarity lies in the mode of inquiry, in that the objects of investigation are studied according to their own intrinsic nature and rational structure, allowing them to reveal and speak for themselves. The difference lies in the approach. Torrance was suspicious of any notion of a *scientia universalis,* a universal principle or methodology applicable to all experimentations.[14] It is necessary for each field of inquiry to develop its own distinctive methods that are faithful to and in accordance

---

10. Torrance, *Reality and Scientific Theology,* 148, 154.

11. Torrance, *Christian Theology,* 22. See also Neidhardt, "Torrance's Integration of Judeo-Christian Theology and Natural Science," 87–98.

12. B23 "The Doctrine of God in Traditional Theology," 1.

13. Schubert, "Thomas F. Torrance," 123–37.

14. Torrance critiques Descartes's vision of a *scientia universalis* applied to all *scientiae speciales* as illogical and inappropriate. See also Torrance's discussion of general and special sciences in *Theological Science,* 106–31.

Scientific, Evangelical, and Trinitarian Soteriology

with the nature of the object of its investigation. Thus, for instance, it is illogical to study a frog using the experimental apparatus employed in astronomy. Torrance identifies the similarity and dissimilarity in terms of *formal* scientific procedure and *material* scientific procedure.[15] That the majority of scientists are wary of granting Torrance's argument consideration (as Schubert narrates) is most probably due to Torrance's insistence that theology is a science in its own right.

Kata Physin and Scientific Questioning

Torrance understands and uses "science" in terms of the German *Wissenschaft*, or "a rigorous and disciplined inquiry of the object according to its unique nature," and argues that this approach is not unique to the natural sciences, but was actually employed in the early Alexandrian tradition, in which Athanasius stood. According to Torrance, Alexandria, influenced by the developing Greek science, espoused an investigative procedure in strict accordance with the nature of the reality under scrutiny, or *kata physin*, which is also "to know things . . . in accordance with their truth or reality (*kat' aletheian*) and thus to think and speak truly (*alethos*) of them."[16] Thus, *kata physin* requires that theologians begin a discussion of the knowledge of God by looking at God himself. "If we are to have any true and precise scientific knowledge of God, we must allow his own nature, as he comes revealed to us, to determine how we are to know him, how we are to think of him, and what we are to say of him."[17] This is what Torrance refers to as the "ethical dimension" of knowing and the *dogmatics* he wishes theology to employ, in contrast to what he rejects as undisciplined free thinking.[18] In terms of methodology, like Barth, Torrance rejects the notion that we can develop an account of *how* we know apart

15. Torrance, *Theological Science*, 112–13.

16. Torrance, *Trinitarian Faith*, 51; *Theological Science*, 116; *Divine Meaning*, 180. Concerning the scientific atmosphere in early Alexandria, see Torrance, "Alexandrian Theology," 185–89.

17. Torrance, *Trinitarian Faith*, 52.

18. Torrance, "The Transcendental Role of Wisdom in Science," 139–40; "Reformed Dogmatics, not Dogmatism," 152–56. Rather than free thinking, we must accommodate our rationality to the object of our investigation. Torrance actually blames "free thinking" as the author of secularism, in B41 "The Secularization of the Church." In his sermons, Torrance uses the analogy of accommodating our vision to what appears in front of us. See B42 "Moses wist not that the skin of His face," 4; and B44 "Watchers at the Cross," 1–7. See also Marianne H. Micks, who understands theology as a disciplined thinking about God in *Introduction to Theology*, xiii.

Communion with the Triune God

from our actual knowledge and its material content.[19] To start speculating on the doctrine of God apart from the givenness of God's revelation, Torrance says, follows Arius's *mythological* thinking, or "thinking from a subjective centre in ourselves, in which we project our fabricated patterns and ideas upon the divine Reality and will accept only what we can conceive in terms of what we already know or what fits in with our own prior self-understanding."[20]

To know things in accordance with their nature requires a proper questioning procedure. This is because "genuine questioning leads to the disclosure and recognition of the Truth in its objective Reality, in its own Majesty and Sanctity and Authority, which cannot be dragged down within our dividing and compounding dialectic in order to be controlled by us."[21] Torrance honors Lorenzo Valla as the one who re-introduced the new kind of inquiry that is most suitable for scientific theology, in which there is an interrogative, rather than a problematic form of inquisition. This is the change from *quaestio* to *interrogatio*.[22] Like Calvin, Torrance prefers the latter because it is "a mode of inquiry in which questions yield results that are entirely new, giving rise to knowledge that we cannot derive by an inferential process from what we already know."[23] Truth is known through revelation, or through a "disclosure method,"[24] and is apprehended through the mind's obedience and submission to the given

---

19. Torrance, *Transformation and Convergence*, ix.

20. Torrance, *God and Rationality*, 46; *Ground and Grammar of Theology*, 114–17. This is what he also calls "the disease of imagination," in B42 "Aaron's Calf," 5. With sarcasm, he writes: "Take the theologian—his use of logic, as though you can understand God's ways by a rule from the human mind! Take the ecclesiastic, who tries to organize the Kingdom of God—might as well try to make the ocean run in particular grooves and channels!" See B44 "The Story of Jairus," 4.

21. See B39 "At the ninth hour Jesus," 5; and similar sermon B42 "My God, my God, Why hast thou forsaken me?"

22. Torrance, *Transformation and Convergence*, 267; *God and Rationality*, 33–35. Valla borrowed the process from the Stoics and from Cicero. See Torrance, "The Historical Jesus," 512. Torrance argues that the nature of true theological questioning, however, does not employ the Cartesian approach of beginning from doubt. Torrance explains that doubting is focused on the self, while theological questioning is directed to the other. See B39 "At the ninth hour," 8.

23. Torrance, *Transformation and Convergence*, 268.

24. Achtemeier, "The Truth of Tradition," 355; Morrison, "Torrance's Critique of Evangelical Orthodoxy," 54. In his other article "Heidegger, Correspondence Truth and the Realist Theology of T. F. Torrance," 139–55, Morrison argues that Torrance is indebted to or at least has appropriated Heidegger's assertion of the priority of truth as disclosure over truth as correspondence.

data. Ho argues that this epistemological procedure constitutes a key weakness in Torrance's revelational theology, because it proposes a non-inferential knowledge of God and consequently downgrades humanity's reasoning capability. Ho understands Torrance's emphasis on the objectivity of the object and humanity's obedient response to imply humanity's passive reception, which for Ho is more fideistic than scientific. Following Jason Yeung, Ho thus confidently concludes that "Torrance's theological science is simply another fancy name for a personal belief which is totally independent of science."[25] Ho's harsh critique here is but one of the many theological criticisms he has of Torrance, and actually reveals his one-sided reading of Torrance. Firstly, Ho conveniently skips Torrance's argument that the *interrogatio* mode of questioning actually enables the knower to be actively self-critical, because it allows what we already know or hold as knowledge to be called in question by the object.[26] Secondly, Ho misses the whole point of Torrance's balance between scientific objectivity and subjectivity, to which we now turn.

Scientific Objectivity and Subjectivity

One of Torrance's major concerns was for theology to begin with and be grounded upon objective reality, not some antecedent external presupposition imposed upon reality. Continuing on Barth's theological mission, he consciously combats residues of Descartes's "return to the subject" philosophy, Kantian transcendental *a priorism*, and liberal subjectivism in theology, and uncompromisingly asserts that an important constituent of a scientific theology is "devotion to its proper object, sheer respect for objectivity."[27] The compelling evidence given by the objective content of reality should govern theology, and theology should begin with an objective reference which is always outward looking—away from the self to a focus on the other reality. This is what Torrance calls "*a theological way of thinking*, not from a centre in ourselves but from a centre in God, not

---

25. Ho, *A Critical Study*, 24–25, 29, 232–33, 236–38, 274.

26. Torrance, *Theological Science*, 120–23; *Theology in Reconstruction*, 67. See also Neidhardt's defense of Torrance's disclosure analogy in "Reflections on Remarks of David F. Siemens, Jr.," 114. Siemens also critiques Torrance's preference for auditory epistemology, in "Two Problems with Torrance," 112–13.

27. Torrance, *Theological Science*, 116; *Belief in Science*, 95; Langford, "Torrance's Theological Science," 159. As such, both *Barth: Introduction* (1962) and *Karl Barth* (1990) are not only about Barth's theology, but about aspects that Torrance gleaned from him.

from axiomatic assumptions which we make but from a frame of reference that derives from God Himself through His Word."[28] As A. E. Taylor argued, authority lies "in a reality that is wholly given and transubjective, and simply and absolutely authoritative through its givenness,"[29] not in the experimental methodology the scientist or theologian invents. Furthermore, this controlling given is not constructed but is received. Torrance's rejection of subjectivism in theology is not only intellectually propelled, as if the issue is contained only in the academy. Rather, he was also concerned that the obsession for self-consciousness, or for "the egocentric I" is actually morally unbecoming for a Christian thinker. Simply put, the maturing Christian must be able to distinguish his presuppositions from the objective reality, in contrast to the immature Christian who is in "stuck adolescence, an adolescence that somehow perseveres in the egocentric direction without breaking into maturity and manhood."[30] This "diseased form of religion," Torrance continues, is the "inability to live outside of himself and to consider the 'thou.'"[31] For Torrance, this self-centeredness is the road to hell, for "whatever hell may be, certainly the hell of it must be to be shut up in yourself, finally to be incarcerated in your own meaninglessness and boredom, to be locked up in yourself for ever and ever."[32]

---

28. Torrance, *Theological Science*, 281 (italics mine). What should be avoided is the "Hellenization" or "Eurocentricization of Christianity." See Torrance, "Being of One Substance with the Father," in *Nicene Christianity*, 50; and on the history of Protestant theology's lapse into this feared Eurocentricization, see Heron, *A Century of Protestant Theology* (1985). Torrance also refers to this as the "Subjectivization of Christianity," in "Hermeneutics According to Schleiermacher," 263–65. But this does not mean that the Christianization of Hellenism that Torrance advocates is completed in the Nicene-Constantinopolitan creed. See Torrance, *Ecumenical Studies*, 73–76. It is rather incomplete as Robert Jenson argues in "Second Locus: The Triune God," esp. 118f. on "The Initial Christianization of Hellenism"; and Schwöbel, "Christology and Trinitarian Thought," in *Trinitarian Theology Today*, 115. Interestingly, Jenson adds that although the Western church has struggled with Hellenic theology through the ages, he argues that "so long as the Western church endures, it must be Hellenic," in *The Triune Identity*, 161.

29. Torrance, *Theological Science*, viii. See Taylor, *The Faith of a Moralist*, 241.

30. B36 "The Heart of the Matter," 2.

31. Ibid. This "false principle" of being inward-looking, Torrance says in another sermon, should be replaced by an "Archimedean point outside of ourselves . . . that can come only from Jesus." See B39 Untitled sermon on 2 Corinthians 8:9, 3.

32. B36 "The Heart of the Matter," 4. The solution to this problem is only found in Christ, who alone "can break into the closed circle of human selfishness and bend man's will until it becomes straight and points beyond itself to complete fulfilment in the purposes of God," in B38 Untitled sermon on Isaiah 21:11–12, 8.

But "why the massive, redundant, and presumptuous assertion of the actuality of the Object of theological inquiry, God Himself?" Donald Klinefelter asks.[33] Ho follows Klinefelter's critique that Torrance's optimism for receptive knowledge in particular and Torrance's theological science in general are founded on a few implicit and explicit presuppositions or ultimate beliefs that are above verification by any other field of inquiry, which is also why Ronald Thiemann and Douglas Morrison see theological foundationalism in Torrance.[34] In all these critiques, the general tenor is that even knowledge of God should be validated by an accepted universal canon of truth. Objectivity is measured by verifiability, and anything beyond proof is considered subjective understanding. Thus, Klinefelter could say that Torrance's use of science and philosophy, "rather than supporting an advance to new theological frontiers . . . serve instead as bulwarks protecting a sophisticated Barthian fideism."[35] It is true that Torrance does not provide evidence for the validity of the presumption that God has revealed himself in Jesus of Nazareth using philosophical apparatuses of verification. Torrance's defence is that objectivity in theology and the validity of its claims should be measured not by canons of truth derived from philosophy or any other field, but from theology itself. Even in the articulation of theological truths, Torrance argues, the use of philosophical apparatuses is unnecessary. Because all special sciences should develop their own investigative procedures to discern objective truths, so does theology have its *theo-logical* procedure, that is, that objectivity should be measured through the "logic of grace."[36]

The central thesis of Torrance's argument is simple: objective reality and self-evidence are given priority over all precedent knowledge or

33. Klinefelter, "God and Rationality," 123.

34. Ho, *A Critical Study*, 26–29. Achtemeier adds that the objectivity of God as God is "an indispensable presupposition," in "The Truth of Tradition," 355. See the basis of Ho's critique in Torrance, *Transformation and Convergence*, 191–208. See also Thiemann, *Revelation and Theology*, 40; and Morrison, *Knowledge of the Self-revealing God*, 65–68. Thiemann argues for a non-foundationalist approach: "narrated promise." See McCall's illuminating discussion in "Thiemann, Torrance and Epistemological Doctrines of Revelation," 148–68. McCall concludes that Torrance offers a much more coherent epistemology than Thiemann, although he thinks that Torrance has a "modern foundationalism."

35. Klinefelter, "God and Rationality," 128.

36. Torrance, *Theology in Reconstruction*, 37–41; *Theological Science*, 12–33. Although Torrance is appreciative of the early Fathers, he thinks that the early Christian apologists wrongly used philosophy and blames them for the beginning of the "baptism of paganism" to Christianity. See B23 "The Doctrine of God in Traditional Theology," 5.

opinion, although Torrance also realizes that an anthropological element is inescapably present in every human endeavor, including theology. Theology remains the discourse of God about himself with humanity as active recipient and interpreter. But the subjectivity that Torrance recognizes is different from that of the subjective *a priorism* which he strongly repudiates, i.e., subjectivism. Critical here is the difference between subjective *starting point* and subjective *participation*. The former refers to the procedure of approaching reality with fixed presuppositions, opinions, and sets of standards to quantify or qualify data. The latter, on the other hand, gives priority to the reality under investigation, but considers the personal element involved. Participatory subjectivity, therefore, refers to the realization that a personal engagement is necessary in order to acquire knowledge of another reality. Torrance redefines *objectivity* and *subjectivity*. Contrary to the claims of old science for a detached experimentation which aims to exclude from scientific knowledge all subjective bias and prejudice so that it can be genuinely objective, Torrance argues:

> It must not be forgotten that only a person is capable of self-criticism and of distinguishing what he knows from his subjective states, and therefore of appreciating the bearing of human thought upon experience. In fact, it is only a person who can engage truly in objective and scientific operations . . . any scientific inquiry pursued in a detached, impersonal, formalistic way isolates itself from man's higher faculties and thereby restricts its range and power of insight and understanding.[37]

In sum, precisely because ontological openness to reality is an essential ingredient in the objectivity of a scientific theory, it "inevitably throws the maintenance and fulfillment of objectivity back upon the personal responsibility of the scientist himself: he and he only is capable, as an active centre of rationality, of establishing the bearing of his knowing upon reality in this way."[38] It is here that Michael Polanyi, James Clerk Maxwell, and Einstein have their important bearings on Torrance's scientific theology. Among the three, it was Polanyi, however, who brought to prominence the particular point of restoring to rigorous scientific activity what he called "the personal coefficient of knowledge" and the centrality of "ultimate beliefs or normative insights."[39]

---

37. Torrance, *Christian Theology*, 61–62.

38. Torrance, *Transformation and Convergence*, 115.

39. Torrance, *Christian Theology*, 61–71; *Belief in Science*, 1–27; "Ultimate and Penultimate Beliefs in Science," 151–76; and *Theology in Reconstruction*, 69–72.

Scientific Theology and Trinitarian Thinking

Scientific theology—in which the nature and being of God take priority and authoritative control—is inevitably trinitarian. Torrance must have realized this upon reading Barth's *Dogmatics* I/1, because the volume exemplifies what scientific theology should look like. Torrance admits the insights he gained from Barth's scientific approach in the volume, but even more gripping for him was how Barth accomplished his scientific theology in structuring the book's contents in explicit trinitarian style.[40]

STRATIFICATION OF KNOWLEDGE

The circular relationship between scientific theology and trinitarian theology becomes more apparent in Torrance's appropriation of Einstein's and Polanyi's hierarchical epistemology. In a realist account of knowing, conceptual knowledge arises from the ground level of human intuitive apprehension of reality, as characteristic of all *a posteriori* investigation. Then from the tacit, experiential level of knowledge, there comes a conceptual advance to another level, although the advance is not a movement away from concrete reality, but a progressive and deepening apprehension of reality.[41] Formalized knowledge remains coordinated with the basic experience of reality. In theology, Torrance writes:

> Formulation of the doctrine of the Trinity develops a stratified structure arising on the ground of our evangelical experience, knowledge and worship of God in the life of the Church, deriving from the historical revelation of God as Father, Son and Holy Spirit mediated to us in the incarnate life and work of Jesus Christ, and directed to the transcendental mystery of God the Father, the Son and the Holy Spirit as he is in his one eternal being.[42]

Polanyi has shown Torrance that positivist and objectivist philosophies of science are inadequate since they try to establish the objective validity of science on impersonal grounds. See Thorson, "Scientific Objectivity and the Listening Attitude," 61; and for an extensive treatment of Polanyi's influence on Torrance, see Weightman, *Theology in a Polanyian Universe* (1994).

40. Torrance, *Karl Barth*, 121.

41. Torrance, *Ground and Grammar of Theology*, 34–35, 156–72; *Reality and Scientific Theology*, 131–36; *God and Rationality*, 83; *Christian Theology*, 37; *Divine and Contingent Order*, 20; and *Transformation and Convergence*, 159.

42. Torrance, *Christian Doctrine of God*, 83; *Reality and Scientific Theology*, 136, 140.

Torrance calls this "Chalcedonism," because the creedal formulations of both Nicea and Chalcedon exemplified a rise to a higher level of knowledge. Borrowing from Einstein's *Physics and Reality*, Torrance describes this Chalcedonian hierarchical model of knowing in three ascending orders.[43]

The level of personal encounter with Jesus Christ in worship and fellowship in the church represents the first level of theological knowledge: what Torrance calls the "*evangelical and doxological level.*"[44] Torrance acknowledges Polanyi's direct influence on his understanding of this level, particularly his discussion of the tacit or inarticulate dimension in human thought.[45] Like the experience of the early church, in this level, an implicit awareness of the threefold act of God expressed in 2 Corinthians 13:14 is imprinted in the Christian psyche: "the grace of our Lord Jesus Christ, the love of God, and the fellowship of the Holy Spirit." However, while such a trinitarian awareness is present at this stage, the focal point of the *evangelical level* is "personal encounter with Jesus Christ within the structures and rationalities of our historical existence in space and time . . . where we are summoned to live and think not out of a centre in ourselves but out of a centre in the Lord Jesus."[46] This *incipient theology*, as Torrance also calls it, although involving no speculative or logical analysis, remains as "the *sine qua non* of the other levels of doctrinal formulation."[47]

Thomas A. Noble, however, discerns an apparent inconsistency in Torrance's view of the evangelical level, especially because Torrance argues that explicit conceptualization and theoretical understanding only proceed at the second level of knowledge: the *scientific or theological level.*[48] The problem is that a completely unconceptual knowledge at the first level seems to contradict the fact that the Christ we encounter in our evangelical experience is "Christ clothed with his gospel,"[49] and that revelation is

---

43. Torrance, *Belief in Science*, 104–6; *Ground and Grammar of Theology*, 156–59. Torrance considers Einstein as a "disguised theologian," in *Theological and Natural Science*, 17.

44. Torrance, *Ground and Grammar of Theology*, 156; *Christian Doctrine of God*, 88.

45. Torrance, *Reality and Scientific Theology*, 132. See also Myers, "The Stratification of Knowledge," 6.

46. Torrance, *Christian Doctrine of God*, 88.

47. Ibid., 90.

48. Private conversation with T. A. Noble, 20 May 2011; Myers, "Stratification of Knowledge," 7.

49. Torrance, *School of Faith*, lxxx; *Reality and Evangelical Theology*, 9. We know

Scientific, Evangelical, and Trinitarian Soteriology

always in and through the eloquent Word in his self-communication. Because our knowledge of God is also always *a posteriori*—achieved through an encounter with the self-revealing Christ—then our knowledge is not merely tacit or unthematic, but is to a certain degree already conceptual. If the tacit dimension is to be truly a *prolepsis*, or "a forward leap of the awakened mind in laying hold of some aspect of reality,"[50] then a conceptual understanding, limited it may be, should be present already. Moreover, one should not forget that the gospel we receive today is the gospel as it was already conceptually articulated by the apostles and biblical writers. It may be that Torrance's desire to categorize neatly the three levels of knowledge led him to dwell on their differences from one another, without giving sufficient space for an elaboration of and about the overlapping intersections between the levels. It would be evangelically more accurate to say that even in the first level of knowledge, an articulate knowledge is already achieved, although not as explicitly or astutely as that which is achieved in the second level, where a movement of penetration into the logical relation between the reality-in-itself and the reality as it is experienced in space and time is reached. Torrance argues that this process requires the invention of theoretical tools and concepts, which should (1) be grounded upon the tacit experience of reality, and (2) function as freely chosen "fluid axioms" that are open to revision in the light of further discoveries.[51]

According to Torrance, the movement from the evangelical to the theological level of knowledge is the attempt to "apprehend more fully the economic and ontological and trinitarian structure of God's revealing and saving acts in Jesus Christ as they are presented to us in the Gospel."[52] As we experience God in worship and in our daily lives, we become aware of the threefold movement of God's revealing and saving nature as Father, Son, and Holy Spirit underlying all our Christian experiences, enabling us to speak of the economic Trinity. As such, early creedal formulations represent an example of the ascent from the first to the second level of knowledge. Torrance particularly refers to the development of the all-important concept *homoousios* to give expression to the reality which the

---

Christ as the Savior: "We know Jesus Christ by what He has done for us. It is by His works that we know his Person. If Christ has not saved you and dealt with your sin and guilt by his Cross, then you don't know Him," in B46 Untitled sermon on 1 Corinthians 2:2, 7.

50. Torrance, *Reality and Scientific Theology*, 84.

51. Torrance, *Reality and Evangelical Theology*, 49–51; *Reality and Scientific Theology*, 77–78.

52. Torrance, *Christian Doctrine of God*, 91.

early fathers had grasped intuitively with God through Jesus Christ. In their personal union and communion with Jesus Christ, the Nicene fathers knew themselves that they had entered into union and communion with the very being of God.[53]

Finally, building upon the progression from the first to the second level of knowledge, we move from an awareness of the Trinity *ad extra* to the Trinity *ad intra*, which Torrance calls the *metascientific or metatheological level* of knowledge. It is here that "we discern the Trinitarian relations immanent in God himself which lie behind, and are the ground of the relations of, the Economic Trinity—that is, we are lifted up in thought to the level of 'the Ontological Trinity' or 'the Immanent Trinity,' as it is variously called."[54] Arrival at this level, Torrance describes, is the arrival at the "ultimate theoretic structure," not because of its superficial abstractive speculation, but because of its logical economy and simplicity.[55] This level of refined conceptualization is "the supreme point in our knowing of God in the inner perichoretic relations of his triune Being," primarily because the perichoretic relations are "the ultimate constitutive relations in God," and as such also constitute "the ground upon which the intelligibility and objectivity of all our knowledge of God finally repose."[56]

Trinity as Nature and Being of God

Torrance's stratification of theological knowledge using scientific investigation ends up with the doctrine of the Trinity *in se* as the nature and

---

53. Torrance, *Ground and Grammar of Theology*, 157; Myers, "Stratification," 9. See also *Christian Doctrine of God*, 93–102, on the centrality of the *homoousion* in the stratification of knowledge.

54. Torrance, *Ground and Grammar of Theology*, 158.

55. Ibid., 171–72.

56. Torrance, *Christian Doctrine of God*, 103, 107. As Noble suggests (Private conversation, 27 July 2011), Torrance's stratification of knowledge, owing perhaps to his dedication to the Nicene formulation, possesses a certain chronological ambiguity. Because Torrance points to the Nicene *homoousion* as the moment of ascent from the first to the second level, the question of when the third level of knowledge is achieved remains unanswered. Torrance hints that the ascent from the theological to the meta-theological level happens around the Nicene-Constantinopolitan period, but Torrance does not say more or make it clear. Noble's suggestions that the assent to the second level (the economic Trinity) was achieved as early as the second century by Irenaeus, Tertullian, and Clement of Alexandria, and that the assent to the third level (the immanent Trinity) occurred during the Nicene-Constantinopolitan period through Athanasius and the Cappadocians, offer a better chronological explanation of the stratification of knowledge.

being of God. He believes that this stratified structure of knowing, using an inductive bottom-to-top pyramidal paradigm, enables him to enter into the inner cohesion of the evangelical narratives deeply in a way that was not possible before.[57] In Christian theology, there would be no greater theological articulation that could be claimed as scientific truth beyond the ontological Trinity. The interrelation between scientific theology and the doctrine of the Trinity is therefore irreversible. The circular interconnectedness may be expressed as several movements within one act of knowing. Firstly, a faithful and rigorous scientific theology should be undertaken *kata physin*, according to the nature of the object of investigation. Since theology is primarily a discourse on God, the being of God becomes the unquestionable starting point and controlling center. The question, however, is: "Who is God"? or "What is the nature of God"? It is here, secondly, that scientific theology, through the stratification of knowledge, is particularly helpful. A multi-leveled view of reality, accompanied by an ascending hierarchical order of knowing, reveals that the nature of God is triune. In one sense, the doctrine of the Trinity is to be seen as the culmination of a scientific theology. Therefore, the doctrine of the Trinity, of the being who God is in himself, constitutes the "ground and grammar of theology."[58] Thirdly, while the Trinity *ad intra*, or the perichoretic relations, forms the basis of all theological reflections, a faithful scientific investigation does not do away with the data found in the evangelical level of knowledge. In fact, a continuous retrospective return to the evangelical data and the theoretical constructs based on them is necessary. This means that the centrality of Christ, and the fundamentality of the concepts *homoousios* and *hypostatic union* should always be referred to. This is one of the reasons why Torrance claimed that the use of scientific theology carries with it an evangelical thrust.[59]

---

57. Torrance, *Transformation and Convergence*, 94–95.

58. This Torrance dictum is also his response, following Barth, to the neglect of the doctrine of the Trinity in modern theology that Rahner brought to the awareness of the church in *The Trinity*, 10–15. For the history of this neglect, see Welch, *In This Name*, esp. chapters 1 and 2. Because of this neglect, Timothy Lull asserts that "the doctrine of the Trinity should be subtitled the guilt-producing doctrine," in "The Trinity in Recent Theological Literature," 61.

59. Torrance, *God and Rationality*, viii.

Evangelical Theology and the Trinity

Admittedly, the description "evangelical theology" is vague,[60] so we need to provide a definition here. Firstly, we are neither concerned with evangelicalism as a movement, nor will we follow the prevailing consensus of understanding "evangelicalism" primarily in non-theological ways, as David Bebbington and Mark Noll, two most influential historians of evangelicalism today do.[61] To a certain extent, Stephen Holmes's assessment that "any attempt to define eighteenth-century British evangelicalism as a theological movement is destined to failure"[62] could be applied to the worldwide evangelical movement, but still, to relegate theological developments to be of lesser importance than the *evangelistic* spirit displays the serious error of assuming that ministry can operate without biblical-theological grounds. As such, secondly, we will not follow Timothy Larsen's procedure in emphasizing the community that identifies itself as "evangelical." Rather, our concern lies precisely in what Larsen intentionally considers as peripheral: *theological* evangelicalism or evangelical *theology*,[63] and on how theology is in itself evangelical and evangelizing.

Torrance understands evangelical theology as an evangelizing movement. He writes: "Evangelical theology is an evangelizing theology, for it is concerned with the winning and transforming of the human mind through conformity to the mind of Christ—not simply the minds of individual human beings but the mind of human society and culture in which individual human beings exist."[64] This is what he desired as "the Christianizing of the Mind of the people, within and without the Church."[65] But this

---

60. Dayton, "Some Doubts about the Usefulness of the Category 'Evangelical,'" 245–51; and see Olson's attempt to offer useful definitions in *The SCM A-Z of Evangelical Theology*, 3–10.

61. Holmes, "British (and European) Evangelical Theologians," in *The Cambridge Companion to Evangelical Theology*, 241.

62. Holmes, "British (and European) Evangelical Theologians," 242.

63. Larsen, "Defining and Locating Evangelicalism," in *The Cambridge Companion to Evangelical Theology*, 1–14.

64. Torrance, *Atonement*, 444; "The Reconciliation of the Mind," 6; Hesselink, "A Pilgrimage in the School of Christ," 60. See also Torrance's *The Christian Frame of Mind* (1985). At the center of this should be Christ. See "Putting First Things First," 10–12; "The Tide has Turned," 14–15; "Where is the Church of Scotland Going?," 24–26; "The Kirk's Crisis of Faith," 15–16; "The Crisis of Community," 16–17; and "A Right-about-Turn for the Kirk," 20–21.

65. B41 "The Task of the Church in Britain in the Eighties," 4. In a fireside chat with students, Torrance argues that rather than attempting to make the gospel relevant by following the contextualizing principles employed by Kuhn, Tillich, and Bultmann,

evangelizing mission could not be accomplished without a theology that is eminently self-critical, "for it is continually exposed to judgment and never relieved of the crisis in which it is placed by its object, or rather to say, by its living subject."[66] This is what Torrance speaks of as theology's "evangelical task."[67] As will be elaborated later, Torrance's evangelical-evangelizing theology is related to the scientific theology that he learned from Barth: "This is the God who reveals himself in the Gospel, who himself speaks to men and acts among and upon them. Wherever he becomes the object of human science, both its source and its norm, there is *evangelical* theology."[68] Two considerations immediately emerge from the quotation from Barth, which will constitute the outline of this section: the *procedure* and *content* that makes theology evangelical.

The Evangelical Procedure of Theology

Because theology should be grounded and guided by the very nature of God as God, according to Torrance's *kataphysic* principle, theology is also inevitably concerned with the doxological-evangelical approach of the early church and Barth's emphasis on revelation, wherein God is known only through his own self-manifestation in the economy of salvation as Father, Son, and Holy Spirit. Knowledge of the Triune God comes *a posteriori*, i.e., from the *euangelion*, with a controlling center

---

which actually made the gospel irrelevant, Christians must "switch back to evangelical foundations." See B40 "Christian Protest and the Power of Evil," 1–4. He warns against a superficial Christianity that makes people stunted, starved, and dwarfed in soul, in B42 "Second-hand Religion," 1–8; and admonishes believers never to make choices that would compromise their faith in B42 "Lot and Daniel," 1–9. See also B45 "Paul and Silas at Philippi," 1–6; and B47 "Communion," especially 5–6, on Torrance's understanding of what Christianity is all about. As someone pessimistic about contextualization, Torrance strongly admonished his parishioners that "No matter how much it hurts them, no matter how much Christian faith will mean the overthrow of their own religion and philosophy, we must point them to the Cross, and tell them that Christianity is a religion of suffering—and only there through that great humiliation can men be forgiven and come to know God in Jesus Christ. Christianity is God's attack upon Man and all his pride. Christ's claims are intolerant and absolutely uncompromising, just because He is God: 'I am the Way, the Truth and the Life . . .'" See B47 "Foreign Mission," 5.

66. Barth, *Evangelical Theology*, 10; and Torrance's appreciation of Barth's theological "ruthless criticism," in *Barth: Introduction*, 21.

67. Torrance, *God and Rationality*, viii. Torrance believes that even the future of ecumenism lies in the Evangelical church, in "Ecumenism and Rome," 62.

68. Barth, *Evangelical Theology*, 6.

> constituted by the incarnation of God's self-revelation in Jesus Christ the Son and Word of God and by the Holy Spirit sent by the Father through the Son who are of one being and act with God the Father, for it is through union and communion with them that we are given to know God as he really is in the inner relations of his Triune Being, and all our understanding of God in his Trinitarian self-revelation is governed.[69]

Knowledge of the Triune God, therefore, is evangelical, i.e., it is grounded in the gospel of Jesus Christ obeying the Father's will in the power of the Holy Spirit. As such, evangelical theology necessarily employs christocentricism, which Bruce McCormack defines as "a methodological rule—not an *a priori* principle, but a rule which is learned through the encounter with the God who reveals Himself in Christ."[70] This is not an arbitrary invention, but is grounded in God's decision to reveal and reconcile us to himself in Jesus Christ. Because Jesus Christ is himself the content of God's objective revelation, all genuine theological knowledge is to be found *via* Christology. This is why, in his 1981 Payton Lectures, Torrance specifically aimed "to cut a swath through the prevailing confusion about the nature of theological and biblical interpretation of divine revelation, so that Christ clothed with his gospel may be allowed to occupy the controlling centre of the church's life, thought, and mission in the world today."[71] Evangelical theology operates "on a Christological basis."[72] This is also why Torrance refers to Barth as a "biblical and evangelical theologian," for at "the heart of Barth's theology is the doctrine of Christ as the divine Reconciler."[73]

Marc Cortez convincingly argues that the term "christocentric" is ambiguous, and everyone who has a Christology could claim to be christocentric.[74] In order to understand Torrance's evangelical-christocentric procedure then, we must follow McCormack's distinction between *formal* and *material* christocentricity.[75] McCormack is concerned that while many theologians may place Christology at the center of their theologies

---

69. Torrance, *Christian Doctrine of God*, 29–30.
70. McCormack, *Karl Barth's Critically Realistic Dialectical Theology*, 454.
71. Torrance, *Reality and Evangelical Theology*, 9.
72. Torrance, *Karl Barth*, 71.
73. Ibid., 20. This is what Torrance refers to as the "uniqueness and centrality of Christ and his Gospel," in "Why Karl Barth Still Matters so Much," 16; "Tom Torrance's Reply on Israel," 33–34. See also Kang, "Concept of the Vicarious Humanity of Christ," 8.
74. Cortez, "What Does it Mean to Call Barth a 'Christocentric' Theologian?," 128.
75. McCormack, *Karl Barth's Critically Realistic Dialectical Theology*, 453–54.

at the *formal* level, the *material content* of their specific Christologies may vary from each other. The issue is: "Who is the Jesus placed at the center"? Like Barth, the *formal* christocentrism of Torrance is grounded in his evangelical Christology, the Christ revealed in the gospels. Theology must proceed in the same manner as Torrance views preaching: "The Gospel must be preached in an evangelical way, that is, in accordance with the nature and content of the Gospel . . . or else it is 'another Gospel.'"[76] Because Jesus Christ is "the very centre of God's self-revelation," he is also "the framework of the New Testament message."[77] Even our understanding of the Triune God, Torrance writes, "must be *soteriologically* conditioned from end to end."[78]

Torrance's evangelical starting point overflows into other aspects of his theology. Firstly, one of the theological imports of his stratification of knowledge is the significance of our evangelical experience as the ground through which deeper knowledge of the Triune God can be attained. The theological constructs that we enjoy are but an articulation of the church's most basic evangelical knowledge, experience, and worship of God the Father through Jesus Christ in the Holy Spirit. Doctrines are conditioned by the realities and events of God's self-revelation and our evangelical and doxological encounter with them. Secondly, Torrance rejects cultural-philosophical ways of thought imposed on theology as starting points. Concerning Barth, he writes:

> It was only through penetrating and subverting the prevailing anthropocentric framework of knowledge, and reconstructing the foundations of modern theology strictly in accordance with the nature and constraints of God's self-giving and self-communication through Jesus Christ and in the Holy Spirit, that Barth was able to build up his massive *Church Dogmatics*, in which evangelical and reformed theology of the Word is given

---

76. Torrance, *God and Rationality*, 58. Knowledge of Jesus Christ, John Webster argues, comes from "an orderly intellectual *exposition* of the divine self-exposition" recorded in the Gospels, in "Incarnation," in *The Cambridge Companion to the Modern Theology*, 204–26.

77. Torrance, *Christian Doctrine of God*, 49. For example, in a draft for a planned third volume of *Conflict and Agreement in the Church*, which never materialized, Torrance calls the World Council of Churches to repentance for its neglect to put Christ at the center of its theologizing in its first eight meetings. He calls a non-christocentric ecumenical involvement as an "ecumenical suicide" in B36 "From Christocentric to a Trinitarian Ecumenism," 1–3. For him, "Christianity is Christ and Christ is Christianity," in B46 Untitled sermon on 1 Corinthians 2:2, 4.

78. Torrance, *Christian Doctrine of God*, 49.

its fullest and most rigorous expression ... Karl Barth's theology is at once evangelical and catholic.[79]

Torrance also follows Barth's rejection of the medieval understanding of natural theology as an autonomous approach to the knowledge of God. Although he deviates later in his theological career from Barth's absolute refusal to grant natural theology any bit of consideration, Torrance still follows Barth's fundamental suspicion of an independent approach to God behind the gospel revelation in Jesus Christ and the Holy Spirit.[80]

The Evangelical Content of Theology

The first clue to knowing what Torrance considers as the evangelical content of theology is in the descriptive subtitle of his book *The Trinitarian Faith: The Evangelical Theology of the Ancient Catholic Church*. The book can be considered as Torrance's "dogmatics in outline" because it incorporates his major theological interests in one book: soteriology, Christology, and the doctrine of the Trinity. Torrance admits later in life that of the many books he has published, he was "most pleased with *The Trinitarian Faith*."[81] What interests us here in particular is that he considers the doctrine of the Trinity as the unchanging content of our evangelical and catholic faith, although, as David Ford properly detects, the book is not just focused on a conceptual presentation of the doctrine of the Trinity, but also on the doctrine's truthfulness and salvific import.[82] Evangelical faith has an inseparable salvific and ontological content: it is (1) the gospel (2) of the Triune God.

Firstly, the content of an evangelical faith is *the gospel* of the Triune God. It is no wonder, therefore, that Torrance prefers to call the Trinity *ad extra* the "evangelical Trinity" instead of the more common "economic

---

79. Torrance, "The Legacy of Karl Barth," 292.

80. Torrance, *Theological and Natural Science*, 93. Torrance's reconstruction of natural theology, which Colyer concludes is one of the most difficult aspects of his theology (*How to Read*, 192, footnote 179), is beyond the scope of this research. But see Torrance's formulation in *Ground and Grammar of Theology*, 75–109; *Reality and Evangelical Theology*, 30–34; *Karl Barth*, 136–59; and *Reality and Scientific Theology*, 32–63. See also Gill, "The Doctrine of Revelation," 107–95; and McGrath, "Torrance and the Search for a Viable Natural Theology," 66–81. Weightman claims that the main figure behind Torrance's later disagreement with Barth's position on natural theology is Polanyi, in *Theology in a Polanyian Universe*, esp. chapters 12 and 13.

81. Bauman, "Thomas F. Torrance," 117.

82. Ford, Review of *The Trinitarian Faith*, 263.

Scientific, Evangelical, and Trinitarian Soteriology

Trinity," because the former highlights more clearly the "truth content of the Gospel."[83] Torrance's purposive opting for "evangelical Trinity" portrays his vision to integrate the doctrine of the Triunity of God with the evangelical message of his saving and redeeming activity in Jesus Christ and the Holy Spirit. This is theologically convincing, because our knowledge of the content of the gospel is only made possible by God's actual, dynamic and salvific relation to the world. "We know nothing of God and can know nothing of him completely isolated in himself and apart from the fulfillment of his creative and redeeming purpose."[84] We do not know a God apart from the God who saves. This affirmation is also evident in Torrance's stratification of knowledge, where he calls the first level of knowledge *evangelical,* because it is knowledge that arises in our salvific and doxological encounter with the Triune God. Although it is primarily Jesus Christ and the Holy Spirit that the church personally encounters, as Colyer beautifully summarizes it, "in hearing the gospel and coming to know God the Father through the Son in the Holy Spirit, we encounter the Trinity as a whole simultaneously."[85] Also, it can only be called evangelical knowledge because it is knowledge through an intimate and saving relationship with God in Jesus Christ.

But the salvific content is essentially inseparable from the ontological content, because "if the economic or evangelical Trinity and the ontological or theological Trinity were disparate, this would bring into question whether *God himself* was the actual content of his revelation, and whether *God himself* was really in Jesus Christ reconciling the world to himself."[86] Thus, secondly, the evangelical content of evangelical faith is the gospel of *the Triune God.* Evangelical theology is concerned equally with the act and Being of God. This is in line with Torrance's refusal to separate the empirical from the theoretical, form from content, or experience from its objective ground.[87]

Lee argues that Torrance has a "critically realist evangelical approach."[88] In a sense, Torrance's realism is an epistemological principle:

83. Torrance, *Christian Doctrine of God,* 7.
84. Ibid., 9.
85. Colyer, *How to Read,* 136.
86. Torrance, *Christian Doctrine of God,* 7.
87. Torrance, *Reality and Evangelical Theology,* 10, 39–42; *Christian Frame of Mind,* 38–39; *Transformation and Convergence,* 61–105; *Christian Theology,* 22–24, 124–25; and *Ground and Grammar of Theology,* 122–24.
88. Lee, *Living in Union,* 20–34; Colyer, *The Nature of Doctrine,* esp. chapter 4; and for an extensive elaboration of Torrance's realist theology, see Morrison, *Knowledge of*

"an epistemological orientation of the two-way relation between the subject and object poles of thought and speech, in which ontological primacy and control are naturally accorded to reality over all our conceiving and speaking of it."[89] On the other hand, realism emphasizes ontological factuality. The key issue in a realist evangelical theology is "the connection between form and being" or between conceptual signs and the realities they signify.[90] In short, critical realism makes sure that the content of theology is grounded in an ontological reality, which, in Torrance's evangelical theology, is the Triune God. Without an ontological reality on which revelation and salvation are grounded, theology is but a speculative exercise. This is what Torrance calls "the principle of coherent integration from above."[91]

Torrance's concern is the objective actuality of the Triune God because it is finally in our understanding of the trinitarian relations in God himself that we have a ground and grammar of a realist theology. From the evangelical to the meta-theological level of knowledge, the objective content is the Triune God in the unity of his being and act. The doctrine of the Trinity is not a speculative movement of thought, but an articulation of the received knowledge of God through God's own self-revealing presence in the actual evangelical and doxological life of the church. It is the *homoousios* that makes it possible for us to know that who God is in his act is who God is in his being. As Myers states, *homoousios* "expresses our most basic and profound evangelical intuition about God: namely, that God is inherently in himself what he is towards us in Jesus Christ, and that the economy of God's grace in Jesus Christ is nothing other than a revelation of the Trinitarian relations of God's own being."[92] As such, *homoousios* is "the ontological foundation for Christian theology" because it points us to knowledge of the Triune God.[93] Colyer is right that Torrance's

---

the *Self-revealing God,* which is devoted precisely to evaluate this aspect of Torrance's thought.

89. Torrance, *Reality and Evangelical Theology*, 60.

90. Ibid., 65–73, 127–34; "Theological Realism," 169–73. The connection between content and form, however, is not a relation of identicality. See "'The Substance of the Faith,'" 327–38.

91. Torrance, *Christian Theology*, 36. Torrance argues that realist thinking is not only applicable to theology, but also to our understanding of political and social laws, in *Juridical Law and Physical Law,* esp. chapter 3; and "Revelation, Creation and Law," 276–78.

92. Myers, "Stratification," 9. See also Torrance, *Christian Doctrine of God,* 93–98, on the centrality of the *homoousion* in the stratification of knowledge.

93. McGrath, *Intellectual Biography,* 158.

theology is fundamentally evangelical because it is ultimately focused on the doctrine of the Trinity.[94]

Scientific, Evangelical, Trinitarian Soteriology

Cass distinguishes two major theological camps within the Reformed Church: federal Calvinism and evangelical Calvinism. Federal Calvinists, according to Cass, possess an essentially forensic doctrine of atonement and salvation, and an Aristotelian logico-causal form of rationality, and teach the doctrines of two covenants with a priority of law over grace, double predestination, and limited atonement. Evangelical Calvinists, on the other hand, possess a "Trinitarian and Christocentric approach to soteriology,"[95] and Cass identifies Torrance under this camp.[96] What interests us here is Cass's recognition of the interpenetration of evangelical theology, trinitarianism, and soteriology. The scientific character of Torrance's theology should be added to Cass's trilateral, but Cass could be acquitted for missing it, because such a theme is beyond the focus of his study. The interrelation between Torrance's scientific theology and trinitarian thinking is highlighted by Colyer's book, but the chapters are treated not in a progressive, sequential manner but as "different facets of an integrated whole."[97] As such, although Colyer presents the evangelical *content* of the gospel (the Trinity), the fact that he thought of his outline as "different facets of an integrated whole" means that he was not consciously appropriating the evangelical *procedure* that Torrance argues for. Also, along with Molnar's *Theologian of the Trinity*, Colyer's concern is primarily to offer an introduction to Torrance's trinitarian theology as a whole. As such, although these two books are extremely helpful in providing a fairly comprehensive guide to Torrance's doctrine of the Trinity, and although they discuss aspects of Torrance's doctrine of salvation, they are not written specifically with the agenda of explicating Torrance's trinitarian

---

94. Colyer, *How to Read*, 25, 29.

95. Cass, *Christ Condemned in the Flesh*, 5–6. See also Peter Toon's elaboration of the various soteriological trends in Reformed theology in *Justification and Sanctification*, 75–87. Particularly interesting is Toon's similar comparison of the different Reformed Confessions with Torrance's *School of Faith*.

96. Heron asserts that Torrance cannot really be called a Calvinist because of his aversion to scholastic Calvinism, in "Calvin in the Theology of Thomas F. Torrance," 46–51.

97. Colyer, *How to Read*, 26.

soteriology or formulating it in the manner that Torrance would have formulated it.

This book, in contrast to the above publications, seeks to integrate all four important factors: scientific theology, evangelical theology, trinitarian theology, and soteriology. In fact, Torrance's integrative approach to theology is best evidenced in his soteriology, which is guided by three principles: (1) theological investigation should proceed *kata physin*, (2) theological formulation should follow the evangelical *taxis* of God's self-revelation in Jesus Christ and the Holy Spirit, and (3) the Trinity is "the ground and grammar of theology." With this, I argue that Torrance espouses a unique and distinct kataphysic, *evangelical, and trinitarian soteriology*.

Kataphysic, *Evangelical Trinitarian Soteriology*

In general, Torrance's *kataphysic* soteriology is related to his insistence that God's being is triune. He writes: "The pattern of coactivity between the Father, the Son and the Holy Spirit in the economic Trinity is. . . a real reflection of the coactivity of the Father, the Son and the Holy Spirit in the ontological Trinity."[98] The doctrine of the Trinity is the ultimate knowledge of *Theos*, and theological formulation, if it is to remain theo-logical, should be guided by an awareness of the triune being of God. Torrance adds:

> In the strictest sense the doctrine of the Holy Trinity is *theologia*, that is, theology in its purest form, the pure science of theology, or *episteme dogmatike*. I myself like to think of the doctrine of the Trinity as the *ultimate ground* of theological knowledge of God, the *basic grammar* of theology, for it is there that we find our knowledge of God reposing upon the final Reality of God himself, grounded in the ultimate relations intrinsic to God's own Being, which govern and control all true knowledge of him from beginning to end.[99]

As such, Torrance's doctrine of salvation reposes in his doctrine of the Trinity. But he argues that this procedure is not just one option among many, but is the only plausible theo-logical procedure. Scientific-trinitarian soteriology *is* theological soteriology. This is even more so because soteriology is primarily an inquiry about the *who*, not the *what* or the

---

98. Torrance, *Christian Doctrine of God*, 198.
99. Torrance, *Ground and Grammar of Theology*, 158–59.

how. The subject of salvation is the Triune God. The nature, range, and attainment of human salvation is inseparable from the being of the Savior, which is another way of affirming that God's being is his act and his act is his being. Salvation "is indeed more than a reflection of [the Trinity], for it is grounded in it, is altogether inseparable from it, and actually flows from it."[100] Torrance's critique of federal Calvinism's reliance on abstract concepts and principles instead of grounding soteriological formulations on the revealed personal being of God is motivated by his commitment to a *kataphysic* theology. His difference from federal Calvinism is primarily theological.

However, a *kataphysic* trinitarian soteriology not only looks at the being of God in an uncritical monotheistic manner. God's being is triune: *mia ousia treis hypostaseis*. Properly speaking, then, God is the Father, Son, and Holy Spirit, and to argue for a soteriology grounded in the being of God is to argue that salvation is the work of the persons of the Triune God. This is *kataphysic* soteriology: understanding salvation in strict accordance with the being of God as triune. God is not only triune in being, but also triune in activity. Because the agent of salvation is the Triune God, for instance, a doctrine of salvation that is formulated in the light of a Jesus Christ isolated from the Father and the Holy Spirit is insufficient. Although there is merit in arguing that Christology is implicitly trinitarian, such implicitness could not be a substitute for a well-expounded trinitarian soteriology.[101]

The challenge, then, is how to formulate a trinitarian soteriology that does justice to both the *one being* of God and the *triune persons* of the Godhead. Seen in the light of his responses to this challenge, grounded in his trinitarian theology, Torrance's soteriology is superior to traditional textbook soteriologies. His consideration of the Triune God's being and Persons and his balance between the Unity-in-Trinity and Trinity-in-Unity in the salvific economy marks a great accomplishment. First, Torrance understands the mediation of reconciliation as the work of the Tri-unity whose being is communion-for and communion-with. Because God's being is personal, he interacts with the created other in the personal mode of his being. This can be called Torrance's trinitarian *kat' ousian* soteriology. In short, the act of the Triune God is in strict accordance with his being as triune. Soteriologies that are not grounded on the being of the agent of

---

100. Torrance, *Christian Doctrine of God*, 198.

101. Reciprocally, as Olson and Hall argue, it is only when we think trinitarianly that the flaws of all non-trinitarian accounts of God are realized, in *The Trinity*, 2.

salvation are both unscientific and non-theological. Furthermore, moving to the second aspect of God's personal agency in the salvific economy requires the doctrine of *perichoresis*, which highlights both unity-in-distinction and distinction-in-unity in God's being and act. Salvation is the "perichoretic coactivity of the Holy Trinity."[102] The triune persons mutually interpenetrate each other not only in their hypostatic relations but also in their salvific agencies: "The Father, the Son and the Holy Spirit always act together in every divine operation whether in creation or redemption, yet in such a way that the distinctive activities of the Father, the Son and the Holy Spirit are always maintained."[103] Thus, in the second aspect of the salvific work of the triune God, there are self-designated and distinct activities that each of the three Persons fulfill. For instance, only the Son is incarnate and only the Son and the Holy Spirit are "sent." This can be called Torrance's trinitarian *kath hypostasin* soteriology.

One important aspect that is still left virtually untouched by Torrance scholars is Torrance's employment of the doctrine of appropriation, which is actually important in the second level of a *kataphysic* trinitarian soteriology. This means that the distinct works of the Persons of the Trinity in the salvific economy are in strict accordance with their distinct hypostases as Father, Son, and Holy Spirit. In *The Christian Doctrine of God*, Torrance's attitude towards the doctrine of appropriation is somewhat negative, because he was combating an "essentialist approach to the doctrine of the Trinity from the One Being of God," but his trinitarian theology in general and his trinitarian soteriology in particular indubitably employs the doctrine as a hermeneutical principle, most especially in that he follows Barth's procedure.[104] The Triune God, Torrance writes, is "engaged in the work of reconciliation in distinctive ways appropriate to each Person."[105] The critique that Torrance obscures the plurality of God's activity and identity by an overemphasis on the unity of God's operations is therefore unwarranted.[106] Chapters 2, 3, and 4 of the book explain how Torrance's trinitarian soteriology employs this *kataphysic* principle.

---

102. Torrance, *Christian Doctrine of God*, 198.

103. Ibid., 198.

104. Ibid., 200. See Barth, *CD* I/1: 373–75, and most evident in chapter 2, sections 10 to 12. See also Jüngel, *God's Being is in Becoming*, 49–53; Gunton, *Becoming and Being*, 150; and McIntosh, "The Doctrine of Appropriation," 278–90.

105. Torrance, *Scottish Theology*, 87; *Christian Doctrine of God*, 252–53.

106. Flett, "Persons, Powers, and Pluralities," 16–17.

Kataphysic, Evangelical *Trinitarian Soteriology*

Application of the doctrine of appropriation in soteriological formulation, however, could not be done arbitrarily. For instance, although the Holy Spirit fulfills a unique salvific agency in accordance with his hypostasis as the Holy Spirit, it is chimerical to outline the whole triune economy of salvation by beginning with the work of the Holy Spirit. The articulation of the doctrine of salvation should follow the economic *taxis* of God's revealing and reconciling activity, or "the movement of saving Love."[107] As such, a *kataphysic* trinitarian soteriology should also employ the evangelical approach, i.e., beginning with the revealed knowledge of God in the incarnate Son. Nevertheless, the consideration of the evangelical *taxis* of the Triune God in soteriological formulation is in a sense only pedagogical, because the evangelical *taxis* could not be read back into the Trinity *in se*. As will be seen in the subsequent chapters, although Torrance accepts a trinitarian economic subordination, he repudiates any talk about priority or superiority that is read back into the Trinity *in se*.[108] Ontologically speaking, there is no one prior or subsequent in the triune persons. Even the Father could not be Father without the Son, for Fatherhood is a relationship that requires a Son.

Torrance argues that the triune evangelical *taxis* is reflected in Paul's benediction formula, "the grace of the Lord Jesus Christ, the love of God, and the communion of the Holy Spirit" (2 Cor 13:14). He even argues that this "constitute[s] the Trinitarian structure of all Christian faith and life," and should be considered as a "statement of the condescension of God to our weaknesses."[109] In the Gospel narratives, the Triune God manifested himself in a profound way as the incarnate Son, who then reveals the Father and the Holy Spirit not only by speaking about them but also by communing with them. This formula is in Torrance's early theology, evident in his employment of this outline in his sermon "The Trinity of Love,"[110] and remained in his later argument in *The Christian Doctrine of God*:

> God's distinctive self-revelation as Holy Trinity, One Being, Three Persons, creates the overall framework within which all Christian theology is to be formulated. . . . The doctrine of the

---

107. Torrance, *Theology in Reconciliation*, 118.

108. Torrance, "Thomas F. Torrance Responds," in *The Promise of Trinitarian Theology*, 316.

109. Torrance, "Crisis in the Kirk," 21–22; *School of Faith*, xxi; and *When Christ Comes*, 183.

110. Torrance, "A Sermon on the Trinity," 40–44; *When Christ Comes*, 180–92.

> Trinity enshrines the essentially Christian conception of God: it constitutes the ultimate evangelical expression *the Grace of the Lord Jesus Christ* who though he was rich for our sakes became poor that we through his poverty might become rich, of *the Love of God* who did not spare his own Son but delivered him up for us all, for it is in that personal sacrifice of the Father to which everything in the Gospel goes back, and of *the Communion of the Holy Spirit* through whom and in whom we are made to participate in the eternal Communion of the Father and the Son and are united with one another in the redeemed life of the people of God.[111]

The whole book, thus, follows this evangelical trinitarian blueprint. Colyer, writing on Torrance's trinitarian and scientific theology, utilizes the same sketch, rightly asserting how Torrance himself argues for such a structure. But unlike Colyer who opted for a non-progressive outline with a hope that Torrance's "theological holism gradually comes into view" at the end,[112] this book follows a progressive sequential argument. This means that rather than presenting Torrance's trinitarian soteriology through a partitive investigation, it attempts a progressive presentation, by which the preceding chapters are the building blocks for explorations that follow. This coheres better with Torrance's overall evangelical procedure, which can be applied in presenting his trinitarian soteriology.

Conclusions

Torrance's trinitarian soteriology is (1) scientific, because it is grounded in strict accordance with the nature of the Triune God, and (2) evangelical, because it proceeds in strict accordance with the economic *taxis* of God's own revealing and reconciling activity. Consequently, Torrance's trinitarian soteriology is also (3) doxological: "In knowing God in accordance with his ultimate divine nature we can know him only through his self-revelation and grace, and thus only in the mode of worship, prayer, and adoration in which we respond personally, humbly and obediently to his divine initiative in making himself known to us as our Creator and Lord."[113] As Torrance writes in a sermon, "Fidelity to the truth of the Gospel, belief in the Holy Spirit, and worship of the Father in and through Jesus Christ

---

111. Torrance, *Christian Doctrine of God*, 2.
112. Colyer, *How to Read*, 26.
113. Torrance, *Theology and Natural Science*, 92.

cannot be separated from one another."[114] The emphasis on the doxological attitude in theologizing is important because Torrance discerns that there seems to be the loss of the affirmation of God's majesty today, which is an evidence of "another decay in our souls."[115] In short, theologians should consider that in theology we are up against God himself in his ultimateness and the absolute Lordly authority of his almightiness,[116] so that in our attempt to expound our limited knowledge of his self-revelation, the ethical approach is that of worship and submission. As will also be seen in the last chapter, salvation, when perceived in the light of the being, persons, and work of the Triune God, results in a dynamic, participatory, and communal soteriology. The integrative-sequential trinitarian approach to salvation as "the grace of the Lord Jesus Christ, the love of God and the communion of the Holy Spirit" paints a more faithful eschatological picture. Of course, the complete view is only available as we begin to paint from the proper starting point, so we turn to a chapter on the Person and work of Jesus Christ.

---

114. B39 and B47 "Ecumenical Service—Kirk of the Greyfriars," 8.
115. B38 "With God is Terrible Majesty," 2.
116. Ibid., 1.

2

The Grace of Our Lord Jesus Christ

> "It is finished!" Finished the temptation! Finished the tyranny of it! Finished the shame of it! The foe is vanquished at last. The snare is broken. The Syrian lies dead upon the field. Glory be to Christ—it is finished! Thank God for the Cross—the arrow of the Lord's deliverance. Glory be to Christ, the Chariot of the Lord, and the horsemen thereof![1]

CONGRUENT WITH TORRANCE'S CRY FOR OBJECTIVITY, REALIST THEOlogy, and *kath hypostasin* soteriology, and in line with a doctrine of salvation that considers the salvific agency of the persons of the Triune God, this chapter presents the Person and work of Christ. This chapter has two sections: (1) *the grace* of (2) *the Lord Jesus Christ*. The Person of Christ will be presented first, because reconciliation can only be properly understood when it is grounded upon the Person of the Reconciler. We are not postulating, however, that the saving work of Christ is only an addendum to the Person of Christ. As Torrance warns, "We must be careful not to state a doctrine of the person of Christ, or of the hypostatic union, and then go on to state the doctrine of the saving work of Christ as atoning reconciliation, as if atoning reconciliation were something that had to be added on to the doctrine of the hypostatic union."[2] The two are interrelated: a presentation of the Person of Christ already involves soteriology. In fact, Torrance's Christology is soterio-conditioned. As will be evident in this chapter, Torrance's understanding of *what* Christ accomplishes for our salvation develops out of his equal concern for *who* Christ is, which is integral to his polemic against the subjectivist tendencies of contemporary

---

1. B42 "Joash and Elisha," 9.

2. Torrance, *Incarnation*, 183–84. See his sermon on reconciliation in B46 Untitled Moderator's sermon on 2 Corinthians 5:18.

soteriological formulations that are apparently more interested in the benefits of Christ's gift of salvation than recognizing the objective reference, i.e., *who* Christ is.[3]

The Grace of *Our Lord Jesus Christ*

Torrance's theological and scientific consistency is unmistakable in his soteriological understanding. To examine "who" Jesus is, prior to discussing his redemptive work, is grounded upon two important rationales: (1) historical-theological and (2) methodological-scientific. First, the identity of the Savior as God-man is essential in understanding his unique role in the whole drama of salvation. Particularly important are his identity as the Son of the Father in the Spirit (trinitarian identity) and his identity as fully human (anthropological identity). Second, and in relation to the first, like Einstein's reaction to Newtonian cosmology and Euclidian geometry, which separated physics and theoretical frameworks, Torrance avoids soteriological formulations purely from theoretical assumptions—that is, a way of thinking grounded upon *a priori* presuppositions. Rationality should be in touch with an equivalent reality, or a theory should be grounded upon an objective and concrete reality for it to be acceptable. Applied to soteriology, a theoretical understanding of redemption should be founded upon the concrete reality of the life and work of the Triune God.

Homoousion to Patri

The central issue in Christology today—as in the fourth century—is the identity of Jesus Christ, particularly in relation to objective soteriology. Colin Gunton rightly asserts that the favorite heresy of the nineteenth and twentieth century was Arianism, evident in the popular theologies of Friedrich Schleiermacher, Rudolf Bultmann, and Paul Tillich.[4] Residues of these soteriologies, which focused more on self-experience rather than relying on Christ's vicarious redemption were frequently mentioned and combated in Torrance's theology. Torrance's argument for a proper understanding of the identity of Christ as *homoousion to Patri* is thus extremely relevant for contemporary theology. In a sentence, the significance of the

---

3. Torrance, *Belief in Science*, 93–95.
4. Gunton, "And in One Lord, Jesus Christ," in *Nicene Christianity*, 35–48.

homoousios is the affirmation that "Jesus is God," which, as will be seen later, has profound implications.

Theological Development and Meaning of the Term

Torrance refers to the critical importance of the *homoousion to Patri* in the development of the creeds in the fourth and fifth centuries, when the church was engrossed with theological challenges. He discerns that the heresies, in various forms and arguments, were all grounded (among other things) in the same foundation: a dualistic frame of thought in which their proponents were trapped. The dualism that characterized Hellenic philosophy proposed a radical separation between the *kosmos noetos* and the *kosmos aisthetos*, so that an unbroken relationship between the incarnate Jesus and God appeared incomprehensible.[5] The result was that

> Conflicting attempts were made to interpret the mystery of Jesus Christ, operating not only from contrasting Hebraic and Hellenistic starting points but from the sharp antithesis between God and the empirical world in the prevailing framework of knowledge. Thus there arose the so-called "ebionite" and "docetic" types of Christology which had the effect in different ways of breaking up the wholeness of the New Testament presentation of Jesus Christ as God and man by separating the divine Christ from the man Jesus.[6]

This happens, Torrance adds, whenever *a priori* presuppositions derived from culture, philosophy and/or experience take precedence in interpreting the reality of Jesus Christ. It was Athanasius, Torrance's patristic hero, who detected this irregularity in the fourth century, particularly in his debates with Arianism. Athanasius clearly showed the early church that it was the axiomatic assumption of a radical dichotomy between the realm of events and the realm of ideas that gave rise to Arius's mythological thinking. Thus, in retrospect, the church fathers that met in Nicea were left with two options: (1) to give in to the prevailing culture and interpret revelation using the tools it provides, or (2) to submit themselves to the objective reality of Jesus Christ as Immanuel, "God with us." Nicea opted for the latter, affirming that "in Jesus Christ the eternal Logos of God had become incarnate in our physical existence" by employing the definitive

---

5. Torrance, *Preaching Christ Today*, 15.
6. Torrance, *Trinitarian Faith*, 111.

phrase *homoousion to Patri*.⁷ Referring to the Nicene solution, Torrance names *homoousios* as a representative of scientific and theological thinking, because objective reality is allowed to speak for itself.⁸ The term does not, however, encompass the whole mystery of the incarnate God. Rather, as Torrance recognizes, it is an attempt, using human words, to give clarificatory expression to the oneness in being and act between Jesus Christ and God the Father, which meant that "the Father and Jesus do not only have a similar Nature, they possess one and the same identical Nature; they have not only one intelligence, one power and one outpouring of goodness, but the 'same' intelligence, power and goodness."⁹ By extension, whatever Christ did should be perceived as the work of the Father himself. This concept was reiterated in the Nicene-Constantinopolitan Creed, and was given its fullest exposition in Chalcedon in 451, when its profound implications for the doctrine of the Trinity were fully realized.

Insofar as *homoousios* can be considered as a decisive response to the question of Jesus's identity, Torrance recognizes that it also served an exegetical function in the conciliar deliberations. Thus he argues that the employment of the *homoousios* was "an absolutely fundamental event that took place in the mind of the church," an event that is of irreversible significance because it changed the course of the church's theologizing.[10] Nevertheless, as is so for every term or concept used in theology, the term *homoousios* is only instrumental, that is, *dianoietic* (letting the mind assume conceptual forms under the pressure of the objective reality of God) and *paradeigmatic* (images and representations taken from the visible world to point to divine realities and not to themselves). As such, it is open for reformulation: "Like any other creative 'definition' of this kind,

---

7. Torrance, *Space, Time, and Incarnation*, 14; "Theological Realism," 184–86. Torrance consistently contrasts mythological thinking and theological thinking, and in B23 "The Doctrine of God in Traditional Theology," he even claims that ultimately, pagan and Christian views of God, owing to their different presuppositions and methodology, are irreconcilable. See also B45 Untitled sermon on Acts 5:3, 4; and B44 "Christ: God or Not," on Torrance's lament on the fact that the world wants a Christ that it can mold to its own liking, not the Christ who reveals himself as he is. Ultimately, with Barth, Torrance is against any domestication of God. See B46 "Ye have known God," 2–4.

8. Torrance, *Theology in Reconstruction*, 33; "Theological Realism," 185, 190–93.

9. Torrance, *Theological Dialogue* 1: 134. Because Jesus is God himself, the appropriate response to his presence is humility, as exemplified in the words of John the Baptist. See B44 "He must increase, I must decrease," 1–6.

10. Torrance, *Christian Doctrine of God*, ix, 80–81; *Theological Dialogue* 1: 98. The *homoousion to Patri* thus constitutes two functions: clarificatory and exegetical (or theological and hermeneutical; *Trinitarian Faith*, 129).

owing to its essentially semantic and interpretative function, this formulation must also be continually tested and revised in the light of what it was coined to express in the first place, as well as in the light of its fertility in the subsequent history of thought."[11] As to whether the contemporary church has already invented a new term with an exegetical function equivalent to *homoousios,* Torrance seems to say "not yet," evidenced by his uncompromising stance for it.[12]

Evangelical Significance of "Fully God"

In terms of the Person of Jesus Christ, the *homoousion to Patri* bridges the apparent gap between the Trinity *ad extra* and the Trinity *ad intra*. To affirm that Jesus Christ is of the same substance as the Father implies that the ontological Trinity became immanent and present in the world, thus "God with us" in its fullest literal sense. The staggering significance of this to soteriology is thrown into sharp relief by posing the question: "What would be implied if there were no oneness in being between Jesus Christ and God the Father"? At stake is the saving work of Christ and the credibility of Christ's atoning reconciliation. As Athanasius once argued, "If Jesus Christ is not himself God, then there is no final authority or validity for anything he said or did for human beings. If he were not divine, he could not act divinely, and if he were not Creator, he would not be able to save and recreate humanity. No creature can ever be saved by a creature."[13] As a concrete illustration, Torrance uses Jesus's words in Mark 2:5, "Your sins are forgiven," to explain that if Jesus were not God himself, then his words are mere human utterances void of saving significance, for only God can forgive sins (Mark 2:7).[14] Thus, *homoousios* has direct bearing upon the

---

11. Torrance, *Christian Doctrine of God,* x. See Torrance's discussion in *Theology in Reconstruction,* 49–52.

12. As such, the entrenchment of most of his theological positions might seem to betray his cry for theological openness, because, as Klinefelter notes, Torrance formulates his theology "in a way as to defy refutation, that is . . . that they must be simply accepted or rejected, not 'refuted.'" Klinefelter, "God and Rationality," 124. This is further evidenced by his statement that the Nicene Creed still "represents the essential and unalterable core of the Church's convictions," in "The Substance of the Faith," 17.

13. Athanasius, *C. Ar.* II.21–31 (*NPNF*² 4): 359–65; II.56–72 (*NPNF*² 4): 378–88; *Adel.* 8 (*NPNF*² 4): 577–8; in *Trinitarian Faith,* 138.

14. According to Torrance, that only God can forgive, coupled with the deity of Jesus Christ, is the heart of forgiveness and justification that is often taken for granted. B39 Untitled sermon on Mark 2:5. He particularly refers to John 5:17, 10:30, and 14:9 to describe the oneness in being and act between the Son and the Father, in "The

The Grace of Our Lord Jesus Christ

saving acts of Jesus Christ, in healing, forgiving, reconciling, and redeeming lost humanity, for it asserts in the strongest possible way that they are all accomplished out of a relation of unbroken oneness and communion between Jesus Christ and God. The *homoousion to Patri*, therefore, is "the supreme evangelical truth,"[15] because it embodies the central fact that in the same way that God is the content of his self-revelation, God is also the content of his saving grace in Jesus Christ. Thus, the *homoousion to Patri* asserts, "not only that there is no division between the being of the Son and the being of the Father, but there is no division between the acts of the Son and the acts of the Father."[16] It is the personal being of God in Christ who is at work in reconciliation: the Mediator is the Mediated. An extrinsicist soteriology, which carries with it an impersonal and instrumental view of grace, has no place in Torrance's theology. The Triune God sends himself and not some other agent or force to effect reconciliation. God himself in Christ is acting in the world for the redemption of humanity. The earthly works of Christ are the eternal works of God.

Epistemological Significance of "Fully God"

Apart from the soteriological significance of Jesus's consubstantiality with God, there are epistemological implications of the same ontological oneness. In particular, it highlights that God's being, Word, and act are one in Christ. The epistemological significance of the *homoousion* cannot be separated from the saving significance of the *homoousion*.[17] To distinguish God's Word from his act in this section is not to make an ontological distinction between the two: the decision is more pedagogical, in the hope that we might see Jesus's unique role in God's historical-theological self-communication more clearly.

Parallel to the importance of understanding the act of Jesus as the very act of God, grounded upon their ontological oneness, it is necessary that we consider the speech of Jesus to be the very speech of God. Torrance's concern for a realist theology, objectivity, and the objective ground of knowledge resurfaces here. He writes: "Everything depends upon the unity of being and act and word between Jesus Christ the only begotten Son and God the Father. If the *homoousion to Patri* were not true, the

---

Evangelical Significance of the *Homoousion*," 165.

15. Torrance, *Trinitarian Faith*, 132.

16. Ibid., 137.

17. Kang, "Epistemological Significance," 342.

Gospel would lack the very foundation in the self-revelation and self-communication of God in Jesus Christ which it needs in order to be Gospel."[18] If Jesus were not God himself speaking, then his words were just empty human utterances, and not the reliable words of God. If this is so, then we do not have genuine knowledge of God, but only knowledge of humanity. But because Jesus Christ is *homoousios* with God, then in Jesus Christ "we have a *Logos* that is not of man's devising but One who goes back into the eternal Being of God for he proceeded from the eternal Being of God."[19] So Torrance insists that in the person of Jesus Christ we have an *analogical reference*, that is, the movement of our thoughts and concepts across another or higher logical level goes back to the source which gives rise to them. What God is toward us in his economic revealing and saving activities in the historical Jesus, he really is inherently and eternally in himself. The earthly words of Jesus, therefore, are the eternal words of God. As Kang puts it, "The doctrine of *homoousion* and the incarnation mean that genuine human knowledge of God as God is possible because, in Kierkegaardian phraseology, the absolute Truth is now also an historical Truth."[20]

However, Jesus is more than the messenger of the truth of God. In Jesus Christ, the incarnate Son, truth is personalized.[21] Jesus is the *truth* (John 14:6). The Word and truth became Human. The Logos therefore is Word and Person: an "embodied Truth." For Torrance, Jesus is "the self-communicating, self-authenticating Word: the *Autologos, Autozoe, Autoexousia*."[22] In "The Deposit of Faith," he writes: "The self-sustaining and self-expressing nature of the Truth is its identity with the living Christ who in his saving work and Person *is* the Truth."[23] The implication for human knowledge of God is precise: our knowledge of God is bound to Jesus Christ who alone is the embodiment of truth, and truth himself. This is why Torrance argues that what God communicates in Christ is not to be understood as *datum*, but as *dandum*, because the Giver is identical with the Gift. He elaborates: "The application of the *homoousion* to the grace of God is to be understood as the impartation to us not of an impersonal

---

18. Torrance, *Trinitarian Faith*, 135.

19. Torrance, *Theology in Reconstruction*, 36.

20. Kang, "Epistemological Significance," 349; Torrance, *Reality and Scientific Theology*, 70–71.

21. Torrance, *School of Faith*, xxiv, xxxii–xxxv.

22. Torrance, *Theology in Reconstruction*, 41.

23. Torrance, "The Deposit of Faith," 5. Torrance adds: "Jesus Christ was the Prophet . . . but he was prophet in the unique sense of being identical with the word which he proclaimed. He was the Word of God," in *Incarnation*, 57.

something (an *aliquid*) from God, but of God himself. In Jesus Christ and in the Holy Spirit God freely gives himself to us in such a living personal way that the gift and the giver are one and the same and cannot be detached from each other."[24]

Homoousion hemin ton auton

Just as Torrance affirms the Nicene conclusion that emphasized the full divinity of Christ, he also affirms the Constantinopolitan, and later Chalcedonian, balance of the full humanity of Christ. For him, the Chalcedonian statement on the humanity of Christ demonstrates the triumph of *theologic* over Hellenic dualistic culture and philosophy. As with the *homoousios* employed in Nicea, referring to Jesus as "fully man" rejects Docetic and Apollinarian dualistic presuppositions. Particularly interesting, however, especially in the Chalcedonian symbol, is the application of the same term *homoousios* to express the full humanity of Christ: "consubstantial with us." Jesus Christ is both *homoousion to Patri* and *homoousion hemin ton auton kata ten anthropoteta*: "consubstantial with the Father according to the Godhead, and consubstantial with us according to the Manhood." That *homoousios* is also used to express Christ's humanity is most probably intentional, so as to emphasize that the full humanity of Christ is as important as his divinity. Rejecting the *homoiousios* alternative, Jesus did not only become like human, but existed as human in a concrete historical manner. "The incarnation," Torrance stresses, "is to be understood as *God really become man.*"[25] Any proposal of partial incarnation in whatever form (partial divinity or partial humanity) should be rejected.

> In the fullness of his Deity he became man in the undiminished reality of human and creaturely being, without of course ceasing to be God the Son. The incarnation was not the bringing into being of a created intermediary between God and man, but the incarnating of God in such a way that in Jesus Christ he is both God and man in the fullest and most proper sense. The incarnation is to be understood, then, as a real becoming on the part of God, in which God comes *as man* and acts *as man*, all for our sake—from beginning to end God the Son acts among us in a human way, "within the measures of our humanity."[26]

---

24. Torrance, *Karl Barth*, 192; *Trinitarian Perspectives*, 104; *Doctrine of Grace*, 31–32.

25. Torrance, *Trinitarian Faith*, 149.

26. Ibid., 150.

The affirmation that Jesus Christ is not just God *in humanity,* but God *as human,* implies a rejection of the idea that the humanity of Christ was merely instrumental in the hands of God. While maintaining this, Torrance also emphasizes the originality and newness of the incarnation: "in the incarnation of the Son something *new* has taken place in God."[27] This, however, does not only refer to the virgin birth, or to the fact that God became human. Rather, the whole life of the incarnate Son is new to God, including being in creaturely space and time, experiencing human emotions and needs, down to the cross and the resurrection. The rationale Torrance provides for this new becoming in the life of the eternal God is tied to his theology of vicarious redemption. Quoting Athanasius, "He was not man previously, but he became man *for our sake.*"[28] And precisely because God himself became human, he himself is the agent of reconciliation. According to Torrance, Athanasius realized the significance of the wholeness of Christ's humanity, particularly because of his emphasis on vicarious atonement. Furthermore, any Apollinarian Christology is also repudiated, because being wholly human involves having a human consciousness, not just physicality.[29]

Soteriological Significance of "Fully Human"

Torrance asserts that the humanity of Christ should be understood in the light of Christ's vicarious Person and work. Inasmuch as the deity of Christ secures for our salvation the objective ontological foundation in God, so that the work of Jesus is nothing other than the work of God himself, the humanity of Christ also secures the objective ontological foundation in humanity *for* humanity *by* the human Jesus. Our salvation is not only worked out by God in Christ, but also by humanity in Christ. Jesus Christ, therefore, appropriately receives the title "Mediator" and "Bridge of God."[30] Our salvation is fulfilled *in* Christ *by* Christ in his synergistic and double redemptive movement expressed as his humanward descent

---

27. Torrance, *Divine Meaning,* 187. Hence, God takes us by surprise, revealing to us himself in a way we are not able to anticipate. See B44 "The Fig Tree," 1–8.

28. Athanasius, *In Ill. Om.* 3 (*NPNF*² 4): 88; in Torrance, *Trinitarian Faith,* 88; *Christian Doctrine of God,* 238. In his article "The Doctrine of the Virgin Birth," 20, however, Torrance argues that the virgin birth means that it was not an entirely new act of creation on the part of God, but rather a recreation within our human existence in the creative action of God.

29. Torrance, *Divine Meaning,* 191–92.

30. B23 "Where is God?," 6.

as God and his Godward ascent as human. In so far as redemption requires both God's initiative and humanity's response, both are seen to have been accomplished by the one God-man, Jesus Christ. What is profoundly important, Torrance argues, is to see "the historical Jesus as a single individual man."[31] Jesus was fully human not only as a physical existent, but as a whole human being, with psyche and emotions like any other human. Torrance wants to avoid two errors: "There is a clear danger in speaking of the assumption of 'a man,' for that savours of adoptionism, but on the other hand, to speak of the assumption of 'man' savours of the idea that what was assumed was only human nature in general, human nature with all its human properties and qualities."[32] Torrance's emphasis here is not only ontological, but also soteriological: Jesus assumed full human nature in order to redeem it. "As the Head of creation, in whom all things consist, he is the only one who really can act on behalf of all and save them. When he took our human nature upon himself, and in complete somatic solidarity with us offered himself up to death in atoning sacrifice for man, he acted instead of all and on behalf of all."[33]

Two emphases may be expounded. First, that Jesus was in "complete somatic solidarity with us" implies not only the assumption of the body and its physical needs, but also of the human condition of sin. The Inhominisation of the Son represents "the coming of God to save us in the heart of our fallen and depraved humanity, where humanity is at its wickedest in its enmity and violence against the reconciling love of Christ."[34] Jesus does not assume a neutral humanity different from our own, but assumes our fallen humanity, which he also sanctifies and redeems through his whole life and work. According to Torrance, this is in line with the patristic

---

31. Torrance, *Incarnation*, 210.

32. Ibid., 210.

33. Torrance, *Trinitarian Faith*, 155. While Torrance is fascinated by the Athanasian emphasis on the divinity of Christ, he admits that he is more fascinated by the humanity of Jesus: "What overwhelms me is the sheer humanness of Jesus, Jesus as the baby at Bethlehem, Jesus sitting tired and thirsty at the well outside Samaria, Jesus exhausted by the crowds, Jesus recuperating his strength through sleep at the back of a ship on the sea of Galilee, Jesus hungry for figs on the way up to Jerusalem, Jesus weeping at the grave of Lazarus, Jesus thirsting for water on the Cross—for that precisely is God with us and one of us, God as 'the wailing infant' in Bethlehem . . . , God sharing our weakness and exhaustion, God sharing our hunger, thirst, tears, pain and death. Far from overwhelming us, God with us and one of us does the very opposite, for in sharing with us all that we are in our littleness and weakness he does not override our humanity but completes, perfects and establishes it." See *Preaching Christ Today*, 13.

34. Torrance, *Mediation of Christ*, 39.

Communion with the Triune God

emphasis that "the unassumed is unhealed," which he considers "the cardinal soteriological principle of the ecumenical Church."[35] Because of Christ's assumption of "our actual fallen Adamic nature," and his becoming human in the ontological depths, Christ "made our sin and misery, our death and fate his own. He really became one with us as we actually are in our flesh of sin and alienation in mind. Otherwise our actual human nature, physical and mental, would not have been brought within the sanctifying and renewing activity of the Saviour."[36] More radically, Torrance proposes that owing to this, Christ's life and death, therefore, should be perceived to have dealt with actual and original sin altogether.[37]

Secondly, the humanity of Christ is a necessary foundation for understanding the priestly office of Christ and the God-humanward and human-Godward activity of Christ. Just as Christ is God himself ministering to humanity, so he is human embodying humanity in himself and vicariously effecting human response to God. Thus, in the incarnation the Son of God "ministered not only the things of God to man but ministered the things of man to God."[38] Torrance adds: "God not only fulfils his promise of love in the covenant in giving himself to humanity in complete and utter grace, but he accomplishes for man, and from within man, man's fulfilment of the covenant, man's appropriation of God's gift of himself."[39]

Torrance's view of Christ's assumption of humanity's fallen nature is one of the few points where others critique his theology. First, Torrance's view, particularly in his allusions to the fathers, lands him in the middle of the debate as to whether or not the early fathers taught Christ's assumption of fallen human nature. There are those, like Donald MacLeod, Matthew Baker, and Matthew Kapic, who argue that Torrance's appeal to Gregory Nazianzen's dictum "the unassumed is unhealed" is unwarranted, and demonstrates how he reads what is really not explicitly said by the early

---

35. Gregory of Nazianzus, *Letter to Cledonius the Priest*, in *NPNF*[2] 7: 440; Torrance, *Karl Barth*, 232. See Kang's more elaborate discussion in "Concept of Vicarious Humanity of Christ," 260–88.

36. Torrance, *Karl Barth*, 103–4; *Scottish Theology*, 209; *Theology in Reconstruction*, 129; and B47 "Christ tempted in all points as we are." See Dawson's instructive article "Far as the Curse is Found," in *An Introduction to Torrance Theology*, 55–74. Athanasius adds: "Though [Christ] used the body as instrument, he shared nothing of its defect, but rather sanctified it by his indwelling," in *On the Incarnation*, chapter 43. Torrance, *Atonement*, 129–34.

37. Torrance, "The Atonement," 237–39; *School of Faith*, lxxxvi; and *Atonement*, 158–60.

38. Torrance, *Trinitarian Faith*, 4, 157, 161–64, 183.

39. Torrance, *Incarnation*, 56.

fathers in general.⁴⁰ The primary issues here are interpretation and emphasis. Ho critiques both MacLeod's and Torrance's (and other theologians's) "excessive claims" and suggests that "the assumption of both fallen and unfallen human natures are found in patristic writings"⁴¹ depending on where one is looking or how one interprets patristic writings. At first sight, this offers a promising solution, but his compromising *via media* does not really solve the problem of orthodoxy. What it proposes and only accomplishes is a sort of theological relativism vindicated by hermeneutical differences, but this certainly is not sufficient. What is needed in the debate is not just a superficial glossing and citing of specific patristic statements on the issue, either *pro* or *anti*, but a sensitivity toward the general tenor or argument of the early fathers, especially those found in the ecumenical councils. For instance, MacLeod's judgment that Torrance's interpretation of Gregory Nazianzen's dictum "the unassumed is unhealed" is "an illegitimate use of a form of words" because Gregory's only concern was to establish Christ's genuine human mind, illustrates an erroneous microscopic analysis that disregards the overall picture.⁴² What MacLeod misses is the inseparable concern of Gregory (and the theologians of the Council of Constantinople) for both ontology and soteriology. Christ assumed all human experiences because he saves humanity by doing so. The rational implication of this, even though not stated verbatim by the fathers, is that what Christ assumed included our fallen human condition, because it is that which he came to heal. By virtue of the intention to heal that which is assumed, then what has been assumed must be in need of healing. Furthermore, if one compares the treatments of both those who are *pro* and *anti* the idea of Christ's assumption of fallen human nature found in the early fathers, one would discern a qualitative difference in the level of patristic scholarship. For instance, if we compare Torrance's treatment of the patristic writings with MacLeod's (who is Torrance's most avid critic on this issue), one would find that the latter's treatment is limited to only a few patristic writings. Torrance's handling of patristic documents, on the other hand, is exceptional and comprehensive.⁴³ In fact, considering

40. See MacLeod, *The Person of Christ*, 221–30; *Jesus is Lord*, 128–29; Baker, "The Place of St. Irenaeus of Lyons," 25–27; Kapic, "The Son's Assumption of a Human Nature," 157, 164.

41. Ho, *A Critical Study*, 77. With MacLeod who rejects the fallen view is Hughes, *The True Image*, 125–35.

42. MacLeod, *The Person of Christ*, 224.

43. For instance, MacLeod only cites Gregory of Nazianzus, Cyril, Augustine, and Leo (and in the most minimal manner) in *The Person of Christ*, 224–25. Contrast

this achievement by Torrance, one cannot but cringe at Ivor J. Davidson's ill-judgment that Torrance is among those whose attempt to prove the classical orthodoxy of belief in the fallen flesh is "in almost all cases too simplistic."[44]

Secondly, MacLeod, Davidson, and Oliver Crisp argue that concomitant to insisting that the human nature of Jesus must be "fallen" if it is to be *real* lies the damaging idea that sinfulness is of the essence of human nature.[45] Davidson adds that this view leads (1) to a denial of the primordial goodness of creation, and (2) to miss the fact that authentic humanity is only marred, not constituted by sin.[46] In this line of thought, Torrance is judged as guilty of failing to distinguish what is *universal* from what is *essential*, i.e., while sinfulness is universal, it may not be truly essential (or necessary) to what it means to be human.[47] In here, instead of differences in hermeneutics lie differences in theological agenda and presupposition. In terms of agenda, it seems that there is a double concern for the proponents of Christ's unfallen humanity not only to affirm the goodness of creation but also, and especially, the sinlessness of Christ. The problem of the latter, however, which Trevor Hart discerns, is that "the more we seek to bolster and secure the sinlessness [using *non posse peccare*], the more we seem to put at risk those very moral conditions which render it [Christ's victory over sins] soteriologically significant."[48] What is at stake, therefore, as Torrance also discerns, is the integrity of Christ's salvific economy, so that there needs to be a worshipful affirmation of Jesus as "in the likeness of sinful flesh" (Rom 8:3) and "yet he did not sin" (Heb 4:15). How this can

---

Torrance's references in *Trinitarian Faith*, chapter 5, esp. 161–68.

44. Davidson, "Pondering the Sinlessness of Jesus Christ," 397. For other writings defending the idea, see Wiles, "The Unassumed is the Unhealed," 47–56; McFarland, "Fallen or Unfallen?," 399–415; and Gunton, *Christ and Creation*, 35–68. Cass argues that no patristic writer explicitly held the assumption and the consequent sanctification of sinful humanity in Christ's life, so Torrance's accomplishment is actually the development of a unique approach to the doctrine of the incarnation, in Cass, *Christ Condemned in the Flesh*, 212. See McCormack, "For us and for Our Salvation," 1–38, for the relationship between *kenosis* and the humanity of Christ in the history of Reformed theology; and on Torrance's view of *kenosis*, see Ho, *A Critical Study*, 242–71. Perhaps the general problem is that it is difficult to maintain how Christ could have assumed fallen human nature and yet not be sinful or commit sin. See Gill, "The Doctrine of Revelation," 55, 255; and Crisp, *Divinity and Humanity*, 115.

45. Crisp, *Divinity and Humanity*, chapter 4.

46. Davidson, "Pondering the Sinlessness of Jesus Christ," 397.

47. This distinction is made by Morris, in "The Metaphysics of God Incarnate," in *Trinity, Incarnation and Atonement*, 116.

48. Hart, "Sinlessness and Moral Responsibility," 40.

The Grace of Our Lord Jesus Christ

be is explained by Torrance: "Far from sinning himself or being contaminated by what he appropriated from us, Christ triumphed over the forces of evil entrenched in our human existence, bringing his own holiness, his own perfect obedience, to bear upon it in such a way as to condemn sin in the flesh and to deliver us from its power."[49]

In terms of differences in theological presuppositions, those who argue that Jesus did not assume a fallen human nature presuppose, whether they are aware of it or not, that sinfulness is not the primordial essence of human nature by adhering to Augustine's thoughts on the difference between pre- and post-Fall humanity. Concomitant to this view is a line of thinking that begins with creation, then works from there to redemption, or from Adam to Christ. Torrance, on the other hand, consistent with his christocentric approach, begins with revelation and redemption in Christ, then from there develops his anthropology and doctrine of creation. What constitutes humanity can only be known in the light of who Christ is and what he has done, not the other way around. Thus, the affirmation of Christ's assumption of fallen human nature is not only a christological statement but is also an anthropological statement, i.e., a statement about humanity in general. If, grounded in Irenaean Christology, Christ assumed and experienced every aspect of human existence, and, as discussed above, Christ assumed fallen humanity, then we can infer that humanity is fallen. Theological anthropology is grounded in Christological anthropology. Statements about Christ's humanity are also statements about our humanity. The problem with the creation-to-redemption or Adam-to-Christ approach is that it presupposes the distinction between an original perfect human *esse* which is corrupted from without because of the Fall, and which Christ assumed. Thus, there are two different types of humanity existing alongside each other—a pre-Fall Adamic humanity and a post-Fall fallen humanity—and it is argued that it is the first type that Christ assumed. Along with this is the idea that sin is like an Aristotelian accident that does not really effect a change in humanity at the ontological level. There is a Platonic *real* perfect human nature different from the *actual* fallen human nature that we now have. But this is certainly not the view of Athanasius, the Cappadocians, or Cyril. Even if we follow the Augustinian theological heritage, especially *via* Calvin, the change that happened in humanity is total and therefore has corrupted every fibre of

---

49. Torrance, *Trinitarian Faith*, 161.

human existence. There are not two types of humanity, but only one, and it is fallen and sinful.[50]

Epistemological Significance of "Fully Human"

Christ's becoming human displays that the Word of divine self-revelation is objectively and subjectively fulfilled and completed in Jesus Christ. The import of *homoousion to Patri* is the actuality and objectivity of the Word of God in Christ, and that God himself has spoken. But this objective self-speech also takes place in the man Jesus, in whom God's truth has become actual for us in space and time. The Son took on human form (*morphe*, Phil 2:6, 7) to reveal the Triune God in reconciling knowledge. Considering humanity's inability to know God because of sin's blinding effect, and the asymmetrical relation between human finite reception and divine infinite knowledge, God had to assume human form and language in order for human reception of revelation to take place.[51] Put simply, "the incarnate person of Christ reveals the person of God in a humanized form."[52] In more technical language, Torrance writes:

> The information density of God is known to us only through contingent mediations; and considering the world and its increasingly complex life, even considering the entropy and negentropy of learning, does not enable more than fragmented glimpses of the information density of God to occur. . . . And this time-encompassing, lived-form event is Jesus Christ. He is the medium in which the information density of God occurs for

---

50. For instance, Torrance argues that even "the goodness of man" could only be discussed in terms of the redemptive work of the humanity of Christ, in "The Goodness and Dignity of Man," 309. He also asserts, opposing the Enlightenment's blind optimism, that the assumption that there is nothing wrong with human nature is not true. See B44 "What manner of child shall this be?," 6–7.

51. See Athanasius, *Incarnation*, 11 (*NPNF*[2] 4): 42; *C. Ar.* III.37–41 (*NPNF*[2] 4): 414–16. Torrance, *Divine Meaning*, 245, 250; *Incarnation*, xxxii–xli; and *Calvin's Doctrine of Man*, especially chapters 1 and 10. The incarnation, therefore, is the only valid ground for all knowledge of God. This is why Torrance, following Barth, was very suspicious of natural theology and all religious attempts to "discern" God apart from God's concrete self-manifestation in Christ. See *Karl Barth*, 136–59. Torrance brands human religion not only worthless, but also the supreme form of sin. See *God and Rationality*, 69; and *Karl Barth*, 7.

52. Torrance, *Ecumenical Studies*, 31; *Christian Doctrine of God*, 15, 21, 23, 30, 34, 71, 82, 107, 110, 111, 115.

The Grace of Our Lord Jesus Christ

mankind, and by which we may understand the domain of God in the inner logic of the world.[53]

Overall, from the side of God, the theological import of this is that Jesus himself is the Word of God to humanity in human form. Just as God's being and act are inseparable, God's being and Word in the human Jesus are one and the same. Thus, in his Didsbury Lectures, Torrance argued: "If, as we believe, Jesus Christ the incarnate Son and God the Father are one, then he embodies the very self-communication and self-giving of God to mankind and constitutes in his own Person the God-given pledge of its truth and reality."[54] Moreover, because Jesus Christ assumed our fallen human language as well, "our human word is now renewed in him and sanctified to be the proper instrument of divine revelation, and that truly understanding the human speech of Jesus Christ is indeed the faithful hearing of his eternal Word."[55]

As such, as both God and human, Jesus Christ is both the Word of God to humanity and the word of humanity to God, for in and through his incarnate life he has grounded and perfected humanity's knowledge of God. In a double movement, Jesus came in order to embody in himself both our questions to God and God's answers to us, as well as God's questions to us and true answers from us to God.[56] Several considerations must be noted. First, Torrance's insights on the assumption of our fallen human nature overlap here. As *the* true human, Christ embodied and exemplified the manner in which blinded humanity might see God. Because Christ sanctified human nature by assuming sinful humanity, he also redeemed our fallen spiritual senses (to use Origen's expression) to enable us to know God. Thus, "revelation is not only the uncovering of God but the uncovering of the ear and eye of man for God."[57] Secondly, in

---

53. Torrance, *Ecumenical Studies*, 108.

54. Torrance, *Mediation of Christ*, 58; *Theology in Reconstruction*, 121.

55. Kang, "Epistemological Significance," 349; Torrance, *Space, Time, and Resurrection*, 167.

56. Torrance, *Theology in Reconstruction*, 122, 126, 127. See also Torrance, "The Place of Christology in Biblical and Dogmatic Theology," 15–17; and "The Word of God and the Response of Man," 172–83.

57. Torrance, *Theology in Reconstruction*, 130, 131. Torrance borrows Augustine's view of *sapientia*, in which knowledge is achieved when humanity discerns an invisible transcendent and immutable truth, in "Transcendental Role of Wisdom," 131–32. See Karl Rahner's exposition in "The Spiritual Senses According to Origen," 81–103. Clement of Alexandria also stressed the priority of faith in the enabling of our spiritual senses, in *Strom.* V.1 (*ANF* 2): 444–47.

the light of human inability and God's priority, Christ is the sole ground of acceptable human response to the Father. As the true human, Christ represented humanity in himself in his conversation with God. Jesus is the "Believer for us, vicariously Believer, whose very humanity is the embodiment of our salvation."[58] The human Jesus is humanity's ear and mouth, hearing and responding to the self-giving of God. This is why Torrance calls Christ "a divinely prepared response to God's revelation."[59] Finally, Torrance emphasizes that only the Son knows the Father. This implies that our knowledge of God is dependent upon the knowledge and relationship of the Son to the Father. Rather than a direct knowledge of God through Christ, therefore, it is only by our participation in the human knowing of Jesus that we know God (this will be elaborated in chapter 3).

Hypostatic Union

In discussing the hypostatic union, Torrance asks: "How can we be faithful in our theological statements to the nature of the eternal being of the Son who became man and who yet remains God, and at the same time be faithful to the nature and person of the historical Jesus Christ?"[60] According to Torrance, heirs of the Alexandria-Antioch christological debates resurface in modern theology owing to the forgetfulness of both biblical and dogmatic theologians in appropriating the hypostatic union as the *theological* hermeneutic in understanding the Person of Jesus Christ. Parallel to the patristic situation, Torrance identifies the root of the problem as the dualistic framework that crept back into the church through Newtonian science and Kantian philosophy. For instance, Torrance identifies two particular movements with the tendency of emphasizing the humanity of Christ at the expense of his divinity: Bultmann's problematic demythologization project and the *Leben-Jesu Forschung* movement.[61] For Torrance, Christ is both theological and historical, or divine and human united in one Person. Jesus Christ is the personal event of the co-existence of divinity and humanity, or *metousia*.[62]

The *hypostatic union* is both foundational and immensely significant for Christian theology. Following the assertion of the early creeds, Jesus

---

58. Torrance, *Ministry and Sacraments of the Gospel*, 81.
59. Torrance, *Theology in Reconstruction*, 132–34, 157.
60. Torrance, *Incarnation*, 182.
61. See Torrance, "The Historical Jesus," 511–26.
62. Torrance, *Ecumenical Studies*, 34; *Incarnation*, 190.

The Grace of Our Lord Jesus Christ

Christ is the one Person in whom a permanent union of God and humanity took place. Torrance sees the centrality of the hypostatic union from two inseparable perspectives. First, the hypostatic union guards the full reality of Jesus Christ. The incarnate Son did not live a split personhood, but lived as one Person, as fully God-man. We can name this to be the *ontological significance*. Secondly, the hypostatic union is at the heart of the saving work of Christ. In fact, the deity and humanity of Christ have no revealing or saving significance for us apart from their hypostatic union in him. Thus, as Colyer concludes, "the hypostatic union of the divine and human natures within the one person of the incarnate Son is always and everywhere the source for all of Christ's atoning activity on our behalf."[63] We name this the *soteriological-epistemological significance*. To elaborate,

> The atonement is the work of the God-man, of God and man in hypostatic union, not simply an act of God in man, but an act of God as man. And so the hypostatic union and atonement belong together. Atonement is possible on the ground of the hypostatic union. . . . If we could divide the two natures of Christ, his divine and his human nature, into a nature of a divine person and a nature of a human person, then the human acts would not be acts of the divine person, and the divine acts would not be in the human person. In that event, the accomplishment of reconciliation would be illusory, for its ultimate achievement, the union of God and man, would not have been carried through. . . . The purpose of atonement is to reconcile humanity back to God so that atonement issues in union between man and God, but it issues in union between man and God because the hypostatic union is that union already being worked out between estranged man and God, between man's will and God's will in the one person of Christ.[64]

For Torrance, therefore, hypostatic union and atoning union imply and interpenetrate each other in Christ's mediation of reconciliation to humankind, which is a unique feature of his soteriology, at least in the light of his Reformed heritage: the hypostatic union is itself the atoning union.[65]

---

63. Colyer, "The Incarnate Saviour," in *An Introduction to Torrance Theology*, 38. See also the article of Kelly in the same book, "The Realist Epistemology of Thomas F. Torrance," 81–83.

64. Torrance, *Incarnation*, 195–96.

65. Cass, *Christ Condemned in the Flesh*, 159, 279; *Mediation of Christ*, 66. That Torrance considers both the divinity and humanity of Christ as important constituents for our salvation is an evidence of his fundamental Anselmic heritage. See *Cur Deus Homo* (1909); and Holmes, *Listening to the Past*, esp. chapter 3.

The Grace of Our Lord Jesus Christ

Reconciliation is Torrance's favored term for his soteriology.[66] This decision has several ramifications in his soteriological understanding and formulation. First, Torrance's soteriology is deeply relational in orientation. Human salvation is not primarily about entering an eschatological state of happiness in heaven or escaping future judgment (which are both characteristics of escapist soteriology), although these aspects are not altogether missing. Rather, salvation is primarily the event of reconciliation between two alienated parties, or "at-one-ment."[67] Secondly, the relational aspect of justification is recovered. Justification should not be viewed only as acquittal from sin, but also as restoration of lost relationship—reconciliation. Being integrative and holistic, Torrance is critical of soteriologies that are grounded solely upon humanity's negative predicament (i.e., sin), to the point of neglecting the positive ground of our salvation that precedes even sin (i.e., God's missional love). Thirdly, relational salvation is grounded upon the personal being and act of the Triune God. As a community of love, the triune being is essentially relational. Consequently, God's acts in space and time with "the other" (created existents) are personal, in that he himself comes to re-establish the broken covenant. Torrance asserts:

> Jesus Christ the Son of God made flesh for us and our salvation, was crucified to bear and bear away the sin of the world, to break down the barrier between God and man, and to reconcile the world to God. Jesus Christ descended into hell, an awful hell of our sin and guilt and its righteous judgment. He has borne our iniquities and suffered for us in his holy sacrifice, that we might be forgiven and restored to the Father as His dear children. That is the deepest reason for our hope, that *God has overcome our alienation and reconciled us to Himself*.[68]

Attached to this, Christ's reconciling work should be understood as the work of the Triune God himself. If Christ is the Mediator, who are the two parties mediated? Biblical statements such as "God was reconciling the world to himself in Christ" (2 Cor 5:18, 19) have a two-sided implication. On the one hand, the Triune God, in Jesus Christ, is engaged in a reconciling mission. The Son does not work autonomously, but vicariously

---

66. Habets, *Theosis*, 93. See *Atonement*, chapter 5 for Torrance's discussion of salvation in the light of the term "reconciliation."

67. The term was coined by William Tyndale to translate the Greek *katallage*. See Fiddes, "Salvation," 178.

68. Torrance, *When Christ Comes*, 153 (italics mine).

The Grace of Our Lord Jesus Christ

from the side of the Triune God. On the other hand, the effected reconciliation in Christ is not only with Christ, but with the Triune God. Just as it is the Triune God who is effecting reconciliation, it is also the Triune God who is reconciled. Jesus Christ, then, is the reconciling link between the Triune God and humanity. "In Jesus Christ," Torrance writes, "God Himself has come into our human life and forged a link between God and man which can never be broken."[69]

Incarnational Atonement

Cur Deus Homo? Throughout the history of Christian theology, theologians have grappled with the question of how Jesus accomplished salvation for us. As early as the second century, Irenaeus already asked the soteriological question, "Why did Christ descend?," prompting him to write his monumental *Against Heresies*. Athanasius's stress on the deity and humanity of Christ was also soteriologically driven. The furious theological debates from Nicea to Chalcedon were fuelled by soteriological implications. Similarly, Torrance's agenda in asserting the Chalcedonian Jesus Christ is primarily soteriological. Torrance's Christology is his soteriology, and *vice versa*. "On the basis of his articulation of *homoousios*, hypostatic union, and the vicarious humanity of Christ," Habets observes, "it is clear that central to Torrance's soteriology is the articulation of Christ's incarnational redemption."[70]

Why did God descend? It is a temptation for theologians to regard this as an anthropological question, that is, to treat it as a question of the human condition requiring anthropological statements, or statements about humanity. Approached from this perspective, the logical choice would be an initial presentation of hamartiology, the human condition in sin. Torrance's approach deviates from this popular Western route.[71] Following

69. Torrance, *When Christ Comes*, 150.
70. Habets, *Theosis*, 50.
71. Molnar, on the other hand, argues that understanding the connection between incarnation and atonement requires an understanding of Torrance's views of sin and evil (*Theologian of the Trinity*, 159). It seems, however, that although Torrance incorporates the discussion of sin in his soteriological formulation, this is not his principal concern. Thus, although he discusses the retrospective aspect of salvation, his primary concern over the prospective aspect seems to overshadow the former. Unfortunately, a fuller discussion of this lies outside the scope of the research. Suffice it to say here that the place of hamartiology in Torrance's soteriology is an area that is still unexplored in Torrance studies. It is interesting, nevertheless, that Torrance's definition of sin is similar to that of Calvin: "the act that you do, even in ignorance or in the impulse of a fleeting moment," in B42 "Sin at the Door," 1–8.

Calvin and Barth, Torrance argues that the human condition should be understood in the light of the doctrine of grace, and within God's gracious creative and redemptive scheme. Sin is illogical and irrational; it does not have a rationality of its own apart from Jesus Christ.[72] The present human predicament cannot stand by itself and be an autonomous ground of any soteriological formulation. Interestingly, amidst Calvin's doctrine of total depravity, he still recognizes the value and dignity of humanity through the lens of grace and of God's creative intention for us. Thus, Calvin and Torrance view true and genuine humanity, not in the light of the Fall, but in the light of God's will and purpose as revealed in Jesus Christ. Christology, theological teleology, and eschatology precede anthropology and hamartiology. Torrance consistently asserts that humanity's purpose is to be in relationship with God, which is our destiny and dignity: "The relation of creature to himself [God] [is] its true end."[73] Our future, then, is bound up with God in Christ, who is the mediator of reconciliation.

In the light of the gospel of grace, i.e., Jesus Christ himself in his life and death, Torrance argues that humanity, whom Jesus Christ came to redeem, is in the state of sin and under its effects. As such, humanity has fallen from its intended existence towards its opposite. "Ours is an existence," Torrance writes, following Calvin, "from nature to de-nature," a state of "fearful deformity."[74] This predicament gives rise to three concomitant states. First, humanity became alienated from God. If "being made in the image of God means being brought into a holy and sacred bond of order with God," and if "human nature set forth in its truth as creature [is] made for a filial relation to the heavenly Father," the perversion of the *imago Dei* consists in a motion against God—a broken relationship.[75]

---

72. Torrance, "Universalism or Election?," 311, 314.

73. Torrance, *Karl Barth*, 123; *Theology in Reconstruction*, 100–102. More elaborately, Torrance writes: "Man was once made for fellowship with God, and the whole structure of his being is built up on that fact. If you want to understand man, and diagnose his troubles, whether it be mental or spiritual or even bodily you will fail altogether unless you take that supreme factor into account." See B46 "God in Christ reconciling the world," 1. Torrance enumerates three gradations of human existence: (1) we have being in God in the same sense as all other created beings; (2) we have motion in the same sense as other living creatures; but (3) we have a higher life in God proper to us as human beings, in "The Word of God and the Nature of Man," 122.

74. Torrance, *Calvin's Doctrine of Man*, 83, 87, 91, 97. Torrance admits that students of Calvin are faced with difficulties with Calvin's view of human corruption after the fall, because even though Calvin teaches that the *imago Dei* "was wholly defaced and wiped out in us," he also believes that "something remains in fallen man." See *Calvin's Doctrine of Man*, 88–90.

75. Torrance, *Calvin's Doctrine of Man*, 36, 44, 47, 113; O'Donovan, "Man in the

The Grace of Our Lord Jesus Christ

Thus we understand that Jesus Christ is the minister of reconciliation. Secondly, our God-given capacity for truth and knowledge of God was also perverted. Torrance notes that Calvin's favorite way of describing humanity's corrupted reason is that humanity has been "*alienated in mind from God.*"[76] Jesus Christ came to redeem our rational faculties as well—epistemological redemption. Finally, sin ushered in death. "Fallen man," Torrance writes, "is dead—not sick, but dead, so that 'there is not a drop of life in him.'"[77] In his resurrection and ascension, Jesus Christ conquered and triumphed over death. Christ came, lived, and saved us according to the nature of our predicament. Expressed as an equation, since the situation is S, Christ dealt with S using methods appropriate to the nature of S. But Christ also dealt with S according to his nature as God-man. This can be called *scientific soteriology*, that is, Christ as God-man enacted God's will according to the nature of the incarnate Son and according to the nature of humanity's needs.

Vicarious Inhomination

Grounded in the realization that Jesus Christ is both fully God and fully human in one person, and that both divine and human work flow from this one person, Torrance stresses that incarnation and atonement are interconnected throughout the earthly life, death, and resurrection of Jesus Christ. The incarnation is in itself an act of salvation, an inauguration of a new humanity.[78] From the virgin birth to the ascension, the salvific work of the Triune God was carried out by the incarnate Christ. Every aspect of Christ's life is salvific.

> Redemption begins with the very advent of Jesus, so that his conception and birth of the Virgin Mary are to be regarded as essential constituents in his saving activity, and his humanity

---

Image of God," 433–59. Primarily, the *imago Dei* has to do with humanity's relation with God.

76. Torrance, *Calvin's Doctrine of Man*, 119.

77. Torrance, *Calvin's Doctrine of Man*, 88–89. On the state of humanity, see B42 "O Lord, Thou hast searched me and known me," 1–11.

78. Torrance, *Scottish Theology*, 12–14; *Ecumenical Studies*, 161–64. Torrance argues that the incarnation is "the ordering force and distinctive pattern of grace . . . that presents us the key for deeper theoretic insight into the saving economy of God," in *Divine Meaning*, 221. In becoming human, Christ "opened out as he grew, the wondrous blossom of perfect humanity such as had never before come from any root, nor grown on the most sedulously cultivated plant." See B42 "Harvest Thanksgiving," 6.

is seen to be not just a means to an end. Atoning reconciliation is to be understood as taking place within the incarnate constitution of the Mediator. His person and his work are one. That is why the New Testament can say that Jesus *is* redemption, he *is* righteousness, he *is* life eternal. He himself in his incarnate person *is* our salvation.[79]

Following Scottish Reformed theology, Torrance explains that Jesus Christ accomplished his incarnational redemption in a two-fold obedience: *active* and *passive*. By active obedience, the whole life of Jesus Christ positively fulfilled and "maintained a *perfect filial relation to the Father*," representing the whole of humanity in his Sonship.[80] As true human, Jesus Christ embodied in himself humanity's true relational nature, thus sanctifying our individualistic selves. With his perfect love and offering to the Father in our name and on our behalf, he enables us now to relate to God as God's sons and daughters. Also, by his passive obedience, or his *perfect submission to the judgment of the Father* upon our sin by assuming our sinful human nature and embodying in himself sin's appropriate penalty, he expiated our sins.[81] Corresponding to Christ's active and passive obedience are the positive and negative aspects of the incarnation. Positively, Jesus Christ fulfilled what true humanity is supposed to be in relationship to God. Torrance follows Irenaeus's appropriation of Romans 5:12–21 and 1 Corinthians 15:42–48, or of the Adam-Christ typology, in which Christ is taught to have vicariously and positively accomplished what the

---

79. Torrance, *Preaching Christ Today*, 58.

80. Torrance, *Theology in Reconstruction*, 154 (italics mine); *School of Faith*, lxxxiv–lxxxv.

81. Torrance, *Theology in Reconstruction*, 154. Torrance does not use the controversial term *punishment*, most probably to avoid being associated with the scholastic Calvinist doctrine of penal substitution. This does not mean, though, that he dismisses this atonement model completely. Rather, along with John McLeod Campbell, he interprets it in the light of the *homoousios*, or of the reality of the God-man on the cross rather than in a purely juridical manner. The difference lies, according to Torrance, in the fact that federal Calvinists separated God and the incarnate Son completely on the cross, therefore failing to recognize that it was actually God himself in Christ who took upon himself the appropriate judgment for sin. Whereas federal Calvinists view Christ's suffering in terms of the Father punishing the Son, Torrance views the cross in terms of what took place in Christ as God-man in one incarnate Person. The Father suffered with Christ. See Torrance, *Scottish Theology*, 301–3; and Torrance, "The Contribution of Campbell," particularly page 304 for his critique of federal theology, which for him inverts the biblical order of the relationship between forgiveness and atonement, or love and satisfaction. For Torrance's theological differences with Scottish theology, see MacLeod, "The Atonement," 39–43; balanced with David Fergusson's "Torrance as a Scottish Theologian," 77–87.

first Adam failed to be and do, thus renewing human capacity to relate again to God.[82] Interesting here is the fact that Torrance's view of human enablement is also christological, in contrast to the common pneumatological emphasis. In and through Jesus Christ, our Adamic alienation met a solution. Negatively, Christ's whole life was a life of retracing and undoing fallen human nature. He assumed and lived the experiences of fallen humanity in order to rectify and sanctify each part.[83] Through Christ's act, now, every aspect of human existence can be glorifying to God. This aspect in Torrance's soteriology, i.e., the emphasis on both the retrospective and prospective aspects of our redemption, is a valuable contribution.[84]

The significance of Torrance's approach is that the atonement is understood as both personal and ontological. It is personal because it is God in Jesus Christ who is at work in drawing himself near to humanity and humanity near to God. The atonement "is not an act of God done *ab extra* upon man, but an act of God become man, done *ab intra*, in his stead and on his behalf."[85] This is also why Torrance rejects exclusively extrinsicist or instrumental views of atonement, where Christ's redemptive work is considered to be an external transaction between God and humanity. He calls this extrinsicist atonement *the Latin heresy*, ascribing it to the dualistic "Western habit of thinking," which, when applied to theology produces a thinking dominated by external relations.[86] In it, Christ the Mediator is viewed as an Arian *tertium quid*, external both to God and to humanity. Contrary to this, Torrance argues that atoning reconciliation takes place within the personal being of the Mediator, and not in some third party

---

82. Irenaeus, *Haer.* III.18 (*ANF* 1): 445–48; III.23 (*ANF* 1): 455–59. See also Minns's discussion of this typology in *Irenaeus*, 86–99.

83. Irenaeus, *Haer.* II.22.4 (*ANF* 1): 391; III.7 (*ANF* 1): 420–21; III.18 (*ANF* 1): 445–48; III.20.2 (*ANF* 1): 450; III.22.2 (*ANF* 1): 454–55; V.14.1–4 (*ANF* 1): 541–44.

84. Even in his pulpit ministry, Torrance teaches these two aspects. He writes: "The great thing about this love [of Christ] is that it does not simply patch up the old centre ruptured by the battle between good and evil. It recreates life and brings a new centre within. The man under the constraint of the love of Christ is a new creature in which the old things pass away, and all things become new; new because he no longer lives unto himself but unto Christ, unto LOVE itself," in B46 "Constraint of Love," 5. See also B38 and B44 Untitled sermon on John 5:17.

85. Torrance, *Trinitarian Faith*, 158.

86. Torrance, *Karl Barth*, 228–29. Torrance sees this tendency in both Roman Catholic and Protestant theologies, and particularly in the Westminster Confession and in Fundamentalism. See *Karl Barth*, 213–40; "The Atonement," 236; *Divine Meaning*, 193–95; and *Doctrine of Grace*, 28.

other than God himself. This also safeguards Christ's sole mediatorship between God and humanity.

Consequently, the personal work of God in Jesus Christ has a personalising effect for humanity as well. In his personal and saving relations with us, Jesus Christ was engaged in a radical personalizing and humanizing activity. The precise relation between the person of Christ, his personal work, and his personalizing mission is that

> In virtue of the fact that the Person who became incarnate in Jesus Christ is the Creator Word of God by whom all men are made and in whom they consist, and is therefore the Person from whom all creaturely being is derived, the Incarnation must be regarded as creative, personalising activity. As the incarnate Son of God Jesus Christ is Person in his own divine Being, but we are called created persons. He is the personalising Person, and we are the personalised persons. . . . With the Incarnation there took place an acute personalising of all God's interaction with us, so that the incarnational union of the Person of the Son with our human nature must be regarded as the most intensive personalising of it that could have taken place.[87]

Moreover, equivalent to his personal agency, Christ's incarnational redemption is also ontological in both its means and end. Reiterated by the *vicarious* nature of Christ's life and work, and as God really becoming human, Jesus "embodies the act and fact of our salvation in his own Person," so that "the incarnation was seen to be essentially redemptive and redemption was seen to be inherently incarnational or ontological."[88] Jesus Christ assumed our human nature in its ontological depths in order to redeem it. The Word became *flesh*, so that within those ontological depths he can forge an ontological bond between God and humanity in and through himself. This is why, following Athanasius, George D. Dragas points to the incarnation as "the vantage point in the divine and human co-existence."[89]

---

87. Torrance, *Mediation of Christ*, 67–68.

88. Torrance, *Trinitarian Faith*, 62, 65, 142, 156, 159. Christ is *Persona personans* and humanity is *persona personata*. See also Torrance, *Theological Dialogue* 1: 11; *Mediation of Christ*, 30. See also Habets's discussion in *Theosis*, 55–59. Habets argues that Torrance's view of ontological atonement is a sufficient response to critiques that argue that Torrance advocates a physical theory of redemption. On Torrance's discussion of the physical theory of atonement, see *Trinitarian Faith*, 156–57.

89. Torrance, *Ecumenical Studies*, 40; *Space, Time, and Resurrection*, 20. It is for this reason that salvation is exclusively and singularly through Christ. See B45 "I am the Way, the Truth and the Life"; B45 "No man cometh unto the Father but by me"; and B45 "The Way, the Truth, and the Life."

The Grace of Our Lord Jesus Christ

The implications are staggering. That Christ's redeeming work reaches humanity's ontological existence and problems means that all our problems, within and without, met their solution in Jesus Christ, and that there is no aspect of human existence, past, present, and future, that Christ did not deal with. Similarly, there is no human problem, no matter how deep, that Christ is unable to mend. Torrance writes:

> Here is a man whose life has become impure and sordid, who has created foul things in his soul; and the wreck of his wasted humanity is haunted ghosts of evil deeds, and hollow with the mocking laughter of sin's remorseless guilt. What power in heaven or earth can make anything of that? Go to Bethlehem, there is a power wrapped in swaddling clothes, but whose name is called Jesus, for He shall save His people from their sins![90]

The Virgin Birth

Torrance offers an early caveat in his discussions of the virgin birth. He asserts that the virgin birth is not a theory explaining how the Son of God became human. The Gospels are silent as to *how* such an event can transpire, violating all the known laws of physics, or *how* the Spirit can conceive the Son of God. Ultimately, the *hows* in the narrative transcend our human comprehension. Rather, for Torrance, the virgin birth is an indication of what happened within humanity when the Son of God became human. In short, the virgin birth is a soteriological event and statement. By virtue of its account being included in the Gospel stories, it should be regarded as an important aspect in the emphasis of both the person and work of Christ. While it is true that the virgin birth can be used, as is the current theological practice, to point to his being human (Greek patristic church) and divine (Western church tradition), it is also a powerful statement about his saving agency. The virgin birth is a salvific event where God is already at work. It is not an unnecessary prelude leading to the main act, but is the beginning of the act itself.[91]

---

90. B43 "The Messenger of Peace," 7–8. See also B43 Untitled Sermon on Isaiah 50:11, 6–7: "The Sun of Righteousness has arisen with healing in His wings. He takes away the sin of the world; He blots out as with a thick cloud all our transgressions; and all the rank weeds that grow wild, the gnawing unrest of a stinging conscience, the evil habits, which at first were as light as a cobweb and as soft as a silken bracelet, and later became heavy and solid like iron fetters upon our limbs, all these are shattered by the blazing rays of God's forgiving Smile and burned up like chaff before the fire."

91. Torrance, *Incarnation*, 94–95.

So how is the virgin birth of Jesus Christ related to his vicarious redemptive activity? Torrance insists that the virgin birth cannot be separated from the whole mystery of Christ, particularly from the new life of Christ in his resurrection. Like the resurrection of Jesus from the virgin tomb (Luke 23:53), the virgin birth points to a new kind of life in the Holy Spirit. If in the virgin birth Jesus is conceived by the Spirit, the resurrection is also the work of the Spirit raising Jesus from the dead (1 Pet 3:18). The virgin birth and the resurrection, therefore, are the christological foundations of Jesus's demand for humanity to be "born of the Spirit" (John 3:5–6). Going back to the Pauline Adam-Christ typology, as Adam's life was through the breathing of the *ruach*, the two beginnings of Jesus's humanity are wrought in the power of the Spirit. This is also the beginning of a new humanity in us. Torrance expands:

> In his truth and obedience Jesus Christ breaks through the continuity of adamic existence and opens up a new continuity in a new Adam, in a new humanity. As such Jesus Christ is the firstborn of the new creation, the head of a new race in perfect union with God. . . . For the first time there is a true man in the midst of our inhumanity, for in the midst of our fallen humanity Jesus is true man. In and through him, therefore, humanity which has been dehumanized through sin, finds its true being and true human nature in union with God.[92]

In the virgin birth, therefore, transpired the re-creation of humanity. The *new* Adam has at last appeared. The virgin birth represents a break in the sinful existence of humanity, because in the birth of Jesus Christ in our depraved existence, he resisted that which was universal to all humanity (i.e., sin), sanctifying the human nature that sin corrupted and uniting it again to the holiness of God. "We cannot but acknowledge," Torrance writes, "that all our human life is involved in sin . . . but the birth of Jesus was a birth of the holy Son into that condition which far from acquiescing in its sin, resists it, sanctifying what sin had corrupted, and uniting it again to the purity of God."[93] But it is not only fallen human nature that Jesus came to resist. As Origen thought, the virgin conception necessitates victory over demons. The *Logos* had to break through a *cordon insanitaire* of celestial powers to get to earth.[94] Jesus came as a conquering King,

---

92. Torrance, *Incarnation*, 94.
93. Ibid., 100.
94. Turner, *The Patristic Doctrine of Redemption*, 49.

triumphing on our behalf over the forces of evil that we as humans can never defeat on our own.

> It is probable, therefore, that since at the birth of Jesus "a multitude of the heavenly host," as Luke records, and as I believe, "praised God, saying, Glory to God in the highest, and on earth peace, good-will towards men," *the evil spirits on that account became feeble, and lost their strength, the falsity of their sorcery being manifested, and their power being broken*; this overthrow being brought about not only by the angels having visited the terrestrial regions on account of the birth of Jesus, but also by the power of Jesus Himself, and His innate divinity. The Magi, accordingly, wishing to produce the customary results, which formerly they used to perform by means of certain spells and sorceries, sought to know the reason of their failure, conjecturing the cause to be a great one; and beholding a divine sign in the heaven, they desired to learn its signification.[95]

The birth of Jesus also possesses an epistemological significance, for it reveals the movement of grace. It connotes a disqualification of human capabilities and powers as possible means for humanity's approach to God. The virgin birth teaches that the movement of the Son of God to become human is from God to humanity, and not the other way around. In other words, Jesus Christ is in no sense a product of causal-historical processes in the world. It powerfully stresses that from first to last salvation is by grace alone. Even faith is not an actualization of human innate capabilities, but is in the power of the Spirit. Faith is *conceptus de Spiritu Sancto*.[96] The virgin birth reveals the pattern of grace and the appropriate human response. Torrance asserts the sovereign initiative that God takes in approaching Mary to proclaim to her the word of election, or that she is chosen not because of previous hard-earned merits, but because of the sovereign freedom of God. Mary's response is also the archetypal response God expects from us: "I am the Lord's servant. . . . May your word to me be fulfilled" (Luke 1:38). It is an act of glad, thankful, and humble submission and surrender to the will of God.

---

95. Origen, *C. Cel.* I.60 (*ANF* 4): 422 (italics mine).
96. Torrance, *Incarnation*, 102.

Communion with the Triune God

The Prokope

Luke curiously writes that Jesus Christ grew in wisdom and knowledge (2:40, 52). The verse actually summarizes the early twelve years of the life of Jesus Christ, and it teaches that the intellectual, moral, and spiritual growth of Jesus as a child was just as real as his physical growth. In short, Jesus Christ developed as a psycho-somatic being like the rest of humanity. Jesus is a true human being who passed through a process of physical and mental growth. The soteriological importance of the *prokope* is that it underscores Christ's vicarious human life. Generally speaking, in the economy of salvation, Jesus Christ assumed and experienced all of humanity's experiences in order to redeem and sanctify each part. In the words of Irenaeus,

> He came to save all through the means of Himself—all, I say, who through Him are born again to God—infants, and children, and boys, and youths, and old men. He therefore passed through every age, becoming an infant for infants, thus sanctifying infants; a child for children, thus sanctifying those who are of this age, being at the same time made to them an example of piety, righteousness, and submission; a youth for youths, becoming an example to youths, and thus sanctifying them for the Lord. So likewise He was an old man for old men, that He might be a perfect Master for all, not merely as respects the setting forth of the truth, but also as regards age, sanctifying at the same time the aged also, and becoming an example to them likewise. Then, at last, He came on to death itself, that He might be "the first-born from the dead, that in all things He might have the pre-eminence," the Prince of life, existing before all, and going before all.[97]

In relation again to Paul's Adam-Christ typology, Jesus Christ assumed everything that Adam experienced in order to undo that which Adam did and to do that which Adam failed to do. In particular, however, and keeping in mind that revelation is inseparable from reconciliation, Torrance highlights the epistemological significance of Jesus's assumption of human growth. Irenaeus taught that Jesus Christ assumed our ignorance and childishness in himself as well, being born as a baby and needing to grow in wisdom and stature. Consequently, Jesus's growth in wisdom can be regarded "as opening a way for man to rise to true knowledge of the

---

97. Irenaeus, *Haer.* II.22.4 (*ANF* 1): 391.

The Grace of Our Lord Jesus Christ

Father."[98] As divine, Jesus Christ himself is speaking on behalf of God, but "he is also Man hearing and obeying that Word, apprehending that Truth throughout his life on earth, so that he provides for us in his own obedient sonship within our human nature the *Way* whereby we are carried up to knowledge of God the Father."[99]

Torrance's strong pneumatic Christology is also evident in his understanding of the *prokope*, and which consequently influences his pneumatic soteriology. The emphasis here is that because Jesus Christ lived in complete dependence on the Holy Spirit from his birth to resurrection—and particularly in his growth—the whole economy of salvation cannot be separated from the saving agency of the Holy Spirit. The whole atoning life of Christ is the economy of the Spirit, which entails therefore that "every operation of God in the economy of our salvation was wrought with the co-operation of the Spirit."[100] And the same Spirit who was active in the *prokope* of Christ is the same Spirit through which we participate in Jesus, and through whom we rise "to true knowledge of, and communion with, God the Father."[101]

Baptism and Temptation

The paradox in the act of the sinless one undergoing a baptism of repentance for the remission of sins (Mark 1:4) is quite difficult to comprehend if we do not consider Christ's whole life as lived vicariously and *pro nobis*. Matthew explains that even John was reluctant to baptize Jesus (Matt 3:14) but Jesus insists that he be baptized, saying that "it is proper for us in this way to fulfil all righteousness" (3:15). In this context, "righteousness" has nothing to do with Jesus's need to become moral. God's righteousness is another way of expressing his saving activity.[102] Donald A. Hagner is on the right track when he states that "Jesus thereby shows his solidarity with his people in their need. The Messiah is a representative person, the embodiment of Israel, whether as King or righteous Servant."[103] Jesus's baptism, Torrance writes, is his consecration to fulfil God's judgment

---

98. Torrance, *Theology in Reconstruction*, 38.
99. Ibid.
100. Ibid., 39.
101. Ibid., 39.
102. Hagner, *Matthew 1–13*, 56.
103. Ibid., 57.

and forgiveness through identifying himself with sinners.[104] Jesus stands where the people he seeks to save stand, in the queue of people awaiting baptism of repentance for the forgiveness of sins, and thus fully identifying with them in their hopes and needs. The righteousness he fulfils is thus his righteous amen to the judgment of God against sin: "He came to fulfil all righteousness and to fulfil every jot and tittle of the law, acknowledging to the fullest extent the divine sanction in the law. He submitted himself under the law and was wholly obedient to the Father's will in the life he lived."[105]

Then after his baptism, he was endued with the Holy Spirit and confirmed as the beloved Son. It was not as if he needed to be baptized or to receive the Spirit, but that they were done vicariously, showing us the way to be called sons and daughters of the Father. He was already of the Spirit and full of the Spirit from conception, so that the drama that unfolded in the Jordan river is but a manifestation of what was already happening in Jesus Christ. Jesus's baptism was a *vicarious baptism,* in which he identifies with us as sinners, as pointing back to his birth by the Spirit to be the Savior of the world. Christ's baptism embraces his sacrificial life and death on our behalf in complete solidarity with us. When he was anointed by the Spirit, it was into our humanity that Jesus received the Spirit, so that we too may receive "the voice of forgiveness"[106] and adoption, and be filled with the Holy Spirit.

Right after his baptism, Jesus is led by the Spirit to be tempted. These two events—baptism and temptation—are inseparable. In both, Torrance argues that Jesus basically accomplished the same thing. He writes: "Repentance . . . is actualized in the submission of the sinner to the divine judgment and pardon—that was the repentance into which Christ was baptised at the Jordan and into which he stepped in his temptations in the wilderness, where he fasted and prayed while suffering the assaults of evil and chose the way of the cross laid upon him by the Father for our sakes."[107] So, just as the baptism of Christ is a salvific moment, his temptation was also a vicarious atoning act. But in relation to evil and sin, there is a distinction between what Jesus accomplished in these two events. In his baptism, he *submitted* to the righteous judgment of God against sin and becoming sinner with and for us, thereby undoing the sins

---

104. Torrance, *Atonement,* 5.
105. Ibid., 31–32.
106. Ibid., 85.
107. Ibid., 69; *Incarnation,* 123–24.

The Grace of Our Lord Jesus Christ

of humanity. In his temptation, however, he *opposed* the power of evil and sin and "invaded the domain of evil and redeemed us out of the power of darkness"[108] so that we too may live victoriously in the new life we receive from him. As such, in the combination of his baptism and temptation, we see not only an undoing of humanity's past, but also a redemption and enabling of the new people of God. Jesus's baptism and temptation have both retrospective and prospective imports.

Vicarious Death

"Why the God-man"? should be followed by another question: "Why the gruesome cross"? It could not be pedagogical, for certainly the cross is "a stumbling block to Jews and foolishness to Gentiles" (1 Cor 1:23). Could it then be that the vicarious human life of God in Christ was insufficient for our salvation, so that Jesus's death was necessary? Torrance responds in the negative. A holistic view of the incarnation includes the death, resurrection, ascension, and Christ's bodily intermediary-intercessory presence with the Father (Rom 8:34; Heb 4:14; 7:25). But does an emphasis on holistic incarnational redemption contradict the New Testament insistence on the centrality of the cross, as MacLeod thinks?[109] MacLeod's critique is an example of a biblicism that Torrance rejects, because it emphasizes certain aspects at the expense of others and therefore fails to see the whole of the gospel story. Torrance insists that the death of Jesus is part of Christ's assumption of all human experiences that need to be redeemed. In assuming the experience of death, he also redeemed and overcame it through his resurrection. Thus, the cross occupies a central place in Christ's redemptive activity. As Torrance writes, "It was his whole life, and above all that life poured out in the supreme sacrifice of death on the cross, that made atonement for sin, and constituted the price of redemption for mankind."[110]

The precise question, however, is "What happened on the cross with the God-man Jesus"?[111] Torrance's view is guided by his emphasis on the

---

108. Torrance, *Atonement*, 32.

109. MacLeod, *Jesus is Lord*, 131–34.

110. Torrance, *Trinitarian Faith*, 169; *Mediation of Christ*, 79; *Ecumenical Studies*, 164–67. James D. G. Dunn also argues that Paul's understanding of Jesus's whole vicarious life is the key that opens up to his understanding of the significance of Christ's death. See "Paul's Understanding of the Death of Jesus," 35–56.

111. From the early church, this question brought about different responses, which are now commonly referred to as *theories* or *models* of atonement. Stephen Holmes calls them *stories* of atonement in *The Wondrous Cross* (2007). The New Testament

vicarious and incarnational nature of Christ's work. As an act of reconciling at-one-ment, it is simultaneously an act from God to humanity and an act from humanity to God. "This is the most astonishing part of the Christian message," Torrance adds, "the identification of the man on the cross with God himself."[112] Biblical metaphors of ransom, sacrifice, propitiation, expiation, and reconciliation are all legitimate expressions of Christ's atoning work. They should not, however, be perceived as referring to any external transaction between God and humanity carried out by Christ, "but to what took place within the union of divine and human natures in the incarnate Son of God."[113] As such, Torrance does not flatly reject forensic atonement metaphors. What he objects to is the *Latin heresy*, or the preoccupation of Western theologians with forensic metaphors to the neglect of ontological considerations. As Cass concludes, Torrance combines both the forensic and the ontological aspects of redemption, although his emphasis clearly slides towards the ontological. Torrance's integrative framework is one of his major contributions to theology that should be taken seriously, especially because his model offers a promising integrative alternative to Aulén's dialectical approach to the Anselmic and Irenaean metaphors, and Aulén's false autonomistic attitude.[114]

The prominence of the vicarious humanity of Jesus Christ led Torrance to combine the themes of substitution and representation in a concept of *total substitution*.[115] On the cross, Jesus as fully human and on

---

itself embraced different images and metaphors, which we are not going to deal with here. Our only concern is to present Torrance's own views, but for a historical study of the doctrine of atonement, see Young, *Sacrifice and the Death of Christ* (1975); Gunton, *The Actuality of Atonement* (1988); and Marshall, *Aspects of the Atonement* (2007).

112. Torrance, *Preaching Christ Today*, 27.

113. Torrance, *Trinitarian Faith*, 168.

114. See Cass, *Christ Condemned in the Flesh*, 176–203; and John Stott's balance and affirmation of Peter Forsyth's "threefold cord" of atonement: satisfactionary, regenerative, and triumphant, in *The Cross of Christ*, 228–30. This does not mean that Torrance rejects Aulén's *Christus Victor* model that highlights the victory of Christ over evil. See B42 "Make Us a King to Judge Us," 1.

115. Colyer, *How to Read*, 112. See also Torrance's discussion in *Karl Barth*, 234–36; and *Trinitarian Faith*, 168–78. Torrance writes: "It will not do to think of what Christ has done for us only in terms of representation, for that would imply that Jesus represents, or stands for, *our* response, that he is the leader of humanity in humanity's act of response to God. On the other hand, if Jesus is a substitute in detachment from us, who simply acts in our stead in an external, formal or forensic way, then his response has no ontological bearing upon us but is an empty transaction over our heads. A merely representative or a merely substitutionary concept of vicarious mediation is bereft of any actual saving significance. But if representation and substitution are

behalf of humanity, took upon himself our sins and their corresponding judgment, in order for us to be reconciled to God. At Calvary, Jesus "penetrates the utmost extremity of our self-alienating flight from God where we are trapped in death, and turned everything round so that out of the fearful depths of our darkness and dereliction we may cry with him, 'Our Father.'"[116] Quoting John McLeod Campbell (1800–1872), the cross

> was essentially an *amen* of the sinner to the righteous judgment of God in being righteously condemned and justly forgiven.... It is important to note that the "perfect Amen" in which Christ confessed our sin, and in which he yielded in body and soul to the inflictions of the Father, was yielded out of the ontological depths of his sinless humanity and in his inseparable relations to sinners, thereby acknowledging and receiving in our place and on our behalf the judicial condemnation of God upon us and absorbing it in himself.[117]

Reacting against the scholastic Calvinist view of penal substitution, Christ's "joyful atonement" through his death, resurrection and ascension, "is not to be understood in any sense as the act of the man Jesus placating God the Father, but as a propitiatory sacrifice in which God himself through the death of his dear Son draws near to man and draws man near to himself."[118] "The self-offering of Christ [is] a voluntary sacrifice to his

---

combined and allowed to interpenetrate each other within the incarnational union of the Son of God with us in which he has actually taken our sin and guilt upon his own being, then we may have a profounder and truer grasp of the vicarious humanity in the mediatorship of Christ, as one in which he acts in our place, in our stead, on our behalf but out of the ontological depths of our actual human being," in *Mediation of Christ*, 80–81.

116. Torrance, *Mediation of Christ*, 79; *When Christ Comes*, 166. This is why Torrance argues that the cross has both a light and a shadow. On the one hand, the cross displays God's overflowing love to humanity. On the other hand, it also shows God's righteous judgment against humanity's sin. See Torrance, *Incarnation*, 239, 255–56; *Karl Barth*, 7; *Apocalypse Today*, 56, 118, 120; and "The Gospel Depends on the Cross," 20.

117. Quoted in Torrance, *Scottish Theology*, 300. In Scottish theology Campbell belongs to a minority group in the tradition of the Marrow men and Thomas Erskine (1788–1870) who did not subscribe to the federal theology of the Westminster Confession, particularly on the doctrine of limited atonement. See Torrance, *Scottish Theology*, 287–305; and Cass, *Christ Condemned in the Flesh*, 80–112. Cass argues that regarding Christ's assumption of fallen human nature, it was Campbell who had the greatest influence on Torrance among Western theologians. Gill disagrees and argues that it was Barth, in "The Doctrine of Revelation," 54. MacLeod lists both Campbell and Barth and adds Edward Irving, in *Jesus is Lord*, 125.

118. Quoted in Torrance, *Scottish Theology*, 19; *Christian Doctrine of God*, 161. MacLeod enumerates "an insistence that the suffering of Christ were penal" as one of

Father for us," Torrance explains, so that "in our place and in our stead and for our sake, Christ took our lost cause upon himself in submitting to the judgment of God upon our sin that we might be absolved from our guilt at the tribunal seat of God."[119] Torrance links Christ's sacrifice on the cross with Christ's priestly office, particularly with the Hebrew *kpr*, which results in the expiation of sin, so that the barrier of sin and guilt between God and humanity is done away with and propitiation is effected between them. Again, while admitting the forensic elements in this, he stresses the personal-ontological.[120]

Vicarious Resurrection and Ascension

Following Mackintosh, Torrance repeatedly stressed that the cross is "the window into the heart of God," for it reveals God's self-giving love.[121] In Torrance's theology, however, centrality does not entail supremacy or priority. The cross definitely fulfils a unique and distinct significance that the other redemptive experiences of Christ do not convey, but it is only a part of the whole, not an aspect that can stand on its own apart from the virgin birth, resurrection, and ascension. This is why Torrance argues that the resurrection and ascension should also be viewed soteriologically. He enumerates two soteriological significances of the resurrection, related to his holistic view of Christ's incarnational redemption. First, just as Christ embodied in himself humanity's predicament in his whole life and ministry, in his resurrection he embodied in himself humanity's final triumph over

---

the characteristic features of Scottish theology in "The Atonement," 39.

119. Torrance, *Scottish Theology*, 18.

120. As the High Priest, Jesus is the One representing the Many at the Holy of Holies. See Torrance, *Atonement*, 125–26; *Ecumenical Studies*, 137–41; and *Incarnation*, 50–52, on Torrance's similar discussion of the representation of the particular for the universal. The other Hebrew terms Torrance used to describe the aspect of divine redemption are *pdh* and *g'l*, respectively representing Christ's dramatic and ontological redemptive acts.

121. Torrance, *Preaching Christ Today*, 27; *Mediation of Christ*, 109. This theme is one that Torrance repeatedly preached about. See B38 and B39 Untitled sermon (Beechgrove Church, Aberdeen, 2 November 1997); B38 Untitled sermon (Penicuik, Midlothian, 5 September 1993); B38 Untitled sermon (Cluny Parish, Edinburgh, 17 October 1993); B38 Untitled sermon (Mcdoland Memorial Church, Bellshill, 7 June 1998); B38 Untitled sermon on Romans 8:32; B39 "'He that spared not his own Son'"; "The Cross—a Window into the heart of the Father"; "Greater love hath no man"; and B46 "God commendeth his love toward us." In all these sermons, Torrance claims that it is "at the Cross that we learn that our heavenly Father loves us, and loves us more than he loves himself."

The Grace of Our Lord Jesus Christ

everything he had assumed. Sin and death were both dealt with through life. It is no wonder, therefore, that Torrance sees the resurrection as the ground of Christian hope:

> The Christian Church that believes in the resurrection of Jesus Christ from the dead has no right to despair of "this weary world" or to be afraid it will crumble away into nothing. Christ is risen! He is completely victorious over the mighty demonic forces of destruction that threaten our world. In him we can lift up our heads and laugh in the face of disaster and death, for in him we are more than conquerors over all, knowing that God who raised Jesus from the dead, wearing our humanity, will not suffer the world for which he died and rose again to see corruption.[122]

Apart from the resurrection, therefore, the death of Jesus Christ on the cross could not take on any sacrificial or vicarious significance. It is precisely because Jesus Christ triumphed over that which he assumed that his life and death become meaningful. "The resurrection is the fulfilment of the incarnate mission of the Son of God who has taken up our worldly existence and history into himself."[123] Thus, secondly, Christ's resurrection *pro nobis* must be understood in the light of his whole vicarious incarnation. Torrance writes:

> The resurrection does not come to its real significance unless it is the resurrection of the incarnate and crucified Son of God, that is, unless there is included in the full material content of the resurrection the concrete historical actuality of Jesus Christ in *the whole sequence of his vicarious human life and passion,* for

---

122. Torrance, *Karl Barth*, 23. In almost similar language, Torrance preached: "The resurrection of the body of Jesus means the end of our world, this wicked warring world of bloodshed and cruelty and sorrow; it means an end to history; and end to the long story of shame and betrayal and the ruthless triumph of unrighteousness; it means the end of time, bad time." See B44 "Then opened He their understanding," 4. The sermon also explains the epistemological significance of the resurrection, along with B44 "Emmanuel," 1–10; and B45 "If a man dies, shall he live again?," 1–8. The centrality of the resurrection in Torrance's thought is further displayed in his other sermons: B46 "If Christ be not risen"; B46 "But now is Christ risen from the dead"; B46 "How are the dead raised up?"; and B47 "Sure and Certain Hope."

123. Torrance, *Space, Time, and Resurrection*, 171; "The First-born of all creation," 12–14; "Barth: Appreciation and Tribute," 262–63; and "*Phusikos Kai Theologikos Logos*," 21–24. See Molnar's discussion of how important it is to understand the resurrection as the resurrection of Jesus himself as the incarnate Word for the doctrines of the Trinity and salvation in "Incarnation, Resurrection and the Doctrine of the Trinity," 147–67.

what we have to do with here in the risen Lord is "the whole of Christ," Christ clothed with his Gospel of saving deeds.[124]

Jesus Christ died and rose again as the "firstfruits of those who have fallen asleep" (1 Cor 15:20) in order that we may share in his life. Human life is grounded solely upon the reality of Christ's bodily resurrection, and it is only in our sharing in his vicarious life that we find true life. Furthermore, because the incarnate Christ is the resurrected Christ, his bodily resurrection is an affirmation of our physical human existence, thus vindicating the possibility of corporeal relation with God. This is affirmed in the ascension of Christ in his resurrected body. Jesus is now in perfect communion with the Father in his hypostatic reality, as fully God and fully human. This has profound implications. Firstly, the ascension is not an addendum to Christ's incarnational redemption, but is an integral part of it. Particularly, the relationship between the incarnation and the ascension can be described in terms of Christ's *katabasis* and *anabasis*, his redemptive descent and ascent, which complement each other. "In the incarnation," Torrance writes, "we have the meeting of man and God in man's place, but in the ascension we have the meeting of man and God in God's place."[125] Important here is the fact that the bodily presence of Jesus Christ, both in the incarnation and ascension, implies the real meeting and interaction between God and humanity. Secondly, the bodily ascension of Jesus Christ vindicates our humanity, rather than demolishing it. It sharply repudiates Gnostic and escapist soteriologies that claim the escape of the soul from the physical body (which will be destroyed) in order to relate to God. Thirdly, the ascension points to the continuing bodily and priestly ministry of Jesus Christ in the throne of God: "Christ Jesus, who died—more than that, who was raised to life—is at the right hand of God and is also interceding for us" (Rom 8:34). Jesus Christ is still the Mediator and the High Priest atoning for the sins of the world, and who will one day return to consummate his work. Finally, we are assured, reading John 14:1–4, that the future is not empty. Jesus Christ has gone ahead of us, and our future is bound up with his.[126]

In his understanding of the ascension, Torrance discerns important soteriological points that theologians often miss. Ho argues that Torrance's

---

124. Torrance, *Space, Time, and Resurrection*, 171 (italics mine); *Karl Barth*, 207–8. See also B47 "Christ the Priest of the Resurrection."

125. Torrance, *Space, Time, and Resurrection*, 129.

126. B45 Untitled sermon on Acts 1:7 and Hebrews 13:8, 5; B46 "God's Arrows," 6; and B47 "Jesus Christ the same yesterday, today and forever," esp. 6–8.

The Grace of Our Lord Jesus Christ

understanding of the ascension is nevertheless vulnerable to some criticisms. Ho accuses Torrance of espousing an "open-ended incarnation," in which the human nature of Christ becomes a permanent reality, because Christ is interceding as human in the presence of the Father.[127] This criticism exemplifies Ho's ignorance of both historical theology and theological orthodoxy. In fact, Torrance is only affirming the position of the whole Christian church since the early fathers on the ascension of the human Christ to the right hand of the Father. The inclusion of the clause "whose kingdom shall have no end" in the creeds, J. N. D. Kelly notes, is precisely to counter all remaining Apollinarianism and Marcellianism in the church, and to stress that the incarnation is not merely instrumental or transient.[128] As such, Ho's critique of Torrance actually comes from a heretical perspective. It is Torrance's affirmation of the soteriological import of the priestly office of the ascended human Christ that represents the faith of the Christian church. Ho perceives that Torrance holds a progressive incarnation which "challenges the effectiveness and sufficiency of Christ's atonement on the Cross" by teaching the need for "a continual maintenance by the incarnate Christ."[129] This is a sharp criticism, perceivably grounded in the presupposition that the atonement is effectively completed in the Cross. However, the recent conclusions by Richard D. Nelson on the role of the High Priest in the *Yom Kippur* favor Torrance's position. Using Old Testament templates of sacrifice from Leviticus 16 and Exodus 24:3–8, Nelson argues that Christ's sacrificial act can be divided into three stages: the (1) death of the victim, (2) passage of the priest into the realm of the holy, and (3) use of blood to effect purification and to create a covenantal relationship. Important in this argument is the fact that the death of the sacrifice is not the end of the atoning process, but is actually just a part of the whole. The real consummation of the atonement is the physical presence of the High Priest in the Holy of Holies sprinkling the blood of the sacrificial animal. The ascent of Christ, the sacrifice and the priest, to the presence of the Father actually constitutes an important aspect of the whole atoning process.[130]

---

127. Ho, *A Critical Study*, 188. Ho considers Christ's humanity as merely a transient phenomenon, which is the ground of his critique (p. 194), and suggests that Torrance's open-ended incarnation fails to distinguish between the economic Trinity and the immanent Trinity (p. 191). The relationship between the incarnation, the evangelical Trinity, and the theological Trinity will be discussed in chapter 5.

128. See Kelly, *Early Christian Creeds*, 266–74, 303, 338–39.

129. Ho, *A Critical Study*, 190.

130. See Nelson, "'He Offered Himself,'" 251–65; Kang, "Concept of Vicarious

Communion with the Triune God

Atoning Exchange

Christ's vicarious work can be summed up in what Torrance calls the "atoning exchange," "reconciling exchange," "blessed exchange," "sacrificial exchange," "wonderful exchange," or "soteriological exchange."[131] Put simply, through the incarnation, Christ took what was ours so that we may partake of what is his. In his entire atoning life, a reconciling exchange is taking place between the Triune God in Christ and humanity in Christ, "between his obedience and our disobedience, his holiness and our sin, his life and our death, his strength and our weakness, his grace and our poverty, his light and our darkness, his wisdom and our ignorance, his joy and our misery, his peace and our dispeace, his immortality and our mortality."[132] This is precisely the "grace of our Lord Jesus Christ, that though he was rich, yet for [our] sakes he became poor, that [we] through his poverty might become rich" (2 Cor 8:9). In his salvific *katabasis*, Jesus Christ assumed our Adamic humanity in order to live and redeem it, so that by sharing in our human experiences, as the second Adam, our humanness is sanctified in him. Colyer summarizes: "Christ's union with us in our broken and sinful nature entails the humiliation and self-sacrifice of the incarnate Son, but also the transformation and the exaltation of our humanity that is lifted up in and through Christ to share in the communion that God is in God's Trinitarian life."[133] One consideration is that although it is an "exchange," it is more unilateral, for everything is the work of God in Christ from beginning to end.[134]

There are at least three profound implications of the atoning exchange. First, it radicalizes our understanding of God's boundless love. Christ's sacrifice has an infinite worth: "The benefits of God's free gift of

---

Humanity of Christ," 292–97; and Torrance's own exposition in B47 "Such an high priest became us," 1–9.

131. Torrance, *Preaching Christ Today*, 32–33, *Incarnation*, 63; *Atonement*, 151–52. See Torrance's sermon on the blessed exchange in B39 Untitled Sermon on 2 Corinthians 8:9, 1–4. See the comprehensive list by Kang on how Torrance uses the word "vicarious" in "Concept of the Vicarious Humanity of Christ," 26.

132. Torrance, *Trinitarian Faith*, 181. This echoes Calvin's understanding of the wonderful exchange, in *Institutes* II.16.5. On the peace of Christ, see B45 "The Peace of Christ," 1–10; and B46 "The peace that passes understanding," Jesus is the "Peacebringer," in B47 "And there was no more sea," 4.

133. Colyer, *How to Read*, 93. Torrance defines grace as "the transcendent Self-impoverishment of Christ for our sakes," in B46 "The Poverty of Christ," 2. In page 4, he also defines grace as "the Pauperization of God."

134. Habets, *Theosis*, 112; Torrance, *Preaching Christ Today*, 32; *Atonement*, 148–50.

The Grace of Our Lord Jesus Christ

Jesus Christ to mankind are as inexhaustible as his love."[135] By virtue of Christ's ontological assumption of the whole human for the whole of humanity, and the evidence of God's unconditional love displayed in Christ, Torrance rejects the Calvin*ist* doctrine (of the Synod of Dort) of limited atonement. But because of this, with his view of the universal range of salvation and his use of universal terminologies, Torrance is accused of holding universalism, or at least possessing a tendency towards it. Torrance himself explicitly rejects universalism, made plain in his quick response to J. A. T. Robinson's article on universalism and in his own explicit denunciations of the concept.[136] Torrance considers both universalism and limited atonement as twin heresies that impiously subjugate the logic of grace to a logico-causal understanding.[137] Nevertheless, as Gunton and George Hunsinger discern, Christology has a natural tendency to universalize.[138] This is true in Torrance, because he argues for the ontological oneness between all humanity and Jesus Christ by virtue of the hypostatic union, which is the ground of the atoning union and atoning exchange. "Since in [Jesus Christ] divine and human natures are inseparably united, the secret of every man, whether he believes or not, is bound up with Jesus."[139] Such a statement is indeed quite misleading if isolated from Torrance's overall theology. What Torrance affirms is the universal scope, range, and sufficiency of Christ's atoning work, but it is not true that he

---

135. Torrance, *Trinitarian Faith*, 181. Similar to Anselm's thoughts, the infinite worth of Christ's sacrifice is necessary to redeem humanity from sin, for "sin is sin against the infinite majesty of God and therefore infinite in its guilt," in B47 "Time and Eternity," 5.

136. See Robinson, "Universalism—Is it Heretical?," 139–45; and Torrance's response, "Universalism or Election?," 310–18; *Atonement*, 185; *Incarnation*, xlii.

137. Torrance, "Atonement," 246–8; *Theology in Reconstruction*, 190–1.

138. Gunton, *Promise of Trinitarian Theology*, 66; and Hunsinger, *How to Read Karl Barth*, 128–35; referenced in Gill, "The Doctrine of Revelation," 40. Robert W. Jenson's understanding of the gospel in the light of Christ also reflects universalism. For instance, he writes "The gospel is an *unconditional* promise of fulfilment. The gospel does not merely launch a quest, upon the success of which salvation must depend. . . . It says rather, "Because Jesus, who has bound himself to you unto death, lives, with death behind him, you will surely be fulfilled." See *The Triune Identity*, 26.

139. Torrance, *Trinitarian Faith*, 183; *Space, Time, and Resurrection*, 47. "It is the divine-human natures of Christ," Torrance writes, "that determines the nature and range of his redeeming work," in "Atonement," 244. Although the gospel is a gospel of God's love, according to Torrance, hell and judgment are real, so Christian love must speak about them, in B44 "What shall we do then?," 1–12. See B47 "What is God Like?—God in Judgment," 1–11; B47 Untitled sermon on Mark 13:33–37; and B47 "Lion of the Lamb," 1–10, where he talks about the "wrath of the Lamb."

is not concerned with the efficiency and efficacy of the atonement, as Ho mistakenly thinks.[140] But we must admit that Torrance does not offer a sufficient buffer against universalism. Although he explicitly rejected it in his writings, still, as Morrison writes, "vigorous assertion does not overcome incoherence."[141] In the end, Torrance's ultimate stance regarding the apparent discrepancy between the universal range of Christ's atoning work and the reprobation of some—or between *possibility* and *reality*—in the last days, is that of necessary apophatism. Like sin, all he could affirm is that the damnation of sinners is a "strange mystery of iniquity."[142]

The second implication of the atoning exchange is the redemption of suffering. God took upon himself the agonies of the human condition in order to redeem it. Using a rhetorical device which Morrison calls "a contrastive juxtapositioning,"[143] Torrance writes: "In Jesus Christ himself God has penetrated into our passion, our hurt, our violence, our condition under divine judgment, even into our utter dereliction, 'My God, my God, why hast thou forsaken me?,' but in such a profoundly vicarious way that in the very heart of it all, he brought his eternal *serenity* or *apatheia* to bear redemptively upon our passion."[144] Furthermore, the redemption of our suffering also entails the redemption of our human weaknesses. Even the economic ignorance of Jesus Christ is vicarious, so that we may know God only according to the knowledge of the human Jesus. Finally, and most importantly, the atoning exchange in Christ reveals the trinitarian structure of soteriology. Torrance writes: "Since this soteriological exchange takes place within the incarnate constitution of the Mediator who is both God and man in his one Person, it takes place not without but within the very Life of God himself."[145] The saving life of Jesus Christ is internal to

---

140. Ho, *A Critical Study*, 134.

141. Morrison, *Knowledge of the Self-revealing God*, 253.

142. Torrance, *Apocalypse Today*, 105. In *Atonement*, 156, Torrance argues that reprobation in the last days is accidental to salvation.

143. Morrison, *Knowledge of the Self-revealing God*, 180.

144. Torrance, *Trinitarian Faith*, 185; *Incarnation*, 66. Torrance adds in a sermon: "God does not keep His Love within the movement of His own heart, but He opens His innermost being to us in our creaturely frailty and need. Through the Incarnation, He has so united Himself to us that He is present in our midst, touched with the feeling of all our infirmities, moved and stirred with us in all our distresses, participating with us in our existence in active sympathy and compassion. No, God in His own being is not closed to us, for He shares with us the innermost movement of His Divine heart and absorbs our hurt and suffering into Himself." See B47 "What is God Like?—God in Mercy," 2.

145. Torrance, *Christian Doctrine of God*, 250–51; *Scottish Theology*, 78.

the saving person of God the Son, issuing from the saving nature of the Triune God. And in a double movement, the descent of the eternal Son is the Triune God's movement to *initiate and enable* reconciliation decisively with humanity, which is then followed by the ascent of the human Christ to *continue the enabled* relationship with the Triune God.

Participation "in Christ"

Salvation "in Christ" flows logically from Torrance's understanding of Christ's incarnational redemption. It is here that the influences of Calvin's participation soteriology and Mackintosh's doctrine of the *unio mystica* in Torrance are readily discernible.[146] As Robert Redman concludes, both Mackintosh and Torrance heavily relied on the Pauline and Johannine expression "in Christ" to express the reality of the relationship between us, the redeemed, and Jesus Christ, the Redeemer.[147] Clearly, therefore, the relational and more participative aspects are highlighted. Another important consideration is that our being "in Christ" should be understood in the light of Torrance's trinitarian emphasis. Our being in Christ implies not only relationship with Christ but with the Triune God. Jesus Christ is the Mediator between humanity and God and by being *in Christ* we are also *in the Triune God*: "This union between humanity and God in Christ entails our adoption as daughters and sons of God in Christ, or *our participation in the communion of God's Trinitarian life, light and love*."[148]

Union with Christ

Habets argues that Torrance scholars generally agree that Torrance's doctrine of reconciliation can be expressed in terms of a theology of "union with Christ."[149] While this conclusion is true, it appears that his fascination

---

146. See Torrance, "Hugh Ross Mackintosh," 163, 166–68. On the participation soteriology of Calvin, see Canlis, "Calvin, Osiander and Participation in God," 169–84; Hart, "'Humankind in Christ and Christ in Humankind,'" 67–84; Mosser, "The Greatest Possible Blessing," 36–57; and Slater, "Salvation as Participation in the Humanity of the Mediator," 39–58.

147. See Redman, "*Participatio Christi*," 201–22; and "Mackintosh's Contribution to Christology," 526–28; and on the relationship between Mackintosh and Torrance, see "Mackintosh, Torrance and Reformulation of Reformed Theology," 64–76.

148. Colyer, *How to Read*, 252 (italics mine).

149. Habets, *Theosis*, 93. He refers to the following writings that support his argument: Kruger, "The Doctrine of the Knowledge of God," 373; and Lee, *Living in Union*.

with the doctrine of *theosis* moved him to presuppose that "union with Christ is . . . informed by the more determinative doctrine of *theosis*."[150] The question, however, is whether this properly represents Torrance's theology, or whether it is not rather an overestimation of *theosis*. Considering Torrance's integrative approach, it is more appropriate to conclude that Torrance employs *theosis* and union with Christ interchangeably to articulate the reality of our salvation "in Christ," not in the manner of categorizing one under the other.

Torrance's understanding of humanity's union with Christ is grounded in the one person of Jesus Christ, the hypostatic union. Union with Christ, therefore, must primarily be understood as the reconciling initiative of God accomplished ontologically through Christ's incarnate life. "Hypostatic union and atoning union implied and interpenetrated each other in Christ's mediation of reconciliation to mankind."[151] In the complete union of the human and the divine in Jesus Christ, vicariously and redemptively, the incarnate Son assumed our humanity and opened his mutual relation with the Father for human participation. This is why Torrance argues that the hypostatic union is "the ground for all Christ's mediatorial and reconciling activity."[152] But what is at stake in Christ's reconciling work expressed in "union with Christ"? First, because of the hypostatic union, there exists now an unbreakable ontological bond between God and humanity, a bond achieved within the personal constitution of Jesus Christ the Mediator throughout his life. This is what Torrance calls "the third dimension."[153] In *Incarnation*, Torrance speaks of "*the once and for all union* of God and man," and the "*continuous union* in the historical life and obedience of Jesus" to balance the already, the on-going, and the not yet.[154] Habets expresses it differently but in a way which is complementary to Torrance's agenda: "Union with Christ has a pretemporal basis (in God's electing will), an historical application (in the incarnate life and

---

150. Habets, *Theosis*, 93. "*Theosis*," for Habets, is "foundational to Torrance's theology and is one way in which he holds together in systematic fashion his diverse theological *oeuvre*," in *Theosis*, ix, 16.

151. Torrance, *Mediation of Christ*, 66.

152. Ibid., 64–65.

153. Torrance, *Karl Barth*, 22. Torrance explains this further by using another metaphor: "There is a *moral matrimony* pledged between Jesus Christ and every man of earth—Bethlehem brought Jesus very near, and Calvary betrothed Him and the sinner together. Therefore what God hath joined together, let no man put asunder." See B44 "Moral Matrimony," 5 (italics mine).

154. In fact most of the book is focused on the hypostatic union, but see particularly chapters 3–6 (italics mine).

The Grace of Our Lord Jesus Christ

death of Jesus Christ and the work of the Spirit), and an eschatological orientation (in both sanctification and glorification)."[155]

Secondly, union with Christ implies our sharing in the benefits of his atoning exchange.[156] To guard against any form of Pelagianism, Torrance stresses the sole mediatorial role of Christ in his Person and act.[157] Jesus Christ already did everything for our salvation in his vicarious life and death. Whether this is a strength or weakness in Torrance's theology can be judged differently from various perspectives, but his christocentric soteriology can lean towards a promotion of human passive participation, in that the only human role in the redemption drama is to share in what Christ already did for us and in us. Indeed, as Colyer writes, this aspect of Torrance's theology is "a controversial area."[158] For instance, concerning faith, Torrance argues that

155. Habets, *Theosis*, 93. Concerning the application of Christ's works in our humanity, Torrance preached that Christ is the link between what has already happened in us and what is yet to be fulfilled. See Torrance, *When Christ Comes*, 170.

156. Dawson, *An Introduction*, 7, 44. In *Theology in Reconstruction*, 158, Torrance writes: "It is only through union with Christ that we partake of the blessing of Christ, that is through union with him in his holy and obedient life. Through being united with him we share in his judgment and his exaltation."

157. See also Torrance, "Covenant or Contract?," 76. Although, interestingly, Torrance preached that there is no believing without doing, or that grace and works go together. See B44 Untitled sermon on John 3:1–21; Luke 10:25–37. In B42 "Prosperity of the Wicked," 9–10, he writes: "Our faith manifests itself not merely by a lazy reliance upon what He once did long ago on the Cross for us; but by daily, effortful revivifying of our consciousness of our dependence upon Him. . . . Darkness will fall, if you neglect to exercise your faith. . . . It should never be forgotten that faith is like muscle, it is strengthened by exercise. The most advanced Christian life needs a perpetual renewal and repetition of past acts of faith." But, it is clear that for Torrance, doing is a consequence of being, and never the other way around. He writes: "There is no more damnable heresy in the Church today than the idea that to become a Christian means to become good. If you become a Christian you WILL become good; but that is the only way," in B42 "Moses wist not that the skin of His face," 8. In another sermon he refers to the crude imposition of earthly notions of wage and pay in the doctrine of salvation as a "satanic thought." He calls the view that salvation consists in what God demands as a "bewitching idea," in B46 "O Foolish Galatians," 8. See also B44 "Labourers in the Vineyard," 4. In a more polemic manner, he writes: "Do, do, do! It is not a question of doing at all[,] . . . it is a question of trusting, of having faith. You must believe in order to be saved." See B45 "The Philippian Jailer," 6. It is precisely our attempt to be righteous through our works that makes us unrighteous, and thus "we must repent of our own goodness." See B45 "The Epistle to the Romans," 1–7; B45 "Romans chapter 2," 4; B42 "Thanksgiving After Communion," 6; B42 "There is a way that seemeth right unto a man," 7–14; and B43 "Cursed be the man that trusted in man," 1–14.

158. Colyer, *How to Read*, 113. In B38 Untitled sermon from 1 Corinthians 2:1–5, 10, he poses a dialectic: "In faith we have the personal act of decision that answers the

Communion with the Triune God

> We must think of Jesus as stepping into the relation between the faithfulness of God and the actual unfaithfulness of human beings. . . . Jesus steps into the actual situation where we are summoned to have faith in God, to believe and to trust in him, and he acts in our place and in our stead from within the depths of our unfaithfulness and provides us freely with a faithfulness in which we may share[;] . . . if we think of belief, trust or faith as forms of human activity before God, then *we must think of Jesus Christ as believing, trusting and having faith in God the Father on our behalf and in our place.*[159]

In being united with Christ, then, "through his incarnational and atoning union with us our faith is implicated in his faith."[160] Similarly, our knowledge of God is a sharing in the knowledge of the incarnate Son, or a "cognitive union with Christ."[161] Furthermore, salvation, faith, worship, and knowledge of God were all accomplished in Christ's hypostatic person for us and on our behalf.[162] This follows logically from Torrance's stress on the vicarious humanity of Jesus Christ, which includes his vicarious response for humanity to God's judgment and love.

> We are to think of the whole life and activity of Jesus from the cradle to the grave as constituting the vicarious human response to himself which God has freely and unconditionally provided for us. . . . Jesus Christ *is* our human response to God. Thus we appear before God and are accepted by him as those who are inseparably united to Jesus Christ our great High Priest in his eternal self-presentation to the Father.[163]

Word of God and responds to God's action in Jesus Christ. The miracle is that as you actively decide to accept Jesus Christ, Jesus Christ becomes alive in you. You choose Christ, but you know that you have not chosen Him. He has chosen You. You grasped the Saviour, but you know the Saviour is there actually grasping you."

159. Torrance, *Mediation of Christ*, 82–83 (italics mine).
160. Ibid., 84.
161. Torrance, *Trinitarian Faith*, 58–59; *Mediation of Christ*, 116.
162. See Torrance, *Mediation of Christ*, chapter 4. On the vicarious nature of worship in Christ, see *Ecumenical Studies*, 128–37. See also Kang's detailed treatment of the vicarious response of Christ for all humanity in "Concept of Vicarious Humanity of Christ," chapter 6.
163. Torrance, *Mediation of Christ*, 80. Torrance's rhetorical question, "Which is greater: the gift or the altar that makes the gift sacred?" is relevant here. Our so-called human response is sanctified by the priest and the altar, so that at the end of the day, it is not our sacrifice that matters, but the One that sanctifies the sacrifice. See B39 Untitled sermon on Matthew 5:23–24, 1.

The Grace of Our Lord Jesus Christ

Torrance's radical emphasis on the objective vicarious act of Christ raises the suspicion of a neglect of the subjective pole in salvation.[164] Torrance's choice of terminologies has made him vulnerable to this critique. For instance, he argues: "We are to think of the whole human race, and indeed of the whole creation as in profound sense already redeemed, resurrected, and consecrated for the glory and worship of God."[165] As noticeable, the critique of universalism against Torrance is the twin sister of the critique of his neglect of *our* human involvement in salvation. Torrance's objection to what Cass calls "soteriological existentialism" is unquestionable,[166] but it is still scripturally inaccurate to ignore the important part played by *our* grace-enabled response as human beings. This is important in our being truly transformed into a new creation, because if our conversion means sharing in the conversion brought by Jesus Christ alone, then it would appear that the only truly converted One is Jesus.[167] But the real danger of Torrance's view of a *totus/totus* vicarious act of Christ is that it logically leads to a coercive divine love, especially because he holds that "no rejection or unbelief on our part can undo what Christ has done on our behalf or can undo the all-decisive impact of his passion and resurrection on our human existence, so that we are quite unable to cut ourselves off from the resurrection of all men, the just and the unjust, at the last day."[168] In the words of Cass, "we are converted against our will in the freeing and renewal of our will."[169] A further implication of Torrance's christocentricism, according to Lee, is that salvation is merely discovery of what has already been fulfilled.[170] Eschatologically, this is untenable, because the Scriptures suggest that in the day of judgment, some people indeed "discover" that they are not saved (e.g., Matt 7:15–23).

On the other hand, while it is true that Torrance's published academic writings seem to reflect a dismissal of the necessity of a God-enabled human response in salvation, his unpublished sermons provide us with important counter balances.[171] For instance, he preached "the need for

---

164. Barth shares the same target of this critique. See Thompson, "Christology and Reconciliation," in *Christ in Our Place*, 221–22; and Nimmo, "Karl Barth and the *Concursus Dei*," 58–72.

165. Torrance, *Trinitarian Faith*, 183; "Atonement," 244.

166. Cass, *Christ Condemned in the Flesh*, 177.

167. Torrance, *Mediation of Christ*, 85; *Reality and Evangelical Theology*, 89.

168. Torrance, "Immortality and Light," 157.

169. Cass, *Christ Condemned in the Flesh*, 202.

170. Lee, *Living in Union*, 314.

171. In *School of Faith*, cvi, Torrance mentions the work of the Holy Spirit in

people personally to call upon the Name of Christ."[172] This is because faith is "an intensely personal thing."[173] Surfacing here is his view that one cannot stand in aloofness in relation to God, for to be neutral before God is to be hostile against God. More importantly, notice the conditional tone of the following quotation: "Christ has triumphed. Yes! But that triumph can only be yours in faith. . . . It is the grace of God—that you can have as your own all the power of God; and can appropriate all that Christ has achieved on the Cross against sin, *if only you will stretch out your hand and take it.*"[174] Furthermore, in a curious sermon that makes one think of John Wesley, he explains the necessity to work out our own salvation, although he emphasizes that it is more a case of working *out* what has already been worked *in*.[175] Ultimately, Torrance uses the importance of human response in order to argue that the fault for not being saved lies not in God, but in us. For instance, he argues that the Word of God "penetrates straight to the heart, demanding personal decision. It places a man in a position of complete responsibility."[176]

Torrance also highlights that the Christian must remain in zeal and faith even amidst difficulties. It is here that he seems to think along the line of conditional perseverance of the saints. For instance, he writes: "If you do not know Him in his poverty, if you do not follow the Christ Who had not where to lay His head, and follow him through to the end, you will not arrive at the Resurrection and then at last at the Ascension to the right hand of the Majesty on High."[177] In another sermon, he spells out the implications of our being united with Jesus Christ in our Christian moral life.

> If you want communion with Him, then you must be prepared to share with Him His board. You must be united with Him

---

"creating and calling forth the response of man in faith," but he goes on to write that "we cannot enter into this in detail here." He never went back to elaborate this important theme.

172. B38 "No Other Name," 2. See also B43 "Conversion," 1–8; and B44 "Why This Waste?," 1–9.

173. B47 "Faith," 8.

174. B47 "Without," 7 (italics mine); and B46 "The Poverty of Christ," 8.

175. See B46 "Work out your own salvation," 1–8; and also B47 "And there was no more sea," 6–7.

176. B43 Untitled sermon on Jeremiah 7:2, 7; B43 "The Lost Sheep," 1–8. Torrance adds that it is precisely God's demand for a personal decision from humanity that is offensive to many in B43 "Keep Thy Foot," 1–9.

177. B46 "The Poverty of Christ," 8; B42 "The Unknown Prophet from Judah," 7; and B42 "Doth Job fear God for naught?," 1–8.

in mind and affections. You cannot sit down with him at His table without sitting in union of spirit and purpose with Him who came not to be ministered unto but to minister and give his life as ransom for many. You must be united to Him in His gentleness and purity, in His love and forgiveness. In short, it means that you must drink His cup, and be immersed with His baptism.[178]

Torrance also argues that someone who wants to be saved without facing his Christian responsibilities for God's service "cannot be saved at all," for "you cannot have the life of Christ . . . without having the life of service, the burden-bearing and the sympathy and the Cross with which it is altogether bound. You cannot have the person of Christ without having the work of Christ."[179]

Thirdly, union with Christ implies our sharing in his relationship with the Father, and our participation in the very life and communion of the Triune God. Redman is right in saying that "in Christ" expresses the continued fellowship of the disciples with Christ even after his ascension.[180] Jesus's admonition to "remain" in him (John 15) stresses the personal element of relationship. But Torrance also emphasizes that relationship with Christ is not the end of Christ's reconciling work. The true *telos* of Christ's reconciling activity is for humanity to enter into communion with the Trinity: "It is not atonement that constitutes the goal and end of that integrated movement of reconciliation but union with God in and through Jesus Christ in whom our human nature is not only saved, healed and renewed but lifted up to participate in the very light, life and love of the Holy Trinity."[181] This is why alongside Dawson and Colyer we are justified in saying that Torrance's soteriology is trinitarian.[182]

Justification in Christ

Torrance's doctrine of justification accomplishes two interrelated aims: (1) positively, to stress the priority of Christ, and (2) negatively, to combat

178. B44 Communion Sermon on Mark 10:38, 5–6.

179. See B47 "The Message to the Church at Philadelphia," 3; and also B42 "National Day of Prayer," 1–10. This is not only on a personal level, but as a church: "If a Church follows Jesus Christ as saviour, then it must devote its work to saving as well," in B42 "Foreign Missions," 1.

180. Redman, "*Participatio Christi*," 202.

181. Torrance, *Mediation of Christ*, 66.

182. Dawson, "Far as the Curse is Found," 72; and Colyer, *How to Read*, 93.

what he calls "a gospel of external relations." Torrance is adamant that justification should be expounded in the light of the vicarious person and work of Jesus Christ. Fuelled by an emphasis on the objectivity of salvation, he explains that justification was accomplished by Jesus Christ for us—the weight being given to *Jesus Christ* rather than *for us*. Torrance is critical of Roman Catholics, evangelicals, and liberals who preach an anthropocentric salvation and stress human, personal, or existential decision to gain salvation. This is why he views "justifying faith" as inappropriate, for it promotes the human act, rather than the mediatorial and vicarious ministry of Jesus Christ. By contrast, Torrance elaborates "justification by faith" from a participative approach, which is grounded in our union with Christ.[183] This implies that *our* faith is actually *Christ's* faith made vicariously for us. It is Christ's faith and vicarious obedience to the Father that is important, not ours. By being in Jesus Christ, we then participate and share in his faith. Quoting the seventeenth-century Scottish minister James Fraser of Brae, Torrance stresses "the correlation of our faith with the faith of God and the faith of Christ," because "human faith derives from, rests on, and is undergirded by divine faithfulness."[184] C. F. D. Moule criticizes this, stating that it does not sufficiently consider the polarities of faith. Moule's view is partly right: Torrance has a tendency towards a one-sided view of the *pistis Christou*. On the other hand, Torrance's program against an existential understanding of faith, prominent in most evangelical theology, is also praiseworthy. He is not really opposed to human faith, and considers it "absolutely essential," but he argues that "the faithfulness of Christ" should be "the main ingredient."[185] At stake, Torrance argues, is the all-sufficiency of Jesus Christ, "for it is on Christ and his all-sufficiency in his obedient life and death, and God's good-will toward sinners incarnated in him, that believing faith is grounded."[186]

---

183. Torrance, *Kingdom and the Church*, 102–3.

184. Quoted in Torrance, *Scottish Theology*, 184.

185. Torrance, "The Biblical Conception of Faith," 221. This article is a response to Moule's criticism of Torrance's earlier article "One Aspect of the Biblical Conception of Faith," 111–14. See his sermons emphasizing the faith of Jesus Christ in B45 "What is Faith"; B45 "The just shall live by faith"; and B45 "Reconciliation through the Person of Christ." In B47 "Sure and Certain Hope," 3, he writes: "Yes, faith is absolutely essential. We must believe in Jesus Christ as our Saviour and Lord, and we have no inheritance in hope apart from faith. But, it is not your faithfulness that counts so much as God's faithfulness."

186. Torrance, *Scottish Theology*, 187; B40 "Implicit Faith," 1–3. The disagreement between Moule and Torrance is reflected later in the debate about whether *pistis Christou* should be interpreted as objective or as subjective genitive, with James D. G. Dunn

The Grace of Our Lord Jesus Christ

Torrance speaks of how our justification happens wholly in Jesus Christ by expounding the complementary relationship between *objective justification* and *subjective justification*. Objective justification refers to what took place in Jesus Christ before the Father as the incarnate Son of God, which Torrance calls Christ's "incarnational fraternity."[187] Through his active and passive obedience, Jesus Christ embodied in himself both God's judgment and love in order to redeem us and reconcile us back to God. Subjective justification, on the other hand, refers to the act of Jesus Christ on our behalf—highlighting his redemptive roles "as our Substitute and Representative who appropriated the divine Act of saving Righteousness for us."[188] What happened to Jesus Christ in his life, death, and resurrection becomes ours, because Christ did them not for his own sake but for our sake.

> Justification has been fulfilled subjectively as well as objectively in Jesus Christ, but that objective and subjective justification is objective to us. It is freely imputed to us by grace objectively and we through the Spirit share in it subjectively as we are united to Christ. His subjective justification becomes ours, and it is subjective in us as well as in him, but only subjective in us because it has been made subjectively real in our human nature, in our own human flesh in Jesus, our Brother, and our Mediator.[189]

Secondly, because justification is accomplished *in* Christ *by* Christ *for us*, Torrance argues that left on their own, forensic and juridical views of atonement are insufficient in expressing Christ's personal agency, because they lead to an instrumental view of Jesus Christ. Justification, following this line of thought, appears like an external transaction between God and humanity through a third party. Furthermore, Torrance argues that several other errors which he found in federal-contractual Reformed theology spring from this extrinsicist perspective, such as double

---

and Richard B. Hays as the main proponents, respectively. See Dunn, "Once More, *Pistis Christou*," 61–81, and Hays, "*Pistis* and Pauline Christology," 35–60, both in *Pauline Theology*, vol. 4. Hays's arguments affirm Torrance's position. See also Hays, *The Faith of Jesus Christ* (2002); Hooker, "ΠΙΣΤΙΣ ΧΡΙΣΤΟΥ," 321–42. For a consideration of patristic interpretations, see Bird and Whitenton, "The Faithfulness of Jesus Christ," 552–62; and Whitenton, "After ΠΙΣΤΙΣ ΧΡΙΣΤΟΥ," 82–109. For the soteriological implications of the positions in the debate, see Stubbs, "The Shape of Soteriology and the *Pistis Christou* Debate," 137–57.

187. Torrance, *Theology in Reconstruction*, 153.
188. Ibid., 157; *Atonement*, 120–24.
189. Torrance, *Theology in Reconstruction*, 160.

predestination and limited atonement.[190] Habets is right that Torrance did not really reject the Reformed doctrine of imputation, but deepened it with the ontological perspective by relocating it within his participation theology.[191] Cass also argues that Torrance's position takes up both Eastern and Western soteriological concerns, in an integrative whole, thus making his position superior to others.[192]

Nevertheless, it cannot be denied that Torrance's position tends more towards the ontological aspect, particularly because of his emphasis on justification, grounded in a "theology of internal relations," and the vicarious nature of Christ's redemptive agency. Justification happens in Christ and consequently, in us. At the cross and in the resurrection, a positive ontological transformation, there and then, happens in us (and all of humanity) through and in Christ. "Justification is ... importing new humanity."[193] Through union with Christ, righteousness is imputed to us—"not just in terms of imputed righteousness but in terms of a participation in the righteousness of Christ which is transferred to us."[194] Thus,

190. Torrance, *Scottish Theology*, 137.

191. Habets, *Theosis*, 100; Hart, "Humankind in Christ," 67–84; Torrance, "Atonement," 253–56.

192. Cass, *Christ Condemned in the Flesh*, 10, 283, and chapter 4 for an elaboration.

193. Torrance, *Scottish Theology*, 20. On putting on new humanity and the need to live the new life in Jesus Christ, see B46 Untitled sermon on Ephesians 4:20–24; B45 Untitled sermon on Romans 6:11, 1–8; B45 Untitled sermon on Romans 7; and B46 "Put ye on the Lord Jesus Christ," 1–8. In B47 "Herein is love," he writes: "Christianity begins at that moment—when the deed of God's love strikes into a man's soul, and creates a new heart and a responsive love of a new order." Having a new life in Jesus Christ also means carrying our crosses, in B42 "Let him curse," 2–5. The new humanity that we become through union with Christ also means the beginning of increase and growth, in Torrance, *Kingdom and the Church*, 94, 100–104. The word "beginning" is important, because Torrance also recognizes the fact that transformation is a gradual process. He writes: "I am not going to be so narrow or so foolish as to say that the Christian life must always begin with a conscious and a sudden change; but this I am sure of, that in the vast majority of cases of really religious men, there must be a conscious change, whether it has been spread through months or years, or concentrated in one burning moment." See B43 "Conversion," 3–4. He has sermons that also discuss the need for growth in Christian life, such as B46 Untitled sermon on Ephesians 4:26; B46 "A Disciplined Life"; and B42 "Harvest Thanksgiving," 7–10. He even argues that being born again is not everything; rather "it is the growth after birth, the growth to maturity that is much more important," in B47 "Leaving First Principles," 4. Torrance also fears and laments what he observes as "spiritual declension" which "is the history of hundreds of nominal Christians amongst us, and I dare say, of some of us," in B42 "Samson," 3.

194. Torrance, "The Distinctive Character of the Reformed Tradition," 6; quoted in Habets, *Theosis*, 100. This is related to Torrance's view of the comprehensiveness of

> Justification means not simply the non-imputation of our sins through the pardon of Christ, but positive sharing in his human righteousness.... It is only through this union of our human nature with his divine nature that Jesus Christ gives us not only the *negative righteousness* of the remission of sins but also a share in the *positive righteousness of his obedient and loving life lived in perfect filial relation on earth to the heavenly Father.*[195]

Justification, Habets properly concludes, is not simply a declaratory act, but an actualization of what was declared and what happened at the cross.[196] Justification and sanctification happen in us "in Christ." Torrance points to the resurrection as the evidence of this reality. Jesus Christ was not only declared righteous by God, but God also raised him from the dead. The Amen of God to Christ was tangible, true, and effective.[197]

Conclusions

Torrance's understanding of salvation in Jesus Christ is grounded in the reality of the incarnation of the Son, who, as fully human, is also *homoousios* with the Father. As the Son, his descent to created space and time is a salvific movement accomplished by the Triune God in drawing himself near to us in revelation and reconciliation. Likewise, his ascent as fully

---

salvation. It reaches the whole life of humanity as a physical, social, and spiritual being. See B45 "Jesus Christ our Saviour," 1–9.

195. Torrance, *Incarnation*, 81–82. "We are now made through justification by grace to share in the righteousness of God in Christ," Torrance writes in "Atonement," 254. See also B45 "Being justified freely by his grace"; B45 "Law and Grace"; B45 "Justification"; and B47 "Handwriting and Forgiveness," 1–8.

196. Habets, *Theosis*, 118.

197. Torrance, *Space, Time, and Resurrection*, 63. Torrance adds that this is not just an eschatological hope, but is also "a continuing act of Christ, in whom we are continuously being cleansed, forgiven, renewed, and made righteous." Justification is accomplished by Jesus Christ in the past, is realized in us in the present, and will find its culmination in the future. See *Space, Time, and Resurrection*, 64–65; and B46 "Ascension and Second Advent." Torrance's incarnational atonement, particularly the inseparability of the cross and resurrection proves useful in ending the history of debate between Wesleyanism and Calvinism on whether justification is imputed or imparted. Put simply, if justification is viewed in the light of Christ's death, then it is imputed, because Christ's death is his own death. He dies so that we should no longer die. The benefits of what he accomplished on the cross are imputed to us. But if justification is viewed in the light of the resurrection of Jesus Christ, then justification is imparted, for we share in his resurrected body. Not only did Jesus Christ resurrect from the dead on our behalf, but he is also the "firstborn from among the dead," giving to us the gift of experiencing what transpired in his own body.

human to the throne of God in his ascension is a salvific movement accomplished from the side of humanity and on behalf of humanity. God's initiative in electing us to salvation is characterized by a double movement: God in Christ's humanward movement and human in Christ's Godward movement.[198] Jesus Christ vicariously redeemed us not only from the side of humanity, but from the side of God. Salvation is accomplished by Jesus Christ not solely in what he did, but primarily in who he is as fully God and fully human. The being, person, and work of Christ are one. His salvific work is his salvific person. This is another way of saying that Christ's distinct salvific agency is also grounded in his hypostasis as the Son, which can be called *kath hypostasin economy*.

Torrance's soteriology, contrary to criticisms of christomonism, is actually far from it. It is indubitable that Torrance is thoroughly Christocentric. However, his christocentricism is just an introduction to his trinitarian theology. His starting point is definitely christological, but he also stresses that our salvation is accomplished by the Triune God in Jesus Christ, not by Jesus Christ alone. Furthermore, the end of the gift of reconciliation in Christ is not reconciliation with one Person, but with the Triune God. Just as the being and work of the Triune God is the origin of reconciliation, the *telos* and end of human salvation is also reconciliation and relationship with the Triune God, accomplished in Jesus Christ. Thus, Torrance writes that the incarnation is "at once the act of God's humiliation and the act of man's exaltation, for he who is such amazing grace descended to make our lost cause his own, ascended in accomplishment of his task, elevating man into union and communion with the life of God."[199] Just as the Triune God is in the world in Jesus Christ, so is humanity in Jesus Christ lifted up to the triune life and love. This chapter focused on the reconciling work of the Triune God in Jesus Christ, but Torrance's trinitarian theology also discusses the distinct salvific agencies of the Father and the Holy Spirit. In fact, even in the life and work of Christ the Son, Torrance admits the co-working of the Father and the Holy Spirit.[200] The next chapter, thus, deals with the person and work of the Father in the economy of reconciliation.

---

198. Torrance, *Ecumenical Studies*, 136, 141–45; *Trinitarian Faith*, 149; *Christian Doctrine of God*, 161.

199. Torrance, *Incarnation*, 57; *Christian Doctrine of God*, 128.

200. This is especially emphasized by Torrance in his discussion of "*perichoresis* and the co-activity of the Holy Trinity," in *Christian Doctrine of God*, 194–202.

3

The Love of God the Father

Father in heaven, from whom comes [e]very good and perfect gift, grant us your blessing and incline our hearts to prayer. Merciful Saviour, who are at the right hand of the Father, fulfil your own promise, and be present with us who are gathered in your name. Holy and Life-giving Spirit, help us in our weaknesses, and enable us to serve you in the beauty of holiness.[1]

THE FATHER IS INVOLVED IN HIS HYPOSTASIS AS THE FATHER IN THE SALvific economy. This in itself stands as a distinct emphasis in Torrance's soteriology, because not so many soteriological formulations even mention the Father's active involvement in the economy. Against binitarian *missio Dei* formulations (grounded in non-trinitarian readings of Irenaeus's "two hands" theology), this, as such, constitutes another important contribution of Torrance to theology, grounded in his two-tiered *kataphysic soteriology*. The first part of this chapter deals with the person of the Father, emphasizing Torrance's Christo-conditioned approach to knowledge of the Father. It is here that his biblical and realist theology is brought into sharp contrast with all abstractive and speculative approaches to the doctrine of the Father. The second section deals with the distinct work of the Father in the economy of salvation. This separation is only pedagogically helpful, because in reality, the person and work of the Father are indivisible, as will be made manifest in the unavoidable overlapping presentations.

---

1. B38 "Lessons on Isaiah 6:1–4 and Ephesians 2:8–16; John 14:1–20."

The Love of God the Father

"No One Comes to the Father Except through Me"

While it is true that the Son takes priority in the order of knowing, Torrance asserts that in the order of being, the Father comes first, precisely in virtue of his being the Father to the Son.[2] This does not mean, however, that the priority of the person of the Father should be understood in terms of temporal priority or ontological superiority. Rather, for Torrance the priority of the Father should be understood in terms of relation: "The relation of the Son and the Father is irreversible, for 'the Son is from the Father, not the Father from the Son.'"[3] That such a priority is inverted in Christian epistemology is a mystery of the gospel, expressed gnomically by Jesus's claim that "no one comes to the Father except through me" (John 14:6). Christian theology (concerned particularly with the trinitarian economy of salvation and the knowledge of God made available for humanity through it), to remain faithful to Jesus's model, should begin precisely where the God-incarnate wants it to begin: "through me [Jesus]." This christocentric approach to the Father is enveloped within Torrance's christocentric approach to the Trinity in general.[4] God can be known only *through* his acts, *by* his acts, and *in* his acts. But it is precisely because God is a personal being that his dealings with humanity are also personal. Humanity through Jesus Christ is in personal encounter with the Triune God, which is why the Nicene *homoousios* plays a vital role: "It is only in him who is both *homoousios* with the Father and *homoousios* with us, that we may really know God as he is in himself and in accordance with his nature."[5] This *kataphysic* requirement in humanity's knowledge of God

---

2. Torrance, *Christian Doctrine of God*, 137. Thus, as Edith Humphrey notes, starting with the Son is of heuristic significance, in "The Gift of the Father," in *Trinitarian Theology for the Church*, 101.

3. Torrance, *Christian Doctrine of God*, 137; quoting Augustine, *Trin.* 4.20.27 (*NPNF*[1] 3): 83.

4. Kevin Giles identifies four possible starting points for thinking about the Trinity practised within semantics: starting with the Father, starting with the divine Three, starting with the idea of a divine substance, or starting with the notion of the Trinity. While these are philosophically plausible, Giles, like Torrance, chooses not to ask the question of possibility. For both of them, this should be rephrased as the question of historicity: "Where *did* thinking about the Trinity begin"? Unquestionably, it began with the doxological apprehension that Jesus is Lord, leading to the creedal affirmation that Jesus is *homoousios* with the Father. See *Jesus and the Father*, 77; and Humphrey, "The Gift of the Father," 85.

5. Torrance, *Trinitarian Faith*, 203; *Ecumenical Studies*, xx.

The Love of God the Father

is related to Torrance's demand that we avoid the idolatrous tendency to create images of God from the created world, and fashion for ourselves something that is familiar and comfortable to us. We cannot create other images to see the face of God, for "God has imaged himself for us in Jesus Christ." He is "the Reality of God, and therefore the sole, exclusive image of God."[6]

Torrance highlights that human knowledge of the Father in Jesus Christ is *participative*: it is only possible through our *participation* in Christ in revelation, worship, and reconciliation.

Participation in Revelation

In Torrance's Christian epistemology, the convictions that only God knows himself fully and that only by God is God known, are fundamental.[7] In essential reality, therefore, only the Father, Son, and Holy Spirit know each other, and only through God's gracious and free decision does God make himself known to created existents. Two aspects are important to consider in our human knowledge of God: (1) God has enabled humanity to know God in Jesus Christ, and (2) God in Jesus Christ has prescribed the way to know him. Torrance speaks of the second as "the covenanted way of vicarious response to God" through and in Christ.[8] Outside of Christ, or "behind the back of Christ,"[9] there is no genuine knowledge of God. The incarnation of the Word in space and time, as God's final and decisive self-communication, not only sets aside all other ways of knowing him, but also creates the parameters within which such self-communication is to be understood, appropriated, and interpreted. Torrance's rejection of both the traditional arguments for natural theology and speculative abstractions concerning God from philosophical presuppositions is rooted here.[10] Because revelation is primarily *disclosure*, not

---

6. B39 Untitled sermon on Exodus 20:1–4 and John 14:6, 9, 2. In page 5, Torrance adds that the image of God in Jesus Christ is permanent and unchangeable. See also B45 "He who has seen me has seen the Father"; and B47 "What is God Like?— God in the Face of Jesus Christ," 1–9.

7. Kang, "Epistemological Significance," 351–53.

8. Torrance, *Mediation of Christ*, 78.

9. Torrance, *When Christ Comes*, 86; *Christian Theology*, 130.

10. B23 "Christian Doctrine of God," 1–2. Related in his dismissal of other approaches to knowledge of God is his view of the interrelationship between revelation and reconciliation. In his sermon B42 "Knowledge of God," 2, he writes, referring to natural theology or nature: "Never once has that sort of thing brought you near to the Lord God, the Father against Whom you have sinned, and from Whom you

anamnesis, or discovery, it implies the refutation of all else that purports to be knowledge about God. Revelation is not an extended version of human rational knowledge, and therefore it subverts human-grounded attempts to approach God. In fact, Torrance argues that it is human foolishness to attempt to know God through other means, when in fact in the incarnation God came to humanity "in a familiar way" already.[11]

Underlying this argument for the covenanted way of response in Jesus Christ is Torrance's strong emphasis on the personal nature of revelation. First, the revelation of God is essentially the revelation of persons, and only secondarily the revelation of facts. This can be perceived dialectically: just as the revealed is a person, so the Revealer revealing is also a person. Thus, the person of the Father is revealed in the person of the Son, for in the revelation of the Son, the Father is also revealed.

> What God the Father has revealed of himself in Jesus Christ his Son, he is in himself; and what he is in himself as God the Father he reveals in Jesus Christ the Son. The Father and the Son are One, one in Being and one in Agency. Thus in Jesus Christ the Mediation of divine Revelation and the Person of the Mediator perfectly coincide. In Jesus Christ God has given us a Revelation which is identical with himself. Jesus Christ *is* the Revelation of God.[12]

---

need pardon and new life." More poetically in B42 "Creation," 10–11, he argues: "The religion of nature will only lead you to the brink of a fearful precipice where nature ends, and where you can only stand helpless with empty beseeching hands stretched out into the blackness of eternal night. Nature has not a single word of comfort for the dying, not a word of peace to the guilty, not a spark of hope for a single son of man. Natural development leads only to death. Thank God, thank God a thousand times that this is not the Gospel."

11. B23 "The Christian Doctrine of Revelation," 7–11, 56. He polemically adds in B42 "Naaman," 3–4: "What a picture of idolatrous humanity wanting to carve out its own gods, and substitute its own Abanahs and Pharpars in place of the river of God. That is the great mistake that we all make. We think we can find out our own religion, and that we can manipulate the ways of God to suit ourselves. We have all sorts of ideas: ideas of beauty, and value, ideas of right and wrong, a whole bag load of preconceptions, and we produce these one by one and expect God to use them and are peeved when He turns away. We set our inventiveness to work, and say, God must be thus and so—and when we encounter God, we are angry, because He always takes us by surprise, and never comes in the way that we prescribe for Him."

12. Torrance, *Mediation of Christ*, 23. Thus, Torrance also argues that the real text of the New Testament is the humanity of Christ—the real text of God's address to us, in *Mediation of Christ*, 78. The influence of Barth here is undeniable. See *CD* I/1: 295–99.

The Love of God the Father

The Father is revealed, therefore, not primarily through semantics or other human symbols, but through the person of Jesus Christ. Secondly, the personal nature of revelation is evident in the way it is received by humanity. According to Habets, "Knowledge is fundamentally relational, not merely cognitive; it is a *personal* knowing that comes only by *personal* participation."[13] This represents Torrance's assertion that knowledge of persons is only possible in reciprocal relations, that no one knows the Father except the Son, and that a perfect and complete knowledge of the Other is only shared by them. Thus, he concludes, "We are given access to the closed circle of divine knowing between the Father and the Son only through cognitive union with Christ, that is, only through an interrelation of knowing and being between us and the incarnate Son."[14] Human knowledge of God involves mediation. On the one hand, humanity has no independent knowledge of the Father apart from sharing in the Son's knowledge of the Father.[15] But on the other hand, we cannot claim that we share in the totality and comprehensibility of the Son's knowledge of the Father for this would imply the infinitization of our creaturely nature and capability. There is a sense, therefore, that "we cannot take up precisely the same attitude to God as Jesus took, that his view, as it were, cannot be ours. We are sinful, and can only approach God through the Mediator."[16]

Participation in Worship

Along with his brother James, Torrance contends for a christocentric and trinitarian view of worship that is guided by the life and work of the incarnate Son.[17] Central to their arguments is the sole mediation of Jesus

---

13. Habets, *Theosis*, 96; Colyer, *How to Read*, 109, 128, 139, 357.

14. Torrance, *Trinitarian Faith*, 59, 56, 58, 212; *Mediation of Christ*, 25; *Christian Doctrine of God*, 77–78; *Reality and Evangelical Theology*, 111; *Theology in Reconciliation*, 223; *Divine Meaning*, 187; *Karl Barth*, 214; and *Doctrine of Jesus Christ*, 44. Torrance further writes: "The relation between the Father and the Son, and the Son and the Father is a *closed relation*, but entry into it is given through the incarnation of the Son, for in the perfect human life of Jesus the love and truth of God are addressed to man in the concrete form of a historical relationship of man to fellow man, of this man to others." See Torrance, *Incarnation*, 128 (italics mine); and Molnar, *Theologian of the Trinity*, 60.

15. Torrance, *Trinitarian Faith*, 55, 56, 60, 82; *God and Rationality*, 174; *Mediation of Christ*, 116. See also Kruger, "Doctrine of the Knowledge of God," 368; Colyer, *How to Read*, 134–35; and Kang, "Epistemological Significance," 349–50.

16. B23 "Christ's View of God," 5.

17. This is characteristic of the Torrance theological tradition. See Torrance,

Christ as the God-man in his humanward and Godward agencies and the concomitant emphasis on the sole priesthood of Christ *pro nobis* both in the past and in the present. In Jesus's earthly human life and perfect obedience to the Father unto death, he is humanity's only and perfect representative, responding to the Father's words and lifting humanity's prayers in his prayers. Likewise, the ascended Christ is still vicariously interceding in his resurrected human body as our high priest in the presence of the Father. As such, as is true in revelation and reconciliation, so in worship Jesus Christ is embodying in himself the covenanted way of human approach to the Father.[18] This is the doxological implication of Christ's incarnation and ascension.

That Christ is the way to the Father in worship also emphasizes the role of the human mind of Christ. Scorning the Apollinarian tendency of contemporary worship, Torrance reiterates that in Christian worship, the essential role of the human mind of Christ in the mediation of our worship to the Father is non-negotiable. "Once we lose sight of the vicarious role of the mind of Christ in its oneness with the mind of the Father, the whole meaning of worship changes and with it the basic structure and truth of liturgy."[19] Because Jesus is the only one who knows the Father and who offers perfect worship to the Father, worship is "the gift of participating through the Spirit in the Son's communion with the Father—of participating, in union with Christ, in what *he* has done for us once and for all in his life and death on the Cross, and in what *he* is continuing to do for us in the presence of the Father."[20] This, according to Torrance, is what makes the Christian view of worship distinct, in that the emphasis is given in what the God-man did and does rather than what other humans do. Absolute priority is given to the sole priesthood of Jesus Christ and our sharing in his priesthood.[21]

Worship, Community, and the Triune God, 20–24, where he refers to this approach, in contrast to the unitarian view of worship, as the Nicene model. See also *Ecumenical Studies*, 135–7; and Torrance, *Persons in Communion*, 360. The crucial point is the vicarious whole humanity of Christ. See *Theology in Reconciliation*, 213.

18. Torrance, *Mediation of Christ*, 87; *Theology in Reconciliation*, 209; *Incarnation*, 120; and Torrance, *Worship, Community, and the Triune God of Grace*, 64. Even praying the Lord's Prayer means that we pray with the prayer of Jesus, in *Theology in Reconciliation*, 211; B39 "The Centrality of Christ"; and B46 "Sacramental Prayer." See also Slater, "Salvation as Participation," 58.

19. Torrance, *Theology in Reconciliation*, 139–40.

20. Torrance, *Ecumenical Studies*, 128.

21. Torrance, *Theological Dialogue* 1: 5, 8; *Theology in Reconciliation*, 140. Torrance describes this participation in the whole liturgical and sacramental life of Christ

The Love of God the Father

Participation in Reconciliation

For Torrance the gospel of salvation depends on the inner relations between the life and activity of Jesus Christ and the Father. As Jesus is the way to the Father in knowledge and worship, so too he is the only way to reconciliation with God. In fact, reconciliation is the necessary presupposition of our knowledge and worship of the Father. This should not be understood in an existentialist I-am-reconciled-therefore-I-know approach but in the light of Christ's work *pro nobis*. Torrance's emphasis that reconciliation precedes humanity's knowledge of God is a further contribution to theology, and is an antidote to the common perspective in existentialist evangelical theology that *Wissen* (knowledge of facts) precedes *Kennen* (personal knowledge). Torrance inverts the *ordo cognoscendi*, arguing that we are reconciled in Christ first, through his vicarious life and obedience, before we can be brought up into the presence of God. This consistently ties with his assertion that God cannot be known at a distance or in detachment.[22] To be in relation and to know are inseparable. Reconciliation in Jesus Christ through his atoning life and death, and union with him in his death and resurrection, enable us to share in the inner relations of God's own circle of knowing. Again, Torrance's emphasis on the objective accomplishment of Jesus Christ two thousand years ago is unmistakable here:

> By his blood Christ has reconciled us to God and thereby opened the way for all who believe in his name to enter with him into the holy presence of God and share in the gift of the Holy Spirit which he received from the Father. Thus through the grace of the Lord Jesus Christ and the Communion of the Holy Spirit we sinful human beings may have access to the love of the Father, and know him not from afar but intimately as he is in himself.[23]

Christ's twofold movement of atoning propitiation in the incarnation and atonement is the Father's appointed way of drawing himself near to us and us near to him. It is only through Christ's sole mediatorial role, his assumption and sanctification of our humanity, and our consequent

---

as "being yoked to Christ," in B38 Untitled sermon outline on Matthew 11:28–30.

22. See Torrance, *Scottish Theology*, 6. In *When Christ Comes*, 135, 138, Torrance also argues that we cannot come before God unclean, or come before God as spectators.

23. Torrance, *Mediation of Christ*, 108–9.

participation in his sanctified vicarious humanity, that we are given access to the life and love of the Triune God.

The Father of the Son

Torrance argues that God may be known only through his own act of self-revelation, and not through any speculative formulation grounded upon abstract principles and presuppositions derived from extrabiblical sources. Thus he opposes the approach employed in most theology textbooks that begins by enumerating the attributes of God prior to a presentation of God's historical acts.[24] For instance, Torrance repudiates attributing omnipotence to God apart from what God actually is and actually has done. More importantly, respecting the nature of God as triune requires that relationship or communion be employed as the primary category in the identification of any of the persons. Correspondingly, "the Father is not properly Father apart from the Son and the Spirit, and the Son is not properly Son apart from the Father and Spirit, and the Spirit is not properly Spirit apart from the Father and the Son."[25] This is very significant, considering that in the doctrine of the Trinity we are concerned with persons-in-relations, whose very nature is what Gregory Nazianzen called *pros ti*, understood as meaning "Being for."[26]

The church fathers, according to Torrance, already discerned the necessity of approaching the Father in terms of Christ's essential relationship with him, as manifested in the Gospels. Therefore, it is only in the light of what the incarnate Son revealed throughout his historical existence that we can know the Father, Jesus's Father. And because Jesus is the incarnate Son of the Father, then the relationship between them in the economy of salvation is *revelation* itself. Fascinatingly, Torrance argues that Jesus's act of calling God "Holy Father" also reveals his distinct view of God, which we must also follow.[27] "God was Father because he was his Father and he was his Son."[28] And, because Jesus called the Father "Abba," and not

---

24. Torrance, *Trinitarian Faith*, 82; and *Christian Doctrine of God*, 14, 19, 21, 204–5. It is postsupposition, rather than presupposition, that is important. See also Torrance, *Persons in Communion*, 26, 36; and McGrath, *Intellectual Biography*, 148.

25. Torrance, *Trinitarian Perspectives*, 141.

26. Torrance, *Christian Doctrine of God*, 163; Colyer, *How to Read*, 312–13.

27. B23 "Christ's View of God," 1.

28. Torrance, *Ecumenical Studies*, 22. "There is only the God and Father who has revealed Himself to us in our Lord Jesus Christ and with whom Jesus is completely one," Torrance writes in "Jesus is God and Man in One Person," 17.

The Love of God the Father

something else, Torrance follows Athanasius's argument that "It would be more godly and true to signify God from the Son and call him Father, than to name God from his works and call him Unoriginate."[29] Athanasius's statement cannot be isolated from his reaction against the Arians, who erroneously approached the being of the Son in terms of creation rather than his relationship to the Father. Torrance argues that personal relations have priority over relations of functions in theology, because knowing the Father in terms of the Creator-creation relation does not provide direct and personal revelation, but only external and negative affirmations. Thinking and speaking about God from the perspective of creation, or from the Unoriginate/originate relation, means "we can only think and speak of him in vague, general and negative terms, at the infinite distance of the creature from the Creator where we cannot know God as he is in himself or in accordance with his divine nature, but only in his absolute separation from us, as the eternal, unconditioned and indescribable."[30] More positively, knowing the Father in terms of the Father-Son relation is knowing him as he is in his being—thus, knowing him *kata physin*.

> If we are to have any true and precise scientific knowledge of God, we must allow His own nature, as He becomes revealed to us, to determine how we are to know Him, how we are to think of Him, and what we are to say to Him. That is what happens when we approach God the Father through Jesus Christ his Son, for the Son is of one and the same nature and being as the Father ... He is God of God, the one way of access to God the Father.[31]

Thus, in both the order of being and acting, and our knowledge of the Father, there is the absolute priority of the Fatherhood of God over his designation as Creator. This is also because "the concept of God as Creator is wholly governed by the coinherent relation between the Father and the Son and the inseparable activity in which they are engaged."[32]

---

29. Torrance, *Trinitarian Faith*, 49; quoting Athanasius, *C. Ar.* I.34 (*NPNF*² 4): 326; *Dec.* 31 (*NPNF*² 4): 171–72.

30. Torrance, *Trinitarian Faith*, 50.

31. Ibid., 52.

32. Ibid., 77. This, Colyer notes, refers to the "Christological qualification of God as Almighty," in *How to Read*, 153, 157. See also Torrance's rejection that God is eternally Creator and the idea that creation eternally existed in the mind of God, in *Ground and Grammar of Theology*, 66. See also Molnar, *Theologian of the Trinity*, 81; and Boff, *Holy Trinity*, 70.

"Father" as God's Name

Knowing the Father based on the Son's relationship with him in the Gospels prevents us from imposing and importing into the Father our own earthly and human categories of fatherhood. Torrance rejects gender issues about God, for gender only belongs to created existents and should not be read back into the nature of God as Father, Son, and Holy Spirit. He objects to the anthropocentric technique in feminist theology of refusing the Fatherhood of God because it is equated with the human experience of (terrible) earthly fathers. Torrance writes: "Human fatherhood may not be used as a standard by which to judge divine Fatherhood, for it is only in the light of the Fatherhood of God that all other fatherhood is to be understood."[33] Torrance's understanding of the Father as loving is grounded upon the Father's eternal being, his relation with the Son, and his work in creation and redemption. First, the Father is love because the being of the Triune God is a communion of love. Secondly, that the Father is love is portrayed in his eternal relation to the Son: "the Father/Son, Son/Father relation belongs to the innermost being of God as God—in fact the flow of love from the Father to the Son and from the Son to the Father reveals that God *is* the ever-living and ever-loving God precisely as this dynamic communion of loving and being loved within himself."[34] Finally, the Father as love is manifested in his creative and sustaining act and redemptive purposes. "By revealing himself in the Lord Jesus Christ as *his* dear Son," Torrance writes, "God reveals that Fatherhood belongs to his eternal Being, and in giving his Son to be the Saviour of the world, he reveals that he loves us to the uttermost with an eternal fatherly Love."[35]

However, although the designation "Father" is derived primarily from the relation of the Son to the Father, "to name God Father is to signify his very Being."[36] Torrance writes:

> When the Father is considered relatively, that is *ad alios* in relation to the Son and the Holy Spirit, he is thought of as Father of the Son, but when the Father is thought of absolutely, that is *in se*, as God himself (*Autotheos*), the name "Father" is often

---

33. Torrance, *Trinitarian Perspectives*, 130. See also Torrance, *Worship, Community, and the Triune God of Grace*, 99–110; and Williams, "The Fatherhood of God," in *The Forgotten Trinity* 3: 91–101, on the difficulties in understanding the Fatherhood of God.

34. Torrance, *Christian Doctrine of God*, 59.

35. Ibid., 55.

36. Ibid., 118; quoting Athanasius, *Syn.* 35 (NPNF² 4): 469.

applied to God (*Theos*) or the Godhead (*Theotes*). The name "Father," then, may refer to the one Being of God or *ousia* of God, but it may refer to the Person or *hypostasis* of the Father.[37]

That Jesus called the Father *Abba* means that he is calling God his own proper name. The New Testament, therefore, through Christ, provides a "radical change in the understanding of God, for 'Father' is now revealed to be more than an epithet—it is the personal Name of God in which the form and content of his self-revelation as Father through Jesus Christ his Son are inseparable."[38] Torrance finds this in the prayer of Jesus Christ in John 17, which he quotes: "'Father, . . . I have finished the work which you gave me to do. . . . I have manifested your Name unto men,'"[39] and in the Lord's Prayer: "Our Father in heaven, hallowed by your name" (Matt 6:9).

Monarchia and the Trinity

In the early church, "Father" referred to two different but interrelated aspects: the being of the Godhead (*ousia*) and the person of the Father (*hypostasis*). However, according to Torrance, the Cappadocian fathers, particularly Basil, combined them together, arguing that the being of the Godhead is in the person of the Father. The result is that the person of the Father became regarded as the source of the being of God, particularly by Basil and Gregory of Nyssa. This means that the divine *ousia* is equated with the uncaused person of the Father, who then becomes the cause or *arche* of the Deity and of the personal nature of the Son and the Holy Spirit. For Torrance, this move represents a partial return to the Origenist position that the Godhead is complete in the Father alone, but mediated in the Son and the Holy Spirit through their origination from the Father, against which Athanasius had insisted on the perfect equality of the Father, Son, and Holy Spirit, in each of whom the Godhead is complete. He also notes Gregory Nazianzen's uneasiness about the attribution of the *Monarchia* only to the person of the Father, and the concomitant combinations of the terms *arche* and *aitia* in speaking of the origin of the Son and the Holy Spirit, for this appeared to imply and import notions of superiority and inferiority in the Trinity.[40] And although Gregory Nazianzen "nevertheless

---

37. Torrance, *Christian Doctrine of God*, 140.
38. Ibid., 56.
39. Ibid., 139; and Colyer, *How to Read*, 143.
40. See Torrance, *Theological Dialogue* 1: 87; *Christian Doctrine of God*, 181. See also Ralph Del Colle's comparison of Torrance and Zizioulas on this issue in "'Person'

spoke of the Father as the *arche* and the *aitia* in order to secure the unity of the Godhead," Torrance adds, "actually he *thought* of them as referring to *relations* or *scheseis* subsisting in God which are beyond all time, beyond all origin, and beyond all cause."[41]

Torrance rejects the ascription of *monarchia* to the Father alone. Guided by his understanding of *perichoresis* and *onto-relations,* he stresses that the Son and the Holy Spirit must be included with the Father in the one originless source or *arche* of the Holy Trinity.[42] Also, Athanasius's legacy and emphasis on the *homoousios* enabled Torrance to formulate his view of the monarchy of the Father and the Trinity: "Athanasius had such a strong view of the complete identity, equality and unity of the three divine Persons within the Godhead, that he declined to advance a view of the Monarchy in which the oneness of God was defined with reference to the

---

and 'Being,'" 70–86. R. P. C. Hanson shares Torrance's interpretation of the Cappadocians, particularly on the Arche, saying that in Basil, the Father's *hypostasis* is the sole origin (*arche*), source (*pege*), and root (*riza*) of the other two hypostases. See *Search for the Christian Doctrine of God*, 693–96. Hanson, however, vehemently argues that Basil and Gregory of Nyssa explicitly rejected subordinationism in the Arche of the Father. (See also Kelly, *Early Christian Doctrines*, 265.) Najeeb G. Awad also thinks that the approaches of Basil and Gregory of Nyssa to the Godhead are different: Basil's approach is "patro-centrically semi-heirarchial" and Gregory's is "reciprocally koinonial," in "Between Subordination and Koinonia," 181–204.

The main reason for divergence of interpretations, even in the early church concerning *ousia* and *hypostasis* is that they were used quite interchangeably, just as their meanings were ambiguously interchangeable. See Kelly, *Early Christian Creeds*, 243–50; and Hanson, *Studies in Christian Antiquity*, 244–48. For a modern theologian who followed Basil's *Monarchia* of the Father, because of his emphasis on person over nature, see Zizioulas, *Being as Communion*, 17–18, 40–44, 88; and *Lectures in Christian Dogmatics*, xii, 60. See also Torrance, *Theological Dialogue* 1: 87–88. Along with Volf, *After Our Likeness*, 79, Humphrey views the consequence of the Monarchy of the Father differently: "The Father's hierarchy, holy leadership and monarchy," she wrote, "does not drive out, but is the condition for mutual honor, responsive love and fruitfulness beyond measure," in "The Gift of the Father," 101. On the contrary, Arthur Williams argues that "monarchy" indubitably entails subordination, in "The Trinity and Time," 65. Boff enumerates the dangers of understanding Father as monarch in politics and religion in *Holy Trinity*, 7–9.

41. Torrance, *Trinitarian Faith*, 239. Noble, on the other hand, argues that Gregory Nazianzen used *arche* and *aitios* and not *aitia* to refer to the Father as the principle of origination in the Godhead, because the third term implies subordinationism and is only used by Gregory Nazianzen to refer particularly to the "external causation of the world." See "Paradox in Gregory Nazianzen," 96–97.

42. Torrance, *Christian Doctrine of God*, 181; *Trinitarian Faith*, 223–24, 328–31. See Torrance's discussion of *perichoresis* in relation to the *Monarchia* in *Trinitarian Perspectives*, 120–21, 125–26, 139–42; and Jenson's rejection of the Father as the sole *arche* of the Trinity in *The Triune Identity*, 141–43, 175.

Father alone or to the Person of the Father."[43] Like Athanasius, Torrance affirms the Father is the *arche* of the Son in that he eternally begot the Son. Nevertheless, "while the Son is associated with the *Arche* of the Father in this way, he cannot be thought of as an *Arche* subsisting in himself, for by his very Nature he is inseparable from the Father of whom he is the Son. By the same token, however, the Father cannot be thought of as an *Arche* apart from the Son, for it is precisely as Father that he is Father of the Son."[44] Thus, that the Father is *arche* of the Son should be understood not in terms of temporal origination or ontological superiority but in terms of an equal eternal relation, "for the Sonship of the Son is as ultimate as the Fatherhood of the Father."[45] In eternity, there was the Godhead, not the Father alone. This is founded on the fact that the Father is not properly known as Father apart from the Son and the Holy Spirit, that the Son is not properly known apart from the Father and the Holy Spirit, and that the Holy Spirit is not properly known apart from the Father and the Son.

The Love of God the Father

Now that we have established the triune identity of the Father, we can proceed to discuss his agency in the mediation of reconciliation. That the Father plays a distinct role in the salvific economy is a given in Torrance's trinitarian soteriology: "There are relative distinctions in his [the Triune God's] three-fold activity appropriate to the Persons of the Father, the Son, and the Spirit, which bear upon creation."[46] Of course, it must

---

43. Torrance, *Christian Doctrine of God*, 183. Thus, "in proclaiming the *Monarchia* we do not err," Torrance adds, "but confess the Trinity, Unity in Trinity and Trinity in Unity, one Godhead of the Father, Son and Holy Spirit. There is one true God, Trinity in Unity; one God, Father, Son and Holy Spirit." Torrance, *Trinitarian Faith*, 223; *Trinitarian Perspectives*, 137–39.

44. Torrance, *Christian Doctrine of God*, 183; *Trinitarian Faith*, 312.

45. Torrance, *Trinitarian Perspectives*, 18. Torrance, quoting Calvin, adds: "The *principium* does not apply to the *Being* of the divine Persons which they have wholly in common, but only to the order of relations which they have with one another within the unity of the Godhead. 'For although we affirm that there is a *principium divinitatis* in the Father in respect of order and position (*ratione ordinis et gradus*), yet we declare it a detestable invention that Being belongs to the Father alone, as though he were the deifier of the Son.' Thus the *principium* of the Father does not import an ontological priority, or some *prius aut posterius* in God, but has to do only with a 'form of order' (*ratio ordinis*) or 'arrangement' (*dispositio*) of inner Trinitarian relations governed by the Father/Son relationship, which in the nature of the case is irreversible." See *Trinitarian Perspectives*, 65–66, 118–19; Calvin, *Institutes* I.13.24.

46. Torrance, *Christian Doctrine of God*, 212; *Trinitarian Perspectives*, 55; *Scottish*

be remembered that in evangelical reality not only are the being and the act of the Triune God inseparable, but in their perichoretic love and life, the work of the Father is inseparable from the works of the incarnate Son and the Holy Spirit. The only theological basis for the possibility of distinguishing the distinctive role of the Father from the work of the Son and the Holy Spirit is that even though the Triune God works as one, the persons of the Trinity are "engaged in the work of reconciliation in distinctive ways appropriate to each Person."[47] So in relation to what we have referred to as Torrance's *kath hypostasin* trinitarian soteriology, this chapter is concerned with the Father's *kath hypostasin economy*, or *kata Patera*.

The Loving Father

The evangelical experience of the Triune God as the way that God willed to make himself known serves as the foundation of all statements of God's character as love. This is why Torrance's view of the Father's character as love is also Christo-conditioned. In particular, he argues that it is through the cross that we learn "the innermost nature of God the Father as holy compassionate love,"[48] which the resurrection also confirms:

> The resurrection tells us that the God and Father of our Lord Jesus Christ is not the kind of God who remained alone and aloof in his eternity, who did not lift even a finger to save Jesus when he was hounded to death on the gibbet and put to an open shame. He is not the kind of God who abandoned his Son in his despairing cry on the Cross.... On the contrary, He is the kind of God who remained unswervingly true and faithful to Jesus and all he revealed through him.[49]

It is no wonder, therefore, that Torrance understands the nature and work of the Father as characterized by love. His use of 2 Corinthians 13:14 is

---

Theology, 87. Using the baptismal formula in the Great Commission, Torrance writes that to be saved indubitably means being saved in the name of the Father, Son, and Holy Spirit. See B44 Untitled sermon on Matthew 28:19, 1–4.

47. Torrance, *Scottish Theology*, 87; *Christian Doctrine of God*, 252–53; Mackintosh, *Doctrine of the Person of Christ*, 526. To maintain the distinction-in-unity is a better alternative than Jenson's rejection of the idea that each person fulfils a distinct economy. Jenson is anxious about what he discerns as the danger of appropriation: "mathematically equal abstract divinity of the triune persons," in *The Triune Identity*, 126–27.

48. Torrance, *Christian Doctrine of God*, 109.

49. Torrance, "The Whole Universe Revolves," 13.

The Love of God the Father

also central. In fact, it is only after an affirmation of this Pauline statement that Torrance expounds how and why love is properly attributed to the Father.[50]

The constancy and faithfulness of God's love in both his being and act is also a major theme in Torrance's theology. Torrance is adamant that God's loving act to bring humanity to relationship with himself is not an afterthought, but he is also adamant in asserting that God's love is faithful throughout the entire movement of salvation. This means that even in the apparent triumph of un-love in humanity's rejection of God in Jesus Christ, God remains faithful and loving. "Why people may want to reject the love of God is quite inexplicable," Torrance writes, "but whether they believe in Jesus Christ as the incarnate love of God or refuse to believe in him, the love of God remains unchangeably what it was and is and ever will be, the love that is freely, unreservedly and unconditionally given to all mankind."[51]

Love as God's Character: God as Communion

Eastern theologian Emilianos Timiadis writes: "God has love for us because he is love himself. We witness a trinitarian relationship based on the mutual love of each Person, where the difference is only apparent, necessary to communion. Each time we speak of the Trinity, we must think of nothing else but Love. . . . God is Love."[52] This is important to Torrance, because of his insistence that human salvation is ontologically grounded in God's being. This means that if God were not love in his innermost being, his loving act in Jesus Christ and the Holy Spirit would be groundless and incomprehensible.[53] This is also related to understanding the Trinity as communion: "The one triune Being of God is to be thought of, then, as essentially and intrinsically a mutual movement of loving self-communication between the Father, the Son and the Holy Spirit, an intensely

---

50. Colyer, *How to Read*, 146–49. This is explicitly found in Torrance's treatment of the work of the Father in creation: "It is to the ultimate Love of God the Father that the 'reason' for the creation is to be traced . . . there is no reason why the creation came to be, why there is something and not nothing, apart from the eternal movement of Love in the inner Life of God, which in love freely overflows from God who does not will to exist for himself alone but for others also. It is then, as grounded in that ultimate Love which God the Father is, that the rational order of the creation is to be understood," in Torrance, *Christian Doctrine of God*, 212.

51. Torrance, *Christian Doctrine of God*, 246.

52. Torrance, *Theological Dialogue* 1: 125.

53. Torrance, *Christian Doctrine of God*, 5.

personal Communion, an ever-living ever-loving Being."[54] But God is love not only *in se* but also *ad extra*. Torrance points to the personal naming of God as the I AM or Yahweh as an illustration.

> The significant point to be emphasized here is that the self-naming of God as *Yahweh* is bound up with the covenant of steadfast love and truth he made with Israel. The divine pronouncement "I am who I am/I will be who I will be," is not isolated from the establishing of a holy fellowship between *Yahweh* and Israel which he backs up with his own Being: "I am the Lord," and reinforces with his promise "I will be with you." The Being of *Yahweh* is his Being-in-union with his people.[55]

The being of God as love flows to his acts in history. It is precisely because God is both personal and a communion of love that he establishes communion and initiates personal relationships with others. And because the being of God as love is essentially personal, dynamic, and relational—he is also personally, dynamically, and relationally involved in reconciling the world to himself.

Love and Creation: God as Open Communion

Torrance's rationale for discussing creation under his presentation of God the Father is that the notion that God is Creator is only intelligible through the primary principle that God is eternally Father to the Son: "God was always Father, not always Creator, but now he is Creator as well as Father."[56] Furthermore, his understanding of creation, and his emphasis on the creative work of the Father rest on the Father-Son relation: "Creation arises, then, out of the Father's eternal love of the Son, and is activated through the free ungrudging movement of that Fatherly love in sheer grace which continues to flow freely and unceasingly toward what God has brought into being in complete differentiation from himself."[57] In relation to humanity and redemption, however, Torrance warns that "While God is Creator in virtue of his being eternally Father, with us the reverse is the

---

54. Torrance, *Christian Doctrine of God*, 133.
55. Ibid., 122; Colyer, *How to Read*, 144.
56. Torrance, *Trinitarian Perspectives*, 88.
57. Torrance, *Christian Doctrine of God*, 209. See Torrance's discussion on the problems that arise out of the failure to distinguish between the generation of the Son and the creation of the world, in *Theology in Reconciliation*, 220–24.

The Love of God the Father

case, for God has become our Father, not by nature but by grace, after he had become our Creator."[58]

Concomitant to this is the fact that God is not a solitary, detached being who is aloof and distant from the completely other. God is an eternal communion of love and personal being in himself, but this is to be understood not in terms of the being of God grounded in an abstract necessitarian-philosophical view of "being," but as *the being of God for others* whom he seeks and with whom he creates fellowship. God's transcendence and immanence, his being-in-himself and being-with-us, or *ousia* and *parousia* are inseparable.[59] In the light of this, creation in general and humanity in particular, in Habets's and Rahner's terms, possess a "transcendental determination," i.e., we are made to commune with the Triune God.[60] "The whole *raison d'être* of the universe lies in the fact that God does not will to exist alone, that he will not be without us, but has freely and purposely created the universe and bound it to himself as the sphere where he may ungrudgingly pour out his love, and where we may enjoy communion with him."[61] Torrance calls this humanity's "supernatural destiny," and attributes the nature and purpose of creation to the triune love,

---

58. Torrance, *Trinitarian Faith*, 90. See also B43 "The Fatherhood of God," 1–11.

59. Torrance, *Christian Doctrine of God*, 123–24. Closely related to this discussion is the relationship between the holiness and love of God. John Webster's article "Holiness and Love of God," 249–68, is of critical importance. In it, Webster argues for their inseparability: "God's holiness is the majestic incomparability, difference and purity which he is in himself as Father, Son and Holy Spirit, and which is manifest and operative in the economy of his works in the love with which he elects, reconciles and perfects human partners for fellowship with himself" (see pp. 256, 258, 261). In "Goodness and Dignity of Man," 314, Torrance similarly states that God's holiness "is far from being merely condemnatory for it is supremely self-imparting and redemptive." See also B43 "The Holiness of God," 1–10; Bradshaw, "Barth on the Trinity," 147; and Molnar, *Theologian of the Trinity*, 56.

60. Habets, *Theosis*, 37; and Rahner, *Spirit in the World*, liii. Rahner views humanity essentially as a transcendental being, and calls humanity *Geist*, which refers to "a power which reaches out beyond the world, and knows the metaphysical." See also "The Concept of Mystery in Catholic Theology," 42; "Anonymous Christians," 392; and "The Theology of Power," 399.

61. Torrance, *Trinitarian Faith*, 94–95. He preached: "You are meant by your very [M]ake[r] to soar up into the heights of the glory of God, and to plunge deep into the abysses of His infinite love and wisdom. Man is made for God, and is a dark creature indeed without Him." See B43 Untitled sermon on Isaiah 50:11, 5. Thus Torrance refers to the dignity of humanity as made for covenant partnership and conversation with God, in "Goodness and Dignity of Man," 314. Alan Torrance also notes that participation in the New Creation, when true personhood is achieved, is the *telos* of creation, in *Persons in Communion*, 365.

but especially to "the activity of divine Love which is peculiarly appropriate to the Father."[62]

Love and Creation: Relation and Redemption

Torrance quotes Calvin: "It is not enough for us to conceive God to be the Maker of the world, and to father all power upon Him, but we must know him to be our Father because He draws us to Him with so gentle and loving a care as if we were His children."[63] Humanity, created by God the Father as love, is essentially covenanted to filial relationship with the heavenly Father: "We come to God not only as Him that created me, but also as Him that hath uttered a fatherly love toward me."[64] But the given goodness and dignity of creation—or anthropology in particular—should also be triangulated with the doctrines of sin and redemption, placed in the context of the Father's love. Sin effects the corruption of the *imago Dei* in humanity. Because sin is rebellion against God, it is therefore the dehumanization of humanity.

> If in Calvin's thought the *imago Dei* has thus to do first of all with God's gracious beholding of man as His child, which is the objective basis of the *imago*, and then with man's response to that decision of God's grace in coming to Him as a Father and yielding to Him the gratitude and honor which are due in such a filial relation, which is the subjective basis of the *imago*, it is implied throughout that God created man just for this relationship with God. . . . Calvin thinks of sin as destroying or utterly defacing the image of God in man. In this way man has become a "double beast."[65]

Important here is the fact that creation and redemption are interrelated, especially when viewed relationally. Torrance argues that it is only on the basis of viewing redemption as reconciliation with God that the inner logic and *telos* of creation is brought to light, because creation is proleptically conditioned by redemption. Colyer explains:

---

62. Torrance, *Theology in Reconstruction*, 100–101; *Christian Doctrine of God*, 212. See also B42 "What is Man?," 1–13.
63. Calvin, *Sermon on Job* 36:1; quoted in Torrance, *Calvin's Doctrine of Man*, 76.
64. Calvin, *Sermon on Job* 35:8; quoted in Torrance, *Calvin's Doctrine of Man*, 77. See also Torrance, "Answer to God," 3, 4.
65. Torrance, *Calvin's Doctrine of Man*, 7–78; *Atonement*, 75.

The Love of God the Father

> What Torrance intends, I believe, is that God's ultimate *telos* for creation from the beginning is revealed and actualized in the incarnation, death and resurrection of Christ, a *telos* in which all creation comes to share in the eternal communion of love that God is. This is the ultimate goal of both redemption and creation. It is actually realised in redemption after the Fall, and it is a *telos* that proleptically conditions the creation.[66]

Interesting here, therefore, is the relationship between the work of the Father and the work of the Son in restoring creation. Torrance argues that although creation possesses temporal priority in terms of existence in space and time, "the actual creation of the universe in the outward movement of the Father's love was proleptically conditioned by the incarnation of that love . . . in order to redeem creation and to reconcile all things, things visible and invisible alike, to himself."[67] The original creation, the restoration of God's creation, and the incarnation of the eternal Son and Word of God in Jesus Christ are interrelated. "The restoration of creation to communion and fellowship with Him in which the peace of God reigns over all, the joy and gladness in God the Father fills the whole of creation"[68] is at the heart of the triune act of creation.

The Electing Father

Theologians must realize that the redemption of humanity and the restoration of communion with God are not divine afterthoughts necessitated by and only consequential to the Fall. This adds significance to Torrance's argument that redemption proleptically conditions creation. Communion with God derives its origin not from temporal moral necessity but from the eternal will and purposes of God, which Torrance refers to as the import

---

66. Colyer, *How to Read*, 164, footnote 34; also quoted in Habets, *Theosis*, 26. This is because through the work of Jesus Christ, we may discern more fully that the origin and *telos* of creation is embedded in his eternal being. See Torrance, *Trinitarian Faith*, 102; *Christian Doctrine of God*, 204; and Lee, *Living in Union*, 180. Torrance is indebted to both Athanasius and Mackintosh concerning this theme. See Athanasius, *C. Ar.* II.21.65–72 (*NPNF*² 4): 383–88; III.26.33 (*NPNF*² 4): 411–12; III.27.38 (*NPNF*² 4): 414–15; IV.33 (*NPNF*² 4): 446; and Mackintosh, *Doctrine of the Person of Christ*, 70. See also Torrance, *School of Faith*, ciii; *Order and Disorder*, 49; and Habets, *Theosis*, 25–28, 142, 148.

67. Torrance, *Christian Doctrine of God*, 210.

68. Torrance, "The Atoning Obedience of Christ," 66; quoted in Habets, *Theosis*, 24.

of *predestination*.⁶⁹ That such intended communion was disrupted in the Fall does not entail the defeat of God's eternal purposes; rather, through the Father's sending of the Son and the Holy Spirit to reconcile humanity back to God, the eternal openness of the love of God is displayed as eternally the same, pre- and post-Fall. The origin of creation is also the *telos* of redemption.

Prothesis, Mysterion, and Koinonia

The doctrine of appropriation and the *kath hypostasin* distinction of works in the economy of salvation are revealed most explicitly in Torrance's threefold categorisation of the triune work as *prothesis, mysterion,* and *koinonia.* Under the banner of "union with Christ," both Lee and Habets affirm this triadic trinitarian action as follows: "The cause of 'union with Christ' is *prothesis*, the election of God [the Father]. Its substance is *mysterion,* the hypostatic union in Jesus Christ, and its fulfilment is *koinonia*, the communion of the Holy Spirit."⁷⁰ This triadic trinitarian work reinforces Torrance's emphasis on the unbroken relation of being and act among the persons of the Trinity. Moreover, in speaking of the triune work in terms of *prothesis, mysterion,* and *koinonia,* the weight falls on continuity and oneness in the economy of salvation. The emphasis here naturally falls on the work of the Father, understood by Torrance as *prothesis,* or election.

To understand better how the three terms are interrelated, it is best to proceed from where Torrance starts: in Jesus Christ. Torrance's theological consistency concerning the epistemological and evangelical priority of Christ even in this triadic movement is displayed in *Incarnation,* and is also purposeful in that it seeks to avoid grounding the doctrine of election behind the back of Jesus Christ or in some divine abstract eternal decree. The eternal will of the Father, therefore, can only be properly understood in the light of the mystery of Christ. Torrance calls it *mysterion,* or mystery, because it refers primarily to the hypostatic union, the union of God and humanity in the one person of Christ.⁷¹ His emphasis on the salvific and

---

69. Torrance, *Christian Doctrine of God,* 210.

70. Lee, *Living in Union,* 201; Habets, *Theosis,* 105. Another triadic distinction almost similar to this is from Basil, and summarized by Habets, whereby the Spirit is "the perfecting cause," the Father as "the originating cause," and the Son as "the moulding cause," in Habets, *Theosis,* 146; and Basil, *Sp. Sanc.* 16.38 (*NPNF*² 8): 23.

71. Torrance, *Incarnation,* 164–65. Habets failed to represent Torrance's theological attitude when he began with *prothesis,* election of the Father, rather than with *mysterion,* hypostatic union in Christ. Habets, *Theosis,* 105–7. See Torrance's own

The Love of God the Father

vicarious humanity of Jesus Christ reverberates: the hypostatic union is a reconciling union in "the form of a dynamic atoning union . . . worked out within the structures of our human existence" throughout his life, death, resurrection, and ascension.[72] This is related to the Father's eternal will for communion.

> Mystery is the secret that lies behind God's creation. In the heart of that creation, God created man, made in the union of male and female as one flesh, to reflect the image of God within their relation of union with God. But that union between man and God was sundered, and the union within mankind making mankind one flesh was sundered: the secret was lost to man, the mystery remained wholly recondite. But the eternal purpose of God remained, and so at last in Jesus Christ after long and patient preparation in God's purpose with Israel, the mystery of God's will became incarnate. It embodied itself in the midst of our humanity, begetting in Jesus Christ the one in whom all mankind is gathered back into communion with God.[73]

Thus, the *mysterion* enacted in the incarnation of Christ, and vividly displayed in the cross, reveals the eternal heart and will (or *prothesis*) of the Father.[74] *Prothesis* has a twofold inseparable meaning: (1) the purpose of God, or election of the Father; and (2) the "setting forth" of God for the redemption of humanity in Jesus Christ.[75] Torrance points to Ephesians 1:11 and Romans 8:28–30 to explain that the eternal election of the Father includes both predestination and future glory (Christologically understood), emphasizing "the purpose of God in Christ reaching out from and into the eternal and infinite mystery of God."[76] In grounding salvation in the election of the Father in Jesus Christ, Torrance follows the Reformation doctrine of *sola gratia*, which epitomizes "a strictly theonomous thinking, from a centre in God and not in ourselves."[77] This is because the doctrine of election essentially refers to "the eternal decision which is nothing less than the Love that God himself is, in action; it is

---

approach in *Ministry and Sacraments of the Gospel*, 82–92; and *Incarnation*, 164–74.

72. Torrance, *Mediation of Christ*, 65.

73. Torrance, *Incarnation*, 165; *Mediation of Christ*, 30. For Torrance's view of Israel as an instrument of revelation, not only in preparing the way for the incarnate Son but until today, see "Salvation is of the Jews," 164–73.

74. Torrance, "Singularity of Christ," 234.

75. Torrance, *Incarnation*, 169, 177–80.

76. Ibid., 169.

77. Habets, *Theosis*, 105; Torrance, *Christian Theology*, 127, 132–33.

the unconditional self-giving of God in the undeflecting constancy of his Grace."[78]

Election and Predestination

It is, therefore, only on the grounds of the eternal love of the Father and the incarnation of the Son that election and predestination should be understood. Torrance is critical of federal Calvinism for importing philosophical, logico-mechanistic apparatuses to explain the doctrine of election theologically, which is precisely the opposite of the meaning of election, for essentially, the doctrine of election "rejects any projection of human ways of thought, speech or behaviour, or any creaturely representation, into God."[79] Election is primarily grounded in God's free sovereign decision in creation and redemption, and is thus "to be equated with the sheer mystery of God's Love which knows no reason beyond its own ultimateness as the Love that God eternally is."[80] As such, it is not an abstract decree; rather, "Christ in His own Person is the eternal decree of God."[81] Torrance rejects the deterministic understanding of election espoused by Scholastic Calvinists such as Samuel Rutherford (1600–1661), who, since he followed Theodore Beza and the Synod of Dort instead of Calvin and Knox, was caught up with a strictly causative understanding of the relation between God's eternal decrees and the efficacy of Christ's atoning work, forcing him to admit limited atonement.[82] This could have been avoided, Torrance says, if election had been understood primarily in Christ, as in the incarnational and corporate view of election held by John Forbes of Corse (1593–1648): "the *compredestination* of Christ and the elect in Christ."[83]

78. Torrance, *Christian Theology*, 127.
79. Ibid.
80. Ibid.
81. Torrance, "Predestination in Christ," 110. Torrance also refers to Jesus Christ as "the permanent purpose of God," in B44 "Palm Sunday," 3.
82. Torrance, *Scottish Theology*, 105. "The concept of limited atonement," Torrance writes, "limits the very being of God as Love," in "Atonement," 236. See Torrance's discussion and rejection of determinism in "Predestination in Christ," 110, 113–16. An interesting unfinished essay by Torrance seems to want to relate Aristotelian rigid logic and the further development of federal Calvinism in Scotland in B40 "Aristotelianism and Calvinism in Scotland."
83. Torrance, *Scottish Theology*, 88; quoting Forbes, *Instructiones*, VIII.30.1–4. Torrance considered this Christo-centric understanding of election not only in his academic writings, because he also preached about it. See B46 "Predestination in Christ."

The Love of God the Father

> Compredestination means not only that God has elected and adopted us in Christ before the foundation of the world, but that he has elected Christ himself in whom he is well pleased, and elected us in Christ, predestinating us in love as those who are redeemed through the precious Blood of Christ as of a Lamb without blemish and spot. He has elected us not on the ground of any holiness or belief on our part, but in order that we may believe. Christ himself is the primary object of election and as such the ground of our election.[84]

That election should be understood in Christ, however, should not overshadow the primacy of the Father's love in the whole process of redemption. Robert Boyd (1578–1627), another Scottish theologian, stressed that the *omnium primo* in election is the act of the Father in willing and delivering up his own Son.[85] This is the eternal priority of the Father's free and gracious decision not only to create but to elect humanity into communion with the Triune God. Torrance quotes Campbell: "the love of God as the cause, and the atonement as the effect. 'God so loved the world, that he gave his only begotten Son.'"[86] Torrance's understanding of the personal, ontological, and relational work of the whole Triune God for humanity's salvation also influenced his view of election.

> The "pre" of predestination cannot be regarded as the *prius* to anything here in space and time; it is not the result of an inference from effect to first cause, or from relative to absolute, or to any world-principle. The "pre" in predestination takes election not out of time but grounds it in an act of the Eternal which we can only describe as "per se" or "a se." In other words, it is grounded in the life of the Godhead, that is, in the personal relations of the Trinity. Just because we know God to be Father, Son and Holy Spirit, we know the Will of God to be supremely Personal—and it is to that Will that predestination tells us our salvation is to be referred.[87]

---

84. Torrance, *Scottish Theology*, 88.
85. Ibid., 69–70.
86. Ibid., 298.
87. Torrance, "Predestination in Christ," 116.

The Sending Father

That the Son became incarnate in accordance with the eternal will of the Father, and that the Holy Spirit is operative in the world for our salvation, logically entails the essentially and eternally dynamic being of God. Torrance elaborates: "Movement belongs to his eternal Being. If God is who he is in his activity toward us through the Son and in the Spirit, then it belongs to the essential Nature of his eternal Being to move and energise and act."[88] This emphasis is indisputably applicable to both the ontological and evangelical Trinity, God *ad intra* and *ad extra*, and can be discerned specifically in the double movement of God's saving love "from the Father, through the Son, and in the Holy Spirit, and to the Father, through the Son, and in the Holy Spirit."[89] James Torrance refers to this *katabatic*, God-humanward, and *anabatic*, human-Godward activity as "a double movement of grace," which is equivalent to Torrance's view of God's "redeeming movement in Love," and the definition of atonement as "the movement of divine reconciling and justifying love."[90] And because the Triune God is a being-in-movement, this immediately implies that God is in essence a God who is self-sending.

Procession of the Son and the Holy Spirit

In the light of the fact that the persons of the Triune God work in strict accordance with their personal nature as Father, Son, and Holy Spirit, it is plausible to say that the sending agency belongs primarily to the Father. It is true that the Son—with the Father—is involved in the sending of the Holy Spirit, and the Spirit—with the Father—is involved in the "sending of the Son," and so both the Son and the Holy Spirit send one another. But the Father is in no way called "sent" by the Son and the Holy Spirit; instead, the Father is depicted to be sending both the Son and the Holy Spirit. This is displayed, for instance, in Irenaeus's understanding of the

---

88. Torrance, *Christian Doctrine of God*, 149. God's being is "being-in-movement" and "being-in-action." Torrance, *Theological Dialogue* 1: 22, 33–40, 49; *Trinitarian Faith*, 130–31; *Ecumenical Studies*, 33; and on the dynamic character of God and his self-revelation, see Torrance, *Karl Barth*, 95–99; and also Bradshaw, "Barth on the Trinity," 160.

89. Torrance, *Theology in Reconciliation*, 118, 251. In *Trinitarian Faith*, 5, Torrance identifies this as the "general formula which the Nicene and post-Nicene fathers employed to speak of the Triune God and his one activity."

90. Torrance, *Worship, Community, and the Triune God of Grace*, 32; Torrance, *Christian Doctrine of God*, 8; *Scottish Theology*, 304; and "Israel and the Incarnation," 3.

The Love of God the Father

two hands of the Father, referring to the Son and the Holy Spirit.[91] The procession of both the Son and the Holy Spirit, therefore, should not only be understood as coming from the divine nature, but also from the will and love of the electing Father.[92] Torrance argues, however, that this should be understood only in the light of the economic relations, and not imposed on the Trinity *in se,* so as to avoid any notion of subordination or hierarchy within the Godhead. Referring to the procession of the Son, he writes: "We believe in Jesus Christ as our Lord and Saviour with the very same faith with which we believe in God the Father Almighty, and we believe that what he is toward us, with us and for us *in his incarnate mission from the Father* he is antecedently and eternally in himself, the eternal Son of the eternal Father."[93] That the mission of the Son is willed by the sending Father does not entail priority or superiority of the person of the Father, or accepting the absolute *Monarchia* of the Father alone.

The same applies to the procession of the Holy Spirit, or the controversial *filioque*.[94] Here too, the Father (together with the Son), again assumes the sending role: "The Spirit is ever *in the hands of the Father who sends* and of the Son who gives him as his very own, and from whom the Spirit on his part receives."[95] However, Torrance maintains that this Athanasian statement should be interpreted "in such a way that the enhypostatic realities and distinctive properties of the Father, Son and Holy Spirit always remain the same in the equality and consubstantiality of the Holy Trinity."[96] Thus the creedal affirmation of Constantinople in AD 381 proves to be an insightful safeguard against subordinationism: "We believe

---

91. In *Theology in Reconciliation,* 101, Torrance also refers to this as "the twofold way in which the one incomprehensible God communicates himself to us," elaborated further in *Trinitarian Faith,* 20: "There is from the Father one grace which is fulfilled through the Son in the Holy Spirit. . . . The Father does all things through the Word and in the Holy Spirit."

92. The procedure here is not to follow Athanasius's differentiation between nature and will, and the exaltation of the former above the latter, but to regard the two as inseparably acting together. This, I believe, is more consistent with Torrance's borrowed understanding from Reformation theology and from Barth concerning the oneness between God's being and act. See also Hanson, *Search for Christian Doctrine,* 711–12, 731.

93. Torrance, *Christian Doctrine of God,* 142 (italics mine).

94. This will be dealt with more extensively in Chapter 4.

95. Torrance, *Trinitarian Faith,* 331, 244 (italics mine).

96. Ibid., 245.

Shaliach of God

That God the Father sends is particularly evident in John 3:16–17, where John refers to the incarnate Son as the *apostolos* of God. The same Johannine emphasis is found in 10:36, where Jesus calls himself the one whom the Father sent into the world (*apesteilen eis ton kosmon*). In the light of these Scripture passages, Torrance argues that the whole mission of Christ can be called "the apostolic mission of Christ from the Father."[98] Using Hebrews 3:1–6, Torrance then equates the apostleship of Christ with the Hebrew concept of the *shaliach* of God. Based on the Hebrew tradition and reflected in both the Old and New Testaments, Torrance concludes that at the basic level, "*Shaliach* referred to the man who speaks for God and acts for God in *semeia*."[99] For instance, in the Old Testament, prophets and leaders like Moses, Elijah, Elisha, and Ezekiel were referred to as *sheluchim*; in the New Testament, the apostles who bore witness to the life and resurrection of Jesus were also called *apostle-shaliachs*.[100] Torrance says, however, that there is a difference when the term *shaliach* is applied to God and to human representatives. For instance, "The whole New Testament doctrine of *shaliach* is one in which the person of the *shaliach* retreats into the background, so that the living person of the risen Christ comes to the fore."[101] When applied to God and the triune persons, however, there is an inseparability of being and act between the Father who sends and the Son and the Holy Spirit who are sent into the world as agents of reconciliation. This is the theological import of the *homoousion to Patri*. Ultimately, it is the incarnate Son and the Holy Spirit who are the *sheluchim* of the Father. Torrance relates this to the apostleship and priesthood of Christ, and his twofold function in the mediation of revelation,

---

97. Ibid., 245. This should be balanced, according to Gunton, with the understanding that the Son is begotten by the Father and the Holy Spirit, in *Father, Son, and Holy Spirit*, 72–73.

98. Torrance, *Order and Disorder*, 24.

99. Ibid., 39; *Incarnation*, 23; *Royal Priesthood*, 11. See also Purves, "The Christology of Thomas F. Torrance," in *The Promise of Trinitarian Theology*, 64; Wanamaker, "Christ as Divine Agent in Paul," 517–28; and Barrett, "Shaliah and Apostle," 89–102.

100. Torrance, *Atonement*, 317–19.

101. Torrance, *Order and Disorder*, 38.

The Love of God the Father

reconciliation, and worship. In *Atonement*, Torrance refers to Christ as the "unique *shaliach* of God in word and deed," to which he adds:

> It is supremely in that sense that Christ is *shaliach*: he is the word of God and the deed of God, who not only brings from God his word of pardon, but effectively enacts it. In Jesus Christ the word and deed of God are identical, identical in his person. He *is* the word of God which he represents, so that his word is not just word about God, but actually *is* God's word, God in his word. His actions not only point to God, but he *is* himself God in action, so that his acts are God's own acts. *Christ was sent from the Father* not only to forgive sin, but to heal, not only to speak of God's pardon but to enact that pardon in our flesh and blood.[102]

Concerning the Holy Spirit as *shaliach*, Torrance also grounds his arguments primarily in the Gospel of John. In 14:26, Jesus says that the Spirit is sent by the Father, but in 16:7, Jesus says that he himself sends the Spirit. When Jesus says that the Spirit is sent both by the Father and the Son (John 15:26), the Spirit's role as witness is also highlighted. From these verses Torrance concludes that inasmuch as Jesus Christ is the *shaliach* of the Father, the Holy Spirit is the *shaliach* of the Son, in that "He [the Spirit] does not draw attention to Himself or speak of His own Person, but speaks only of Christ."[103] Nevertheless, both the Son and the Holy Spirit, as the two hands of the Father, are the *sheluchim* of the Father in the economy of salvation.

It is unfortunate that Torrance offers no explanatory statements on Irenaeus's view of the "two hands of the Father," which would have helped him elaborate the sending agency of the Father. Perhaps his concern and polemic against subordinationism imported to the intra-divine Trinity prevented him from emphasizing this Irenaean phraseology. In fact, it is this neglect that led Gunton to think that Torrance holds "a homogeneous view of the persons of the economy," or that the three persons of the Triune God share *equal* divinity even in the economy.[104] Gunton perceives Torrance's position as a double-edged sword: it is profitable in the light of the Arian controversy, but it also offers a complication in the light of the issue of economic subordination. Although Torrance himself affirms

---

102. Torrance, *Atonement*, 318 (italics of last six words mine).
103. Torrance, *Order and Disorder*, 40.
104. Gunton, "Being and Person," 121.

economic subordination,[105] his polemic against ontological subordinationism prevented him from elaborating important aspects that may be interpreted to mean or imply the latter (in this case, "the two hands of the Father"). On the one hand, Torrance's silence illustrates his determination for theological consistency; but on the other hand, it may portray his purposive evasion of selected topics that could open a critique to his position.

The Receiving Father

For Torrance, there is a reciprocity in the saving movement made by the Father from beginning to end in the one economy of salvation in accordance with his person and nature as Father. As was shown above, he ascribes to the Father the electing and sending offices—"*from the Father* through the Son in the Spirit"—with special emphasis on the eternal will and love of the Father, which is then reciprocated by a Godward movement: "in the Spirit through the Son *to the Father*." From this double movement of grace, one can immediately recognise that for Torrance, in the economy of salvation, the Father is both the electing-sending and receiving person: *from* the Father and *to* the Father.

Torrance's understanding of "*to* the Father" as a salvific event is best discerned in the language of adoption. According to Torrance, there are three senses that God is Father: (1) God is the Father of Jesus Christ, (2) the Father is the Father of all by virtue of creation, and (3) "He is the Father of those who are born again, of those who were lost, but are found, of those who are dead but are now alive."[106] It is the third sense in which we are interested, because it is here that Fatherhood is understood "in terms of redeeming grace toward us and free adoption of us as his children."[107] The church, as the community of the reconciled, is "the universal family of God the Father sharing brotherhood with Jesus Christ and therefore sharing with him sonship to the Father."[108] In one of his sermons, Torrance refers to our adoption as children of the Father as the morning that comes after the night. Humanity's history is dark and is doomed to destruction, but "When men shall really be sons of God, children of God, and that means when men shall no longer be beasts . . . when man really becomes a child of God, a son of God in the image of God, then the eternal morning

---

105. Torrance, "Thomas Torrance Responds," 316.
106. B23 "Christ's View of God," 3.
107. Torrance, *Scottish Theology*, 7.
108. Torrance, *Atonement*, 360.

The Love of God the Father

has come."[109] This is grounded in and accomplished by Jesus Christ *pro nobis*. Thus, Torrance argues, "new birth refers ultimately to [Jesus's] own birth," in which humanity shares, and "it is in Christ and through Christ only that we are born again."[110] Interpreting John 3:16 and quoting John 1:12 in this light, he argues that "to all who did receive him, to those who believed in his name, [Jesus] gave the right to become children of God." Again, humanity's filial relation with the Father is mediated through Christ, in consistency with his whole soteriological framework that access to the Father happens only through Jesus Christ in the Spirit.[111]

There are two kinds of sonship: one by nature and one by grace, and we must distinguish one from the other. The former refers to the relation of the Son to the Father; the latter to humanity's adoption into the family of God: "Our being children *of* God falls outside the Being of God, for we are created beings, utterly distinct from the Being of God. But Jesus Christ is Son *of* God in a unique sense, for he is Son of God within God, so that what he is and does as Son of the Father falls within the eternal Being of the Godhead."[112] This distinction is important, because it maintains the creaturehood of humanity and safeguards the intrusion of the dangerous traditional Western misinterpretation of *theosis* into soteriology. "The Son became man without ceasing to be divine in order to make creatures participate in the divine communion without ceasing to be creatures."[113] Nevertheless, Torrance asserts, because of the incarnation, we are called sons of God by sharing in the Sonship of Christ. Thus, as our *Frater*, "the Son of the Father has made himself our Brother, for through his incarna-

---

109. B38 Untitled sermon on Isaiah 21:11–12, 8. See also B47 "Behold what manner of love"; and B47 "Everyone that loveth is born of God." The new birth also includes the death of death, in B47 "Your life is hid with Christ in God," 2.

110. Torrance, *When Christ Comes*, 72. Even little children, when baptized, "are no longer strangers but members of the household of God," in Torrance, "The Bible's Guidance on Baptism," 17.

111. Torrance, in *Theology in Reconciliation*, 181–82, writes: "While it is through Christ that we have access to God the Father, that takes place *in one Spirit*. All things are wrought by the Father through the Son and in the Spirit, and proceed from the Father through the Son in the Spirit. Correspondingly, all service from man towards God is rightly mediated through the Son and in the unity of the Spirit." See also B46 "The Spirit itself beareth witness," 1–9.

112. Torrance, *Mediation of Christ*, 54; *Doctrine of Grace*, 74; *Ecumenical Studies*, 32–33. George D. Dragas describes "sonship by grace" further using three terms: grace (χάρις), position (θέσις), and virtue (ἀρετή): meaning, respectively: sonship from the side of God, sonship from both the side of God and humanity, and sonship from the side of humanity. These three are all fulfilled in Christ's vicarious humanity.

113. Habets, *Theosis*, 36.

Communion with the Triune God

tional union with us, he has established our union with him. By making himself our Brother, he has made us brothers of his and therefore sons of the Father."[114] This is what Torrance calls Jesus's "incarnational fraternity" with us.[115]

> According to one central strand of biblical soteriology, the Christian life is fundamentally a sharing in the Son's relationship with the Father in the power of the Spirit through the economic earthing of that same relationship in the particular flesh of Jesus of Nazareth. We do not share in the person of the Son, but precisely in the relationship which he has with the Father and the Spirit in the triune life of *koinonia*. This is the trinitarian shape of the kerygma and of the Christian experience of God.[116]

The quotation above from Trevor Hart expresses two important reminders: (1) that our adoption is a sharing by grace in the Sonship of Christ and (2) that our sharing in Christ ultimately means sharing in the triune *koinonia*. Inasmuch as humanity's adoption into the family of God is effected by "the third dimension,"[117] referring to the union of God and humanity in the one person of Jesus Christ, Torrance also maintains a trinitarian view of adoption. We become sons and daughters of the Father through Christ in the Spirit. "The work of spiritual rebirth is performed in unison by the Father, Son and Holy Spirit."[118] James Torrance expresses trinitarian adoption more beautifully:

> Firstly, I have been a child of God from all eternity in the heart of the Father. Secondly, I became a child of God when Christ the Son lived, died and rose again for me long ago. Thirdly, I became

---

114. Torrance, *Theology in Reconstruction*, 153. Briefly sketching the economy of salvation, he expounds: "We have all sold our birthright, but we have a Brother in whom we may win it back, the elder Brother of us prodigals. . . . Whatever we are, whatever has been our past, however imbruted in evil, however entangled in material gains, we have but to turn ourselves to that gracious Lord our Brother, in whom the Father blesses us with all heavenly blessings, and we shall share in the birthright of His firstborn Son, 'being heirs of God and joint-heirs with Christ.'" B47 "Esau's Birthright," 8. See also, Moltmann, *History and the Triune God*, 31–41.

115. Torrance, *Theology in Reconstruction*, 153. Humphrey follows Torrance's Christocentric assertions: "Because of the person and work of Christ Jesus, we become children, or more properly, 'sons' of the Father," in "The Gift of the Father," 92. Gerald L. Bray proposes the view that sonship to God is unique to Christianity, in "Out of the Box," 46–54.

116. Hart, *Regarding Karl Barth*, 108.

117. Torrance, *Karl Barth*, 22.

118. Torrance, *Theological Dialogue* 1: 140.

a child of God when the Holy Spirit—the Spirit of adoption—sealed in my faith and experience what had been planned from all eternity in the heart of the Father and what was completed once and for all in Jesus Christ.[119]

That adoption should also be construed from a trinitarian perspective is completely consistent with Torrance's conception of the nature of human salvation as sharing in the life and love of the Triune God. Filial relation, reconciliation, and union with God are inseparable: "Through his Sonship, that is, through his obedient Life in filial relation toward the Father, and through his brotherhood with us in our estrangement, Christ is the active Agent who reveals God to us and reconciles us to God . . . [bringing] us back to union with God."[120] In other words, adoption into the Father's household is a conceptual equivalent of participation in the life and love of the Triune God. This is what Torrance calls "our adoption into the communion of the divine life," the fulfilment of God's eternal plan to invite creation to himself as sons and daughters.[121] In the light of this, and recalling that union with Christ also implies communion with the Triune God, a trinitarian pattern is already apparent in Torrance's soteriology: the salvific agency of the persons and the relationship with each of them imply more than a relationship with individual hypostases, because each relationship means a lifting up into the triune communion to which each of the hypostases belong. This will be made evident again in the salvific agency of the Holy Spirit, and will be explained in chapter 5 as humanity's *mediated* participation in the triune life.

Conclusions

As demonstrated, the distinct nature and work of the Father in the salvific economy could be best described in terms of his love as Almighty Creator, his electing and sending agency, and his receiving role, whereby

---

119. Torrance, *Worship, Community, and the Triune God of Grace*, 76.
120. Torrance, *Theology in Reconstruction*, 153.
121. Torrance, *Theological Dialogue* 1: 34, 139; *Mediation of Christ*, 66; *Atonement*, 167; Habets, *Theosis*, 101. Torrance's tone finds striking similarity with Moltmann's in *History and the Triune God*, 38: "In communion with the only-begotten Son of God, human beings become children of God, born again from the eternal Spirit of God, and in this way taken up into the eternal life of the Triune God." Torrance himself writes: "In God there is a Holy Fellowship of Love—and you cannot know God without being caught up into that fellowship, without becoming a son of God in Christ through the Holy Spirit," in B46 "The Trinity," 9.

the Father accepts through Jesus Christ in the Holy Spirit humanity as children of God. Of course, all of these should be tied to four of Torrance's important emphases. First, the person and work of the Father are one and inseparable. It is precisely because God is the Father who loves the Son and the Holy Spirit that he is able to love and invite the creaturely other into communion with himself. Torrance quotes John Knox: "We call him Father not so much because he has created us, but by reason of his free adoption by which he has chosen us in Jesus Christ."[122] Secondly, the eternal will of the Father and the sending of the Son and the Spirit are one: his will and act are one. In relation to the latter, thirdly, the electing, sending, and receiving roles of the Father are inseparable. In other words, the origin and goal of trinitarian salvation are one. "Bringing humanity back from estrangement to communion with the Father," Torrance argues, is the mission of Christ.[123] Fourthly, trinitarian salvation involves a "glorious exchange,"[124] willed by the Father through the Son in the Holy Spirit, enabling humanity to participate in the love of the Father, the Sonship of the Son, and the fellowship of the Holy Spirit.

---

122. Quoted in Torrance, *Scottish Theology*, 7.

123. Torrance, *Incarnation*, 114.

124. Hart, "Humankind in Christ," 82, 84.

4

The Communion of the Holy Spirit

Heavenly Father, who has preserved and extended thy Church in our land by the continual outpouring of the Holy Spirit, accept us now as we offer ourselves to thee through Jesus Christ our Saviour, for renewed service in his Name. May he, in whom all fullness dwells, have the pre-eminence in all we think and say and do; may we be more deeply grounded in the truth which he taught us that we may be united with one another and all who call upon His Name, that the Gospel of divine peace and reconciliation may take root in the lives of our people. Hasten the day when in thy mercy the kingdoms of this world shall become the Kingdom of thy dear Son, our Lord Jesus Christ.[1]

THERE IS A NOTICEABLE ASYMMETRY IN TORRANCE'S TREATMENT OF THE Father, Son, and Holy Spirit in his writings, demonstrated clearly by a non-existent separate and lengthy treatment of the Holy Spirit amidst the large corpus of his works (at least in comparison to his numerous treatises on Jesus Christ). As Gary Deddo argues, however, Torrance's reflections on the Spirit and the Spirit's relation to both the Trinity *ad intra* and *ad extra* are scattered throughout his writings.[2] As such, far from lacking a mature theology of the Holy Spirit, Torrance actually has a well-developed pneumatology that is integrated and integral to his whole theological cogitation. C. Baxter Kruger justifiably adds pneumatic thinking (and eschatological thinking) on Robert Palma's list of six cardinal facets of Torrance's theology (trinitarian, Christocentric, unitary, rational, and natural theology).[3]

1. B38 "That in everything he might be preeminent," 5.

2. Deddo, "The Holy Spirit," in *The Promise of Trinitarian Theology*, 103–4.

3. Kruger, "Doctrine of the Knowledge of God," 366–89; Palma, "Thomas F. Torrance's Reformed Theology," 13–23. Kang argues that Torrance's theology is also evangelical, humanist, catholic, Reformed, ecumenical, and doxological in "Concept

Overall, Torrance's pneumatological approach is both christocentric and trinitarian, and is thus consistent with his entire theological program. "There is no separate activity of the Holy Spirit in revelation or salvation in addition to or independent of the activity of Christ, for what he does is to empower and actualize the words and works of Christ in our midst as the words and works of the Father."[4] Torrance's pneumatology thus "comes to fruition in an onto-relational and Trinitarian formulation."[5] This is why a presentation of the person and work of the Holy Spirit in Torrance's trinitarian soteriology may advance only after treatment of the persons and works of the incarnate Son and the Father.

The Communion of *the Holy Spirit*

Torrance admits that the doctrine of the Holy Spirit is the weakest of all the doctrines of the church, owing to the difficulty of the subject. He hints that weak pneumatology in Christian theology goes back to as early as the first century. He cites the Apostles's Creed as an illustration, because it offered a laconic treatment of the Holy Spirit, then moved quickly on to the church.[6] Hing Kau Yeung critiques Torrance for ironically falling into the same pit, arguing that his distinct treatments of the Holy Spirit are overly brief. While this is true to a certain extent, Yeung's consequent judgment that Torrance's doctrine of the Holy Spirit is "more or less only significant to the knowledge of God" is unacceptably harsh.[7] Rather, Deddo's analysis, presented above, does more justice to Torrance's theological scheme. Also, in Torrance's defence, presentation of the nature and person of the Holy Spirit requires a deliberate degree of apophatism in accordance with the nature of the Spirit as Spirit.

Torrance recognizes that as in Christology and the doctrine of the Trinity, the deity of the Holy Spirit was initially only implicit in the worship of the early church.[8] But after clear knowledge of the Father and the

---

of Vicarious Humanity," 449–66.

4. Torrance, *Christian Doctrine of God*, 196.

5. Deddo, "The Holy Spirit," 82.

6. Torrance, *School of Faith*, xcv. Interestingly, Kevin Hector argues that the neglect of the Holy Spirit in Western theology should find a solution by going back to Schleiermacher, in "The Mediation of Christ's Normative Spirit," 1–22.

7. Yeung, "Being and Knowing," 223.

8. Following Mackintosh, Torrance can say, therefore, that the origin of the idea of the Holy Spirit in its trinitarian meaning is not in philosophical thought, but in history and life. See Mackintosh, *Doctrine of the Person of Christ*, 519.

The Communion of the Holy Spirit

Son had been achieved by the church, the necessity for explicit statements on the Holy Spirit also became increasingly imperative. The task was undertaken by prominent theologians such as Athanasius, Basil, and Gregory of Nazianzus. Following Athanasius, Torrance's understanding of the Holy Spirit consistently proceeds from the doctrine of the Son, particularly in the *homoousios* as applied both to the incarnate Son and the Holy Spirit. The difference of application of the *homoousios* to the Son and the Holy Spirit, is only that "it is only [Christ] who is both *homoousios* with the Father and *homoousios* with us," while the Spirit is only *homoousios* with the Father, but not with humanity.[9] Clearly, Torrance's approach to the doctrine of the Holy Spirit is integrated in his understanding of the triadic relation between the Triune God and the world, which highlights his consistent contention that knowledge of the Holy Spirit is in line with the knowledge of the Son.

God Is Spirit

A discussion of the person of the Holy Spirit faces serious ambiguities in relation to God's being. This is owing to the fact that while the doctrine of the Trinity delineates the *hypostasis* of the Holy Spirit from the *ousia* of God, it is clear in various passages of Scripture that God's being and nature is in itself Spirit (John 4:24). Torrance identifies this distinction between thinking of the Spirit *absolutely* and thinking of him *relatively*.[10] Concerning the former, Torrance succinctly admits: "*Spirit* is the specific nature of God's eternal being (*ousia*), whether as Father, Son or Holy Spirit."[11] Three important ontological-epistemological implications follow. First, calling God *Spirit* has a dialectical or comparative merit, because it underlines the fact that God's nature is infinite, transcendent, invisible, immaterial, and immutable, in contrast to the contingent, transient, and limited nature of creaturely beings.[12] Secondly, that God is Spirit is important in a realist and imageless epistemology: "God is Spirit, and therefore he is to be known and thought of by us in a reverent and spiritual way without the crude use of creaturely or material images."[13] Thirdly, and in relation

---

9. Torrance, *Trinitarian Faith*, 201–4, esp. 203; *God and Rationality*, 167; *Theology in Reconciliation*, 233.

10. Torrance, *Christian Doctrine of God*, 147; *Trinitarian Faith*, 205.

11. Torrance, *Trinitarian Faith*, 194.

12. Ibid., 205.

13. Ibid., 207, 194.

to the latter, the spiritual nature of God should re-shape our thinking of God even when we use human language. Thus, Torrance writes: "terms like ουσία, ὑπόστασις, or φύσις when applied to God must be understood in a wholly spiritual, personal yet genderless way."[14]

Thinking of the Spirit in the absolute sense, however, does not rule out the distinction between the persons of the Father, Son, and Holy Spirit. The Western tradition, following Augustine, turned the ambiguous use of the term "Spirit" into a positive advantage by conceiving of the Spirit as the bond of love between the Father and the Son. Torrance takes this position when he speaks of the Holy Spirit as "a kind of consubstantial Communion (*communio quaedam consubstantialis*) between the Father and the Son," and by speaking of the Holy Spirit as "*the Bond of Nature* in the Holy Trinity."[15] Torrance elaborates: "The fact that the Holy Spirit is both the hypostasis of the whole Being of God, and, considered absolutely in himself as God, is identical with that Being, for God *is* Spirit, means that he *is* the consubstantial bond of the Holy Trinity."[16]

God the Holy Spirit

Torrance, consistent with his realist and historical approach, owes his pneumatology to patristic and creedal theology. His engagement and critique of liberal theology's subjective understanding of the Holy Spirit and the human spirit, along with the failure to distinguish one from the other, probably marks his only active engagement with recent pneumatological issues. Although Torrance shows optimism concerning the renewal of interest in pneumatology as part of the renewed interest in the Trinity and in ecumenism,[17] his silence concerning Pentecostal theology evidences his lack of involvement—at least at a formal level—with fresh understandings of the Holy Spirit's person and work developed by other contemporary traditions. Deddo mentions in passing that Torrance "makes suggestive comments . . . on Pentecostal/Charismatic movement," but he nevertheless admits that such statements by Torrance are largely undeveloped.[18]

---

14. Torrance, *Trinitarian Perspectives*, 124.

15. Torrance, *Christian Doctrine of God*, 167; quoting Augustine, *Trin.* 15.27.50 (*NPNF*[1] 3): 227; and then referencing Basil, *Sp. Sanc.* 45 (*NPNF*[2] 8): 28 (italics mine).

16. Torrance, *Trinitarian Perspectives*, 67–68; Deddo, "The Holy Spirit," 86.

17. Torrance, *Theology in Reconciliation*, 289–93.

18. Deddo, "The Holy Spirit," 107. This is another aspect in Torrance studies that needs special attention. Deddo lists Torrance's *Space, Time, and Resurrection*, 119, 121–22, 137, 149, as places where one can see Torrance's engagement with Pentecostalism

The early fathers regarded the concept of *homoousios* as inspired by the Holy Spirit in determining and expressing the consubstantial relation of Jesus Christ to the Father, and of the Holy Spirit to the Father and the Son. Torrance asserts that it was Athanasius who "had little hesitation in applying the term *homoousios* to the Spirit as well as to the Son."[19] In this way, the person of the Holy Spirit is established on the same ontological and soteriological grounds as the person of the Son. Yet again, Torrance's concern in the application of the *homoousios* to the Holy Spirit, like Athanasius's, is soteriological, and not exclusively ontological *per se*. Torrance's pneumatology, like his Christology and Pateriology, therefore, is soterio-conditioned. Moreover, Torrance's affirmation of this is deliberate, and is entirely consistent with his realist theology.

> The doctrine of the Holy Spirit is derived, therefore, not merely from biblical statements, nor from doxological formulae alone, but from the supreme truth that God reveals himself through himself, and therefore that *God himself* is the content of his revelation through the Son and in the Spirit. That is to say, far from being an extraneous intrusion, the doctrine of the Spirit was developed naturally and properly out of the inner structure of knowledge of the one God grounded in his *self*-revelation and *self*-communication as Father, Son and Holy Spirit.[20]

By employing *homoousios*, Torrance's argument that knowledge of the Spirit, like knowledge of the Father, is controlled and grounded by knowledge of the Son is further solidified. His hierarchical epistemology is also strengthened, for the movement from knowledge of the Son to knowledge of the Spirit "tells us how our thought moves from the first to the second theological levels . . . in determining how we are to think of the dynamic and spiritual nature of the ontological relation that obtains between the economic Trinity and the ontological Trinity."[21] Colyer justly concludes that Torrance follows "a biblical, evangelical/doxological and trinitarian approach" to his pneumatology.[22]

---

and the Charismatic movement.

19. Torrance, *Trinitarian Faith*, 202; *Divine Meaning*, 195; *Ecumenical Studies*, xx; *Theology in Reconstruction*, 213–15.

20. Torrance, *Trinitarian Faith*, 202.

21. Torrance, *Christian Doctrine of God*, 97.

22. Colyer, *How to Read*, 212–16. Torrance critiques and rejects both Romanism and Protestantism which have often confounded the identity of the Spirit with either the spirit of the church or the human spirit, and used such misunderstandings to ground knowledge of the Holy Spirit. See Torrance, *Theology in Reconstruction*, 227–28.

Torrance's confidence in identifying the person of the Holy Spirit, however, should be balanced with his reluctance in offering a definitive statement concerning the distinct person of the Holy Spirit. He reserves an element of mystery in his pneumatology, and quotes Cyril of Jerusalem's words that "to define accurately the *hypostasis* of the Holy Spirit is impossible."[23] Torrance adds:

> The Holy Spirit is not cognoscible in himself. In the doctrine of the Spirit we are concerned with the ultimate Being of God before whom the very cherubim veil their faces, for there God the Spirit hides himself not only by the very mode of his Being as Spirit, but by his exaltedness, his greatness and majesty, that is, by his infinite holiness. Because he is infinitely greater than we can conceive, we can think and speak of him in his revelation to us only with awe and awareness of the weakness of our minds to apprehend him.[24]

This apprehensiveness is intertwined with the self-effacing nature of the Holy Spirit (which will be elaborated later). By the very mode of the being of the Holy Spirit, he hides himself from us behind the Father in the Son and behind the Son in the Father, so that we do not know him face to face in his own hypostasis. Thus, ultimately, "the difficulty of the doctrine of the Spirit derives from this hiding of himself on the part of the Spirit behind the Face of the Father in the Son and the Heart of the Son in the Father."[25] Therefore, Torrance concludes, the identity of the Holy Spirit remains a mystery that needs to be honored.

The Holy Spirit and the Trinity

Our approach to the doctrine of the Holy Spirit must be from his inner *enhypostatic* relation to the triune being of God. Torrance's use of *enhypostasia* concerning the Spirit highlights the fact that the person of the Spirit is inseparable from the one being of God. As such, coupled with his divine personal nature, the personal objective subsistence of the Holy Spirit in God is an identity in being with the undivided Trinity. Consistent with Torrance's trinitarian emphasis on the doctrine of God, the Holy Spirit, like the Father and the Son, cannot assume an autonomous position, for

---

23. Torrance, *Theology in Reconstruction*, 210, 226; quoting Cyril of Jerusalem, *Cat.* 16.11 (*NPNF*² 7): 117–18.

24. Torrance, *Theology in Reconstruction*, 213.

25. Ibid., 226–27.

The Communion of the Holy Spirit

knowledge of the Holy Spirit is inseparable from knowledge of the Son and the Father, and therefore knowledge of the Triune God. Similarly, in our explicit knowledge of the Holy Spirit, we encounter the Trinity as a whole simultaneously, albeit in an implicit and inarticulate manner.[26]

Homoousios and Consubstantiality

Following Athanasius, Torrance is adamant that similar to our knowledge of the Father, knowledge of the Holy Spirit should not proceed from the divine person's relationship with created reality.

> Athanasius would have nothing to do with an understanding of the Spirit beginning from manifestations or operations of the Spirit in creaturely existence, in man or in the world. Instead . . . he took his controlling point of reference from what he called "the propriety" of the Spirit to God on the divine side of the line dividing between the Creator and the creature, and therefore from the inner relation of the Son to the one being of the Godhead.[27]

As such, Torrance's pneumatology develops out of the Holy Spirit's essential relation to the one God and his undivided consubstantiality with the Father and the Son. This explains why Torrance follows Athanasius and the Nicene-Constantinopolitan application of *homoousios* to the Holy Spirit. Because the Holy Spirit is wholly God and is also inseparable from the Father and the Son both in eternity and in the economy of salvation, it is proper that the early fathers applied *homoousios* not only to the Son's relation to the Father but also to the Holy Spirit's relation to the Father and Son.[28]

The important consequence of the *homoousios* of the Holy Spirit is the necessary equal ascription of divine attributes to the Holy Spirit. Thus, like the Father and the Son, with the Holy Spirit, "these three are one, *eternal* God, the same in substance, *equal* in power and glory."[29] As Gunton

---

26. Torrance, *Trinitarian Faith*, 218; *Christian Doctrine of God*, 29: "The doctrines of the Father, Son and the Holy Spirit are thus each implicitly Trinitarian."

27. Torrance, *Trinitarian Faith*, 201; *Theology in Reconciliation*, 231; *Divine Meaning*, 195.

28. Torrance, *Divine Meaning*, 196; Molnar, *Theologian of the Trinity*, 195. Crump argues however that in John's Gospel, even though the Spirit is described as a distinct person, his status as a divine person is not explicitly clear, in "Re-examinining the Johannine Trinity," 408.

29. Torrance, *School of Faith*, xcvi; *Trinitarian Faith*, 222. "He who grants that the

writes, one of the greatest pneumatological errors in Christian theology is the depersonalization of the Spirit in equating him with the concept of "grace" as substance, or thinking of the Spirit impersonally, as in Pannenberg's "force field."[30] This is not so far from Torrance's rejection of the tendency in the second and third centuries to think of the Holy Spirit as "an immanent *Pneuma* emanating from God" that "led to the notion of [his] creatureliness."[31] Torrance quotes Epiphanius: "When you pronounce the *homoousion*, you assert that the Son is God of God, and that the Spirit is God of the same Godhead."[32] As such, with the Father and the Son, the Spirit is equally honored, adored, worshipped, and glorified. But Torrance also offers a caveat concerning the use of *homoousios* in the doctrine of the Trinity. He holds that the term not only stresses Oneness in being in the Trinity, but also implies a distinction of persons in God. This is because "one Person cannot be consubstantial with himself . . . each of the three Persons has real, substantial, true and perfect subsistence in the one being of God, and indeed that the whole being of the Spirit is the same as the whole being of the Son and the whole being of the Father."[33] In short, tautonomy should not be inferred from the Nicene *homoousios*. Even though the Holy Spirit is ever with the Father and the Son, coinhering with them in the one being of God, it is an "enhypostatic coinherence" in such a way that in the one being of God, the Holy Spirit is always Spirit, as the Father is always Father and the Son is always Son, and each possessing distinct marks and properties that are incommunicable or non-transferable to the other two persons.

Holy Spirit is God," Torrance writes, following Gregory of Nyssa, "has granted all the rest," in *Theology in Reconstruction*, 226.

30. Pannenberg, *Systematic Theology* 1: 381–84. See Moltmann's four-fold metaphor for the experiences of the Spirit in *The Spirit of Life*, 269–85. While his classification is appealing, it gives an uneasy suggestion that the non-personal metaphors are on the same level as the personal metaphors. See also Gunton, *Father, Son, and Holy Spirit*, 79. Torrance discerns that this error emerges from what Epiphanius abhorred as "partitive thinking of God either as he is in himself or as he is toward us," evident when the Giver and the Gift are separated, or more particularly, when "grace" is conceived to be that which is other than God's own self-gift. See Torrance, *Theology in Reconstruction*, 169–91; *Trinitarian Faith*, 222; *Doctrine of Grace*, 139.

31. Torrance, *Theology in Reconstruction*, 212; Yeung, "Being and Knowing," 224.

32. Torrance, *Trinitarian Faith*, 221, 233.

33. Ibid., 220–21; *Trinitarian Perspectives*, 49, 116.

The Filioque Controversy

Torrance's theology offers a great solution to the misunderstandings and misgivings attached to the *filioque* controversy. In fact, his reiteration of an Athanasian stress on *homoousios* and its consequent ramifications on both the East's and West's arguments on the procession of the Holy Spirit is one of Torrance's greatest contributions to both pneumatology and ecumenical theology.[34] Torrance's contribution to the subject is not, however, in providing an answer to the question of *how* the Spirit proceeds from God, for this is tantamount to "an ungodly attempt to intrude into the holy mystery of God's Being."[35] Torrance even contends that like the idea of the Son's "begottenness," we do not know what the "procession" of the Holy Spirit really means. It is rather his argument that the procession of the Spirit should be understood in the light of the theology of Nicea—particularly on the consubstantial and perichoretic relation among the triune persons—that is important.[36]

Theologically, it is evident that the *filioque* debates revolve not specifically around the deity or person of the Holy Spirit *per se*, but on the being and person of the Father in the Trinity, understood differently by the fathers.[37] Torrance follows Athanasius's theology in affirming the double procession of the Holy Spirit, in contrast to single procession as grounded in the theologies of Basil and Gregory of Nyssa through their ascription of *monarchia* and *arche* only to the person of the Father. Owing to the *homoousios*, which argues for the consubstantial relation between the Father, Son, and Holy Spirit, Torrance's solution is logical and precise: "Since the Holy Spirit like the Son is of the Being of God, and belongs to the Son, since he is in the Being of the Father and in the Being of the Son, he could not but proceed from or out of the Being of God inseparably from

---

34. See Molnar, *Theologian of the Trinity*, 217; Baker, "The Eternal 'Spirit of the Son,'" 398–403.

35. Torrance, *Christian Doctrine of God*, 188. An appeal to mystery is certainly one of the important themes of Torrance's theology. In fact, he even preached about the necessity of acknowledging the "utter indescribability of God," in B38 "With God is Terrible Majesty," 1–8; *Christian Doctrine of God*, 192; Colyer, *How to Read*, 240–41.

36. Torrance, *Theology in Reconstruction*, 229–30; *Theological Dialogue* 1: 11.

37. Torrance, *Theological Dialogue* 1: 16; and see Torrance's elaborate discussion in *Trinitarian Faith*, 231–47. We are not dealing with the historical and political issues revolving around the clause here. For this, see Heron, "The *Filioque* Clause," in *One God in Trinity*, 63–75; and Smail, "The Holy Spirit in the Holy Trinity," in *Nicene Christianity*, 154–65.

and through the Son."³⁸ Athanasius's application of *homoousios* to the Holy Spirit, added to Torrance's stress on the concept of *perichoresis* and triune *Monarchia*, has the effect, not only of asserting that the Spirit is also of one being with the Father, but also that the procession of the Spirit is from the *being* (*ousia*) of the Father, in which the Son shares, and not from the exclusive *person* (*hypostasis*) of the Father. This means that in both Trinity *ad intra* and *ad extra*, any proper understanding of the procession of the Holy Spirit must be of procession from the whole spiritual being of the Triune God, which the Holy Spirit has entirely in common with the Father and the Son. This equally applies to the salvific mission of the Holy Spirit.

Discussions concerning the *filioque* serve the purpose of challenging theologians to rethink the internal and eternal relation of the Holy Spirit to the Father and the Son. In particular, what is needed is the overcoming of what Moltmann calls "monarchical pneumatology."³⁹ Ho argues, however, that because Torrance (unlike Zizioulas) grounds the procession of the Spirit in the being of the Godhead and not in the person of the Father, he destroys the personal-relational aspect of the Spirit's procession. As such, even though Ho admits that articulating procession not from God the Father but from God who is Father is a "creative move," he concludes that Torrance's solution "does not really solve the issue of *filioque*."⁴⁰ Ho's critique also represents Zizioulas's concern that the Holy Spirit, as a person, should proceed from a person (the Father) and not from an abstract being. But as to why Ho thinks that Torrance disagrees with this basic contention is a mystery. Ho's misjudgment lies in his fundamental error of regarding being (*ousia*) as essentially impersonal, which he then crudely imposes on Torrance, when in fact Torrance holds a personal view of being more similar to Zizioulas than Ho recognizes.⁴¹

Conclusions: The Holy Spirit in the Trinity

In a sense, the doctrine of the Holy Spirit completes the doctrine of the Trinity. Only after developing an explicit awareness of the consubstantial relation of the Spirit to the Father and the Son did the church explicitly understand the triune being of God. But the Spirit, *enhypostatic* with the

---

38. Torrance, *Christian Doctrine of God*, 188; following Athanasius, *Dec.* 12 (*NPNF*² 4): 157–58.

39. Moltmann, *History and the Triune God*, 58.

40. Ho, *A Critical Study*, 156, 276.

41. This will be elaborated further in chapter 5.

Father and the Son, does not just fill an empty seat in the triune communion. The Holy Spirit, for Torrance, is the bond of love and communion in the life of the Triune God, or "the consubstantial Communion of the Father and the Son in the Trinity."[42] Consequently, concerning the Spirit's salvific agency in the divine economy, because he "comes to us from the inner communion of the Father, Son and Holy Spirit" he is also "the bond of truth and faith who creates unity among us and brings us into communion with the Father, Son and Holy Spirit."[43] The person of the Holy Spirit, thus, reinforces Torrance's assertion of an *onto-relational* God, *ad intra* and *ad extra*. This also solidifies what we have repeatedly referred to as Torrance's *kath hypostasin* soteriology, which in this chapter, focuses on the distinct agency of the Spirit in the salvific economy in strict accordance with his hypostasis as the Holy Spirit, or *kata Pneuma*. Furthermore, that the Holy Spirit is relation- and communion-constituting also implies that the Holy Spirit is in himself personal. The Holy Spirit is not an impersonal emanation, force, or energy of God but is "at once intensely personal reality."[44] Moreover, the Spirit clarifies the nature of God as both holy and spiritual: "The very designation of God's spiritual nature as *holy* and the third person as *Holy* Spirit emphasizes the otherness, the utterly transcendent glory and majesty of God."[45]

The Communion of the Holy Spirit

The saving work of the Holy Spirit is inseparable from his saving person. As Torrance writes, "To be 'in the Spirit' is to be 'in Christ,' and to be in Christ is to be in God, for the operations of the Holy Spirit in us, like the work of Christ for us, is empty of evangelical substance or saving validity unless it is grounded in God and flows from God."[46] Torrance's soteriology is uncompromisingly trinitarian, so that even his view of the salvific agency of the Spirit is grounded in his affirmation of the perichoretic co-activity of the triune persons. This is appropriate, because a proper understanding of the gifts and diverse operations of the Spirit is possible only from

42. Torrance, *God and Rationality*, 180.
43. Torrance, *Trinitarian Faith*, 250. See also Kruger, "Participation in the Self-Knowledge of God," 203–4.
44. Torrance, *Trinitarian Faith*, 192, 218, 226.
45. Colyer, *How to Read*, 217.
46. Torrance, *Christian Doctrine of God*, 61. Thus, to know the Spirit and to be acted on by Him is to be concerned with the very being of God, in Torrance, *Theology in Reconstruction*, 214.

the perspective of their source and ground in the divine Trinity, from the Father, through the Son, and in the Spirit. The activities of the Holy Spirit, therefore, are the activities of the Triune God working in our midst the salvation wrought by the grace of the Son and the love of the Father, but in particular, the Holy Spirit is the "holy presence of God in and through whose communion we may know the grace of the Lord Jesus Christ and the love of God the Father."[47] Pentecost, or the universal outpouring of the Holy Spirit to the church for the world, thus, belongs to the salvific economy. In fact, Torrance argues that the last times "are fully inaugurated by the descent of the Spirit, for it is through the Creator Spirit that the saving work of Christ is actualized in the Church as redemption."[48] Moreover, the *eschatological* Spirit is also the *teleological* Spirit, for it is the agency of the Holy Spirit, in relation to the work of Christ, to bring to completion the mediation of reconciliation.[49]

The Holy Spirit and Jesus Christ

Because of Torrance's emphasis on the *homoousios*, he argues that the doctrine of the Son requires the doctrine of the Holy Spirit, and *vice versa*.[50] In the economy of salvation, the work of the Holy Spirit is never independent from the work of the incarnate Son, just as his person is never independent from the persons of the Son and the Father. This means that Pentecost should be understood as Jesus Christ himself ministering to the church. Torrance summarizes: the Holy Spirit "comes to us *in the Name of the Son* and is sent by him. Hence he is known as 'the Spirit of Christ' (Rom 8:9), 'the Spirit of Jesus Christ' (Phil 1:19), 'the Spirit of the Son' (Gal

---

47. Torrance, "The Christ who Loves Us," in *A Passion for Christ*, 19. In *Trinitarian Faith*, 4, Torrance also writes: "It is only through the communion of the Holy Spirit, the Spirit of the Father and of the Son, that we may share in the saving, regenerating and sanctifying work in the life, death and resurrection of the Lord Jesus Christ, and thus share in his eternal offering of himself, and of us as redeemed and consecrated in him, to God the Father."

48. Torrance, *Royal Priesthood*, 23. The Spirit's descent means the era of revelation and reconciliation. See "The Apocalypse Now," 19–20.

49. Flett, "Persons, Powers, and Pluralities," 51–55.

50. Torrance, *Theology in Reconstruction*, 213. More radically, Torrance argues that the doctrine of the Spirit has Christology for its content, in *Royal Priesthood*, 25. Nevertheless, this should be balanced by Torrance's other arguments that Christocentricism should not be at the expense of pneumatology, as Lee, Deddo, and Habets argue in *Living in Union*, 315–16; "The Holy Spirit," 84; and *Theosis*, 145. In contrast, see the critique of Smail, *The Giving Gift*, 111.

The Communion of the Holy Spirit

4:6), 'the Spirit of the Lord' (2 Cor 3:17), 'the Spirit of Jesus' (Acts 16:7)," and the other Paraclete whom Christ sends in his place (John 14:16). In short, the Holy Spirit is "Christ's *Other Self*."[51]

Nevertheless, there is an apparent asymmetry in Torrance's attention to the triune relationships in the economy of salvation. As previously demonstrated, Torrance develops the economic relation between the incarnate Son and the Father. This section will present the economic relation between the Holy Spirit and the Son. What is missing, then, apart from discussions on the *filioque* and *shaliach*, is Torrance's attention to the relationship between the Holy Spirit and the Father. Therefore, from a *systematic* theologian's point of view, Torrance's failure to devote the same amount of detailed presentation of the Father-Spirit relation found in his presentation of the Father-Son and Son-Spirit relations is unfortunate. In a sense, however, and in Torrance's defence, to identify the specific economic relation between the Holy Spirit and Father would certainly prove difficult, particularly since the Bible itself does not clearly discuss the Father-Spirit relation. So from a *biblical-evangelical* theologian's perspective, Torrance's silence on the matter is an appropriate doxological response to the Scripture's silence.

Mutual Mediation of the Son and Holy Spirit

To encapsulate, Jesus Christ and the Holy Spirit mutually mediate one another. Christ's revealing and reconciling work should be interpenetrated by the doctrine of the Holy Spirit, for the Holy Spirit is wholly present (albeit behind the curtains) in the life and ministry of the incarnate Son.[52] Reciprocally, the coming of the Holy Spirit at Pentecost is not a coming of an isolated Spirit, but rather the Spirit "charged with all the earthly encounter of the historical Jesus," and that "the new mode of activity on the part of the Spirit is [actually] conditioned by the evangelical events that

---

51. Torrance, *Theology in Reconstruction*, 227; *Christian Doctrine of God*, 65; Habets, *Theosis*, 61. Thus, Torrance also calls the Spirit the *shaliach* of Christ, or as Christ's official representative, in Torrance, *Atonement*, lvi, 320–23; *Order and Disorder*, 40–42. See also Lee, *Living in Union*, 143; and Kruger, "Participation in the Self-Knowledge of God," 201.

52. In particular, Torrance highlights the virgin birth, baptism, temptation, prayer, and offering of Jesus as specific moments where the active presence of the Holy Spirit is evident. See *Theology in Reconstruction*, 222, 246; *Incarnation*, 135–36; and Bobrinskoy, "The Indwelling of the Spirit in Christ," 48–65. Lee writes in *Living in Union*, 316: "The Spirit is the hero behind the curtain of Torrance's theological stage."

Communion with the Triune God

lie behind it."[53] This salvific relationship between the Spirit and the Son goes back even before the incarnation, because the Holy Spirit is co-active with the Son in all acts of creation as well as all acts of redemption and sanctification. This double mediation is summarized by Torrance: "The co-activity and co-essentiality of the Spirit with the Son meant that the doctrine of the Spirit must be allowed to interpenetrate the doctrine of Christ and his revealing and reconciling work, for it is the Spirit who mediates the Son as it is the Son who mediates the Spirit."[54] Therefore, even in our knowledge of the Son and the Spirit, the two persons are at work.

In what way, however, is the present presence and work of the Holy Spirit in and to the world Christ-mediated? First, the Spirit became universally available for all only after Christ's Spirit-filled earthly human life. Jesus Christ vicariously received the Holy Spirit in his incarnate life in order to achieve for us a life of perfect communion with the Father in the power of the Holy Spirit. Torrance writes:

> Since he is himself both the God who gives and the Man who receives in one Person, he is in a position to transfer in a profound and intimate way what belongs to us in our human nature to himself and to transfer what is his to our human nature in him. That applies above all to the gift of the Holy Spirit whom he received fully and completely in his human nature for us. Hence in the union of divine and human natures in the Son the eternal Spirit of the living God has composed himself, as it were, to dwell with human nature, and human nature has been adapted and become accustomed to receive and bear the same Holy Spirit.[55]

Secondly, the Holy Spirit is mediated by and through Christ's finished redemptive activity. This is coherent with Torrance's thought that unredeemed humanity cannot approach God face to face. In other words, the Holy Spirit could not be mediated to the rest of humanity while

---

53. Colyer, *How to Read*, 31.

54. Torrance, *Karl Barth*, 209–10; *Theology in Reconstruction*, 213. Our knowledge of the Spirit, Torrance argues, is through the Son as well, in *Trinitarian Faith*, 306. See James D. G. Dunn's elaboration of the relationship between the Holy Spirit and the incarnate Son in *Jesus and the Spirit*, esp. chapter 3. That Torrance upholds the mutual mediation between Jesus Christ and the Holy Spirit is one of the instances that Mun-Chul Shin takes to illustrate Torrance's fundamental dialogical theology in "A Dialogical Trinitarian Pneumatology," esp. chapters 6 and 12.

55. Torrance, *Theology in Reconstruction*, 246; *Incarnation*, 125.

The Communion of the Holy Spirit

humanity is yet in sin, or if Christ's atoning work was not complete. Expressed negatively,

> Until he had sanctified himself and perfected in our human nature his one offering for all men, until he had made once and for all the sacrifice to take away sin, until he had vanquished the powers of darkness and overcome the sharpness of death, until he had ascended to present himself in propitiation before the Father, the Kingdom of Heaven could not be opened to believers and the blessings of the divine Spirit could not be poured out upon human flesh or be received by sinful mortal men.[56]

This is why Torrance insists that Pentecost and Calvary intersect together.[57] Because the world is already reconciled in Jesus Christ, and the enmity between God and humanity is already overcome in the history of Jesus Christ himself, the Holy Spirit could now be poured out without consuming humanity in judgment in the process.

THE SELF-EFFACING SPIRIT AND JESUS CHRIST

Gunton argues that the self-effacing nature of the Holy Spirit encapsulates the central asymmetry of the triune relation in the economy of salvation.[58] Torrance admits that there is indeed an economic subordination in the Trinity, and the self-effacing Spirit evidences this, but his difference with Gunton is his approach to the subject matter. Gunton proceeds from the economic superiority of the Father, which he takes from Basil and Zizioulas, while Torrance primarily takes his cue from his *kataphysic* theology, i.e., that the Spirit's self-effacing activity is in strict accordance with the Spirit's nature as imageless and transparent.[59] Torrance's approach is also more biblically founded, for he takes his arguments from the Gospels, particularly from Christ's statements concerning the Holy Spirit. As such,

---

56. Torrance, *Theology in Reconstruction*, 247, 236, 252; *Atonement*, 178. Thus, David H. McIlroy says that from a relational trinitarian perspective, Jesus dies in order that the Holy Spirit might be released upon the people of God, in "Towards a Relational and Trinitarian Theology of Atonement," 30.

57. Torrance, *Christian Doctrine of God*, 64; "Atonement," 243. Even in our knowledge of Christ, Torrance argues that the Spirit could only reveal Christ after the resurrection and ascension, in *Atonement*, 324–29.

58. Gunton, *The Promise of Trinitarian Theology*, 199; and *Father, Son, and Holy Spirit*, 80.

59. Gunton, *The Promise of Trinitarian Theology*, 197; Torrance, *Theology in Reconstruction*, 253.

Molnar regards this as one of the most important aspects of Torrance's pneumatology, in contrast to theologians who spend more effort concerning the identity of the Holy Spirit.[60] For Torrance, the self-effacing nature of the Holy Spirit is evangelically purposive. The Spirit's function is not to bear witness to himself, but to Jesus Christ. As "the Spirit of Testimony and the Spirit of Truth, the Holy Spirit does not utter himself but utters the Word. He does not incarnate himself but incarnates the Son. He does not show his own Face, but shows us the Father in the Face of the Son."[61] This is why Smail refers to the Holy Spirit as a "Person without a face."[62] Calling the Spirit "the invisible Spirit of truth," Torrance adds that he is sent from the Father in the name of the Son, and does not speak of himself but speaks only of the Father and the Son.[63] This is one of the distinct activities of the Holy Spirit in the mediation of both revelation and reconciliation.

> That is the self-effacing nature of the Spirit who hides himself behind the Father in the Son and behind the Son in the Father, but also the enlightening transparence of the Spirit who by throwing His eternal Light upon the Father through the Son and upon the Son in the Father, brings the Being and Reality of God out of His hiddenness to bear upon man, and brings man out of his darkness to have communion with God, in Jesus Christ.[64]

Consistent with his Christocentric theology, Torrance argues that the agency of the Holy Spirit is to focus our attention on the person and Truth of Jesus Christ. Just as Jesus Christ revealed the Holy Spirit to his disciples, the Holy Spirit reveals Jesus Christ and points the church to him. "The office of the Holy Spirit in the Church is not to call attention to himself apart from Christ but to focus all attention on Christ, to glorify him, to bear witness to his deity, to testify to his mind and will, and in him and through him to lead us to the Father."[65] As Paul Fiddes notes, "the anonymity of the Holy Spirit is thus an eschatological self-effacement in God, and a self-effacement in human life which enables our participation in God."[66] Torrance's emphasis here is on the personal character of the self-effacement

---

60. Molnar, *Theologian of the Trinity*, 201–3.

61. Torrance, *Theology in Reconstruction*, 252; *Atonement*, lvi; "The Christ who Loves Us," 18.

62. Smail, *The Giving Gift*, 30.

63. Torrance, *Trinitarian Faith*, 211.

64. Torrance, *God and Rationality*, 167–68.

65. Torrance, *Theology in Reconstruction*, 253.

66. Fiddes, *Participating in God*, 262.

The Communion of the Holy Spirit

of the Holy Spirit and his witness to Jesus Christ. "The Holy Spirit is indeed personally present among us, but in his transparent and translucent mode of being, who as *homoousios* with the Father and the Son throws his eternal light upon the Father in the Spirit and the Son in the Father."[67] Through the presence of the Spirit's mode of being, he confronts humanity with the sheer presence of God, so that we are in immediate touch with God himself. Thus, "it is not just that the Spirit throws His Light upon a distant Christ but actually connects us with Christ Himself."[68]

Subjective Actualization of Christ's Objective Work

Torrance uses the phrases "objective union in Christ" and "subjective union in the Spirit" to signify the difference-in-unity in the one movement of salvation between the finished work of Jesus Christ, which he accomplished in his whole life, death, resurrection, and ascension, and the continuing work of Jesus Christ in the world through the agency of the Holy Spirit. The work of the Spirit in redemption has two sides: "from the side of Christ in the application of His finished work, and from the side of man in receiving the fruits of that work."[69] Like Calvin, Torrance's view concerning how the benefits of Christ are applied to humanity is deeply shaped by pneumatology. Humanity's sharing in the saving work and benefits of Christ is through union and participation in him, which "takes place through the Communion of the Holy Spirit."[70] As Torrance asserts, "the work of the Spirit in God's people [is] actualizing subjectively in them what has been accomplished for them once and for all objectively in the Incarnation."[71] Interestingly, it is these clarificatory statements that Ho disregards when he considers Torrance's view of the *finished objective*

---

67. Torrance, *Trinitarian Faith*, 212.

68. Kruger, "Participation in the Self-Knowledge of God," 209.

69. Torrance, *School of Faith*, ciii. This does not mean that these two sides are the only roles of the Holy Spirit in the salvific economy. While the Holy Spirit operates in a twofold way in the subjective actualization of Christ's objective work in humanity, the Holy Spirit has been active in the whole life of Jesus Christ in his working out the objective aspect of our salvation. Hence, the Holy Spirit is dynamically operative both in the realization of the objective work of Christ and in the subjective actualization of the objective work of Christ.

70. Torrance, *School of Faith*, xcv; Calvin, *Institutes* III.1.1; in Kruger, "Participation in the Self-Knowledge of God," 194. See Gunton's enumeration of three deficiencies of speaking of the Spirit as applying the benefits of Christ, in *Father, Son, and Holy Spirit*, 196. Nevertheless, Torrance still employed the terminologies and concept.

71. Torrance, *School of Faith*, cvi.

work of Christ on the cross and the *continuing subjective activity* of the Holy Spirit in believers as contradicting each other. Ho believes that Torrance's view of the ascended Christ's continuing priestly work and the Spirit's subjectivation of Christ's work in us is equivalent to belief in an on-going redemptive process that renders the cross insufficient.[72] While Torrance would support Ho's emphasis on the objective aspect of salvation in Christ, it is obvious that Ho's non-trinitarian thinking misses the soteriological import of Torrance's pneumatological soteriology. That Torrance actually involves the Holy Spirit in the appropriation of Christ's saving benefits marks his difference from thinkers like Ho who possess no robust trinitarian perspectives on salvation.

As stated, the subjective work of the Spirit is also encompassed within Torrance's trinitarianism. Torrance borrows Basil's view of the Father as "the originating cause," the Son as "the molding cause," and the Spirit as "the perfecting cause" in the economy of salvation, with emphasis on the act of the Spirit in bringing "to completion the creative purpose of God for human persons in the Son."[73] Torrance also borrows Barth's emphasis on the unity of God's act and being, and argues that "when we speak of the 'subjective' operation of the Holy Spirit in us, or of our being 'in the Spirit,' that is to be understood in an objective, ontological sense, as a being *in God*."[74] Because the Holy Spirit operates as the *enousios energeia* of God, Torrance affirms that in the Spirit, not only that God's activity towards us is grounded in his own being, but that God's being is present with us as Spirit in a dynamic and creative way.

Union with Christ through the Holy Spirit

For Torrance, the communion of the Holy Spirit is the vital link between Jesus Christ and humanity. "The Reformed doctrine of the Communion of the Spirit," is "a doctrine of Communion in Christ through the Spirit, or, to put it otherwise, of *union with Christ through the Communion of*

---

72. Ho, *A Critical Study*, 129.

73. Torrance, "Soul and Person in Theological Perspective," 111. See also Gunton, *Father, Son, and Holy Spirit*, 86; MacKinnon, "The Relation of the Doctrines of the Incarnation and the Trinity," in *Christ, Creation, and Culture*, 96; and Habets, *Theosis*, 146.

74. Torrance, *Karl Barth*, 209; *Divine Meaning*, 196; *Christian Doctrine of God*, 148: "This means that when the New Testament speaks of us as being 'in the Spirit' or of the Spirit being 'in us' . . . this is to be understood not in a subjective sense but in a profoundly *objective* sense."

The Communion of the Holy Spirit

the Spirit."[75] Thus, the objective union which we have with Jesus Christ through his incarnational assumption of our humanity into himself is subjectively actualized in us through his indwelling Spirit. The communion of the Holy Spirit, though a new relationship with humanity in accordance with the person and nature of the Spirit, has an original christological content. Thus, the communion of the Spirit does not create a union that is not already a reality in Jesus Christ.[76]

As Habets notes, Torrance follows Calvin: "the Spirit is the bond by which Christ effectually unites us to himself."[77] This incorporation into Christ can be regarded in two interrelated ways, yet as both works of the Holy Spirit. Humanity is incorporated into Christ as the subjective actualization in us through the Spirit of the objective revelation and reconciliation fulfilled in the incarnation and atonement. On the other hand, "this incorporation into Christ through the Spirit is to be regarded as our participation in the new covenant in Christ."[78] This is both individually and corporately. The entire Christian life is a participation in union with Christ in the Holy Spirit, which takes place within the corporate fellowship of love in the church. This is intertwined with Torrance's view of the church "rooted and grounded in Christ by being incorporated into him through his Word and Spirit. It is called into fellowship with him and united to him by his baptism of the Spirit, so that its members are made to share in Christ's obedient life and are assimilated to his new humanity."[79] Thus, Torrance can also say that by virtue of the personalizing person of the Holy Spirit, the humanizing work of the human Jesus, and our being united with Jesus Christ through the Holy Spirit, humanity finally becomes the humanity God intends us to be, that is, to be in relation with both God and others.[80]

---

75. Torrance, *School of Faith*, cvi.

76. Kruger, "Participation in the Self-Knowledge of God," 196.

77. Habets, *Theosis*, 144; quoting Calvin, *Institutes* III.1.1.

78. Torrance, *Atonement*, 368. See how Torrance discusses the church as the new covenant people of God in *Theology in Reconciliation*, 61–62.

79. Torrance, *Atonement*, 368; *Trinitarian Faith*, 250–51. The church, thus, is both *Ecclesia de Trinitate* and *Ecclesia de hominibus*, in Torrance, *Theological Dialogue* 1: 154.

80. Deddo, "The Christian Life," in *An Introduction to Torrance Theology*, 143. Deddo also enumerates four ways in which union with Christ is not to be understood: (1) *moral* union, (2) *psychological* union, (3) *volitional* union, and (4) *telic* union (p. 139); see also Lee, *Living in Union*, 97.

The Holy Spirit and the World

The specific importance of the office of the Holy Spirit in Torrance's soteriology is this: "Apart from the Communion of the Holy Spirit, we could not enjoy the Grace of our Lord Jesus Christ and the Love of God the Father."[81] As such, although this chapter focuses on the particular salvific works of the Holy Spirit in the world, this does not mean that the distinct works of the Holy Spirit could be isolated from either the Son's or the Father's being and act. Rather, what is argued here is that the Spirit fulfils aspects in our salvation that are unique and in accordance with his nature as the Holy Spirit, the third person of the Triune God, or, that like the Father and the Son, therefore, the Holy Spirit has a *kath hypostasin* agency in the salvific economy.

THE SPIRITUS CREATOR

Torrance develops his understanding of the Spirit's agency in creation in the light of the creedal confession that the Holy Spirit is the "Lord and Giver of Life." He argues that this possesses a fundamental trinitarian background, for it is related to the creative works of the Father and the Son. He elaborates:

> The Holy Spirit shares in the *Sovereign Power* of the Father and the Son, but his distinctive sovereign activity is that of quickening or giving life to the creature. That is to say, while there is only one creative activity of God, from the Father, through the Son and in the Spirit, the special work of the Holy Spirit is to be discerned in that he brings the life-giving power of God to bear upon the creature in such a way that through his immediate presence to the creature and in spite of its creaturely difference from God he sustains it in its being and brings its relation to the Creator to its true end in him.[82]

The primary work of the Holy Spirit, then, is to uphold creaturely existence and prevent it from lapsing into nothingness from which it was created. This stresses the contingency of creation and assures the Lordly presence of God himself in creation. God does not "deistically abandon" creation,

---

81. Torrance, *Christian Doctrine of God*, 18.

82. Ibid., 217–18; *Theology in Reconstruction*, 215. In *Christian Doctrine of God*, 216, Torrance writes: "The Holy Spirit is also Creator in union with the Father and the Son, no less than they... but Creator in his distinctive nature and activity as *Spirit*."

The Communion of the Holy Spirit

Torrance argues, but indwells it for its continuing existence.[83] Torrance's pneumatology, however, is not pantheistic or panentheistic, explicitly or implicitly.[84] The personal agency and presence of the Holy Spirit in creation is precisely Torrance's safeguard against such errors, because he understands the Holy Spirit to be the power of God in action over against that which is not God. The Holy Spirit in Torrance's thought balances the theological pendulum regarding God's transcendence and immanence.[85]

Using the 1581 *Craig's Catechism*, Torrance demonstrates that the Spirit's work "in the order of nature" is to "keep all things in their natural state" though he adds that all alterations in creation are also the work of the Holy Spirit, who works "diversely in nature."[86] This highlights the fact that the Holy Spirit, though God himself immanent in the world, does not destroy the creaturely different (or the wholly other), but upholds creaturely being while maintaining the distinction of Being from being. In short, the Holy Spirit in his freedom and sovereignty maintains the order of nature or the order of created reality, keeping it as it should be, as creation. Torrance holds an important dialectical view of the work of the Holy Spirit here, because the Holy Spirit *maintains* and *transforms* creaturely existence at the same time: "Far from crushing our creaturely nature or damaging our personal existence, the indwelling presence of God through Jesus Christ and in the Holy Spirit has the effect of healing and restoring and deepening human personal being."[87] This is related to the creative work of the Holy Spirit in *renewing* and *sanctifying* creation, or of consummating the intended relation between the creature and the Godhead. The Holy Spirit, "in upholding living, rational creatures from below and within them and

---

83. Torrance, *Christian Doctrine of God*, 218. Torrance adds that the transcendent action of the Spirit in time and space is a proof of God's continuing involvement in creation, in *Theological Dialogue* 1: 43. See also B23 "Where is God?," 4.

84. John W. Cooper rightly does not name Torrance in his list of panentheists in *Panentheism* (2007). See Moltmann, *The Spirit of Life* (1992) for a panentheistic understanding of the Spirit's relation to the world.

85. "The name Holy Spirit," Torrance writes, "gave expression to the recognition that the immanence of the Spirit was the immanence of the Spirit in his irreducible transcendence," in *Trinitarian Faith*, 192. In contrast, Gunton, following Zizioulas, argues that talk about the Spirit is more concerned about God's transcendence, not immanence, in "The Spirit in the Trinity," in *Forgotten Trinity* 3: 123.

86. Torrance, *School of Faith*, c.

87. Torrance, *Trinitarian Faith*, 230. Thus, Torrance adds, the Holy Spirit also works in personalizing persons.

in bringing them to their true end or *telos* in God, makes them participate in the very life and holiness of God himself."[88]

The Spiritus Redemptor

Torrance presents the work of the Holy Spirit in redemption in relation to Christ's *triplex munus*.[89] In relation to Christ's prophetic office, the Holy Spirit "continues to utter Christ the Word and utters the Word with all the quickening, life-giving power of God."[90] In regard to Christ's priestly office, the Holy Spirit subjectively actualizes in us Christ's objective work for us. Following Hippolytus, Torrance refers to the Holy Spirit as "the high-priestly Spirit."[91] And finally, in regard to Christ's kingly office, "the Spirit works as the power and operation of God, effectively applying Christ's victory over the powers of darkness to us, and so delivering us from bondage into the freedom of the sons of God."[92] In all these, the emphasis in on the fact that the fulfilment and realization of the work of the incarnate Son is effected by the coming and indwelling of the Holy Spirit. The coming and presence of the Holy Spirit, thus, belongs to the triune mediation of reconciliation, for the presence of the Holy Spirit is the actualization of the new and redeemed life, which sons and daughters of the Father have in Jesus Christ.

> With the coming of the Holy Spirit at Pentecost God's redemptive and his creative acts merged together. It was a movement of recreation through atoning sanctification, for through the *Holy Spirit* the full creative impact of the divine Word broke in upon the apostolic Church constituting it a new creation in Christ, fulfilling in it the sanctifying and regenerating of our human nature that has already taken place in Christ, and so bringing it

---

88. Torrance, *Trinitarian Faith*, 229.

89. Torrance, *Atonement*, 178. The distinction between the work of Jesus Christ and the work of the Holy Spirit should also be identified: "through the blood of Christ we are redeemed from the guilt of sin, but through the Spirit of Christ we are redeemed into the life of God." Torrance understands the ministry in the church as a continuation of this threefold anointing and Christo-ministry, in *Ministry and Sacraments of the Gospel*, 30–57.

90. Torrance, *School of Faith*, ciii.

91. Quoting Hippolytus, *Apostolic Tradition*, 3.5; in Torrance, *Trinitarian Faith*, 249.

92. Torrance, *School of Faith*, civ. See also B46 "Freedom from Bondage."

into a new stage of being in which it was renewed in the image of God.[93]

Torrance's emphasis at this point is the dynamic recreating, incorporating, and sanctifying work of the Holy Spirit in our continuous and progressive Christian experience: "We grow in the grace and knowledge of Christ as we surrender to the creative impact of the Holy Spirit upon us."[94] Elsewhere Torrance refers to the Holy Spirit as "the Spirit of Holiness, the Spirit of Redemption and the Spirit of Glory."[95] This is because it is through the Holy Spirit "that we come to participate in God and experience his vivifying power toward us, for he is himself the Author and Source of our justification and sanctification, of truth, of grace and every good thing."[96] David Crump properly refers to the Holy Spirit as "the Spirit of regeneration," because new birth is of spiritual origin, and is the Holy Spirit's work.[97]

Interestingly, Torrance also believes that being reborn in the Spirit involves a radical transformation. This is why he thinks that spiritual birth is painful, because "man must be unmade and remade, be broken and recreated, be slain and made alive again."[98] Using the analogies of old and new humanity, Torrance argues that in being born of the Spirit, a new nature is given to humanity to displace the old. Thus, his ethics, far from missing in his theology, is found under the Pauline umbrella "new life in the Spirit."[99] In fact, Torrance is uncompromising in his agreement with his father: "To dwell with God, man must be godlike and to be godlike

---

93. Torrance, *Theology in Reconstruction*, 254; *Trinitarian Faith*, 216; "The Uniqueness of Divine Revelation," 99.

94. Torrance, *Theology in Reconstruction*, 256.

95. Ibid., 248.

96. Ibid., 53.

97. Crump, "Re-examining the Johannine Trinity," 405. In *Trinitarian Perspectives*, 53, Torrance argues that the Spirit is "the Author of regeneration and of immortality, not by some borrowed power but by his very own." See also Torrance, *When Christ Comes*, 69; and Torrance (T. F.'s father), *Expository Studies*, 40. Jesus Christ is the example of being born from above. Following Irenaeus, and in line with incarnational atonement, T. F. Torrance argues that faith is ultimately *conceptus de Spiritu Sanctu*. See *Incarnation*, 102; and B38 Untitled sermon on 1 Corinthians 2:1–5, 11.

98. Torrance, *When Christ Comes*, 71. God does not override humanity, Torrance writes in *Theology in Reconstruction*, 237, but recreates him. See also Kruger, "Doctrine of the Knowledge of God," 387. Going back to Torrance's understanding of the interrelationship between revelation and reconciliation, he argues that even knowledge of God must involve a moral transformation in B23 "The Christian Doctrine of Revelation," 2.

99. Torrance, *Atonement*, 177.

requires a fundamental change of heart and mind. That is: he needs a new righteous disposition which will hate the evil and love the good. This is what it means to be born again and receive new spiritual life by the Holy Spirit."[100] Whether this is a well-developed aspect of Torrance's publications, however, is another question. It seems that Torrance's definitive view of the Holy Spirit's specific active role in daily Christian life is only on the role of the Holy Spirit in affirming the Lordship of Christ.[101] In a sense, this objective grounding of the self in Jesus Christ in the power of the Holy Spirit is what contemporary Christian theology and spirituality needs, in response to the subjectivist distortion characteristic of the modern confusion of anthropology and pneumatology.[102] But still, Torrance did not fully elucidate the Pauline expression "life in the Spirit" in his writings, which is truly regretful. One also wonders whether his anxiety over a moralistic version of Christianity became an unhealthy prejudice that purposely prevented him from articulating this aspect of the Spirit's agency in the world.[103] Unlike Calvin, Torrance's theology lacks a strong emphasis on the vivifying agency of the Spirit in the lives of maturing believers.

Connected to this are two other relevant critiques related to Torrance's Christology. First, as discussed in chapter 2, Torrance's view of human response vicariously accomplished by Christ *pro nobis* in a *totus/totus* manner, and thus an emphasis on the *"in Christ"* of salvation, could be pointed to as a source of his neglect of the *"in the Spirit"* of salvation. In short, because Torrance views the vicarious human response of Jesus Christ for humanity as objective and final, the work of the Holy Spirit in liberating and enabling humanity to respond is undermined. The gift of

---

100. Torrance, *Expository Studies*, 41. The true Christian life, Torrance preached, is characterized by walking in the light of God, but this does not necessarily mean sinlessness, in B47 "If we walk in the light," 1–2. See also B42 "Who is like unto thee?," 3–7; and B43 "Be ye therefore perfect," 1–11 on Christian holy life. Torrance's sermons provide evidence that he was concerned for his parishioners's daily Christian life and witness. Notice, for example, the practical applications found in B43 "The First Temptation of Jesus," 1–14; B43 "The Second Temptation," 1–13; and B43 "The Third Temptation," 1–14. Also, although discipleship is not dealt with in his published writings, Torrance preached about it in B44 "These Candidates for Discipleship," 1–10; and B43 Untitled sermon outline on Matthew 16:24–25, 1–2.

101. Torrance, *Theology in Reconstruction*, 238; *School of Faith*, cv.

102. Torrance, *Theology in Reconstruction*, 238.

103. Ray S. Anderson says that Torrance "seldom ventures onto the turf where practical theologians ply their trade," in "Torrance as a Practical Theologian," in *The Promise of Trinitarian Theology*, 176. Torrance's calls to proper Christian life are found mostly in *Life and Work*. See "A Serious Call for a Return to Devout and Holy Life," 14–15; and "The Crisis of Morality," 15–16.

The Communion of the Holy Spirit

"responsiveness" by and in the Spirit is neglected.[104] The second critique is related to Torrance's unsatisfactory treatment of the kingly office of Christ, which Kruger discerns.[105] Like Kruger, it is not suggested here that Torrance offers no place for the kingly office of Christ in his soteriology. To claim this is just plain absurdity. Torrance, being a true follower of Calvin, places great emphasis on the *munus triplex*, which inescapably deals with Jesus as king. For instance, his treatment of *padah* redemption, which he correlates with the kingly office of Christ, is noteworthy.[106] Nevertheless, at least in comparison to his greater and more in-depth treatments of the prophetic and priestly offices of Christ, the kingly office in Christ's incarnate economy and its implications for Christian life are noticeably less discussed. In particular, he does not elaborate the important implications of Christ's vicarious victory over sin and death for Christians now. One wonders whether Torrance's anxiety over the active part of humanity for salvation thus became a hermeneutical key for him to avoid discussing (1) the kingly office of Jesus Christ and its implications, and (2) the vivifying agency of the Holy Spirit in the lives of believers, which are interconnected. Moreover, one wonders if he avoided these themes because he thought of them as incoherent with his emphasis on the objective work of Jesus Christ.

The Spirit of Truth

Basic to Torrance's epistemology, and cohering with his scientific theology is the realization that because God is Spirit, he can only be known in a spiritual way. As such, Torrance places emphasis on the epistemological significance of the Holy Spirit. First, Torrance distinguishes "epistemology of the Spirit" from the "epistemological relevance of the Holy Spirit," and considers the latter the proper aspect: "In epistemology we are concerned with the *formal* aspects of knowledge, the forms of the *how* and the forms of the *what* . . . whereas in the Spirit we are concerned rather with the *non-formal*, with the given reality or object of our knowledge as it outruns all forms of our understanding."[107] Secondly, the work of the Holy Spirit in Christian epistemology should not be interpreted as an abstract, detached enabling. Rather, because the Holy Spirit is "the living action and personal

---

104. Smail, *The Giving Gift*, 170–75.
105. Kruger, "Participation in the Self-Knowledge of God," 324–34.
106. Torrance, *Atonement*, 27–33, 58–60.
107. Torrance, *God and Rationality*, 166.

presence of God himself among men,"[108] his revealing agency should be understood as God's dynamic activity. The Spirit is the "speaking Spirit," and "who speaks to us in Person."[109] Thirdly, the revealing work of the Holy Spirit is the revelation of the Triune God. There can be no independent epistemology of the Spirit as if he has his own epistemological ground apart from the Father and the Son. Finally, and consistent with the argument for a transformational encounter with the Holy Spirit, "the epistemological relevance of the Spirit lies in the dynamic and transformational aspects of this knowledge."[110]

The Holy Spirit and Knowledge of the Triune God

Torrance had reservations about establishing an "epistemology of the Holy Spirit" because it implicitly presupposes that knowledge of God is accessible by humanity on autonomous grounds. Consistent with his evangelical approach, Torrance insists that "we do not have any knowledge of God apart from the Spirit, for God is Spirit."[111] This can be explored from two trinitarian perspectives: in relation to the self-effacing nature of the Holy Spirit, and in relation to the participative nature of our knowledge of God. First, the Holy Spirit deliberately hides his own *hypostasis* behind the Father and the Son and throws his eternal light upon the Father in the Son and upon the Son in the Father. The Holy Spirit is the "speaking Spirit," but speaking only in order to reveal the Father and the Son. Secondly, knowledge of God is primarily participation in the Son's knowledge of the Father in the Holy Spirit. "It is through the gift of His Spirit to us and by the presence and power of the Spirit," Torrance writes, "that we are enabled to share in the knowledge of God grounded and established and once and for all made accessible to us in Jesus Christ."[112] Fundamental to this argument is that only God knows himself, and that consequently, our knowledge of God is participation in God's self-knowledge through the Son in the Holy Spirit. Furthermore, this participation is not possible from the human side; it is only "through Jesus Christ [that] we are given access

---

108. Torrance, *Theology in Reconstruction*, 92–93.

109. Torrance, *Trinitarian Faith*, 247; Kang, "Epistemological Significance," 359.

110. Torrance, *God and Rationality*, 166.

111. Ibid., 165. Torrance argues that the coming and presence of the Holy Spirit breaks humanity's own sinful creative imagination and abstraction, in *Theology in Reconstruction*, 255.

112. Torrance, *Theological Science*, 52; quoted in Bevan, "The Person of Christ," 134; Kruger, "Doctrine of the Knowledge of God," 368.

The Communion of the Holy Spirit

to the Father *in one Spirit*."[113] This is the epistemological relevance of the Holy Spirit in the knowledge of God: that even though God infinitely transcends the grasp of human minds, the Spirit "lifts us up to the level of participation in God where we are opened out for union and communion with him far beyond the limits of our creaturely existence."[114]

The Holy Spirit and the Scriptures

Kruger argues that for Torrance, Holy Scripture is one of the earthly means of the communion of the Holy Spirit. As long as "earthly means" is not equated with the Augustinian and Medieval concept of "means of grace," Torrance would agree.[115] The Holy Spirit has a double relation to the Scripture: in inspiration and in interpretation. First, Torrance affirms that the Scripture is inspired, through "the witness of the Holy Spirit," not as in literal and verbal dictation, but as the operation of the Holy Spirit to holy people obedient to the Spirit's guidance. Moreover, the inspiration of the Scripture is not an isolated work of the Holy Spirit, but is coordinated within the whole history of God's revealing act in Israel and in the human Christ, where the Word of God and the word of humanity are perfectly bonded within the *hypostatic union*. But specifically, it is the Holy Spirit who empowered and helped the biblical writers to fulfil the special role in their written witness to Jesus Christ.[116]

Secondly, regarding the interpretation of Scripture, Torrance's primary concern is in the relation between human language and divine meaning. Torrance argues that the Holy Spirit makes the human words of the Bible transparent, so that the reality of God embedded in them shines or sounds through.[117] He is also concerned that human words do not sufficiently reflect the realities they refer to, and that most times linguistic forms are opaque. He solves this interpretative problem by identifying the

---

113. Torrance, *Trinitarian Faith*, 55 (italics mine).

114. Torrance, *Trinitarian Perspectives*, 87. Deddo, "The Holy Spirit," 101; *Theology in Reconstruction*, 226, and in 252: "He creates in us beyond all creaturely or human capacities the ability to know the Unknowable, and therein reveals himself as Creator Spirit of the living God."

115. See Torrance, *Ministry and Sacraments of the Gospel*, 7–8. Kruger, "Participation in the Self-Knowledge of God," 215–16. He includes the church and the sacraments as the other two.

116. Torrance, *Karl Barth*, 102; *Divine Meaning*, 274; *Order and Disorder*, 44; *Theology in Reconstruction*, 137.

117. Torrance, *Theology in Reconstruction*, 94. Torrance adds that the action of the Spirit in making the Scriptures transparent for us results in the *perspicuity* of the Scripture.

two-fold character of the Scriptures: *somatic* and *pneumatic*. "We cannot break through the physical sense of the Scriptures without the direct help of God and the enlightenment of his Spirit, but when our ears and eyes are trained and adapted to the divine truth we will be able to interpret the Scriptures in accordance with their deeper message."[118] Thus, "interpretation," Torrance concludes, "requires spiritual perception or *theoria*, if the divine acts and words are to be discerned in the historical, prophetic or apostolic statements of the Scriptures."[119]

The Holy Spirit and the Truth of Being

Torrance is also concerned about the nature of theological statements and their relation to and function for the Truth. This area is both technical and related to general epistemology, but we will discuss this here only in relation to the agency of the Holy Spirit. Torrance critiques both Roman Catholic and Protestant theologies for their nominalistic tendencies in focusing on human statements, and their failure to differentiate truths of statement from truth of being, or between signs and the thing signified.[120] This is important in Torrance's realist and objectivist theology, in which the truth of statement is but a medium and has no objective reality on its own. Its only function and significance is to serve the truth of being by directing attention to the reality on which it is grounded and which it signifies at the same time. With the aid of the Holy Spirit, its function is to

---

118. Torrance, *Divine Meaning*, 359. Torrance explains the dynamic relationship between the work of the Holy Spirit and the human interpreter in this way: "It is ultimately the Holy Spirit which animates the words of the Bible and makes the Word of God in them really contemporaneous, but it is done through the preacher whose business is simply that of a translator or interpreter." See B43 Untitled sermon on Jeremiah 7:2, 3.

119. Torrance, *Divine Meaning*, 275. See also Richardson, "Revelation, Scripture, and Mystical Apprehension," in *The Promise of Trinitarian Theology*, 188. Torrance is hesitant to use the words "mystical" and "mysticism" in his understanding of the Holy Spirit and the Scripture, but Richardson thinks that Torrance fosters "a *mystical realism* of reading Scripture in communion with God by the Spirit who inspired the Scripture" (p. 195). Overall, the Holy Spirit is "the creative agent in our reception and understanding of revelation," in *Ground and Grammar of Theology*, 166; *God and Rationality*, 168. But Torrance also underscores that God cannot be found so easily in the Scriptures. In B44 "Search the Scriptures," he argues that reading the Scriptures demands effort and diligence in spiritual struggle, prayer, and agony.

120. Morrison, "Torrance's Critique of Evangelical Orthodoxy," 53–69. Torrance writes that Calvin battled against the Renaissance that separated signs from realities and the Roman Church that fused form and content, in "History and Reformation," 280.

show through and *point towards* or *beyond* itself. "Apart from the Spirit, we would not break through to the divine Being, or rather the divine Being would not break through to us in His reality as Being and thus in His distinction from our thought and speech of Him."[121] Theological statements, therefore, operate as "open concepts" that reveal God and allow God to reveal himself to us, and it is the Spirit who is "the act of God upon us which keeps our concepts or cognitive forms open, so that our thought and speech are stretched out beyond themselves toward the inexhaustible nature of the divine Being."[122]

The Holy Spirit and the Social Coefficient of Knowledge

In Torrance's understanding of God's revelation, human reception requires participation in three ways: personal participation, participation in the movement of grace, and participation in the social coefficient of knowledge. First, he emphasizes that knowledge of God requires the personal coefficient of knowledge, and the consequent participation and wilful humility of the human mind to the objective claims of God's revelation. "To know the Truth is to become a participant to it."[123] Alan Torrance follows the same argument in rejecting the idea of the neutral theologian, arguing that "to be absolutely neutral before God is to be absolutely hostile to God," because knowledge of God entails intellectual obedience and submission.[124] To know God truly is to be transformed. Secondly, knowing God involves "participation and coordination with its communicated pattern and inner organization."[125] Just as the movement of grace has a pattern, so too has the knowledge of God: "Knowledge of God takes place through a movement of divine revelation from the Father through the Son *in the Spirit* and an answering movement of faith *in the Spirit* through

---

121. Torrance, *God and Rationality*, 175.

122. Ibid., 187; and his elaborate discussion in *Reality and Scientific Theology*, 140–46.

123. Torrance, *Theological Science*, 87; *Ministry and Sacraments of the Gospel*, 62.

124. Torrance, *Persons in Communion*, 12–15; Torrance, *God and Rationality*, 166. In a sermon, Torrance himself argues that the attitude of sheer indifference is one of the ways humanity can say "No" to God. See B42 "Make Us a King to Judge Us," 2. It is a pre-requisite that the knowing subject must engage the personal Subject. It is impossible to know Christ without falling in love with him first. Torrance rhetorically asks: "How can you have HIM as your Saviour without being passionately devoted to Him?" See B44 "Christ: God or Not," 8; and B44 "Faith and Doubt," 7.

125. Torrance, *Transformation and Convergence*, 92; *Theological Dialogue* 1: 96.

the Son to the Father."¹²⁶ The emphasis here is that knowledge of God is only possible *in the Spirit*. Finally, the motion of grace involves a social coefficient of knowledge: the church. In the context of the church, where one develops *tacit knowledge* through *indwelling*, Torrance adds, following Polanyi, our minds gain thought patterns and semantic tools that are common to the Christian church.¹²⁷ But what exactly is the role of the Holy Spirit? Torrance asserts that it is the personalizing Spirit who creates the earthly communion of the church, grounded in the inter-personal communion of the Triune God, not only as the social coefficient of knowledge, but also as a "circle of knowing."¹²⁸

The Spirit of Participation

Torrance's theological reflection is imbued with participation theology. This is not surprising, because several of the Reformed theologians to whom Torrance is indebted, like Calvin and Campbell, had strong participatory languages in their own theologies.¹²⁹ In Torrance's theology, the Spirit is the "Agent of participation."¹³⁰ But the pneumatological element cannot be dissected from the christological and the trinitarian elements, because participation in the Spirit implicitly refers to participation in Christ's relation to the Father in the power of the Spirit. Alan Torrance rightly argues that participation in Jesus Christ means: (1) participation in his worship of the Father in the Holy Spirit, (2) participation in his knowledge of the Father in the Holy Spirit, and (3) participation in his mission from the Father in the Holy Spirit.¹³¹ Our only concern here however is participation in the Son's union with the Father in the Holy Spirit.

Torrance repeatedly emphasized that sharing in the life and love of the Trinity is the goal of salvation, and the Holy Spirit, the Spirit of

---

126. Torrance, "Karl Barth and the Latin Heresy," 461 (italics mine); *Divine Meaning*, 201. Torrance adds: "Unless theological activity is grounded upon, and made to conform to, this motion of grace, then every step of theology can only be from alienation to alienation in the continued self-assertion of self-will," in *Theology in Reconstruction*, 116.

127. Torrance, *Transformation and Convergence*, 93. See *Reality and Scientific Theology*, chapter 4 for Torrance's elaborate discussion; and also Flett, "Persons, Powers, and Pluralities," 209–14.

128. Achtemeier, "The Truth of Tradition," 60; Torrance, *God and Rationality*, 189.

129. Concerning Campbell's participation theology, see particularly Torrance, "Contribution of McLeod Campbell," 310.

130. Habets, *Theosis*, 151–65.

131. Torrance, *Persons in Communion*, 360.

The Communion of the Holy Spirit

communion and love, with Jesus Christ, is also sent in order to sanctify us and facilitate our communion with the Trinity. "By coming *into* man," Torrance writes, "the Holy Spirit opens him *out* for God."[132] Through the incarnation and the Holy Spirit, humanity, without being consumed or overwhelmed by the presence of God, is able to commune with the Trinity, though this sharing and indwelling in God is "not ours but is the Spirit's who is in us and abides in us."[133] Torrance refers to this experience in the Spirit as "objective inwardness."[134] Elaborately, "As the Father, Son and Holy Spirit dwell in one another, so God is in us by the indwelling of the Spirit and by participation of the Spirit we are in God, and thus our being in the Father is not ours but is the Spirit's who is in us and dwells in us."[135]

Therefore, in the triune order of mediation, "from the Father through the Son and in the Spirit [and] to the Father through the Son in the Spirit," it is undeniable that the Spirit himself fulfils a mediatorial role between humanity and God. Like the Son, referred to by Torrance as "the One and the Many" in the light of his vicarious incarnate redemption,[136] the Holy Spirit fulfils a similar office in his God-humanward descent and human-Godward ascent: "By his nature the Holy Spirit not only proceeds from the Father but *lifts up to the Father*. . . . Not only is he God the Holy Spirit descending to us, the Spirit by whom God bears witness to himself, but God the Holy Spirit lifting up all creation in praise and rejoicing in God, himself the Spirit of worship."[137] This raises the question why Torrance did not explicitly call the Spirit "Mediator," arguing that Jesus Christ is the "One Mediator" between God and humanity instead.[138] This is another area where Torrance differs from Barth, who considered the Spirit as "*Mediator* of communion."[139] It would have been more consistent for Torrance,

---

132. Torrance, *Theology in Reconstruction*, 238; *Karl Barth*, 211, 214.

133. Torrance, *Trinitarian Faith*, 268; quoting Athanasius, C. Ar. III.25.24 (*NPNF*² 4): 407.

134. Torrance, *Divine Meaning*, 198.

135. Torrance, *Theology in Reconciliation*, 232; *Trinitarian Faith*, 208–9, 213.

136. Torrance, *Incarnation*, 105–14; *School of Faith*, cxi, cxxiii.

137. Torrance, *Theology in Reconstruction*, 242 (italics mine). Torrance also relates this to the two-fold activity of the Spirit, in conjunction with the humanward and Godward work of the incarnate Son, so that he refers to the Holy Spirit as One "who goes forth from God and returns to God . . . supervening upon the Church and lifting it upwards in its faith and rejoicing in God," in *Theology in Reconstruction*, 248.

138. Torrance, *Trinitarian Perspectives*, 12.

139. See Hunsinger, "The Mediator of Communion," in *The Cambridge Companion to Karl Barth*, 177–94. Aside from his disagreement with Barth on natural theology, Torrance critiques Barth in (1) the element of subordinationism in his doctrine

especially since he faithfully employs the Athanasian soteriological formula "from the Father through the Son in the Spirit and in the Spirit through the Son to the Father," if he also unreservedly called the Spirit *Mediator* mediating reconciliation in accordance with his hypostasis as the Holy Spirit. In a sense, what is missing is just Torrance's explicit affirmation of this, because he himself implicitly considers the Holy Spirit fulfilling a mediatorial office like Christ, evident in his appropriation of the *topos* to both Jesus Christ and the Holy Spirit. Notice the double *topos*-ascription in the following quotations: "Jesus Christ is the *place* (*topos*) where God and man meet, where God stoops down to man and man draws near to God: the one place where we have access to the Father in the Spirit"[140] and "the Holy Spirit is the 'place' (*topos*) where men may meet with God and are enabled to have communion with him, receive his revelation and worship him."[141]

The Holy Spirit and the Church

In *Trinitarian Faith*, Torrance observes two central affirmations that can be gleaned from the Nicene-Constantinopolitan Creed regarding the church. First, the doctrine of the church belongs to and follows from the doctrine of the Holy Spirit, "for *holy* Church is the fruit of the *Holy* Spirit."[142] Secondly, the church belongs to the articles of saving faith, so that the ministry of the gospel as embodied in the church is affirmed.[143] In relation to the first, that the church belongs to the doctrine of the Holy Spirit in particular and to the doctrine of the Trinity in general, is important to Torrance, particularly in his affirmation that the church cannot be considered as an institution founded on human ideals and beliefs. He asserts that the church is founded in Jesus Christ, indwelt by the Holy Spirit, and is rooted in the Holy Trinity. The indwelling presence of the Holy

---

of the Trinity, which in turn affects his views on the *filioque*, (2) his failure to offer a fully trinitarian view of creation, (3) his limited treatment of the implications of the *enhypostasia* for his ecclesiology, (4) his neglect of the ascension of Christ as high priest, and (5) his interpretation of Calvin's doctrine of election. See Torrance, *Karl Barth*, 131–5; *School of Faith*, lxxvii.

140. Torrance, *Theology in Reconciliation*, 210. That Jesus is the place or Temple where God and humanity meet face to face is a theme that Torrance preached about on several occasions. See B41 Untitled sermon on 1 Corinthians 3:16, 1–2; B41 Untitled sermon; B41 "The Sanctification of the Temple," 1–4; and B45 Untitled sermon on Acts 1:11, 1–3.

141. Torrance, *Trinitarian Faith*, 229.

142. Ibid., 252.

143. Torrance, *Atonement*, 358.

Spirit, and the infilling of the Holy Spirit in the church, however, must be understood as the church being possessed by the Spirit, rather than the church possessing the Spirit. This is why Torrance is critical of the Roman Catholic Church for thinking that she can dispense the Holy Spirit.[144]

Owing to Torrance's integrative approach, his doctrine of the church is intertwined with several elements of his theology, such as Christology, pneumatology, eschatology, and soteriology. Here, however, we will only deal with three specific aspects: the church as (1) the Body of Christ, (2) the Community of the Holy Spirit, and (3) a communion-constituting community.

The Church as the Body of Christ

Torrance's soteriology balances the personal and the corporate elements of salvation. He considers salvation as union with Jesus Christ through the Holy Spirit as a one-on-one relationship, but also emphasizes that the Holy Spirit unites us to Jesus Christ by incorporating us into an earthly-historical community "which the Lord Jesus Christ through the quickening power of the Holy Spirit has formed and continually renews."[145] The church, then, is the communion of the Holy Spirit where our union and communion with Jesus Christ is actualized in the actual structure of our human, personal, and social being. The relationship between Jesus Christ and his Body, however, should not be understood only analogically or metaphorically. Rather, precisely because reconciliation is achieved by Jesus Christ through his own incarnate constitution as true God and true human in one person, the church is internally and ontologically related to Jesus Christ, made possible by Christ's incarnational and atoning union

---

144. Torrance, *Trinitarian Faith*, 254. In *Order and Disorder*, 18, Torrance spells out the importance of pneumatology in the church to keep the church from being a hierarchical institution, and to maintain the centrality of Christ and of the reconciled life. B39 "Ecumenical Service," 4.

145. Torrance, *Karl Barth*, 25. The church, Torrance writes in *School of Faith*, cxxiv, is "a corporate Communion, that is, a Communion of mutual participation through the Spirit in Christ and His graces, and a personal Communion which each may have with Christ within the corporate Communion. That is the doctrine of the church as the Communion of Saints, in which each shares with the other and all share together in the life and love of God in Jesus Christ. In that Communion no one can live for himself alone, or believe or worship alone, for he is nothing without his brother for whom Christ died, and has no relation to Christ except in Christ's relation with all for whom He died."

with us and our consequent union with him through the Holy Spirit.[146] This is consistent with Torrance's overall theology of internal relations, which must also govern the doctrine of the church as the Body of Christ. Because of the ontological relation between Jesus Christ and the church, Torrance thus argues that "Body of Christ" is the best designation for the church, although the emphasis should not be on the *Body*, but on the *of Christ*, stressing that Christ himself is the Head, King, and Savior of the Body.[147] "That is what a Christian community is: a community of people whose selves have been displaced by Christ, so that he is their true selves . . . 'not I but Christ,' St. Paul said."[148] This is interesting, because although Torrance argues that the doctrine of the church is "a function of belief in the Spirit,"[149] following the creedal formulations, he still defines the church primarily as the Body *of Christ*. At first sight, this might appear both as a contradiction and another evidence of Torrance's undervaluing of the Holy Spirit. But actually, Torrance is being consistent here with his view of the self-effacing nature of the Spirit. The church is primarily the Body of Christ and not the Body of the Holy Spirit because it is Jesus Christ to whom believers are united in the church in the Holy Spirit. The Spirit's *kath hypostasin* agency is not to create a new communion or a new union apart from that which Jesus Christ has already established. Although there is a sense in which the church is the *koinonia* of the Holy Spirit (as will be elaborated later), it is not a unique communion isolated from Christ's union with us.

Moreover, the church as the Body of Christ has several implications. First, it implies that Jesus Christ is the law of the church's life, although it

---

146. Torrance, *Atonement*, 368–69; "Where Do We Go from Lund?," 57; Lee, *Living in Union*, 221. Referring to the church, and following Irenaeus, Torrance thus optimistically believes that in the Body of Christ, there takes place "a soteriological and ontological unification of people in whose midst God himself dwells through the presence of the Holy Spirit," in *Trinitarian Faith*, 254.

147. Torrance, *Order and Disorder*, 105–6, 134; "The Pre-eminence of Jesus Christ," 54–55; *Atonement*, 362–63. One of the marks of the church, for Torrance, related to the headship of Christ, is having the mind of Christ. See B45 "The Marks of the True Church," 5–6. This christocentric approach to ecclesiology, he argues, should come as a safeguard against the socio-political thinking that even the World Council of Churches has fallen into, and which has consequentially clouded its doctrines of Jesus Christ and the church. See B36 "From a Christocentric to a Trinitarian Ecumenism," 3; and B46 Untitled sermon on Philippians 2:2–8, 1–8.

148. B41 Untitled sermon on Matthew 18:18–20, 2, given on two occasions: The Canongate Kirk, Edinburgh, 18 July 1978 as an introduction to Rev. Charles Robertson; and Northmavine, Hillswick as an introduction to Rev. Dr. Iain R. Torrance.

149. Torrance, *Trinitarian Faith*, 252.

is through the Holy Spirit that the church is able to share in Christ's obedience. The incarnate Son is "the regulative centre with reference to which all the worship, faith and mission of the Church take their shape."[150] Secondly, the church, therefore, can never justify itself by claiming historical succession or doctrinal faithfulness, or by referring to its own place and time in history. The church should not displace Jesus Christ as the Head of the church by any human agenda, be it in the form of institutional regulations or political authorities.[151] The relation between Jesus Christ and his church is the irreversible relation between the *Head* of the Body and the *members* of the Body. Thirdly, the irreplaceable Headship of Christ in the church also forms the foundation of the proper understanding of the "catholicity" and "ecumenicity" of the church: "The essential nature of the church is catholic because it is the one Body of Christ, and the essential life of the Church is ecumenical because it consists in the sanctification and gathering of mankind into a unity in Christ the Head of all creation."[152] Finally, Jesus Christ is and remains the model of how ministry and mission is done and accomplished in and by the church. In particular, the church must imitate Christ's humility and servanthood, but also minister in his authority.[153]

150. Torrance, *Theological Dialogue* 1: 83; *Kingdom and the Church*, 57–60; *Ministry and the Sacraments of the Gospel*, 17; Lee, *Living in Union*, 253. Even ministry is sharing in Christ's incarnation and humiliation, in B41 "Diaconate Service," 3. Torrance also argues that the Spirit of Truth should inform all authentic magisterium in the church, in *Transformation and Convergence*, 332.

151. Torrance, *Order and Disorder*, 12–13; *Theology in Reconciliation*, 19, 34–40. Torrance critiques both Roman Catholicism and Liberalism as falling into this error. Gunton also critiques ecclesiology defined in terms of the clergy, like the church of England, or when theology of the church is derived by analogy of an earthly empire, in *The Promise of Trinitarian Theology*, 57–59.

152. Torrance, *Theology in Reconciliation*, 17; and *Order and Disorder*, 263–83. See also Bobrinskoy, *The Mystery of the Trinity*, 132–34. As a true follower of Calvin's Christology, Torrance also understands the function of the church in terms of the *munus triplex*. He writes, "She is the Heirarchical Community, the Messianic Kingdom on earth. She is the Liturgical Community, the prime function of which is to offer the Sacrifice of Christ and bestow its benefits in the sacraments. She is the Prophetical Community, custodian and mediator of the Word," in B36 "What is the Church?"

153. B44 "Following Christ in Service," 1–8. See also B44 "Who is This?," 4, particularly on humility as constitutive of Christ's "mystery of personality." In B44 Untitled sermon on Matthew 28:19–20, 1–4, Torrance forcefully asserts that the church, because it participates in the ministry of Christ, has the right (1) "to go and upset the faith and religion of other people and claim them for Christ" and (2) "to go and pull down and destroy, and plant and build in the name of Jesus." It is for this reason that the world considers Christianity as not only unattractive, but also repulsive, in B46 "The Cross a Stumbling Block," 1–8. But also, because of the church's commission,

Communion with the Triune God

The Church as the Community of the Spirit

The Holy Spirit's personalizing and incorporating agency could be understood as (1) uniting us to Jesus Christ, and (2) forming "a community of reciprocity" on earth that reflects the trinitarian communion in heaven.[154] In Torrance's theology, the Holy Spirit plays a dominant role in creating a threefold relationship. The Holy Spirit is the bond of love of the Father and the Son, and therefore of the Triune God. This can be called the *onto-horizontal* relationship. The Holy Spirit also makes possible our union with Christ to the Father, ushering us into sharing in the very life and love of the Triune God. "The Spirit creates not only personal union but corporate union between us and Christ and through Christ with the Holy Trinity, so that it is the Holy Spirit who creates and sustains the being and life of the Church, uniting the Church to Christ as his one Body."[155] This could be referred to as *economic-vertical* relationship. The Holy Spirit also creates, within space and time, "a community of reciprocity among ourselves."[156] This can be called the *creature-horizontal* relationship, which is only possible in the light of the first and second relationships.

In the economy of salvation, the communion of the Holy Spirit means communion with Jesus Christ and with others. This highlights Torrance's stress on the primary and secondary meanings of *koinonia* in the church as participation in Christ and communion with one another in Christ, respectively.

Christianity always poses a threat to the world. Torrance writes: "Christianity is dangerous; the Gospel is dangerous; Jesus Christ is Dangerous; dangerous because the new destroys the old[;] . . . you cannot have a Christianity without its being dangerous. It will always take you unawares and leave you gaping with wonder at its sheer audacity—that is a vital element in Christianity, and that is why faith too is always such a daring matter," in B42 "Wonder in Christianity," 4.

154. Deddo, "The Holy Spirit," 98; Flett, "Priests of Creation, Mediators of Order," 170. Gunton refers to the church as "a living echo of the communion that God is in eternity," in *Father, Son, and Holy Spirit*, 200.

155. Torrance, *Trinitarian Faith*, 9. In *Trinitarian Perspectives*, 106, Torrance argues that the indwelling presence of the Spirit in the church establishes "full communion between the divine Persons [of the Trinity] and the Church."

156. Torrance, *Trinitarian Faith*, 250. It is true, however, as Kang discerns, that Torrance does not elaborate this aspect more fully. Apart from his preoccupation about communion in the church, his theology as a whole lacks positive and active involvement or wrestling with social and political concerns. See "Concept of the Vicarious Humanity," 433–36.

> It is only through a vertical participation in Christ that the Church is horizontally a communion of love, a fellowship of reconciliation, a community of the redeemed. Both these belong together in the fullness of Christ. It is only as we share in Christ Himself, that we share in the life of the Church, but it is only as we share with all saints in their relation to Christ that we participate deeply in the love and knowledge of God. Participation is a conjoint participation, a participation-in-communion, but the communion is above all a communion-in-participation in Christ.[157]

The emphasis here is on the conjoint participation in Jesus Christ effected by the agency of the communion-constituting Spirit. Because the church is created in the power of the Holy Spirit, the communion shared by its members is a "communion of love," grounded in the *agape*-love of God. The church "represents that area within humanity where the love of God is poured out by the Holy Spirit and where men and women are given to share together in their life on earth, and within the social cohesions of humanity, in the overflow of the divine Life," and is therefore "the great communion of saints."[158]

The Church as a Communion-Constituting Community

The church as a communion-constituting community can be regarded in three distinct ways. First, the church is an *already communion-constituted community*. The church embodies the already existing union with Jesus Christ in the communion of the Holy Spirit. It is the community of the already reconciled in Christ, living in communion with God through the Holy Spirit.[159] Those who are already engrafted into Christ and who share in his objective and finished work through union with him are unified in

---

157. Torrance, *Order and Disorder*, 109, 115; *Theological Dialogue* 1: 90; "Reconciliation in Christ and in His Church," 29–31. Torrance follows the Orthodox Church's position that interpreting *koinonia* as "fellowship" is weak and superficial, and that it should rather be interpreted as "communion," in B39 "Ecumenical Service," 3.

158. Torrance, *Order and Disorder*, 116. Torrance elaborates: "The Holy Spirit creates a community of people who are bound one to another in the closest of all relations, because He binds them one and all to Jesus Christ. That is what the Bible means by a Church: a community of people who experience the communion of the Holy Ghost—a community of people who are bound to each other in such a way that they only find themselves by losing themselves in the community." See B46 "Communion of the Holy Spirit," 5–6.

159. Torrance, *Atonement*, 361.

the Spirit in the earthly community for co-sharing, co-participation, and co-fellowship. The church is a community constituted *by* the communion of the Holy Spirit *for* communion with the Triune God and with others.

Secondly, the church is a *continuing communion-constituted community*. This highlights the fact that relationship with God and others is a dynamic and an on-going event. Just as Jesus Christ himself through the Holy Spirit is active in continuous self-giving and receiving, the members of the *koinonia* should be active participants in self-giving and receiving, according to our own finite and creaturely natures. The communion in the church, thus, allows for and encourages a deepening of both vertical and horizontal relationships. This is also evident in Torrance's understanding of the sacraments "as signs and seals of the saving grace of Christ given to the Church *to preserve and deepen* its union with Christ and the participation of its members in all his benefits in regeneration and sanctification."[160] In differentiating between baptism and the Lord's Supper, Torrance refers to the former "as the sacrament of what has taken place once for all in Christ, and the other [as] the sacrament of the continuing union and communion of the believers in Christ."[161] Thus, while baptism is administered once, the Lord's Supper is celebrated continuously in the church as the sacrament of our continuous union, communion, and participation in the Body of Christ in the power of the Holy Spirit.[162]

---

160. Torrance, *Scottish Theology*, 88 (italics mine). According to Torrance, the understanding that new birth transpires at baptism is already clearly understood in Judaism, in "Proselyte Baptism," 150–4; and *Ministry and Sacraments of the Gospel*, 93–105.

161. Torrance, *Scottish Theology*, 147; *Ministry and Sacraments of the Gospel*, 131. Christian baptism is our participation in the one baptism of Christ, in *Ministry and Sacraments of the Gospel*, 106–25. Baptism, for Torrance, involves a threefold sealing: (1) being sealed in the name of Christ, (2) being sealed with the seal of Christ, his cross and resurrection, and (3) being sealed by the Holy Spirit. See B39 Untitled sermon on Titus 3:4f. Another sermon that deals with baptism as a seal is B41 Untitled sermon on 1 Corinthians 1:22. Baptism also speaks about our being engrafted into Christ and the fact that he has bound us to himself in covenant. See B42 "For how shall I go up," 5.

162. Torrance, *Mediation of Christ*, 91; B47 "The Christ who came by water and blood," 1–9. But Torrance says elsewhere that the Eucharist does not only focus on the present and the continuous. He enumerates the three dimensions of the Eucharist: "one relating to the past, to the crucifixion of Christ in atoning sacrifice for our sin and guilt, one relating here and now, as often as we celebrate it, to the risen and ascended presence of Christ, but one also relating to the future . . . anticipation of the marriage supper of the Lamb." See B38 "Communion Sermon." The whole Christian life, therefore is "a sacramental communion," in B46 "Ye drink the cup of the Lord and the cup of devils," 3. But still, this unity between the church and Jesus Christ is grounded in "the greatest sacrament of unity [which] is the undivided humanity of Christ," in B46

The Communion of the Holy Spirit

Thirdly, the church is a *reconciling communion-constituted community*. Deddo argues that in Torrance's theology, the church is the immediate sphere of the Spirit's work and the world is the mediate sphere.[163] This assessment is true, and could be explained more fully by examining the interrelationship between the work of the Holy Spirit in the church, the work of the Holy Spirit in the world, and the mission of the church empowered by the Holy Spirit in the world. The Holy Spirit is "poured out immediately only upon the Church, and yet through the Church it was destined for all men, for the Church is sent out on a mission to all nations . . . that they too might receive the promise of the Spirit and be incorporated in the One Body."[164] The church is the community where reconciliation is intensively actualized through the Holy Spirit, but it is also a "royal priesthood," a reconciling community participating in the ministry of the Spirit in restoring alienated humanity to fellowship with God and ordering our disrupted existence through the ministry of proclamation and reconciliation.[165] The nature and mission of the church are inseparable. Thus, the church should live the reconciled life, as a witness to the world. Torrance affirms that the Holy Spirit is quenched when the church fails to fulfil its mission.[166] In a sermon he preached at the centenary celebration of Craiglockhart Parish Church, Torrance declares his critique of the Church of Scotland because he judges that his own church tradition seems to be doing the opposite of what Jesus Christ did on earth, i.e., that the church is more concerned with itself, or "with the sheep in the fold, than the lost sheep."[167] It is evident that Torrance wants to maintain

---

Untitled sermon on Galatians 3:26–29, 1; and B46 "Incarnation," 9. For a discussion of Torrance's views of the sacraments, see Kang, "Concept of the Vicarious Humanity," 385–98; and Hunsinger, "Dimension of Depth," 155–76.

163. Deddo, "The Holy Spirit," 99; Torrance, *Order and Disorder*, 16.

164. Torrance, *Royal Priesthood*, 26. See also Vassiliadis, "Reconciliation as a Pneumatological Mission Paradigm," 30–42.

165. Torrance, "Atonement and Oneness," 259; *Atonement*, 378–80; *Order and Disorder*, 118; and "The Place of Christology," 21–24.

166. Torrance, "Concerning Amsterdam I," 265. This is one of the primary reasons for Torrance's major involvement in the ecumenical movement, and his expressed remorse concerning worldwide church divisions. He argues that "by failing to achieve reconciliation in its own life, the Church is acting a lie against the gospel of reconciliation it proclaims with its mouth," in "Reconciliation in Christ," 33. Again, recognition of Jesus as Lord is Torrance's solution, in "The Way of Reunion," 204–5. See also Molnar, *Theologian of the Trinity*, 279–82, for the relationship between the church as a community of reconciliation and issues like Intercommunion and ecumenism.

167. B38 "Christ in the Centre of Mission," 2.

the balance between the church as a communing community and as a reconciling community. As the eschatological community reaching out to the age to come, the church embodies the unified and reconciled life, and is thus inescapably "always thrust forward into the world and into world history in the fulfilment of the divine purpose for the reconciliation and unification of the world ... for the realization in the world of the coming *oikoumene*, the universal community in which the redeemed life of the people of God and the life of all mankind will be one and the same."[168]

Conclusions

As with the Persons and works of the Father and of the Son, the Person and work of the Holy Spirit in the economy of salvation is important in Torrance's Trinitarian theology. Torrance does not offer a lesser appropriation of ontological and soteriological significance to the Holy Spirit, although there are instances that could be developed more fully in his Christ-Spirit equality in order for him to be completely freed from criticisms of pneumatological neglect. Torrance follows Athanasius's application of *homoousios* to the Holy Spirit, which in turn entails the Spirit's consubstantiality and co-equality with the Father and the Son. The role of the Holy Spirit as the bond of communion is also critical not only to the triune life, but also in understanding the Spirit's work in the economy of salvation. In fact, Torrance uncompromisingly states that "apart from the Communion of the Holy Spirit we could not enjoy the Grace of the Lord Jesus Christ and the Love of God the Father."[169] Moreover, the Spirit's salvific agency should be understood in his triadic relation to Jesus Christ and the Father, the world, and the church. These three relationships overlap and intermingle with one another, and one cannot be isolated from the others. The Holy Spirit, in his communion with us, unites us to Jesus Christ, actualizing in us Christ's finished and objective work for us. This applies to the Spirit's office in creation, redemption, and revelation, in which he enables us to participate in Christ's vicarious humanity and knowledge of the Father. Furthermore, the Holy Spirit unites us to Jesus Christ and to one another by creating an earthly communion, the Body of Christ, through which our union and reconciliation with Jesus Christ—and the Triune God— and with others are continuously renewed and reinvigorated by the Spirit's indwelling presence. In addition, the Holy Spirit through the reconciled

168. Torrance, *Theology in Reconciliation*, 71; *Atonement*, 433–36.
169. Torrance, *Christian Doctrine of God*, 18.

community also reaches out to the world in the ministry of reconciliation, embracing every race and tongue, and incorporating everyone into the family of God.

5

Communion with the Triune God

> Almighty and everlasting God, who has revealed yourself as Father, Son and Holy Spirit, and who ever lives and reigns in the perfect unity of love; Grant that we may always hold firmly and joyfully in this faith, and, living in the praise of your divine majesty, may we finally be one with you, who are three Persons in one God, world without end.[1]

IN THE PRECEDING CHAPTERS, THE PERSONS OF THE TRINITY WITH THEIR distinct works in the salvific economy were presented. These chapters are both important and evangelically purposive, because they reveal that a robust and biblical doctrine of salvation, instead of being neatly encapsulated as "accepting Jesus Christ as Lord and Saviour," should actually be perceived from a trinitarian angle: salvation means union with Christ and being adopted as sons and daughters of the Father in the incorporating communion of the Holy Spirit. Even the tempting alternative that salvation in Jesus Christ involves an *implicit* awareness of the Triune God should be regarded as insufficient. In fact, in theology and ministry alike, it is precisely this assumed adequacy of implicit trinitarianism that paved the way towards both implicit neglect and explicit rejection of the doctrine of the Trinity. In this chapter, the primary point of discussion revolves around Torrance's trinitarian soteriological dictum, scattered throughout his writings, that humanity is enabled to "share in the inner relations of God's own life and love."[2] Two aspects need consideration: (1) the inner relations of the Godhead, or the Trinity *in se*, and (2) humanity's sharing in the primordial community of love. These aspects are interrelated and inseparable. Therefore, in the first place, Torrance's soteriological

---

1. B38 "Lessons on Isaiah 6:1–4 and Ephesians 2:8–16; John 14:1–20."
2. Torrance, *Mediation of Christ*, 64.

trinitarianism will be discussed, and then, based on this, the final shape of Torrance's Trinity-conditioned soteriology will be expanded.

Soterio-conditioned Trinitarianism

Torrance's theological hermeneutic rejects any approach to theological formulation grounded in abstract principles or pure idealism. Theologizing follows a different path, for instead of coming from anthropocentric procedures and starting points, theology proceeds from the "logic of grace."[3] True knowledge of the Triune God is possible in the incarnate Son and the Holy Spirit. Knowledge of the Trinity *in se* derives from the activity of the Triune God *ad extra*. And it is precisely because it is knowledge rooted in the triune economy of salvation that Torrance's trinitarianism is soterio-conditioned. Our knowledge of the triune being of God is derived from God's dynamic self-revealing and reconciling act in the world. Torrance explains this further by using the analogy of light. In particular, he argues that when we see Jesus Christ, we do not see just a spot of light, but the real light that comes from God himself. "The real light was Jesus in whom the invisible Light of God was embodied."[4] And yet this light is a light that has adapted itself to our human condition. This has two soteriological implications: (1) we only see the Triune God if we align ourselves to the manner in which God chose to reveal himself, i.e., in the "logic of grace," and (2) because light means transparency, we only realize our sinfulness when we are in the presence of God's revealing light.

But is Torrance's soteriological approach different from his brother James's doxological approach? The answer is No. Both agree that the initial formulation of the doctrine of the Trinity originated from the worship of the early church, but the defining factor of their agreement

---

3. Torrance, *Theology in Reconstruction*, 37–41; *Theological Science*, 128–33. Kruger is right to claim in "Participation in the Self-Knowledge of God," 15, that Torrance's "methodological discussion is a footnote of massive proportions to his theology."

4. B38 Untitled sermon on John 1:6–9. That Jesus is "the light" is perhaps the most preached theme in Torrance's sermons. This is evident in the numerous sermon outlines and manuscripts on this topic. See B38 Untitled sermon on 1 John 1:5; B38 "I am the light of the World"; B38 "The Real Light"; B38 Untitled sermon on John 1:34; B39 "A Faith for Hard Times: The Living Light"; B39 "Light: Its Theology and Physics"; B39 "Light"; B41 "Christ the Light of the World"; B41 "The Christian Faith and the Physics of Light"; B43 Untitled sermon on Isaiah 50:11, 1–8; and B45 Untitled sermon on 1 John 1:1–10; 2:1–11. For a discussion of light in relation to daily Christian life, see B47 "If we walk in the light," 1–8.

is their understanding of "worship." In the words of James, worship is "our participation through the Spirit in the Son's communion with the Father, in his vicarious life and worship."[5] The definition itself carries soteriological overtones. In fact, the definition above is precisely how T. F. Torrance understands what constitutes salvation. Furthermore, worship and knowledge are inseparable in his theological epistemology. Put simply, knowledge of God involves a self-prostrating subjection of the human mind to the rationality and revelation of God in Jesus Christ. *Theologia*, which is properly the knowledge of the Holy Trinity, and *eusebia*, defined through Jesus Christ the Son of God incarnate, are inseparable: "The more truly God is known in accordance with his nature, the more godliness is advanced, and the more godliness is advanced the more likely we are to know God in a godly way that is worthy of his nature as God."[6] In Torrance's theology, therefore, the soteriological, the doxological, and the scientific approaches are cohesive.[7]

The Evangelical and Theological Trinity

Although Torrance frequently employs the conventional terminologies "economic Trinity" and "ontological Trinity," he suggests that it is better to speak of them as the *evangelical Trinity* and *theological Trinity*. His proposed alternative *evangelical Trinity* is particularly important, for it is related to his overall approach to theology in general and to the doctrine of the Trinity in particular: that knowledge of the Trinity is evangelically grounded, because "it is revealed to us through the incarnate or human economy which Christ undertook toward us, in the midst of us, and for

---

5. Torrance, *Worship, Community, and the Triune God of Grace*, 15.

6. Torrance, *Trinitarian Faith*, 38; *Theological Dialogue* 2: 4, and 159–60, where it is argued that the intention of theology is not "gnosiological" but doxological. See also Colyer, *How to Read*, 374. In B36 "Liturgy and Apocalypse," 3, Torrance relates liturgy and theology in the following way: "Unless liturgy and theology go hand in hand each tends to become impoverished and one-sided. Theology is essentially rational worship and unless its statements are made with the recognition that the Truth is more to be adored than expressed, those statements become arbitrary and arrogant. Theology divorced from wonder is not divine. Liturgy divorced from theology is not service to God, but the expression of aesthetic experience as itself redemptive, like a Beethoven Mass, for example, or even a Greek Tragedy." In the sermon he preached at the death of his colleague John Baillie, he also affirms that "the rational worship of God is necessarily a *way of life, an ethic*. Therefore the purer theology is, the greater its fruit in the *way of love.*" See B47 Untitled sermon on Romans 12:1, 5 (italics mine).

7. Colyer, *How to Read*, 287.

our sakes."[8] Torrance opts for the term *evangelical* Trinity because of his emphasis on the evangelical-soteriological nature of the Triune God, because there is no God who is not a redeeming God.

Torrance holds a more lenient position than, for example, Catherine LaCugna, a Roman Catholic trinitarian theologian who not only avoided using Rahner's terminologies but also criticized them for their several supposed weaknesses.[9] Whereas LaCugna considers the terms "economic" and "immanent" misleading altogether, Torrance considers them only insufficient. She is not only opposed to such terminologies, but is also prejudiced against talks regarding the Trinity *in se*. Gunton does not exaggerate when he judges that LaCugna deems ontology as the enemy in trinitarian theology.[10] LaCugna blames the Cappadocians for speculating on the intra-divine Trinity, leading the church to abstraction and the neglect of the practical aspects of the doctrine.[11] Torrance, by contrast, never considers ontology as the enemy, and argues that the historical manifestations of God as Father, Son, and Holy Spirit have evangelical significance only when they have "a transhistorical and transfinite reference": the Being of God himself.[12] Even though LaCugna proposes *oikonomia* and *theologia* to replace "economic" and "immanent," her interest lies only in the former. Bordering towards agnosticism, she writes: "There is neither an economic nor an immanent Trinity; there is only the *oikonomia* that is the concrete realization of the mystery of *theologia* in time, space, history and personality."[13] For Torrance, it is clear that LaCugna's position dangerously confuses the relation between the being and work of God.

Interestingly, LaCugna's position is a result of her zealous soteriological trinitarianism. That Torrance reached quite different conclusions lies in his richer theological method and realism. While LaCugna considers the discussion of the Trinity *ad intra* as an exercise in speculative abstraction, Torrance considers it as indispensable. This is portrayed

---

8. Torrance, *Christian Doctrine of God*, 7.

9. See Groppe, "LaCugna's Contribution to Trinitarian Theology," 730–63, for her list of these weaknesses.

10. Gunton, "Being and Person," 122. See also Mackintosh's responses to objections to the immanent Trinity in *Doctrine of the Person of Christ*, 515–18.

11. LaCugna, "The Trinity," 8. Jason E. Vickers sees in English Protestantism what LaCugna saw in the Cappadocians in the loss of the doctrine of the Trinity. He argues that a shift from *invocation* to intellectual *assent*, or from *doxology* to *epistemology*, is the culprit. See *Invocation and Assent*, 1, 19–20, and particularly chapters 2 and 3.

12. Torrance, *Christian Doctrine of God*, 6.

13. LaCugna, *God for Us*, 223.

in his insistent scientific epistemology, where the stratified structure of knowledge dictates that knowledge progresses from experiential, intuitive knowledge to knowledge of being *in se*.[14] In line with this, Torrance's proposed terminologies "evangelical Trinity" and "theological Trinity" are closely related to his scientific theology. The similarity in terminologies is just too weighty to dismiss. But if Torrance's trinitarian terminologies are consistent with, if not completely grounded in, his stratified epistemology, then one may wonder why Torrance opts to use "theological Trinity" rather than "meta-theological Trinity," which is human knowledge (and description) of God at its apex. Certainly, Torrance's use of *theological* Trinity is purposive, grounded in a worshipful apophatism. It may be that Torrance wishes to avoid possible misunderstandings if his terminologies were juxtaposed with Rahner's dictum "the economic Trinity is the immanent Trinity, and *vice versa*."[15]

The first part of this axiom, "the economic Trinity is the immanent Trinity," if interpreted to mean that knowledge of the Trinity *ad intra* is possible through the Trinity *ad extra*, resonates well with Torrance's epistemology, because it "has the effect of making the Economic Trinity the norm of all our thought and speech about God."[16] Unfortunately, Rahner's grounding of the economic Trinity in the immanent Trinity, and his making the economic Trinity universally immanent and available in human consciousness prior to God's free act of self-communication, make his understanding of the relationship between the economic Trinity and the immanent Trinity radically different from Torrance's. This is because Rahner's epistemology is primarily grounded in his theological anthropology, in which knowledge of God is an existential capacity of human-ness, while Torrance's is grounded in God's concrete self-revelation in Jesus Christ and the Holy Spirit.

> The element of abstraction which Rahner, in spite of his axiom of identity, has introduced between the Immanent and the Economic Trinity has to do only with a logical movement between sets of concepts taken from official declarations of the Church, and with an underlying desire on his part finally not to break with scholastic formulations of dogma. On the other hand, it must be recognized that Rahner poses the identity of the Economic

---

14. Torrance, *Transformation and Convergence*, 94–101; *Ground and Grammar of Theology*, 156–73; *Reality and Scientific Theology*, chapter 5; Yeung, "Being and Knowing," 167–70.

15. Rahner, *The Trinity*, 22.

16. Torrance, *Trinitarian Perspectives*, 78.

Trinity and the Immanent Trinity, first only as a methodological principle, as an instrument to reveal and organize understanding of the material presentation of God's self-communication, which in the course of his arguments results in the conviction that in reality there is only *one Trinity*, for the Economic Trinity is found to be the same thing as the Immanent Trinity.[17]

This demonstrates that although Torrance perceives Rahner as essentially "a prisoner of a scholastic metaphysical framework,"[18] he notes the profound implications of Rahner's aphorism when perceived from Athanasius's and Barth's perspectives of the oneness between God's being and act. "The Trinity *ad extra* and *ad intra* are identical because the self-communication of God to us in the Son and in the Spirit would not be a self-communication of God to us, if what God is for us in the Son and in the Spirit were not proper to God himself."[19] Thus, to say that the self-communication of God in his revelation and the self-giving of God in his being are one and the same is just another way of saying the economic Trinity and the immanent Trinity are one, and *vice versa*.

However, because Torrance agrees with Rahner's identification of the economic Trinity with the immanent Trinity, he has made himself vulnerable to the same critiques posed against Rahner's axiom on the problem of identicality. This may be posed as a question: what is the degree of the is-ness in the statement "the economic Trinity *is* the immanent Trinity, and *vice versa*"? In recent Protestant theology, this problem can be seen in the debate between Bruce McCormack and Paul Molnar, both followers of Barth, concerning the relationship between God's triunity and self-determination, or more particularly on the identicality of the *logos asarkos* and the *logos incarnandus*. For McCormack, God's economic triunity reveals that God is being-toward the economy of grace, and that God's self-determination to be God with us is logically prior to God's triunity.[20] There is no Triune God who is not always a redeeming God. But Molnar suggests that such a logical identification blurs the distinction between the

---

17. Torrance, *Trinitarian Perspectives*, 80; See Molnar, "God's Self-Communication in Christ," 288–320; and on how Rahner's epistemology influenced his trinitarian dictum, see Badcock, "Karl Rahner," in *The Trinity in a Pluralistic Age*, 143–54; and Molnar, *Theologian of the Trinity*, 67–70.

18. Torrance, *Trinitarian Perspectives*, 81.

19. Ibid., 80; "The Christ Who Loves Us," 20; Barth, *CD* I/1: 479.

20. McCormack, "Grace and Being," in *The Cambridge Companion to Karl Barth*, 92–110.

economic Trinity and immanent Trinity, following Torrance's argument.[21] Torrance argues that both creation and incarnation, God's activities *ad extra*, are *new* even to God.[22] Epistemologically and ontologically, complete and logical identifications grounded in necessitarian, projectionist, and mechanistic relations, and not encased within the boundaries of God's concrete act in the economy, whether they are analogies *from above* (logical deductions from the immanent Trinity imposed on the economic Trinity) or analogies *from below* (projectionist deductions from the economic Trinity imposed on the immanent Trinity), simply have no place in Torrance's theology. The only identicality that Torrance allows is based on soteriological-evangelical foundations, not metaphysical considerations.

Finally, Torrance's epistemological optimism must be balanced with his worshipful apophatism. Thus, although humanity is given the privilege to know God at the highest human level, the meta-theological level of knowledge, humanity could not claim that the meta-theological level is everything. To know God "does not mean that we can know *what* the being of God is, but it does mean that we are given knowledge of God that is directly and objectively grounded in his eternal being."[23] Torrance adds:

---

21. Molnar, "The Trinity, Election and God's Ontological Freedom," 297. Kevin Hector, who jumped into the middle of the debate, agrees with Molnar's argument, in "God's Triunity and Self-Determination," 246–61. Aaron T. Smith, on the other hand, agrees with McCormack's position in "God's Self-specification," 1–25. Robert Jenson seems to align himself with McCormack's position in his interpretation of the "for us" in the incarnation when he argues that "creaturely circumstances are the occasion of an event in the life of God," and "that creaturely circumstances are involved in what it means for God to be God" (Jenson, "For Us . . . He was Made Man," in *Nicene Christianity*, 77). Gunton appropriates the Athanasian distinction between the *being* and *will* of God in order to highlight the difference between economy and theology, in "Being and Person," 123. See Bruce D. Marshall's discussion of the problems of complete identification in "Trinity," in *The Blackwell Companion to the Modern Theology*, 193–97; and Schwöbel, *Trinitarian Theology Today*, 6–7.

22. Torrance, *Theology in Reconciliation*, 223, 224. Thus, although Jesus is identified as Creator, "this does not mean that somehow the humanity of Christ existed before the Incarnation," Torrance writes in "Pre-eminence of Christ," 54. This also marks the difference between Moltmann's panentheistic trinitarianism and cosmology and Torrance's doctrines of creation and the Trinity. See the discussion in Molnar, *Theologian of the Trinity*, 79–82, 84.

23. Torrance, *Trinitarian Faith*, 67; *Trinitarian Perspectives*, 37–38; *Christian Doctrine of God*, 26, 50, 73–75, 81, 110–11; *Theology in Reconstruction*, 30; "Implications of Oikonomia," 230, 235. The agreed statement between Reformed and Orthodox churches is guided by the conviction that "while the Trinity captures our minds, our minds cannot capture the Trinity," in *Trinitarian Perspectives*, 111. Elsewhere, Torrance writes that "the Trinity is more to be adored than expressed," in *Theological Dialogue* 1: 7; *Ground and Grammar of Theology*, 167; *Scottish Theology*, 83, 86. Torrance also

"Only God can comprehend himself, and only God can name himself . . . What God ultimately is in the essence of his eternal being we cannot know, but we are given by God to know *who* he is."[24] Two interrelated realities are evident in Torrance's view of the incomprehensibility of God. Just as knowledge of God is predicated in God's own act of self-revelation and humanity's ability as a recipient, so too is the incomprehensibility of God. In the former, God's being is essentially inexhaustible by human knowledge. Rahner's description of God as "Holy Mystery" perfectly fits Torrance's apophatism: God is "Mystery" "in the fact that we experience it as that which cannot be encompassed . . . and hence it cannot be defined."[25] In this sense, incomprehensibility is both a religious and an anthropological category: it is a statement *about* humanity as a limited creature incapable of exhausting the being of God in both comprehension and articulation.

Substantial versus Relational Trinity

One of Bruce Marshall's six theses characterizing recent trinitarian theology is an overall recourse, particularly among Protestant theologians, to the Eastern or Greek approach to the doctrine of the Trinity as a better alternative to the Western or Latin model.[26] Christoph Schwöbel agrees and explains the reasons for this phenomenon: (1) the recent encounter with Eastern Orthodoxy in the ecumenical context, (2) the interplay between the inspiration of Eastern trinitarianism and the self-critical examination of the history of Western trinitarianism, and (3) Eastern Orthodoxy's criticism of Western trinitarianism.[27] Deeply entrenched in this is the gen-

---

adds that there is a basic impropriety in all human language about God, in *Trinitarian Faith*, 43–44. Fiddes furthers Torrance's linguistic apophatism in arguing that images and symbolisms do not do justice to the personal and relational nature of God, in *Participating in God*, 11.

24. Torrance, "The Christian Apprehension of God the Father," 136; *Theology in Reconstruction*, 30; *Trinitarian Perspectives*, 42.

25. Rahner, *Foundations of Christian Faith*, 65. Torrance adds that "God will always be ultimately incomprehensible, but there shall be no mystery in God or His ways, except the most blessed mystery of feeling that the fullness of His nature still passes our comprehension," in B47 "And there was no more sea," 3.

26. Marshall, "Trinity," 190. The other five characteristic theses are: (1) "the Trinity is the most essential, basic, or distinctive Christian doctrine," (2) "the doctrine of the Trinity is the Christian way of identifying God," (3) "the 'economic' Trinity and the 'immanent' Trinity are the same," (4) "Father, Son and Spirit are genuine *persons*," and (5) "the doctrine of the Trinity should suffuse the whole of Christian theology."

27. Schwöbel, "The Renaissance of Trinitarian Theology," 3–6.

erally accepted difference (and even incompatibility) that Rahner made in *The Trinity* between Eastern and Western approaches to the doctrine of the Trinity. He suggested that the Western church—by looking mainly at Tertullian's famous formula "*tres personae, una substantia*," Augustine's psychological Trinity, and Aquinas's bifurcation and placing of *De Deo Uno* before a section on *De Deo Trino*—has approached the doctrine of the Trinity through the category of substance, or an abstract property that is shared by the Three Persons.[28] It is then argued that this substantialist perspective should be abandoned in favor of the Eastern-Cappadocian view of the priority of three *hypostases* in one *ousia*. As John R. Franke notes, at the heart of this proposal is "the apparent incompatibility of an eternal, essentially immutable God with the portrait in the biblical narratives of a God who has entered into loving relationship with creation."[29] Rather than perceiving God in the light of Aristotelian immutable substance, God should be seen as a relational God, a person-in-relation. Consequently, as LaCugna argues, "person, not substance, is the ultimate ontological category."[30]

Veli-Matti Kärkkäinen's comment that the "move to relationality is also in keeping with the dynamic understanding of reality and the human being" resonates with Torrance's views on the necessary relational change of frame of thought in theology, parallel to the changes in the structure of natural sciences from Newtonian to Einsteinian physics.[31] Is Torrance thus in agreement with the rejection of the Western substantialist approach in favor of the Eastern relational approach? No. Richard A. Muller's judgment that Torrance has driven a wedge between patristic trinitarian Orthodoxy and Western, Latin Christianity, is unfounded.[32] In

---

28. Rahner, *The Trinity*, 15–21, 45–46; Bloesch, *God the Almighty*, 167. See LaCugna's argument that Aquinas, contrary to Rahner's assessment, actually espoused a relational view of God, in "The Relational God," 647–63.

29. Franke, "God is Love," in *Trinitarian Theology for the Church*, 112.

30. LaCugna, *God for Us*, 14–15. See also LaCugna, "The Trinity," 6, in which she adds: "The doctrine of the Trinity is primarily a teaching about our salvation and about the God who saves us, not about essences." For a counterargument regarding the viability of a substantialist understanding of the Trinity, see Aliston, "Substance and Trinity," in *The Trinity*, 179–201; and for a different reading of Gregory of Nyssa's approach to the Trinity, see Coakley, "'Persons' in the 'Social' Doctrine of the Trinity," in *The Trinity*, 125–43.

31. Kärkkäinen, *The Trinity*, 387; quoted in Franke, "God is Love," 114. See also Torrance, *Theological and Natural Science*, 13, 15; *Preaching Christ Today*, 21–23, 42, 60; *Transformation and Convergence*, 70–73; "The Paschal Mystery of Christ," 10–11; "Theological Realism," 182–85; and "The Light of the World," 10–11.

32. See Muller, "The Barth Legacy," 684.

fact, as Mun-Chul Shin argues, Torrance holds a "dialogical" approach.[33] Torrance's comments in *Trinitarian Perspectives* on the agreed statement by the Reformed and Orthodox churches illustrates his stance:

> The Agreed Statement is also of considerable ecumenical significance in offering an approach to the doctrine of the Trinity which is neither from the Three Persons to the One Being of God, nor from the One Being of God to the Three Persons. As such, it cuts across the *mistaken views* of the doctrine of the Trinity according to which Western theology moves from the One Being of God to the Three Persons of the Father, Son and Holy Spirit, while Eastern theology moves from the Three Persons of the Father, the Son and the Holy Spirit to the One Being of God. It is preeminently a statement on the *dynamic Triunity* of God as Trinity in Unity and Unity in Trinity.[34]

Torrance is not trapped into choosing from two neatly categorized opposing options. In this aspect of his trinitarian theology he transcends all others. His trinitarian theology refuses to be categorized as either essentially substantialist or relationalist. His trinitarian discourse does not operate either from the unity detached from the distinction or from the distinction detached from the unity. In Torrance, it is not a matter of choosing between two *wrong* independent approaches, but developing or rediscovering an integrative approach that does justice to both biblical revelation and patristic theology, and that considers the best of both Eastern and Western theological traditions. Torrance, therefore, does not reject theologizing concerning the *ousia* of God *per se*. Theological ontology occupies a central place in Torrance's trinitarian theology, but it is not a speculative ontology grounded in *a priori* abstract philosophical categories imposed on theology, but an ontology that is primarily a *reflection* grounded in *a posteriori* evidences provided by God's own self-naming and self-revealing activity in space and time. In other words, Torrance's trinitarian ontology is both soteriological and relational.

---

33. See Shin, "A Dialogical Trinitarian Pneumatology." Roger Newell thinks otherwise. He writes that Torrance's "prescriptive style lacks a dialogical quality and this has at times rendered his thought inaccessible to the sceptic," in "Torrance, Thomas Forsyth," 550.

34. Torrance, *Trinitarian Perspectives*, 113–14 (italics mine).

The Personal Triune God

Like Zizioulas and Gunton, Torrance believes that a significant contribution of the church fathers is the concept of "person" and its concomitant implication that being is essentially personal-relational.[35] This patristic contribution developed slowly. The Cappadocians's identification of *hypostasis* with *prosopon* to refer to a self-identifying personal being or reality paved the way for *hypostasis* to be redefined to become "suitable for theological speech expressing the objective, identifiable self-manifestations of God as Father, Son and Holy Spirit."[36] Three things are noteworthy. First, Torrance argues that it is the concrete self-evidencing manifestation of the Triune God as Father, Son, and Holy Spirit that required the early theologians to question and abandon the Greek static view of God. Secondly, an acknowledgment of God's Triunity required redefinition of terms, so that *ousia* and *hypostasis*, when applied to God, could no longer be framed without regarding them as essentially relational terms. Thirdly, this redefinition of *old terms* resulted in the development of the *new concept* of personhood. Subsequently, in Christian theology, ontology and relationality could no longer be separated. Unlike Greek tragedy, Christian theology could no longer view relationality or personhood as a secondary quality attachable to and detachable from primordial nature.[37] To be and to-be-in-relation are the same. Appropriating his two favorite patristic terms, *homoousios* and *perichoresis*, Torrance writes:

> It was in connection with this refined concept of *perichoresis* in its employment to speak of the intra-trinitarian relations in God, that Christian theology developed what I have long called its *onto-relational* concept of the divine Persons, or an understanding of the three divine Persons in the One God in which the ontic relations between them belong to what they essentially are in themselves in their distinctive *hypostases*. Along with this there developed out of the doctrine of the Trinity the new

---

35. Zizioulas, *Being as Communion*, 18, chapters 1 and 2; Gunton, *Father, Son, and Holy Spirit*, 13–15.

36. Torrance, *Divine Meaning*, 208–9.

37. See Zizioulas's discussion in *Being as Communion*, 27–38. Harriet A. Harris disagrees from sociological, cultural, and psychological perspectives, in "Should We Say that Personhood is Relational?," 214–34. Even here, Torrance's scientific theology surfaces. For him, Harris's negative response to a theological and trinitarian ground for understanding personhood exhibits what he calls "an analytical dissection of human social relations" by an "imposition of artificial frameworks designed for certain pragmatic and political ends." See B39 "Violence in Society," 2.

concept of person, unknown in human thought until then, according to which the relations between persons belong to what persons are.[38]

Put simply, relation possesses an ontic value. Torrance admits that his concept of persons as "substantive relations" owes much to Gregory Nazianzen's alternative to the concept of *tropos hyparxeos* proposed by the other Cappadocians. Torrance asserts that the relations among the divine persons are not just modes of existence but "hypostatic interrelations which belong intrinsically to what Father, Son, and Holy Spirit are coinherently in themselves and in their mutual objective relations with and for one another."[39] In short, the relations among the persons are as substantial as they are in themselves as persons. In this area, Torrance deviates from Barth and Rahner, who both refused to use the term "person" in their trinitarian discourses. Also, this is where Alan Torrance fills in Torrance's unexpressed critique of Barth's mistaken preference for *Seinsweise* over the more theologically robust *person*.[40] Moreover, Torrance's use of *perichoresis* in his understanding of personhood in God also explains his difference from Zizioulas, who anchored his understanding of person only in the person of the Father as the *Arche* and *Aitia* of the Son and the Holy Spirit.[41] Zizioulas and other Orthodox theologians defend Basil's view of the *Monarchia* of the Father on the ground that it refers to the fact that the source of divineness is a personal one, or that the ground of the personhood of God is in a person, the person of the Father. Torrance's alternative follows Gregory of Nazianzus, who argued for the indivisibility of the *Monas* from the *Trias*, and *vice versa*. Molnar encapsulates Torrance's argument: "The *homoousion, perichoresis,* and the *onto-relational* concept

---

38. Torrance, *Christian Doctrine of God,* 102-3; *Trinitarian Perspectives,* 99; *Reality and Scientific Theology,* 171-78. Torrance understands God's being as self-identifying personal being, i.e. that personhood is a characteristic of his inner being and not derived from a necessary relation to the world.

39. Torrance, *Christian Doctrine of God,* 157. See particularly *Ground and Grammar of Theology,* 172-78, on the help of *perichoresis* in understanding the essential Trinity.

40. Barth, *CD* I/1, esp. chapter 2: section 9; and Rahner, *The Trinity,* 73-76, 103-15; Torrance, *Persons in Communion,* 121, 214-301; and also Hart, *Regarding Karl Barth,* 100-116. See Dennis W. Jowers's presentation of what is at stake in Barth's decision in "The Reproach of Modalism," 231-46.

41. Torrance, *Trinitarian Faith,* 317-18. See Paul M. Collins' discussion of the difficulties and differences of approaches to the concept of triune personhood in *Trinitarian Theology West and East,* 107-61.

of persons function together with the result that God is understood as fully three distinct persons in communion with one another within the eternal Godhead."[42]

Being as Communion

One of the immediate implications of understanding God as a relational being is the realization that communion is what makes being "be." Christian discussion of God's being cannot proceed *via* speculating from a neutral impersonal essence, but *via* an acknowledgment of dynamic personal being, "for God is who he is in the act of his revelation, and his act is what it is in his Being."[43] The doctrine of the Trinity cannot be an addendum to the doctrine of God; rather, the doctrine of the Trinity *is* the doctrine of God. In God, being and communion, *Ousia* and *Koinonia*, are one and the same.

> The Being of God is to be understood, therefore, as living and dynamic Being, fellowship-creating or communion-constituting Being, but if it is communion-constituting Being toward us it is surely to be understood also as ever-living, ever-dynamic *Communion* in the Godhead. By his very Nature he is a Communion in himself, which is the ground in the Being of God for his communion with his people.[44]

In the light of the above quotation, Collins is clearly mistaken in saying that Torrance understands the personhood of the Godhead in terms of an Absolute Subjectivity with its roots from Augustine.[45] Also, Torrance cannot be subject to LaCugna's critique of theologians who neglect the practical import of the Trinity by focusing entirely on the being *in se* of God, because Torrance's doctrine of God's being is not a neutral

---

42. Molnar, *Theologian of the Trinity*, 63. See also Torrance, *Theological Dialogue* 1: 156; and *Trinitarian Faith*, 319.

43. Torrance, *Christian Doctrine of God*, 4, 117. Related here is Torrance's appreciation of Athanasius's preference in using verbs rather than nouns in speaking of God, whose nature is dynamic.

44. Torrance, *Christian Doctrine of God*, 124, 104, 133. Thus, although Torrance is critical of Basil in several aspects of his theology, he favors Basil's conception of the Trinity as *koinonia*. See Basil, *On the Holy Spirit*, 37–47; in *Christian Doctrine of God*, 126. See also Zizioulas, *Being as Communion*, 17. "Community," Boff says, "is the deepest and most fundamental reality that exists," in *Holy Trinity*, 4.

45. Collins, *Trinitarian Theology West and East*, 125.

Communion with the Triune God

uninvolved communion, but is rather a being for others.[46] The divine *ousia* is also *parousia*, God's communing presence with others. "The Being of God," Torrance writes, "known only in the fellowship created through his personal self-naming, self-affirming and self-giving to his people, is the living dynamic Being of God's redeeming presence *to* them, *with* them and *for* them."[47] Thus, the being of God should not be understood simply in terms of a self-grounded being, but as "*the Being of God for others* with whom he seeks and creates fellowship."[48]

One of the characteristic features of Torrance's theology is his purposive comparative approach, which highlights the distinctiveness of Christian, trinitarian, and scientific ways of thinking, in contrast to strictly philosophical, cultural, and dualist points of view. It is therefore surprising that he does not fully elaborate, given his deep knowledge of early Greek philosophy (as his discussion and critique of Platonic and Stoic views of space reveal),[49] some aspects of the profound change in Christian theology from the Greek mindset, when personhood and relationality were given an elevated status equal to that of being.[50] For this, we should turn to Zizioulas's writings. In *Being as Communion*, Zizioulas argues that in Greek ontology, nature, as a neutral essence, is given priority. In the relationship between God and the world, for instance, one possesses a *hypostasis* given by the gods, which is subject to fate (or the will of the gods). In this deterministic worldview, personality and personhood are like masks (*prosopon*) worn by an individual, but these do not constitute the being or *hypostasis* of the person. Personhood and relationality are extrinsic elements attachable to and detachable from one's given nature, and they possess no ontological content. While Zizioulas admits, following Basil, that this might be the case for created beings (grounded in creation *ex nihilo*), this cannot be made into a metaphysical principle to be applied to the being of God. Rather, the fact that God exists simultaneously as

---

46. Torrance, *Christian Doctrine of God*, 133. "The doctrine of the Trinity teaches us that the Godhead is essentially a fellowship of persons—it speaks of Grace and love and communion," in B46 "The Trinity," 1.

47. Torrance, *Christian Doctrine of God*, 123.

48. Ibid. "Unless we begin with God-as-God-is-toward-us and think first of all in terms of God in relation to us and we in relation to God," Toon writes, "we shall miss the biblical emphasis upon the Holy Trinity," in *Our Triune God*, 234.

49. Torrance, *Space, Time, and Incarnation*, 4–10; *Divine Meaning*, chapter 9.

50. In Torrance's defence, Molnar argues that Torrance's understanding of personhood derives primarily from his view of Christ as the personalizing person and his understanding of the Father, Son, and Holy Spirit in perichoretic relations rather than from an analysis of Greek culture and philosophy. See *Theologian of the Trinity*, 348.

the One in Three and Three in One means that personhood should be given equal ontological primacy. In God, it is neither being/nature preceding persons nor persons preceding being/nature. Rather, being/nature is person-in-relation and *vice versa*. In short, being is communion.[51] Even Torrance, who is usually critical of Zizioulas's preference for Basil and Gregory Nyssen over Gregory Nazianzen and Athanasius in his trinitarian formulation, acknowledges Zizioulas's and other modern Orthodox theologians's weighty contribution to the centrality of thinking of God's being as a personal and communal being.[52]

Perichoresis and Personhood

According to Torrance, the term *perichoresis* was first used "in a verbal form" by Gregory of Nazianzus as a christological device to express the hypostatic union. As trinitarian debates continued, the term came to refer to "the way in which the three divine persons mutually dwell in one another and coinhere or inexist in one another while nevertheless remaining other than one another and distinct from one another."[53] Refined further, *perichoresis* means the "complete containing and interpenetration of the three divine persons—Father, Son and Holy Spirit—in one God."[54] *Perichoresis*, therefore, carries an intensely personal meaning. As Bevan concludes, "The true nature of personal being is revealed to us in the *perichoretic* relations of the Trinity as a communion of persons."[55] Furthermore, *peri-*

---

51. See Zizioulas's discussion in *Being as Communion*, 27–64; and in "The Doctrine of the Holy Trinity," in *Trinitarian Theology Today*, 44–60; Melissaris, "The Challenge of Patristic Ontology," 467–90; and also Cumin, "Looking for Personal Space in Zizioulas," 356–70. Lucia Turcescu, however, thinks that Zizioulas misreads the Cappadocians and that Zizioulas's main sources are actually from modern philosophy and theology, in "'Person' versus 'Individual,'" 527–39; and see Aristotle Papanikolaou's response to Turcescu in "Is John Zizioulas an Existentialist in Disguise?," 601–7.

52. See especially Torrance, *Trinitarian Perspectives*, 98 footnote 48. Nevertheless, as Gunton remarks, it is unfortunate that it is only this aspect in Zizioulas's theology that Torrance engages with, and that he did not engage with Zizioulas's work more positively than he did do. See Gunton, "Being and Person," 131. Torrance's response to Gunton gives a hint as to why Torrance does not engage with Zizioulas, particularly on the doctrine of the Trinity. Torrance writes that Greek Orthodox theologians themselves disagree with Zizioulas "in spite of some of his very fine theological works." See "Thomas Torrance Responds," 314.

53. Torrance, *Christian Doctrine of God*, 102. See also Moltmann, "Perichoresis," 111–15, for a short history of the term.

54. Torrance, *Christian Doctrine of God*, 102.

55. Bevan, "The Person of Christ," 112.

choresis also highlights the real enhypostatic relations in the Triune God so that personal distinctions are acknowledged and retained. Torrance writes: "While the three Divine Persons differ from one another precisely as Father, Son and Holy Spirit, they are nevertheless conjoined in all their distinctiveness, for the entire and undivided Godhead resides in each Person, and each Person dwells in or inheres in the Other; so that the whole of one Person is imaged in the whole of the Other."[56] As such, *perichoresis* safeguards against the tendency towards a generic view of *ousia*, which can result in a tautological view of the persons and a partitive view of distinctions. Following Athanasius, coinherent relations within the one being of God imply "not merely a linking of intercommunication of the distinctive properties of the three divine Persons but a completely mutual indwelling in which each Person, while remaining what he is by himself as Father, Son and Holy Spirit, is wholly in the others as the others are wholly in him."[57] In the economy of salvation, the doctrine of appropriation, Eberhard Jüngel stresses, provides balance to the doctrine of perichoresis.[58]

Finally, *perichoresis* not only expresses the relational and personal being of the Triune God, but also implies the essential dynamism and activism of the Triune God. God's self-revelation in the world is grounded in God's own and primordial essential dynamic being. Activity and movement are not something external and only economic to God. The dynamism of the *enousios energeia* is grounded in the dynamic *enousios logos*. Perichoresis thus "gives expression to the dynamic nature of the consubstantial Communion between the three Persons," which should be interpreted "in an intensely personal way, not in a static, but in a dynamic yet ontological way, as the movement of Communion which the Triune God ever is within himself."[59] Thus, in contrast to Aristotle's God as the "Unmoved Mover," the biblical God is a dynamic active being. Life, Movement, and activity are intrinsic to the very being of God.[60]

---

56. Torrance, *Theological Dialogue* 2: xv; *Reality and Scientific Theology*, 168.
57. Torrance, *Trinitarian Faith*, 305.
58. Jüngel, *God's Being Is in Becoming*, xv.
59. Torrance, *Trinitarian Perspectives*, 141.
60. Torrance, *Christian Doctrine of God*, 4–8, 149–55; *Divine Meaning*, 200; *Trinitarian Perspectives*, 105. See also Molnar, *Theologian of the Trinity*, 51; and Nicole, "The Meaning of the Trinity," in *One God in Trinity*, 6–7.

Trinity-conditioned Soteriology

Colyer's statement that the Trinity is "the ultimate focus of Torrance's theology" appears to contradict Torrance's 1959 statement that his "main theological work or interest" is "in the field of Christology and Soteriology."[61] Colyer's assessment, however, is based on Torrance's later trinitarian writings. In an interview with Michael Bauman in 1990, Torrance admits that of the [many] books he had published, he was "most pleased with *The Trinitarian Faith* (1988)."[62] From merely a retrospective view, it appears that Torrance's main interests have shifted from Christology and soteriology to the doctrine of the Trinity, but did they? As Fred Sanders notes, the word "Trinity" encompasses an "extraordinary range of dogmatic material," and even though Christology and Pneumatology are the obvious immediate subjects, the doctrines of revelation and salvation soon follow.[63] Thus, Torrance's trinitarian theology did not abandon Christology and soteriology, but subsumed these fields under the doctrine of the Trinity. And, conversely, even from a chronological perspective, Torrance's earlier fascination with Christology and soteriology could only lead to the doctrine of the Trinity. This double movement is what Torrance refers to as the circular character of Christian theology.[64]

If the word "Trinity" is a comprehensive term, so is the word "salvation." "Salvation," Fiddes writes, "is a concept of the widest scope."[65] This is especially the case in recent theological formulations, where an integrative frame of thought is prevalent, i.e., that doctrines are treated not as isolated but intertwined components. To a certain degree, therefore, firstly, to seek to integrate two of the most encompassing doctrines in Christian theology, Trinity and salvation, is an ambitious project. The only major parameter that delimits the study is that the discussions revolve primarily around Torrance's theology and not the whole of the Christian theological tradition. Secondly, in a sense, the phrase "trinitarian soteriology" is redundant, in that there should be no doctrine of the Trinity which is not also a doctrine of soteriology. As Sanders asserts, "the task of the doctrine of the Trinity is to describe the connection between God and the economy

---

61. Colyer, "Thomas F. Torrance," 464; Torrance, *Order and Disorder*, 7.

62. Bauman, "Thomas F. Torrance," 117.

63. Sanders, "The Trinity," in *the Oxford Handbook of Systematic Theology*, 35. See also Torrance, *Theological Dialogue* 2: 80–82.

64. Torrance, *Christian Doctrine of God*, 27–28.

65. Fiddes, "Salvation," 176.

of salvation,"[66] or as Jenson writes, the Trinity has to do with "the simplest mysteries: that we may in God's own Spirit approach him as Father, because we do so with the man Jesus."[67] Nevertheless, the phrase is used here for emphatic purposes, and also to underline our attempt to make explicit the inseparable connection between two often separated aspects in Christian theology.

Atonement and the Trinity

Emphasized throughout this book is the claim that Torrance's soteriology is trinitarian. Unlike the traditional models of atonement, which seem to be interested only in the crucified Christ and the efficient benefits, Torrance's incarnational approach inquires into ontological aspects that are overshadowed by mere causal and logical considerations. Although traditional models of atonement appear to value the necessity of Jesus Christ being fully God in order for redemption to be possible, their statements are not robustly trinitarian. At best, these models's view of Jesus Christ as God is unqualifiedly monotheistic and primarily apologetic. Torrance, by contrast, grounds and views the deity of Jesus Christ not in Jesus's relation to a generic term "God," but in Jesus's relation to the persons of the Father and the Holy Spirit. "Since Jesus Christ the only-begotten Son of God is of one being with the Father, and since he is God and man inseparably united in his incarnate Person, then, like the incarnation, the atoning work of the incarnate Son falls within the inner life of the Holy Trinity."[68]

While it is perhaps inevitable for a theologian of the Trinity to think of salvation trinitarianly, there are reasons why Torrance is emphatic about perceiving salvation in terms of the Triune God at work in the economy. Historically and ecclesially, Torrance is reacting against some disturbing tenets prevalent in his own theological tradition. Torrance is an outspoken critic of the fascination of federal Calvinists with the benefits of the death of Jesus Christ, understood in a mechanistic-logical manner.[69] Kevin Kennedy identifies these Calvin interpreters as particularists

66. Sanders, "The Trinity," 35; Thompson, *Modern Trinitarian Perspectives*, 21–25. Fiddes writes: "The Trinity will always be about humankind, including us within the richness of the divine life," in "The Atonement and the Trinity," in *The Forgotten Trinity* 3: 120.

67. Jenson, *The Triune Identity*, 187.

68. Torrance, *Mediation of Christ*, 112.

69. This critique flows throughout his book *Scottish Theology*. See also Torrance, "The Incarnation and 'Limited Atonement,'" 32–40; "The Covenant Concept of Scottish

who espouse an *ex opere operato* view of salvation that ultimately leads to limited atonement.[70] At the root of this view, according to Torrance, is a logical one-to-one mechanistic view of the relationship between what Jesus Christ accomplished and what humanity receives (i.e., because not everyone is saved, Jesus Christ died only for the elect) without consideration of the dynamic nature of the triune salvific economy (i.e., Jesus Christ is elected by the Father in the Holy Spirit for the world). Thus, one effect of an explicit trinitarian view of atonement is that the dynamic nature of redemption is highlighted. Instead of perceiving atonement primarily in terms of a transaction, it is perceived as a dynamic movement that "begins with the Father, extends through the Son and reaches its fulfilment in the Holy Spirit," so that humanity through the incarnate Son in the Holy Spirit may become sons and daughters of the Father.[71]

The effects of a robust trinitarian view of atonement could be portrayed in Torrance's view of the suffering of Jesus Christ on the cross. Although distinctions should be made concerning the agencies of the persons of the Triune God in the economy of salvation (grounded in their distinct hypostases as Father, Son, and Holy Spirit), the oneness in being and the perichoretic relations in the Triune God highlight the interpenetration in both God's being and act. As such, although it is not the Father who is crucified, the Father suffers with the Son in the Son's agony on the cross. Torrance even writes that the "passion of the Father" and "the passion of the Lord Jesus Christ" "is a passion in which the Holy Spirit shares equally."[72] Furthermore, if Jesus is not the true Son of the Father, Molnar writes, "his death could easily be construed as immoral,"[73] for it would indeed portray a sadist Father leaving a masochist Son to suffer and die. If such were the case, the critique of liberation and feminist theologians of an immoral Father would be justified. Torrance finds no problem with the idea that Christ suffered on the cross, but views it not in terms of the Father punishing the Son. Rather, he understands the cross in terms of

---

Theology," 225–43; "Calvin and Puritanism in England and Scotland," 264–86; "Covenant or Contract?," 51–76; and Cass, *Christ Condemned in the Flesh*, chapter 2, for an excellent elaboration.

70. Kennedy, *Union with Christ*, 40, 106, 151.

71. Torrance, *Theological Dialogue* 2: 112; Torrance, *Worship, Community, and the Triune God of Grace*, 32.

72. Torrance, *Christian Doctrine of God*, 252–53.

73. Molnar, "The Centrality of the Trinity," 92. Elsewhere, Torrance writes that the cross destroys our faith in God if we only see there the story of a human being and not the Son of God, in B46 "He loves us and gave himself for us," 1–4.

what took place in Jesus Christ as the incarnate Son of God the Father, in which obediently and joyfully, he took upon himself, in the power of the Holy Spirit, the predicament of humanity.[74] Torrance even asserts that because the atonement is a "*joint act* of Christ and God, . . . the blood of Christ shed on the Cross could be spoken of as 'the blood of God.'"[75]

Participation in the Life and Love of God

For Torrance, salvation is *grounded in* the Communing and Communal being of the Triune God, whose perfection and fullness of love "will not be confined within the Godhead but freely and lovingly moves outward toward others whom God creates for fellowship with himself so that they may share with him the very Communion of Love which is his own divine Life and Being."[76] Salvation is also the *work of* the Triune God. Salvation is not only willed and initiated by the Triune God, but is also enacted and accomplished *pro nobis* by the persons of the Triune God in their Unity-in-Distinction and Distinction-in-Unity. Finally, salvation is *oriented toward* the Triune God, because the final goal of salvation is ultimately communion with the Triune God.[77] Among Torrance's favorite terms in depicting our at-one-ment with God are our "sharing," "joining," and "participation" in the inner life and love of the Triune God. These are relational terms, and there is no question that Torrance's soteriology is relational. The phrase "relational soteriology," however, is not strong enough to convey Torrance's thoughts. Rather, the alternative "participation soteriology" is a

---

74. See Torrance, *Scottish Theology*, 18, 301–3; and Torrance, "Contribution of McLeod Campbell," particularly 304 on his critique of federal theology, which for him inverts the biblical order of the relationship between forgiveness and atonement, or love and satisfaction.

75. Torrance, *Scottish Theology*, 171. In *Christian Doctrine of God*, 252, Torrance adds: "The passion of Christ considered apart from the passion of the Father would be no more than the noblest martyrdom for it would be empty of ultimate divine validity." Where he beautifully pictures the humanity and divinity of Jesus Christ on the cross, see B42 "The Well at Bethlehem," 5, where he writes: "There is only One who has broken through the ranks of evil . . . all the hosts of the Philistines are against Him . . . who is this who comes from Bethlehem . . . look there are stains upon his garments—there is blood upon His brow, and a wound in His side—but in His hand there is a Cup of God's Salvation—what a shambles he had to go through in order to bring it to us! Surely if any cup had the life of a Man in it, it is this one—but more than that. This has the blood of God in it."

76. Torrance, *Christian Doctrine of God*, 6; *Trinitarian Faith*, 90–91.

77. Habets, *Theosis*, 101.

better choice.[78] It must be noted that participation theology is not new in the history of the Christian faith. Early and contemporary theologies from both Catholic and Protestant traditions have their representatives to name. There are three theological schools in particular that deserve mentioning.

The first of these is a movement within Roman Catholicism, particularly Thomism. There are five principal schools of modern Thomism: (1) modern defenders of the commentators, (2) existential Thomism, (3) participation Thomism, (4) transcendental Thomism, and (5) Thomistic linguistic analyses. The third, which is our only concern at this point, was initiated by Cornelio Fabro and Louis Bertrand Geiger, in which Aquinas's metaphysics are withdrawn from the essentialism of Aristotle and interpreted using neo-Platonic emanationism instead.[79] Cosmologically, this means that everything is nothing other than a derivation or emanation from God. The problem is that the emanation process did not arise out of God's volitional willing, but just involuntarily flowed out of God's brimful being. Consequently, because the existence of all beings-other-than-God come from the very being of God, a certain amount of God's *esse* is transferred to all other degrees of reality.[80] One would therefore understand Aquinas's interrelated views on the relationship between nature and grace, *analogia entis*, *vestigia Dei*, and natural theology, in which in all four, a necessary and unbreakable proportionality between God's *esse* and creaturely *esse* is presupposed. To exist is, by default, to possess a certain degree of divine *esse*. By the sheer act of existing, humanity, whether consciously or unconsciously, and wilfully or unwilfully, are ontologically related to God. This is reinforced by the fact that existence is dependent upon God, and that in itself, created nature is nothing. Echoing Augustine, whose Platonic indebtedness is well-recognized, "matter participates in something belonging to the ideal world, otherwise it would

---

78. Webster even suggests that Torrance presents theology "in a manner not wholly dissimilar from the way in which it is presented in contemporary theologies of participation," in "T. F. Torrance," 370.

79. Their discovery instigated acrimonious conflicts over Aquinas's Aristotelianism. Other than transcendental Thomism, which regards Aristotle's philosophy as dominant in Aquinas's thoughts, the prevailing view now is that Aquinas's thoughts are best interpreted as neo-Platonic. See the informative study by Hankeys, "Denys and Aquinas," 139–84. For an appreciation and argument for the appropriation of Aristotelian metaphysics in theology, particularly with the doctrine of the Trinity, see Aliston, "Substance and Trinity," in *The Trinity*, 179–201.

80. Along with participation Thomism, this position was also advocated by the existential Thomist and Anglican theologian Eric Mascall. See Kerr, *After Aquinas*, 145–47.

not be matter."[81] Overall, participation in God is understood primarily in mechanical ontological-substantival terms.

While the approach of this participation theology is noteworthy, in that it articulates the being of created realities in terms of the being of God, it has several disagreeable overtones. First, although it is an attempt to overthrow Aristotle in Aquinas's thoughts, the substantive aspect of Aristotle's metaphysics still remains, so that emphasis is still given to substantial participation. This view leads to a serious misunderstanding of *theosis*. Secondly, in connection to the first, the nature-grace relationship it advocates leads to panentheism with its emphasis on immanence, which consequently overlooks the wholly otherness of God.[82] In comparison, although Torrance also advocates the real presence of God in the world, he does not view it as an infused involuntary presence, but as a *parousia* grounded in God's free and gracious act of self-communication. And finally, because ontological participation is a presupposed given, whether creatures will it or not, there is also the tendency to undervalue human created and contingent autonomy. This has a further implication in soteriology. With this approach, the eschatological options are either universalism, when everything returns back to God, or annihilationism, when some existents are reduced to absolute nothingness, *nihil absolutum*.

The second participation model emerged out of Cambridge in the late 1980s in the movement known as Radical Orthodoxy, whose major proponents pronounced that their central framework is "*participation* as developed by Plato and reworked by Christianity."[83] James K. A. Smith outrightly questions whether their foundation is really Platonic, instead of neo-Platonic.[84] Smith's critique is well grounded, for Radical Orthodoxy owes its participation theology to Aquinas's metaphysics.[85] John Milbank, probably the first proponent of the movement, encapsulates their starting

---

81. Augustine, *Ver. rel.* 11.21; cited in Hanby, *Augustine and Modernity*, 87.

82. This panentheistic tendency is particularly most evident in Buxton's *The Trinity, Creation, and Pastoral Ministry*. Molnar argues that there is no panentheism in Torrance, in *Theologian of the Trinity*, 139.

83. Milbank, *Radical Orthodoxy*, 3.

84. Smith, *Introducing Radical Orthodoxy*, 198.

85. Having said this, although Thomistic participation is evident in the whole of Radical Orthodoxy's participation theology, there are significant traces of influence from Anglican theology as well, as advocated by seventeenth-century theologian Richard Hooker and the Cambridge Platonists, particularly on John Milbank. See J. Todd Billings's arguments in "John Milbank's Theology of the 'Gift,'" 93. On Anglican participation theology, see Newey, "The Form of Reason," 1–26; and Allchin, *Participation in God* (1988).

point: "Once upon a time, there was no secular."[86] In response to the supposed secularization of the world, Radical Orthodoxy seeks to re-integrate the metaphysical to the physical in their understanding of theology and reality. This is their understanding of participation, which "refuses any reserve of created territory, while allowing finite things their own integrity" and that "every discipline must be framed by a theological perspective; otherwise these disciplines will define a zone apart from God, grounded literally in nothing."[87] Particularly, they blame John Duns Scotus's teaching on the univocity of being, where being is given an autonomous existence and without necessary dependence upon being, leading to modern secularization. "In opposition to the ontology of immanence produced by the shift to the univocity of being," Smith analyzes, "RO proposes a participatory ontology that understands transcendence as an essential feature of material reality."[88] This participatory ontology is in turn the supposed "antidote to both nihilism and fundamental dualism."[89] Moreover, with a participatory hermeneutic, instead of understanding being as being-towards-death (which Rahner critiques in Heidegger's philosophy as *ontochronistic*), being is understood to be being-toward-perfection.[90]

Radical Orthodoxy's ambitious project to re-integrate the metaphysical in every aspect of human life, not only in theology and in the life of the church, but also in politics, economics, and other areas of society, is revolutionary. Their pronounced *telos* for humanity and social renewal explicated in terms of "divine friendship" that is grounded on an ontology of peace is also enticing.[91] Nevertheless, however agreeable the objective

---

86. Milbank, *Theology and Social Theory*, 9. This publication is identified as the birth of the Radical Orthodoxy movement.

87. Milbank, *Radical Orthodoxy*, 3.

88. Smith, *Introducing Radical Orthodoxy*, 185. Catherine Pickstock is the proponent of Radical Orthodoxy who traced this back to Scotus. See her book *After Writing*, 122–23.

89. Smith, *Introducing Radical Orthodoxy*, 189.

90. Karl Rahner defines *ontochrony* as "a science showing that the meaning of all being as such and the meaning of being in the absolute, is *nothingness*," in "The Concept of Existential Philosophy in Heidegger," 136. Levering, "Participation and Exegesis," 587–601. Significantly interesting is Levering's analysis of Aquinas's participatory exegesis of John 3:27–36, which is very trinitarian and christocentric, particularly his emphasis on the humanity of Jesus Christ in pages 592–97.

91. See particularly Moss, "Friendship," in *Radical Orthodoxy*, 127–42. An ontology of peace is the alternative that Radical Orthodoxy seeks to establish against a "differential ontology" or "an ontology of violence" which Milbank finds in Jacques Derrida, Gilles Deleuze, and Michael Foucault, stemming from the influence of Friedrich Nietzsche in their philosophies (see Milbank, *Theology and Social Theory*,

of the movement is, their particular method or system of participation is grounded upon theologically questionable foundations. Their recourse to neo-Platonic and Thomist ontology comes among the first series of their grave errors, as they then become vulnerable to the similar critiques posed above against participation Thomism.

The third participation model can be found in recent Reformed studies, where scholars are rediscovering a distinct participation theology in Calvin. In an interesting article, J. Todd Billings makes the connection, albeit comparatively, between Milbank and Calvin on the doctrine of participation, with particular attention to the former's critique of the latter's understanding of grace in the light of Milbank's understanding of "gift." Billings concludes that Milbank's critique is unfounded, especially that the concept of "gift" (which Milbank borrows from Marcel Mauss, Jacques Derrida, and Jean-Luc Marion) is foreign to Calvin. In fact, Milbank is anachronistically imposing categories on Calvin that Calvin himself did not think of. Nevertheless, he adds that amidst their differences, "Calvin has much in common with Milbank's concerns in developing a theology of 'participation as deification.'"[92] The same argument is forwarded by Carl Mosser, who asserts that evidences (which unfortunately he does not provide) are noticeable in the language and imageries that Calvin used in his soteriology, eschatology, and trinitarianism.[93]

Nevertheless, although both Billings's and Mosser's interpretation of Calvin are stimulating, they are wrong. Jonathan Slater was right when he asserts that Calvin's understanding of participation should not be equated with deification or *theosis*. Slater is definitely sensitive about what "deification" connotes, especially if it is interpreted in the light of the Petrine phrase "partakers of the divine nature" (2 Pet 1:4, NKJV). In Calvin's theology, he stresses, what is dominant is not the idea of participation in the divine nature, but of participation in the humanity of Jesus Christ. He writes:

278–325). According to Milbank, the problem with a differential ontology is that differences are construed as competing and thus ultimately oppositional. In short, being ultimately leads to war. To counter this myth of differential ontology, says Milbank, "one cannot resuscitate liberal humanism, but one can try to put forward an alternative mythos, equally unfounded, but nonetheless embodying an ontology of peace, which conceived differences as analogically related, rather than equivocally at variance" (Milbank, *Theology and Social Theory*, 279).

92. Billings, "John Milbank's Theology of the 'Gift,'" 97.
93. Mosser, "The Greatest Possible Blessing," 36–57.

> Although Calvin speaks of Christ uniting us to God, it is not clear that our unity with God involves a sharing in the divine nature, or that Christ performed this work according to his divinity. Without in any way denying that it is the eternal Son who is our mediator, Calvin's emphasis is on the humanity of the mediator. It is as our substitute, which Christ is according to his human nature, that we are included in Christ.[94]

This emphasis on the humanity of Jesus Christ is explicit in Calvin's *Institutes*. Discussing the work of the Mediator "to restore us to God's grace as to make of the children of men, children of God," Calvin writes:

> Who would have done this had not the self-same Son of God become the Son of man, and had not so taken what was ours as to impart what was his to us, and to make what was his nature ours by grace? Therefore, relying on this pledge, we trust that we are sons of God, for God's natural Son fashioned for himself a body from our body, flesh from our flesh, bones from our bones, that he might be one with us. Ungrudgingly he took our nature upon himself to impart to us what was his, and to become both Son of God and Son of man in common with us.[95]

The emphasis on union with the substitutionary work of the humanity of Christ, and our participation in the same humanity, is what Trevor Hart calls "the twin aspects of redemption in Christ."[96] Hart even argues that union with Christ and participation in him is the central theme of Calvin's theology.[97]

Julie Canlis observes that although participation theology is indubitably present in Calvin's theology, Reformed theology in general has been hesitant to speak about it because of Calvin's own negative reaction to the theology of participation taught by his contemporary, the Lutheran theologian Andreas Osiander.[98] Osiander's participation theology is a product of his critique of and alternative to Reformation theology's stress on the

94. Slater, "Salvation as Participation," 43.

95. Calvin, *Institutes* II.12.2.

96. Hart, "Humankind in Christ," 82.

97. Ibid., 81. Disagreements with such notions of a central theme in Calvin, particularly on the sovereignty of God, are becoming more and more the sentiment of modern scholarship. See Billings, "John Milbank's Theology of the 'Gift,'" 98; and especially Partee, "Calvin's Central Dogma," 191–200. Partee argues that Calvin's writings, particularly the *Institutes*, would be better interpreted using the theme "union with Christ."

98. Canlis, "Calvin, Osiander and Participation in God," 169.

Communion with the Triune God

doctrine of justification, with its twin concept of imputed righteousness, which for him fails to consider the ontological transformation corresponding to justification.[99] The problem, however, was Osiander's formulation of participation in the righteousness of Christ, which is at best Apollinarian. As Mosser puts it, what was problematic in Osiander's view was "that justification was an in-pouring or infusion of Christ's divine essence into the believer which rendered the believer righteous."[100] It is this exact concept that Calvin could not digest. Without abandoning the doctrine of participation altogether, Calvin approached the doctrine from a different perspective. He first and foremost rejected the ontological-substantival interpretation of Osiander, then employed a christologically-conditioned trinitarian theology to formulate his theology. The result is that instead of Osiander's justification by the divine essence within, Calvin insisted that we participate in Christ's own righteousness through being united with him. As Canlis asserts, "It is a non-substantial participation in the person of Christ, made possible by Calvin's innovative doctrine of the Holy Spirit who is a safeguard against substantial participation."[101]

As is evident, Calvin's debate with Osiander reveals that his understanding of participation in God is different from the one promoted by participation Thomists and Radical Orthodoxy theologians. Their dissimilarities seem to summarize the two options for understanding participation theology throughout its historical development and manifestation: it is either a neo-Platonic substantival participation, or a relational, Christ-centered participation. Torrance's views are more akin to Calvin's participation theology, although Torrance's soteriology far exceeds Calvin in terms of trinitarian depth. This might be because while Calvin wrote on the doctrines of the Trinity and salvation, they were only among the other doctrines that Calvin was interested in. On the other hand, Torrance, because his main line of interests are in both the doctrines of the Trinity and salvation, has given more time to unpacking their relation. So the question is: What is Torrance's distinct participation theology? Here, to elaborate the nature and shape of Torrance's trinitarian participation soteriology, a trifurcated discussion is presented for the purpose of elucidation, although these three aspects are inseparable in reality and experience. First, the concept of *mediated participation* comprehends chapters

---

99. See Weis, "Calvin Versus Osiander on Justification," 31–47; also reprinted in *Calvin's Opponents*, 353–69,

100. Mosser, "The Greatest Possible Blessing," 48–49.

101. Canlis, "Calvin, Osiander and Participation in God," 184.

2, 3, and 4, and emphasizes union with the Son and communion of the Holy Spirit so that humanity may become children of the Father. Secondly, the concept of *perichoretic participation* describes the nature and shape of what it means to "share in [God's] own eternal Life and Love."[102] Finally, it is argued that humanity's participation in the triune life and love is a genuine *human participation*.

Mediated Triune Participation

Chapters 2, 3, and 4 highlighted salvation as the work of the persons of the Triune God. Torrance espouses a doctrine of appropriation in the evangelical Trinity, grounded in the distinction-in-unity and unity-in-distinction in the Trinity *in se*. But the unique agencies of the Father, Son, and Holy Spirit should be understood in the light of the one act and goal of the "mediation of reconciliation," in which "men and women are savingly reconciled to God by being taken up in and through Jesus Christ to share in the inner relations of God's own life and love."[103] In short, the mediating act of the incarnate Son is *an act within the act* of the whole Triune God which culminates in humanity's reconciliation with God. The same is true with the Holy Spirit's mediating communion with us, whereby the Holy Spirit enables us to participate in the primordial communion.

Union with Jesus Christ in the Holy Spirit to the Father

On the work of Jesus Christ, the concept of mediated participation is best portrayed in Torrance's view of the interpenetration of the hypostatic union and atoning union in Christ and the double movement of the mediation of reconciliation, *katabasis* and *anabasis*, in which the incarnate Son mediates the Father in the Holy Spirit to humanity in his incarnation and correspondingly mediates humanity to the Father in the Holy Spirit in his ascension. It is in this sense that Torrance first understands Jesus Christ as Mediator. "The essential nature of the Gospel message of reconciliation through the mediation of Christ," Torrance writes, is "reconciliation with the divine Trinity."[104] As in Calvin's participation in Christ, our union with Christ's humanity, grounded in his prior union with us in the incarnation, enables us to receive the benefits of Jesus Christ. But Torrance

---

102. Torrance, *Trinitarian Perspectives*, 2.
103. Torrance, *Mediation of Christ*, 64.
104. Torrance, *Scottish Theology*, 86, 87.

transcends Calvin because he argues that the benefits of Christ do not end in justification and sanctification, but ultimately in relationship with the Triune God: "It is not atonement that constitutes the goal and end of that integrated movement of reconciliation but union with God in and through Jesus Christ in whom our human nature is not only saved, healed and renewed but lifted up to participate in the very light, life and love of the Holy Trinity."[105] Participation theology does not have union with Jesus Christ as its final goal; rather, union with Jesus Christ mediates us to union with the Triune God. The difference is perhaps found in Torrance's emphasis on the fact that "the hypostatic union is grounded in, derived from and is continuously upheld by what is called the 'consubstantial communion' within the Trinity."[106] Consequently, this implies that to be "in Christ" ultimately means to be in relationship with the Triune God.

> The eternal communion of love in God overflows through Jesus Christ into our union with Christ and gathers us up to dwell with God and in God. This is another way of saying that the Incarnation, and the reconciliation that took place within it, fall within the life of God . . . for in Christ our human relations with God, far from being allowed to remain on merely external basis, are embraced within the Trinitarian relations of God's own Being as Father, Son and the Holy Spirit.[107]

This, according to Torrance, "is what the Christian Gospel is all about": the fact that in Jesus Christ God descended from the heavenly realms to assume, live, and dwell with humanity, so that personal relations with the Triune God may be re-established.

Adoption as Children of the Father through Jesus Christ in the Holy Spirit

The Father, in virtue of his distinct *hypostasis* as the Father, is not sent into the world in the manner that we understand the missions of the incarnate Son and the Holy Spirit. The best summary of the role of the Father in the mediation of reconciliation is that, with some qualifications, the Father is the Mediated One, because his love is the ground of the election of the Son and the communion-constituting activity of the Holy Spirit in the salvific economy. Torrance quotes McLeod Campbell: "the love of God [is]

---

105. Torrance, *Mediation of Christ*, 66.
106. Ibid., 65.
107. Torrance, *Mediation of Christ*, 64; "Karl Barth," 4.

the cause, and the atonement [is] the effect."[108] Mediation has a starting point: the love of the Father. Nevertheless, that the Father is the Mediated One does not mean that the Father is only passively involved in the mediation of reconciliation. In Torrance's Athanasian formula "from the Father, through the Son and in the Holy Spirit, and to the Father, through the Son and in the Spirit,"[109] the phrases "*from* the Father" and "*to* the Father" are both regarded as the distinct and active mediating agencies of the Father in the reconciling economy. Remove or disregard these two phrases and the trinitarian economy will collapse. The phrase "to the Father" is particularly noteworthy. The Father's acts of sending and receiving not only enable us to enter into relationship with the Father as children, but also enables our actual participation in the familial communion of the Triune God. In this sense, adoption could not be interpreted only as a two-way relationship between the person of the Father and humanity. Rather, adoption refers to the dynamic relationship between humanity as brothers of Jesus Christ in the fellowship of the Holy Spirit with the loving and electing Father. Adoption is trinitarian adoption. Put differently, adoption is another metaphor for participation in the triune communion. As Clark Pinnock writes, "God has not left us outside the circle of his life. We are invited inside the Trinity as joint heirs together with Christ. By the Spirit we cry 'Abba' together with the Son, as we are drawn into the divine filial relationship and begin to participate in God's life."[110]

Communion in the Holy Spirit with the Father through Jesus Christ

The concept of mediated participation finds its clearest expression in the agency of the communion-constituting Spirit. Because the Holy Spirit is "the Bond of the Trinity" and is "the Communion of the Father and the Son in the Godhead," his distinct work in the reconciling economy is discernibly to enable human communion with the Triune God as well.[111] The Holy Spirit accomplishes this on two levels. First, the Spirit's communion enables us to be united with Jesus Christ so that we may both enjoy the benefits of Christ's atoning work and be united in relationship with Jesus

---

108. Campbell, *The Nature of Atonement*, 17; quoted in Torrance, *Scottish Theology*, 298; *Christian Doctrine of God*, 238.

109. Athanasius, *Ser.* 1:6, 9, 12, 14, 28, 3:5; 4:6 (*NPNF*² 4); in Torrance, *Theology in Reconciliation*, 251; *Trinitarian Faith*, 5.

110. Pinnock, *Flame of Love*, 153.

111. Deddo, "The Holy Spirit," 86; Torrance, *Christian Doctrine of God*, 167; *When Christ Comes*, 190–92.

Christ our Brother. The Holy Spirit mediates Jesus Christ to us and us to Jesus Christ.[112] As the "agent of participation," the Spirit enables us to participate in Christ's own worship and knowledge of the Father.

> The Holy Spirit who is the consubstantial Communion of the Father and the Son in the Trinity, is the Spirit through whom the Word was made flesh in the hypostatic union of the divine and human natures in the Person of the Son, but it is the same Spirit through whom we have union with Christ and partake of the communion between the Father and the Son and the Son and the Father.[113]

The last part of the quotation hints at the second level of the Spirit's communion-constituting work, and is the main focus here: the mediating role of the Spirit in bringing us into the life and love of the Triune God. The Spirit's saving communion with us and our communion with the Spirit does not function as an ultimate end in itself. Rather, through the Spirit's communion, we are lifted up to share in the triune communion. "As the Father, Son and Holy Spirit dwell in one another," Torrance writes, "so God is in us by the indwelling of the Spirit and by participation of the Spirit we are in God."[114] Again, this is related to the "from the Father . . . to the Father" economic formula. The Spirit comes from God and returns to God. Torrance explains this double movement: "By coming into man the Holy Spirit opens him out to God," and when the Spirit returns to God, he "raises us up in Jesus to participate in the worship of heaven and in the eternal communion of the Holy Trinity."[115]

Perichoretic Triune Participation

As argued above, all persons of the Triune God, in their own distinct hypostatic agencies, have their part in the mediation of reconciliation. Also, the mediatorial work of each person has its ultimate end in humanity's participation in the triune life. It can therefore be said that *mediated participation,* or reconciliation through the agencies of the Triune God, forms the ground of our actual *perichoretic participation,* or our inclusion, by grace, into the eternal communion that the Triune God is. *Perichoretic participation* is derived from Torrance's thoughts that *perichoresis* is the

---

112. Torrance, *Theological Dialogue* 2: 9.
113. Torrance, *God and Rationality,* 180; "The Mission of the Church," 136.
114. Torrance, *Theology in Reconciliation,* 232; *Trinitarian Faith,* 208–9.
115. Torrance, *Theology in Reconstruction,* 238, 150.

highest possible semantic expression of the co-inherent triune relations, and is an eternal movement of communion in which humanity is invited to participate.[116]

> [The triune persons] coinhere in one Another by virtue of their one Being for one Another and by virtue of the dynamic Communion which they constitute in their belonging to one Another. Hence in establishing communion with us through his Son and in his Spirit God wants us to participate in his living Communion which as Father, Son and Holy Spirit he eternally is.[117]

Torrance's theological corpus is replete with similar statements and arguments concerning our sharing in the triune communion. He does not, however, elaborate on the nature or shape of such a trinitarian participation. Perhaps Torrance purposefully left this unarticulated for fear of abstract speculation, but to leave such a prominent aspect of his soteriology to mere indicative statements without further elucidation is regrettable, and seems un-Torrance-like, and opens him to broad interpretation. The work of Habets that argues for *theosis* as a hermeneutical linchpin in reading Torrance's soteriology, is perhaps the first attempt to explain the nature and shape of Torrance's participation theology. Habets's overall study is excellent, but his insistence that Torrance's soteriology should be understood in the light of *theosis* is quite unwarranted, because although Torrance employs the concept in his theologizing, it does not occupy the exalted position in Torrance's theology that Habets ascribes to it. As an alternative, we are arguing that Torrance's trinitarian participation soteriology could be better explained in the light of the concept of *perichoresis*, coupled with his understanding of "relational space."

At one level, *perichoresis* is an ontological concept, for it expresses the tension that should be maintained between enhypostatic relations and hypostatic distinctions in the triune being of God. Thus, in its most developed meaning, *perichoresis* refers to the co-inherent relations or the mutual indwelling of the triune persons. On another level, and of primary interest here, *perichoresis* is a spatial concept. This is evident in *chora*, "space" or "room," or *chorein*, "to contain" or "to make room," as its etymological roots.[118] Thus, the eternal triune perichoretic relation is involved in an eternal movement of mutual space-giving and space-receiving, in cor-

---

116. Torrance, *Christian Doctrine of God*, 102–3.
117. Ibid., 132–33.
118. Ibid., 102; *Trinitarian Perspectives*, 141.

relation to each of the persons's reciprocal self-giving and self-receiving in the triune life. The Father opens himself for the Son and the Holy Spirit; the Son opens himself for the Father and the Holy Spirit; and the Holy Spirit opens himself for the Father and the Son. In other words, each of the persons is room-giving and room-receiving at the same time. The persons of the Trinity, Torrance writes, "wholly dwell in each other and . . . each have room fully for the others in the one God."[119] Our participation in the life and love of the Triune God could be said to follow the same shape, and is only made possible by the inherent space-giving and space-receiving nature of the persons of the Godhead. Torrance argues that the triune relations must be thought of "in terms of 'abiding' and 'indwelling,' in which each wholly rests in the other." He adds: "This is the doctrine of *perichoresis.*"[120] Expressed using the concept of love: "That God is Love means that he is the eternally loving One in himself who loves through himself, whose Love moves unceasingly within his eternal life," and it is "the perfection and fullness of Love that will not be confined within the Godhead but freely and lovingly moves outward toward others whom God creates for fellowship with himself so that they may share with him the very Communion of Love which is his own divine Life and Being."[121] God's being is being-for-*Others* (i.e., persons within the Trinity) and being-for-*others*. God's life and love allows beings-essentially-created-for-the-purpose-of-fellowship to participate. This can be called *perichoretic participation*.

Torrance's relational view of space sheds more light in understanding *perichoretic participation*. Our entry into the Divine space is not an intrusion into the Divine life. Contrary to the static receptacle views of space held by Plato, Aristotle, and the Stoics, the Christian view of "space" is subject-oriented. "Space," Torrance writes, "is a predicate of the Occupant."[122] This means that it is God himself who creates what we call "space," the arena of God's gracious communion-creating activity. As such, the Newtonian and Kantian view of space as a transcendental that limits the interaction between God and the world should be abandoned, for God, as the author of space, could not be confined both within himself and by our human categories. In God, space "is a sort of differential con-

---

119. Torrance, *Space, Time, and Incarnation*, 16; Moltmann, *History and the Triune God*, 87.

120. Torrance, *Divine Meaning*, 367.

121. Torrance, *Christian Doctrine of God*, 5, 6.

122. Torrance, *Divine Meaning*, 366. See Torrance's larger discussion of the early fathers's struggle with cultural-philosophical spatial concepts in pages 289–342.

cept that is essentially open-ended."[123] To put it more vividly, the Divine space, or the arena of God's dynamic communion of love, is essentially open to creatures. Through the creative and salvific activity of the Triune God, creatures are embraced in the perichoretic communion that God is.

Furthermore, perichoretic participation is only possible from above, that is, from the side of God. "Mere creatures are unable to make 'room' for God in their natures."[124] It is only because God's being is being-for-others that our participation in God is made possible. But this participation is also neither automatic nor could be interpreted in a mechanistic necessitarian manner. To make the logical connection between God's open being and our participation in God's life and love is something that Torrance would immediately reject. Thus, Torrance's appropriation of *perichoresis* in his trinitarian soteriology differs from Moltmann's *pericherotic* panentheism, which is rigid and deterministic, in that God and creation cannot but be in perichoretic relation. For Moltmann, because God's nature and love "is a self-evident, unquestionable 'overflowing of goodness' which is therefore *never open to choice at any time*,"[125] God *must* be in an eternal relation with creation. Creation, too, cannot escape this perichoretic oneness with God. Torrance, however, understands humanity's perichoretic participation in the triune life and love as completely gratuitous. God *elects* and humanity *participates* freely and only by grace. Perhaps the distinguishing factor between Moltmann and Torrance is the latter's emphasis on *mediated participation*. For instance, in elaborating the mediating agency of Jesus Christ, Torrance writes: "Now when the Son, who abides in the Father in that way [i.e., mutual indwelling] became incarnate, He became for us the 'place' where the Father is to be known and believed, for He is the *topos* or *locus* where God is found."[126] In short, participation in the life and love of God is through mediation. Humanity participates in the perichoretic communion of the Trinity only when we participate in the Son's internal relationship with the Father in the communion of the Holy Spirit.

Torrance's high optimism and soteriological vision is not grounded in humanity's achievement or capability. It is actually quite the opposite. Torrance's optimism is grounded in the power and love of the Triune God as revealed in the saving economy to redeem and reconcile hopeless,

---

123. Ibid., 371.

124. Ibid., 366.

125. Moltmann, *Trinity and the Kingdom*, 55; quoted in Molnar, *Theologian of the Trinity*, 84.

126. Torrance, *Space, Time, and Incarnation*, 16.

depraved, and fallen humanity. Nevertheless, firstly, the ultimate *telos* of human salvation as participation in the communion of the Triune God could be mistakenly interpreted to imply humanity's absorption into the life and light of God at the cost of human individuality (in its weak form), or loss-of-being through substantial re-absorption into a primordial mass of substance (in its strong form). The participation theologies of Aquinas and Radical Orthodoxy are susceptible to the strong form, although the weak form could also be implied. Because their cosmology facilitates Neo-Platonic emanation philosophy, their teleological vision for gradated existents could not be other than the gradual return of borrowed essence to their source of being.[127] This "cosmonistic communion," or that persons would disappear in "one vast ocean of being,"[128] is a serious implication, although Torrance's trinitarian soteriology is not susceptible to it. His appropriation of creation *ex nihilo*, and rejection of both *analogia entis* and vestigial anthropology are sufficient safeguards against this substantialist absorption. Therefore, even though, as Groppe writes, "we exist in a being-from and being-toward God and as such we have an ontological relation to eternity,"[129] this should be understood primarily in relational and not essential terms. Our relation to the Triune God is not a partitive sharing, but a relational sharing.[130] The question, however, is whether Torrance's soteriology possesses the propensity towards the weak form: that participation in the triune life implies the loss of human identity. Is there, in Gunton's words, "the loss of the manysidedness of our humanity in the undifferentiated unity of the whole"[131] in Torrance's soteriological vision? Torrance does not explicitly deal with this problem in his writings, but his position is discernible. In fact, it is similar to adherents of social trinitarianism who ground their defense in the eternal hypostatic distinctions among the persons of the Trinity in the triune perichoretic communion.

127. O'Donoghue, "Creation and Participation," in *Creation, Christ, and Culture*, 136–38. This seems to be the case for ideas of participation in the Triune God understood in and resulting in panentheistic cosmologies and soteriologies, such as Moltmann's unqualified use of *perichoresis*. Buxton's *The Trinity, Creation, and Pastoral Ministry*, and Fiddes's *Participating in God* ultimately fall into this category, which Fiddes unashamedly admits (p. 292).

128. Volf, *After Our Likeness*, 87.

129. Groppe, "LaCugna's Contribution to Trinitarian Theology," 752–53.

130. Torrance, *Trinitarian Faith*, 53; O'Donoghue, "Creation and Participation," 138. Interestingly, Torrance detected and combated this way of thinking in Scottish theology during his lifetime, referring to this thinking as "'A Dark Whirlpool of Error," 18–19.

131. Gunton, *The Promise of Trinitarian Theology*, 86.

Communion with the Triune God

The important point here is that *personal distinction* is a necessary ingredient of *onto-relation,* because only persons who are different from one another can establish a relationship of intimacy, mutual surrender, and love that ground a communion and a community.[132] Thus, in communion, there happens "a new and paradoxical conception of united separation and separated unity," or a "personological unity."[133] The mediation of Jesus Christ and the Holy Spirit play important roles here as well. Just as Christ as truly human in his resurrected body communes with the Father, so does and will humanity commune with God in our resurrected bodies, distinct from God and from other fellow human beings. Also, because the Holy Spirit enables us to recognize the utter Godness of God in our communion with him, our finitude as contingent created existents, along with our finite consciousness, are retained.[134]

Secondly, the relationship between created and uncreated realities that Torrance advocates can be an issue to both philosopher-metaphysicians and theologians. At the basic level, metaphysicians would immediately dismiss the idea of *personal* relationship between the two. This attitude is portrayed by Arius, who thought that the only relation between Uncreated and created realities is that of separation, or at best, subordination. This, of course, is grounded in Greek dualism, where *personal* relation between entities of the *kosmos noetos* and *kosmos aisthetos* is inconceivable.[135] But as Lee argues, Torrance's theology embodies a funda-

---

132. Volf, "The Trinity is Our Social Program," 407–11; *After Our Image,* 87, 182–83; Boff, *Holy Trinity,* 57. As Ellen K. Wondra also argues, elements of asymmetry are present in mutual relationships in "Participating Persons," 57–73.

133. Gunton, *The Promise of Trinitarian Theology,* 94; Smail, *The Giving Gift,* 187.

134. Torrance, *When Christ Comes,* 153–54; *Theology in Reconstruction,* 242–45. Some theologians use the distinctions and "plurality" of persons in the Trinity as the ground to vindicate religious pluralism, or to say that pluralism is inherent, essential, and primordial in reality. This is not a major element in my research, but suffice it to say that these approaches dangerously appropriate the doctrine of the Trinity to absurd proportions. See for instance Johnson, "Does the Doctrine of the Trinity Hold the Key," in *Trinitarian Theology for the Church,* 142–60; and Vanhoozer, "Does the Trinity Belong in a Theology of Religions?," in *The Trinity in a Pluralistic Age,* 41–71. Gunton's response to this agenda is sufficient: "The doctrine of the Trinity is concerned with unity in plurality, not an absolute pluralism," in "The Trinity, Natural Theology and a Theology of Nature," 89. See also Hart, "Karl Barth, the Trinity, and Pluralism," in *The Trinity in a Pluralistic Age,* 124–42. For another argument against wrongly using trinitarian concepts, see Otto, "The Use and Abuse of Perichoresis," 366–84.

135. Torrance, *Christian Theology,* 22–24. Thus, as Alan Torrance writes, what was missing from Arius was God himself active in the world in Christ, in "Being of One Substance with the Father," 53.

mental rejection of cosmological and epistemological dualisms.[136] In the relationship between God and creatures, Torrance admits "a mutual, but not a symmetrical, relation of detachment," but only in order to safeguard the distinction between "the Godness of God" and "the naturalness of nature."[137] His overall position concerning the relationship between God and creature is optimistic, not because of inherent creaturely potentiality or capacity, but because of God's gracious act of self-giving.

> The distinction between Grace and nature must not be interpreted as a dichotomy, as if there were only a deistic relation between the creature and the Creator. There is a relation of being between the creature and the Creator immediately maintained by the Creator, but it is the irreversible relation of Grace which He freely posits and preserves in love. It is a Creator-creature relation which God establishes freely out of pure Grace; as such it is neither explainable from the side of the creature nor logically definable, and therefore is not reversible.[138]

Thus, it could be concluded that rejections about the possibility of creaturely communion with the Divine are propelled by philosophical presuppositions, rather than thinking out of the "logic of grace."[139] In short, impossibility is perceivable only if anthropocentric considerations (i.e., finite limitations) form the underlying and controlling factor. But if the controlling foundation is predicated in the dynamic being of God, then Creator-creature relationship is essentially not impossible at all. In the first place, God's being is being-for-others —"others" understood as every being that is not God. In the words of Jenson, God's essential being is "roomy."[140] In soteriology, therefore, the most important considerations are the active and dynamic being of God and the mediation of reconcilia-

---

136. Lee argues that in Torrance, dualism is a "perpetual foe," in *Living in Union*, 11–17; see also Torrance, *Divine Meaning*, 181; and Gunton, "Being and Person," 117–18. Still, Morrison argues that Torrance never really overcame dualism in his theology because of his indebtedness to Kierkegaard and Barth, in *Knowledge of the Self-revealing God*, xiii, 294–319, 359–61.

137. Torrance, *Transformation and Convergence*, 26; *Theological Science*, 66.

138. Torrance, *Theological Science*, 66; *Theology in Reconstruction*, 64–65.

139. Torrance, *Theological Science*, 214–22.

140. Jenson, "Aspects of a Doctrine of Creation," in *The Doctrine of Creation*, 27. Earlier, on page 24, Jenson writes: "for God to create is for him to open a place in his triune life for others than the three whose mutual life he is. John of Damascus again: 'God is . . . his own place.' In that place, he *makes room*, and that act is the event of creation."

tion in Jesus Christ and the Holy Spirit. As Gunton discerns, "If God and the world are ontologically other, some account of their relation—some theology of *mediation*—is indispensable."[141] Through the incarnation of the Son in the Holy Spirit, Torrance writes, "God in himself is no longer closed to us, but has opened himself" so that "we may now enter into personal communion with God without being limited by our creaturely incapacities or being obstructed by our alienation."[142]

For Torrance, the indwelling participation of humanity in the communion of the Triune God is not only metaphorical, allegorical, or psychological, but real. Because the coming of God in Jesus Christ and the Holy Spirit is a genuine *parousia*, the presence of God in space and time, this reciprocally enables us to share in God's communion.[143] Torrance repudiates the invented concepts of uncreated grace, created grace, and "means of grace" whereby it is thought that God does not directly or personally act with us without a created medium, often called "grace."[144] He is also suspicious of the Eastern distinction between ineffable divine essence and uncreated energies.[145] The reason is that this distinction undermines genuine and intimate contact with God, and has "the effect of restricting knowledge of God to his divine energies, and ruling out any real access to

---

141. Gunton, *Father, Son, and Holy Spirit*, 93; Torrance, *Transformation and Convergence*, 29.

142. Torrance, *Trinitarian Faith*, 67. The fact that the incarnation of the Son of God in the world falls within and not without the inner life of God, Torrance argues, teaches us about both the openness of God for others and the openness of the world for God, in *Trinitarian Perspectives*, 101. The question of possibility and impossibility of communion with God is tied to the question of the incarnation. See the debates in Hick, *The Myth of God Incarnate* (1977); Goulder, *Incarnation and Myth* (1977), and Skarsaune, *Incarnation: Myth or Fact?* (1991).

143. Torrance, *Ministry and Sacraments of the Gospel*, 157; *Theology in Reconciliation*, 130–31; *Divine Meaning*, 19. In "Deposit of Faith," 6, Torrance speaks about "the *oikonomia* of the divine *ousia*." Elsewhere, Torrance explains, "in God, *logos* and *pneuma* are not separated from *ousia* and *physis* or therefore from *aletheia*," in *Transformation and Convergence*, 304. In *Divine Meaning*, 182, Torrance argues that the *ousia* of God should be interpreted as both *being* and *presence*: presence in being and being in activity.

144. Sanders, "The Trinity," 50. See Torrance, *Theology in Reconstruction*, chapter 10 on Torrance's critique of both Roman Catholic and Protestant views of grace.

145. One of the arguments of Eastern theologians against the *filioque*, for instance, is grounded in this distinction. See Zizioulas, *Lectures in Christian Dogmatics*, 71–73. Palamas asserts that the procession of the Holy Spirit from the Son is only at the level of the divine energies, not essence. See Heron, "The *Filioque* Clause," in *One God in Trinity*, 72. On page 74, Heron adds that this distinction in general is dubious.

Communion with the Triune God

knowledge of God in the intrinsic relations of his eternal triune being."[146] Consequential to this held distinction is the view, particularly expressed by Lossky, that *theosis* is participation only in the energies of God.[147] "Union with the Trinity," Timiadis writes, "means union with the divine energies not the divine essence. We do not become the Father or the Son or the Holy Spirit; rather we share so intimately in their life-creating energies that we are joined to them."[148] On the contrary, for Torrance, God's *energeia* inheres in God's being. God's being is in his act and his act is in his being. To separate the two in our knowledge of God means knowing God's being apart from his act or knowing his act behind his being.[149] To separate the two in God's salvific economy implies a loss of genuine relationship between God and humanity. In fact, reconciliation is diluted to reconciliation only with the act of God. The economic Trinity is then all that there is in both the doctrines of the Trinity and salvation. Against this, Torrance argues that our participation in the Triune God is a sharing "in the inner communion of his divine Being so that we are given to share in the mutual knowing of the Father and the Son in the Holy Spirit in the immanent relations of Father, Son, and Holy Spirit."[150]

A serious question relating to Torrance's view of humanity's participation in the triune communion concerns the element of temporality, or more precisely, the origin and event of participation. Ironically, the confusion emerges from Torrance's understanding of relational space and his view of the oneness between the act and being of God. Put plainly, it appears that in Torrance, there are several levels or moments of participation in God, and their relation is not articulated. For example, because Torrance regards space as the sphere of God's activity, it implies that by default, created existence is already embraced in God's life and love. He writes: "God is not contained by anything but rather . . . He contains the entire universe, not in the manner of a bodily container, but by His power."[151] Contingent creaturely being only finds its existence within the

---

146. Torrance, *Trinitarian Faith*, 336. See also Jenson, *The Triune Identity*, 126–27; and Sanders, "The Trinity," 49.

147. Papanikolaou, "Divine Energies or Personhood," 358.

148. Torrance, *Theological Dialogue* 1: 128. See also Bobrinskoy, *The Mystery of the Trinity*, 73–76.

149. Torrance, *Ground and Grammar of Theology*, 151–53.

150. Ibid., 154. For Torrance, the key to the oneness of God's act and being and our actual participation is the *homoousios*. See *Mediation of Christ*, 111; and *Ecumenical Studies*, xx.

151. Torrance, *Space, Time, and Incarnation*, 11.

sphere of God's creative and sustaining activity. Outside of God's activity is *nihil*, nothingness, and therefore non-being. Could we then say that there is a pre-salvific participation in God? The fact that Torrance rejects the idea that God "deistically abandon[s] what he has brought into existence" could imply that God and creaturely existence are in an unbroken relationship in the first place.[152] Could this be a pre-incarnation, pre-atonement, and pre-Pentecost participation in the triune life and love? Furthermore, when Torrance discusses our participation in the Triune God through the incarnate Son and the communion of the Holy Spirit, whereby we share in the life and love of God in his inner being, could this be different from the first level presented above? The problem is heightened by Torrance's view that the incarnation and Pentecost are *new* to God. We can add that these events also have their temporal and spatial beginning, and thus are *new* to creation. Torrance explains that the incarnation and Pentecost are "decisive" moments in the economy of salvation, because God deals with humanity at a whole new personal level.[153] But then this would seem to mean that there are also degrees of God's *personal* relation with the created order. God is already involved personally in creation and providence, so is there a new and higher level of personal relation inaugurated by the incarnation and Pentecost that is distinct from the first?

Torrance recognized this issue in *The Christian Doctrine of God*, but he did not offer any elaboration. He passingly comments: "The transcendent Spirit of God had always been actively present in the world immanently sustaining its continuing relation to God the Creator, but what happened at Pentecost manifested a change not only in the form of his activity but in the mode of his immanence which is difficult for us to conceive or express."[154] In his sermons, he expands the concept of God's presence a little bit more. He differentiates between God's *sustaining presence* to all creation and his *saving presence*. Discussing the presence of God in the Temple, for instance, he writes that "God is present everywhere, in creation and beyond," although what he really wanted to focus on was about "God's presence to us, to us where we are in the world, to each of us. God adapts his presence to us, and comes to us in our place where we are; this is the *special presence of God*, where he draws near, makes himself known to us, speaks to us, and gives us his grace."[155] In another sermon, he

---

152. Torrance, *Christian Doctrine of God*, 218.
153. Torrance, "Goodness and Dignity of Man," 314–22.
154. Torrance, *Christian Doctrine of God*, 238.
155. B41 "The Sanctification of the Temple," 2 (italics mine).

adds: "Jehovah was there [i.e., in the Temple].... There He forgave sins.... *We need not go into the question of how all that was related to His universal presence*. We need not even stop to remind ourselves that God could be more actually present in the Holy Place than He was on any breeze height of Galilee or in the crowded streets of Babylon. *It is of His manifested and felt presence that we are speaking*."[156] It is not clear whether the saving presence of God is similar to what he calls elsewhere God's *convicting presence* that leads to justification, although this seems to be the case. He writes:

> The nearer a man gets to God, the more he feels himself a sinner. You can only be conscious of sin in the presence of God. . . . It is the presence of God that discovers a man's sin to that man, but just because there is awakened the consciousness of sin, we inevitably feel at enmity to God and far away from Him. We implore Him for pardon and reconciliation, that He may come near us in mercy and not in wrath.[157]

The saving presence of God is necessary because Torrance claims that salvation must involve a *personal encounter* with Jesus Christ himself and a *personal relationship* with Jesus Christ.[158] This personal encounter seems to be the goal of humanity to be saved, as is evident in his statement: "They who become Christ's by the great change of yielding their hearts to Him, and who live here as pilgrims and sojourners, pass dry-shod through the stream *into* His presence."[159] But Torrance also argues, looking at the Pharisees and Sadducees, that spiritual immunity in the presence of God is possible.[160] Part of the problem is how Torrance uses the word "presence." For instance, he can say that one can pray "in such a way as to mean the absence of the presence of God" and add that "if the presence of God is absent in our lives, it is because . . . we have shut Him out." In the first quotation, "the absence of the presence of God" is only figurative, but the said absence is real in the second quotation, where God's presence has something to do with our volitional acceptance of God.[161]

156. B43 "The Little Sanctuary," 4 (italics mine).

157. B44 "The Pharisee and the Publican at Prayer," 6; and B43 "O Man greatly beloved," 1–5; and B47 "The Condemning Heart," 5–6.

158. B44 "Behold the Lamb of God," 3; and B45 "The Conversion of Paul," 1–5 (italics mine).

159. B42 "Abram the Hebrew," 9 (italics mine).

160. B43 "Beware the leaven of the Sadducees," 1–11.

161. B44 "The Pharisee and the Publican at Prayer," 2, 4; and B43 "The Hem of His Garment," 4–5. Elsewhere, he states that there is no greater hell than the hell of someone who cannot get into the presence of God. See B47 "Prayer without ceasing," 3–4.

Communion with the Triune God

Human Participation: *Theosis* and *Theopoiesis*

The revival of interest in Eastern theology equally ushered in renewed interest in the doctrine of *theosis*, neglected for centuries in Western theology due to the categories it employed—categories that are incomprehensible and misunderstood in Western theology. Equally disturbing are the translations "divinization" and "deification" which, when interpreted using Aristotelian substantial philosophy rather than through the triune mediation of reconciliation, create theological problems. Such was the case for Aquinas's doctrine of participation modelled on Neo-Platonic philosophy, and adopted in contemporary theology by Radical Orthodoxy. Torrance quotes Georges Florovsky:

> The term *theosis* is indeed embarrassing, if we would think of it in "ontological categories." Indeed, man simply cannot become "god." But the Fathers were thinking in "personal" terms, and the mystery of personal communion was involved at this point. Theosis means a personal encounter. It is the ultimate intercourse with God, in which the whole of human existence is, as it were, permeated by the Divine Presence.[162]

Theosis, therefore, is primarily a relational concept. Torrance himself defends his use of the term: "Let us not quarrel about the word *theosis*," he writes, "offensive though it may be to us, but follow its intention."[163] He makes clear that in his use of the term, he does not employ it as "divinization," but as the grace of God in redeeming human weakness and allowing us to commune with him in his glory. Torrance interprets *theosis* in its interconnected two-fold significance. First, *theosis* refers to "the emancipation of man from imprisonment in himself," the alienation from God and self-centeredness which is sin. Secondly, and consequently, "*theosis* describes man's involvement in such a mighty act of God upon him that he is raised up to find the true centre of his existence not in himself but in [the] Holy God."[164]

A systematic study of Torrance's appropriation of *theosis* in his soteriology was undertaken by Habets in his book *Theosis*. Although Habets admits that *theosis* is not the central point of Torrance's dogmatics, he

---

162. Torrance, *Christian Doctrine of God*, 96; quoting Florovsky, "St Gregory Palamas," 115.

163. Torrance, *Theology in Reconstruction*, 243.

164. Ibid., 243, 244. This is why Torrance writes that "the idea that he [humanity] is like God, that he has got a spark of divine within him" is "the madness of the devil," in B42 "Creation," 5.

argues that the concept "is of fundamental importance" in Torrance's soteriology in particular, and "is a necessary crucial integrating theme within his overall theological *oeuvre*" in general.[165] Based on this conclusion, the book thus shows how *theosis* can be a justifiable hermeneutical key in a presentation of Torrance's soteriology. Habets admits that he undertakes his project with an assumption that Torrance employs "conceptual equivalents" of *theosis* in his writings, such as "union, communion, participation, transcendental determination, reordering, humanising, personalising and atoning exchange."[166] Although Habets failed to represent the scientific character of Torrance's soteriology by placing cosmological and anthropological discussions as the basis and background of his presentation of Torrance's soteriology, Habets's appropriation of the incarnate Son's and the Holy Spirit's agencies in bringing humanity into relationship with the Triune God are noteworthy. It serves to reinforce the argument for mediated participation in the triune life and love. In Torrance's words, God, "through the Son and in the Spirit lifts us up to the level of participation in God where we are opened out for union and communion with him far beyond the limits of our creaturely existence—which is another way of describing *theosis*."[167] Even the Athanasian term *theopoiesis*, which essentially refers to our adoption as sons and daughters of God by grace, is indubitably communal, for it refers to "the staggering act of God in which God gives himself to us and *adopts us* into the communion of his divine life and love through Jesus Christ and in his one Spirit."[168]

In Torrance's theology, the primary significance of *theosis* is not that it affirms (or restates) his trinitarian participation soteriology. Rather, negatively, Torrance rejects the interpretation of *theosis* in the Thomist and Radical Orthodoxy tradition as substantial metamorphosis or absorption into one divine *esse* that negates all human characteristics. Positively, grounded in the saving agency of the incarnate Son from the incarnation to his ascension in his resurrected body and the Spirit's affirmation of creaturely otherness, *theosis* in Torrance means the personalization and humanization of humanity. *Theosis* or *theopoiesis* is not divinization or deification but the adaptation of humanity in our contingent nature for knowledge of and fellowship with the Triune God.[169]

165. Habets, *Theosis*, 16.
166. Ibid., 15.
167. Torrance, *Trinitarian Perspectives*, 87.
168. Torrance, *Mediation of Christ*, 64; *Theology in Reconciliation*, 230–31.
169. Torrance, "Soul and Person," 113.

Communion with the Triune God

> The Athanasian doctrine of *theopoiesis* (or *theosis*) through the Spirit, in which we are sanctified, renewed and enlightened through adoption in the Incarnate Son to be sons of God, does not import any inner deification of our human nature, but the assuming of us into the sphere of the direct and immediate activity of God himself in such a way that our human being is brought to its *teleiosis* in relation to the Creator and we find our real life hid with Christ in God.[170]

Our participation in the communion of the Triune God is a *human participation*, and could not be anything other. Just as the resurrected human body of Christ has ascended and is in the presence of the Father, so our fellowship with the Triune God is bodily, tangible, and real. This is only possible, Torrance argues, because of the personal power of God, which is "not power that overrules the creature but sustains the creature, ... power therefore that sustains the relation and freedom of the creature before God, for it is always creative, and in relation to his human creatures always personalising and humanising power."[171]

Communion with the Triune God in the Church

Torrance's consistent argument that the Trinity is "the ground and grammar of Christian theology," and therefore the foundational element of all doctrinal formulations, is reflected in his ecclesiology. As to the specific relationship between the church and the Trinity, three categories merit discussion: (1) the church is grounded in the Trinity, (2) the church images the triune communion, and (3) the church is a communion within communion.

---

170. Torrance, *Divine Meaning*, 198; *Theology in Reconciliation*, 234.

171. Torrance, *Christian Doctrine of God*, 206. Torrance refers both to Jesus Christ and the Holy Spirit as personalizing persons, while humanity is referred to as personalized persons. See *Theology in Reconstruction*, 243; *Mediation of Christ*, 67–72; *Trinitarian Faith*, 188, 250; *God and Rationality*, 189. The humanity of Christ is the ground of our humanization in B46 Untitled sermon on Galatians 3: 26-29, 1–6. In other places, Torrance just refers to God as a whole as effecting a personalizing ministry. See *Reality and Scientific Theology*, 173–74; *Christian Doctrine of God*, 126, 206; "Soul and Person," 116; and Colyer, *How to Read*, 178. His definition of sin as "fundamentally self-contradiction," is related here. See B47 "Contradiction of Sinners," 6. This is what Bobrinskoy calls the *reciprocal* element of our participation in the divine life, in *The Mystery of the Trinity*, 61. In beautiful language, Torrance writes about our relationship with God: "Walk before me! What does that mean? Walk before God Almighty—scale the steep scale of Heaven, get into stride with God, keep pace with Eternity!" See B42 "Oh that Ishmael might live before Thee," 8.

Communion with the Triune God

Firstly, as the Archbishop Simon of Ryazan and Kasimov writes, "the Holy Trinity is the Beginning and Archetype of the life of the Church, as well as the ultimate goal of all its spiritual aspirations."[172] Torrance is critical of churches that turn into social institutions posing as gods in themselves, and thus, rather than serving God, oppose him.[173] He argues that the church's being is rooted in the being of God, and does not have any independent existence. More elaborately, Torrance relates both the being and mission of the church to the Head of the Body, Jesus Christ, and to the communion-constituting Holy Spirit. Torrance agrees with Zizioulas's suggestion that "the Church is the outcome of the Father's will, a will he shares with the Son and the Holy Spirit, and which is realized through the economy in which each of the persons of God is engaged."[174] Torrance's long history of ecumenical endeavors and his critical stance against his own ecclesiastical tradition also have influenced his argument for grounding ecclesiology into the doctrine of the Trinity. This is one of the conclusions in both volumes of *The Theological Dialogue between Orthodox and Reformed Churches*.[175]

Secondly, inasmuch as the communion of love is the source of the church's life, the communion in the church also images the triune communion. Torrance's emphasis here is primarily on the unity in the church, which, Timiadis writes, reflects "the Trinity's inner love, like a mirror-image."[176] Gunton, too, following both Zizioulas and Torrance, refers to the church as "a living echo of the communion that God is in eternity."[177] However, this does not imply a direct analogy between the Trinity and the church. Gunton's concern about inferring logical and analogical deductions between the being of the church and the being of God is also

---

172. Torrance, *Theological Dialogue* 1: 202; *Theology in Reconstruction*, 192, 204–5.

173. See Torrance, "Babylon," 16–17; *Apocalypse Today*, 138–48. Included here is Torrance's critique of ecclesiologies centered on the bishop, rather than on Jesus Christ, the Sole Head of the Body. See Torrance, *Doctrine of Grace*, 71–74. Torrance is referring particularly to the Church of England (see *Order and Disorder*, 48–68), the Roman Catholic Church, and even without mentioning his name, Zizioulas (see *Being as Communion*, 136–37, 152–53, and *Lectures in Christian Dogmatics*, 145–48). See also Gunton's critique in *The Promise of Trinitarian Theology*, 57–60.

174. Zizioulas, *Lectures in Christian Dogmatics*, 132, 149–50. Roland Walls argues that this is one of the greatest contributions of Zizioulas to ecclesiology, in "The Church: A Communion of Persons," in *Christ in Our Place*, 103. See also Yves Congar's view of the church in the Trinity in *I Believe in the Holy Spirit* 2: 5–14.

175. See for instance Torrance, *Theological Dialogue* 1: 121–56.

176. Ibid. 1: 131.

177. Gunton, *Father, Son, and Holy Spirit*, 198, 200.

the reason why Torrance himself did not deal too much with the idea of the church's mirroring relation with the Triune God.[178] In places where this idea surfaces, it is usually qualified by the assertion that the church is grounded in the being and act of God. For instance, in *Reality and Scientific Theology*, where Torrance deals with personhood in general, he writes: "What images the Trinity is our interpersonal structure, and not least the interrelations of love which reflect the fact that God is love in the consubstantial Communion of Father, Son and Holy Spirit, although in the nature of the case our inter-personal relations of love have properly to be understood from the Communion of Love in God which is both their source and their goal."[179]

Finally, precisely because the source and goal of the church are in the eternal love of God, which freely and graciously overflows in creation and redemption, the church could be considered as a communion of people within the communion of God. Torrance explains this by referring to the vertical and horizontal relations in the church.

> Through God's self-communication to us within the personal structures of our human being we are drawn into the "vertical" relation of the incarnate Son on earth to the heavenly Father, and thereby share in the relation of mutual knowing and loving between the Father and the Son. At the same time God communicates himself to us in another act by pouring out upon us the Spirit of the Father and of the Son in such a way that there is set up on the "horizontal" level within our social or interpersonal existence a communion of love as a created counterpart or reflection of the trinitarian Communion of Love within the

---

178. For critiques of this idea, see Kilby, "Perichoresis and Projection," 432–45; Husbands, "The Trinity is *Not* Our Social Program," in *Trinitarian Theology for the Church*, 120–41; Tanner, "Trinity," 328–9; Rea, "Relative Identity and the Doctrine of the Trinity," 431–45; Clark, "Trinity or Tritheism," 463–76; and Leftow, "Anti-Social Trinitarianism," in *The Trinity*, 203–49. For those who strongly adhere to this idea, particularly in the so-called "social Trinity," see Plantinga's "Social Trinity and Tritheism," 21–47, and Brown, "Trinitarian Personhood and Individuality," 48–78, in *Trinity, Incarnation, and Atonement*; Plantinga, "Gregory of Nyssa and the Social Analogy of the Trinity," 325–52; LaCugna, "The Trinity," 11; Volf, "'The Trinity is Our Social Program,'" 405–23; and Volf's book *After Our Likeness*. Roland Walls encapsulates the whole principle operating in social trinitarians in "The Church," in *Christ in Our Place*, 109: "God created the human race to be a communion of persons 'in his image' so that they might reflect the glory of the Three in One."

179. Torrance, *Reality and Scientific Theology*, 178; *Theological Dialogue* 2: 78, 83. This "profound unity arises ultimately from the Holy Trinity," in *Trinitarian Faith*, 270. See also Torrance, "The Doctrine of the Trinity in our Contemporary Situation," in *The Forgotten Trinity* 3: 14–15.

> Life of God ... Through the Communion of the Holy Spirit we are given to share in a meeting with God with himself within the structured relations of our personal and social being and are thereby enfolded within the divine Self-Communion of the Holy Trinity.[180]

This illustrates that although it is true that the horizontal interpersonal communion in the church mirrors the triune communion, it is clear that for Torrance, this mirroring function does not constitute the *telos* of the church. As in Kathryn Tanner's argument, a trinitarian ecclesiology does not end with merely human social functions, but rather, "we should seek to understand what it means to participate in the fellowship of the Triune God."[181] This is appropriate because the true being of the church is not found in its horizontal relation, but primarily in its vertical relation with the Triune God. "The Church is truly Church in so far as it dwells in the Holy Trinity," and "it is only through vertical participation in Christ that the Church is horizontally a communion of love, a fellowship of reconciliation, a community of the redeemed."[182] Thus, in Torrance, the church is a communion within a Communion, "*ecclesiola in Ecclesia*." This is a vital element in ecclesiology, because it prevents the church, through the Holy Spirit, from remaining content with its own fellowship, and leads the church to the awareness that its purpose and end are found outside of itself.

To be in the church essentially means to be in the life and love and communion of the Triune God. Torrance thinks that in participating in Christ in his Body, there transpires "a soteriological and ontological unification of people in whose midst God himself dwells through the presence of his Spirit."[183] As God dwells in the church, we also dwell in God. In a more Eastern formulation, Timiadis argues that the church "is the mystical ladder on which man ascends and God descends, so that a real ascent and descent take place, resulting in the blessed meeting of Creator and creature."[184] The way in which the church becomes the avenue where

---

180. Torrance, *Reality and Scientific Theology*, 186–87.

181. Tanner, "Trinity," 16.

182. Torrance, *Trinitarian Faith*, 268; *Order and Disorder*, 109; Moltmann, "Perichoresis," 121. In *Atonement*, 373, Torrance writes: "The term communion or *koinonia* applied to the church refers primarily to our participation through the Spirit in Jesus Christ and therefore in the holy Trinity."

183. Torrance, *Trinitarian Faith*, 254; Colyer, *How to Read*, 219–20.

184. Torrance, *Theological Dialogue* 1: 44. Even the traditional marks of the church, *una, sancta, catholica, apostolica*, in relation to ecumenism, should be understood in

humanity participates in the communion of the Triune God—as consistently stressed by Torrance's argument for mediated participation in the triune life—is in the incarnate Son and in the Holy Spirit.[185] The church, therefore, performs a secondary mediatorial role in our participation in the Triune God, but only because the church is the Body of Christ and the communion of the Holy Spirit. Nevertheless, although reference to Jesus Christ as the Head of the Body abounds, the communion-constituting agency of the Holy Spirit seems to take primacy in this discussion. In *Trinitarian Faith*, Torrance writes that "the church to be *in the Spirit* in an objective and ontological sense, is to be *in God.*"[186] Later on, he then refers to the church as a "divine dimension in the world" and "the direct fruit of God's Holy Spirit."[187]

Conclusions

Tityu Koev writes that there are three fundamental truths in trinitarian theology. These are (1) that God is trihypostatic: *mia ousia, treis hypostaseis*, (2) that each of the three persons possesses personal, hypostatic quality, and (3) that creation and redemption are the works of these persons.[188] It is fair to say that Torrance's trinitarian soteriology, presented in this chapter, encompasses all these three considerations. Moreover, if, as Barth asserted, the doctrine of the Trinity distinguishes the Christian doctrine of God as Christian,[189] could we not also add that salvation understood and formulated in the light of the doctrine of the Trinity is the exclusive Christian understanding of soteriology? If so, then Torrance's accomplishment in his trinitarian soteriology cannot be overrated. As demonstrated in this chapter, Torrance's soteriology consistently makes the doctrine of the Trinity both the source and goal of human salvation.

The doctrine of the Trinity, in Torrance's thought, is not just concerned with the being of God as such, but is concerned with the being of

---

the light of "the sanctification of the church through and in the Spirit whereby it participates in the eternal life of the Triune God," in Torrance, *Theology in Reconciliation*, 17.

185. Torrance, *Trinitarian Faith*, 274–75.

186. Ibid., 251.

187. Ibid., 254.

188. Torrance, *Theological Dialogue* 2: 62.

189. Hart, "Karl Barth, the Trinity and Pluralism," 137. The doctrine of the Trinity, Wolfhart Pannenberg writes, is "the specifically Christian idea of God," in "The Christian Vision of God," 28.

God in relation to others: "The doctrine of the Trinity gives expression to the fact that through his self-revelation in the incarnation God has opened himself to us in such a way that we may know him in the inner relations of his divine Being and have communion with him in his divine life as Father, Son and Holy Spirit."[190] Because God's triune being (or nature) is a dynamic communion of love, he does not remain closed to us but has opened up his being both for knowledge and communion. As Moltmann asserts, the Trinity is an "open Trinity. It is open for its own sending.... It is open for men and for all creation. The life of God within the Trinity cannot be conceived of as a closed circle . . . [and] is open to man, open to the world and open to time."[191] Furthermore, God's openness is reciprocated by God's radical closeness to his creatures. In contrast to Eastern thought regarding the ineffability of God's *esse* and therefore the necessity of viewing God's relation to his creatures in terms only of God's energies, Torrance perceives God's presence as the real presence of God in the fullness of his being in Jesus Christ and the Holy Spirit. Thus, the evangelical Trinity is the theological Trinity. In the economy of salvation, God is with us, *Immanuel*, in the most literal sense.[192]

The possibility of real sharing in the life and love of the triune communion hinges on God's free and gracious act of real self-giving and real self-presence in the world. Torrance's optimism, predicated on (1) God's being as essentially being-in-act-for-others and (2) God's act in his own being in the world, is justifiable. His foundations are purely *theological*, within the logic of grace. The only way, albeit wrong, to critique real relations with God's communion is by grounding the impossibility

---

190. Torrance, *Trinitarian Perspectives*, 1.

191. Quoted in Bauckham, "Jürgen Moltmann," in *One God in Trinity*, 126; Thompson, *Modern Trinitarian Perspectives*, 69. See also Torrance, *Trinitarian Perspectives*, 86; *Reality and Evangelical Theology*, 23; and *Theological Dialogue* 2: 65: "It is this trinitarian interdependence and conditionality within the love of God which precludes the thought of selfishness in God." As indicated earlier, Torrance's difference from Moltmann is that for Torrance, the openness of the Triune God, even though stemming from his nature as love, is also gratuitous and free. See Molnar, *Theologian of the Trinity*, 84.

192. Torrance, *Mediation of Christ*, 29; *Preaching Christ Today*, 11, 14, 27; *When Christ Comes*, 40. He adds in the ensuing pages that "God with us" means God *is for us*, and God is *on our side*. This is the meat of Torrance's sermon "The Sanctification of the Temple," where he preaches that what matters most is "God's presence to us, where we are in the world, to each of us. God adapts his presence to us, and comes to us in our place where we are; this is the special presence of God, where he draws near, makes himself known to us, speaks to us, and gives us his grace." See B41 "Sanctification of the Temple," 2.

in humanity's creaturely nature. This is an *anthropo-logical* reasoning, grounded in human principles, which Torrance abhors.[193] In accordance with the logic of grace, or in the double movement of salvation from the Father to the Father through the Son and in the Holy Spirit, there transpires a *mediated participation* in the salvific persons and works of the Triune God so that we are lifted up into the inner communion of his divine being.[194] In Torrance's words, God "assimilates us into the communion of love in his triune Being."[195] This is humanity's enabled *perichoretic participation* in the triune life, love and communion, which Torrance refers to as humanity's destiny.[196]

---

193. Christos P. Voulgaris strongly argues that anything anthropocentric is ultimately satano-centric, in *Theological Dialogue* 2: 127. John McIntyre, however, argues that a tension in our understanding of theology is inevitable because it still remains a human endeavor, in "Theology and Method," in *Creation, Christ, and Culture*, 205.

194. Torrance, *Ground and Grammar of Theology*, 161; *Reality and Scientific Theology*, 186.

195. Torrance, *Ground and Grammar of Theology*, 154.

196. Torrance, *Transformation and Convergence*, 98–99.

Summary and Conclusions

AN ANALYSIS OF TORRANCE'S THEOLOGICAL CORPUS REVEALS *THAT* HIS soteriology is trinitarian. In fact, it could only be trinitarian, especially because he follows Athanasius's insistence that *Christian* salvation could not but be trinitarian: "This is the salvation of Christians, that believing in the Trinity, that is in the Father and the Son and the Holy Spirit, and being baptized into it, we may indubitably believe the Trinity to have the Same One True Godhead and Power, Majesty and Substance," and that "he who should fall away from it would no longer be a Christian and should no longer be so called."[1] This is rightly so, because as Gunton argues, "the only satisfactory account of the relation between the Creator and creation is a trinitarian one."[2] Also, Torrance consistently applies his scientific and evangelical theology to every aspect of his theology, which results in a soteriology grounded in the gospel of the Triune God. Torrance's doctrine of the Trinity is soteriologically conditioned and his soteriology is conditioned by his doctrine of the Trinity, although this is just an instance of Torrance's general insistence about an appropriate inherent circularity in the relationship between Christian doctrines and the doctrine of the Trinity. In *Belief in Science and in Christian Life,* Torrance speaks about and employs in his theology what he calls "the fiduciary programme," or a self-expanding system of belief in which initial beliefs and subsequent beliefs mutually relate to one another.[3] This "fiduciary programme" is the doctrine of the Trinity, lodged at the very center of his theological system. The assessment that Torrance's works originate and terminate in the Triune God, therefore, is not an overstatement.

Torrance understands salvation as having *one reconciling purpose, proceeding in two movements, and accomplished by three Persons.* Although it would appear that salvation is trinitarian only explicitly at the

---

1. Athanasius, *Ser.* 1.28; quoted in Torrance, *Theological Dialogue* 2: 33, 48, 115.
2. Gunton, *Christ and Creation,* 92.
3. Torrance, *Belief in Science,* 17–18; *Transformation and Convergence,* 195–96.

last aspect in this compressed soteriological formula, each facet is actually fully trinitarian. First, there is only one origin and goal of salvation: the life and love of the Triune God. Thus, although the Father, the incarnate Son, and the Holy Spirit fulfill distinct reconciling agencies in accordance with their *hypostases*, there are not three separate salvation stories. Rather, the mediation of the Father, the mediation of Jesus Christ, and the mediation of the Holy Spirit form the mediation of one salvation that culminate in our being reconciled to the Triune God. Secondly, the whole salvific economy proceeds through a double movement of divine *katabasis* and *anabasis:* from the Father through the Son in the Holy Spirit and in the Holy Spirit through the Son to the Father. And finally, salvation is accomplished through the agency of the persons of the Triune God, each fulfilling a distinct role in strict accordance with his hypostasis as Father, Son, and Holy Spirit.

But if Torrance's soteriology is trinitarian, how may it be articulated? The primary concern is the qualifying term *trinitarian*. Torrance himself did not formulate a "systematic" trinitarian soteriology, nor did he enumerate guidelines or institute a canon that would warrant the trinitarian-ness of a specific soteriological formulation. The challenge, thus, for Torrance scholars is to formulate his trinitarian soteriology in a manner that he himself would most likely have done. This is what this research sought to accomplish. By considering Torrance's own theological methodology and concerns, this research appropriates his evangelical theology and scientific theology as guidelines in sketching his trinitarian soteriology. This decision has significances in several ways. First, it does justice to Torrance's integrative approach. Like any aspect of his overall theology, his soteriology could not be divested of both his theological hermeneutic, methodology, and holism. Secondly, as a follower of Barth, Torrance's evangelical theology dictates that the salvific economy cannot be separated from God's triune self-revelation. The content of the gospel of salvation is none other than the Triune God in his gracious reconciling work. Moreover, presentation of soteriology should follow the *taxis* of triune revelation and reconciliation. Thirdly, in the light of Torrance's *kataphysic* theology, soteriology is perceived primarily in the light of the agents of reconciliation. Torrance does not have an *ex opere operato* soteriology. His soteriology is subject-oriented. As such, his soteriological position offers a promising alternative to utilitarian soteriologies and their primary fascination with the benefits of salvation. For Torrance, the blessing, the gift, and salvation cannot be understood apart from the Blesser, the Giver, and the Savior.

Summary and Conclusions

As such, and in relation to Flett's assessment that Torrance's view of the being of God as personal is "the most important, yet understated feature" of his theology,[4] this book actually argues that the personal being of God is indispensable in Torrance's soteriology. But here, the personal God is understood on two levels. First, it is highlighted that God's personal being could be understood in the light of his personal *ousia* by arguing that God's being is essentially communion-for- and communion-with-others. In the light of his personal being, his interaction with the created other is also personal and personalizing. We have called this the Triune God's *kat' ousian* soteriology. Secondly, God is personal in the light of the personal activities of the three Persons. The persons interact with the created other in the salvific economy in the light of their hypostatic uniqueness, acting personally and dynamically in the mediation of reconciliation. This is why chapters 2, 3, and 4 begin with the *who* of the persons, because it is only in the light of their personal hypostases that their salvific agency could be properly understood. We have called this the Triune God's *kath hypostasin* soteriology.

Chapter 1 discussed Torrance's *scientific, evangelical, and trinitarian* soteriology, and how the three qualifying adjectives are interrelated. As such, the chapter served as an explanatory account of the outline of the whole book, and the foundation upon which the subsequent chapters may be understood. Highlighted there is the fact that theological *procedure* inevitably affects its theological *product*, or that methodology affects theology. The decision to follow the evangelical formula "the grace of our Lord Jesus Christ, and the love of God, and the fellowship of the Holy Spirit" (2 Cor 13:14) is therefore not arbitrary, but is in the light of Torrance's own insistence on it, and which reflects his scientific, evangelical, and trinitarian approach to soteriology. By outlining the succeeding chapters in the light of the benediction formula, the research also responds to Gunton's critique of Torrance's tendency to obscure the plurality of God's activity and identity by an overemphasis upon the unity of God's operations in the economy of salvation.[5] As was shown here, the distinction in the works of the persons in Torrance's soteriology does not neglect the unity, and *vice versa*.

Chapter 2 presented the person and work of the incarnate Son in the economy of salvation. Highlighted there is Torrance's emphasis on incarnational redemption, so that even in the discussion of every aspect of

---

4. Flett, "Persons, Powers, and Pluralities," 221.
5. Gunton, "Being and Person," 121–29.

the person and life of Christ, soteriology is already discussed. Nevertheless, in the light of Torrance's *kath hypostasin* soteriology, the God-man fulfills distinct roles in the salvific economy in strict accordance with his person as the Son, or *kata Christon*. In contrast to the Holy Spirit and the Father, only the Son is incarnate and crucified on a wooden cross. Only the incarnate Son is both *homoousion to Patri* and *homoousion hemin ton auton*. In his oneness with the Father and with us, the Son fulfills a God-humanward and human-Godward mediation in his own incarnate constitution, and reconciles us to the Father and mediates to us the Holy Spirit through his vicarious life, death, resurrection, and ascension. As such, through the hypostatic union and atoning union, we are not only united to Jesus Christ, but are also invited to share in the life and love of the Triune God. "It is not atonement," Torrance argues, "that constitutes the goal and end of that integrated movement of reconciliation but union with God in and through Jesus Christ in whom our human nature is not only saved, healed and renewed but lifted up to participate in the very light, life and love of the Holy Trinity."[6] Torrance's incarnational view of redemption and its ultimate end in the participation in the triune communion makes his soteriology surpass that of many others.

Two interconnected problems-by-implication of Torrance's emphasis on the objective and finished work of Christ *pro nobis* are also discussed in chapter 2: universalism and de-emphasis of human response. First, Torrance himself vigorously rejects universalism, and considers it a heresy like limited atonement. Both, he argues, arise through a logico-mechanistic way of thinking about the *beneficia Christi*. Nevertheless, Torrance's vicarious incarnational redemption does not completely dispel all possible universalistic interpretations. It is undeniable that his optimism about Christ's atoning exchange tends to lean towards universalism. Secondly, with his tendency to emphasize the objective pole of salvation *in Christ* comes views of salvation as passive reception (weak form) or coercive reception (strong form). Torrance's *totus/totus* understanding of the vicarious and atoning exchange may lead to undervaluing humanity's contingent freedom. In its weak form, human freedom is unnecessary, and in its strong form, human freedom is overpowered. It was discussed that this specific problem is only evident in his published writings, because his sermons provide us with counter balancing statements. Perhaps we can say that Torrance was addressing two sets of audience. In his published writings, he was consciously engaging the existentialist understanding of

---

6. Torrance, *Mediation of Christ*, 66.

Summary and Conclusions

salvation prevalent in the evangelical movement that emphasizes human decision in the salvific process. In his dealings with his parishioners, however, he was engaging a group of people deeply rooted in federal Calvinism that emphasizes divine fiat at the expense of human responsibility. In the former he was addressing an excess; in the latter he was addressing a deficiency. Nevertheless, Torrance is consistent throughout his published and unpublished writings that the objective aspect of salvation takes precedence and priority over humanity's subjective response. Salvation primarily involves an active reception, not cooperation, on the part of humanity.

The beginning of chapter 3 explains why a presentation of the agency of the Father has to proceed only after a chapter on the Son's person and work. On the one hand, it takes seriously Jesus's statement, "No one comes to the Father except through me" (John 14:6). The concern here is not the order of being, but the order of knowing the Father in revelation and reconciliation. The Torrance theological tradition's strong participatory theology highlights that we only know the Father by participation in the knowledge of the Son in the Holy Spirit. Moreover, it is Jesus Christ the Son who knows the Father, and so his revelation of the Father must be considered as absolute authority. Knowing the Father behind the back of Jesus Christ or from any speculative abstraction does not have any place in Torrance's theology and methodology. On the other hand, the outline follows the Pauline benediction formula. It could be said that this chapter is quite unique to the book, because the person of the Father is normally invisible in soteriological discourses. For Torrance, the Father, like the Son and the Holy Spirit, fulfills a distinct role in the salvific economy in strict accordance with his hypostasis as the Father, or *kata Patera*. This is another unique aspect of Torrance's soteriology. Whereas the economy of salvation is typically treated only in the light of the two missions (of the Son and of the Holy Spirit), Torrance considers the "from the Father" and "to the Father" in the double movement of salvation as soteriological statements depicting the Father's active involvement in the mediation of reconciliation. In terms of the "from the Father" aspect, the chapter elaborated that the Father's loving, electing, and sending roles are distinct to him in the salvific economy. In terms of the "to the Father" aspect, the concept of adoption into the family of God as sons and daughters of the Father was highlighted. But again, the reconciling paternity of the Father has as its ultimate goal sharing in the life and love of the Triune God. Adoption into the family of God is a conceptual equivalent of participation in the triune communion.

The person and work of the Holy Spirit is then discussed in chapter 4. The asymmetry in Torrance's treatment of the persons and works of the Triune God, first noticeable in comparing chapters 2 and 3, is further confirmed in this chapter. Like his treatises on the Father, the Spirit's agency, in comparison with his treatment of the Son's agency, is not as intensively treated. This asymmetry reflects Torrance's acceptance of economic subordination in the Trinity. This does not mean, however, that Torrance does not have a robust pneumatology. The chapter has actually demonstrated that the Holy Spirit plays many central roles in the economy of salvation. Using human analogy, it is the Holy Spirit who is actually over-worked in the economy! It was demonstrated that the Spirit operates in the salvific economy in the light of his hypostasis and nature as the self-effacing Spirit, which consequently requires worshipful apophatism on the part of the theologian. Again, this is in line with Torrance's *kath hypostasin* soteriology, which, in this case, is *kata Pneuma*. Therefore, it is not as if Torrance held an instrumental pneumatology.[7] Rather, it is the Spirit's self-effacing hypostasis and will that his agency in the salvific economy is that of being the *vinculum caritatis* on three levels of relationship: (1) *onto-horizontal*, or between the Father and the Son (and also even in the incarnate life of the Son); (2) *economic-vertical*, or in humanity's union with Jesus Christ to the Father; and (3) *creaturely-horizontal*, or in humanity's relationship with one another in the church. This is the *koinonia* of the communion-constituting Spirit.

Again, just as in the case of the Father and the Son, the work of the Holy Spirit has as its origin and goal the lifting up of humanity into participation in the communion of love that God is. And it is precisely because of this that the book critiqued Torrance's reluctance to affirm fully the Holy Spirit as Mediator. The Holy Spirit also fulfills a mediatorial office between God and the world in accordance with his hypostasis as the Spirit, which does not contradict the mediation of Jesus Christ, who reconciles the world to the Triune God in the light of the hypostatic union of God and humanity in Christ's own person. Of course it is not a mediation-in-isolation, because like the Son, the mediating work of the Holy Spirit has its ground, origin, and goal in the triune communion.

Another aspect in Torrance's pneumatology that is left undeveloped by Torrance is the important Pauline concept of "life in the Spirit" and its moral-ethical implications. (He has a robust understanding of the

---

7. Kruger accuses Torrance of this error in "Participation in the Self-Knowledge of God," 321–24.

Summary and Conclusions

trinitarian and relational implications of the term.) In a sense, this neglect corresponds to Torrance's non-engagement with practical theology as a distinct branch of theology, and he should thus be acquitted of blame. But there is also a sense in which this neglect portrays a fundamental weakness in Torrance's overall theological framework, and which is also reflected in his view of the passive role of humanity in the salvific economy discussed in chapter 2. As a consolation, this void has given others, like Ray S. Anderson, the opportunity to extract the practical implications of Torrance's theology.[8]

As repeatedly asserted throughout the book, the reconciling agency of the person of the Trinity has its goal in the participation of humanity into the life and love of the Triune God. Union with Jesus Christ means being united to the Father in the Holy Spirit; to be children of the Father means to be a brother of Jesus Christ in the Holy Spirit; and to be in the *koinonia* of the Holy Spirit means to be united with Jesus Christ to the Father. The three Persons all fulfill distinct roles in the economy, but there is ultimately one purpose: for humanity to be mediated into the triune communion. In a chiasmus, and elaborating the Athanasian "from the Father through the Son in the Spirit and in the Spirit through the Son to the Father" soteriological formula, the katabatic and the anabatic reconciling activities of the Triune God could be portrayed as:

p, Communion *of* the persons of the Triune God as the *origin* of human salvation
    m_1, The Father sends the Son and the Holy Spirit to the world
        m_2, The Son mediates the Father in the Holy Spirit to humanity
            m_3, The Holy Spirit mediates the Son of the Father to humanity
            m_3, The Holy Spirit lifts humanity in union with Jesus Christ to the Father
        m_2, The Son unites humanity to the Father in the communion of the Holy Spirit
    m_1, The Father receives humanity as brothers of Jesus Christ in the Holy Spirit
p, Communion *with* the persons of the Triune God as the *goal* of human salvation

---

8. See "The Practical Theology of Thomas F. Torrance," 49–65; and "Reading Torrance as a Practical Theologian," in *the Promise of Trinitarian Theology*, 161–83.

Chapters 2, 3, and 4 emphasized the three Persons's mediation of reconciliation and humanity's *mediated* participation in the triune life and love (m_1, m_2, and m_3), and they form the basis for chapter 5's emphasis on humanity's *perichoretic* participation. The outline is heuristic because humanity's *perichoretic* participation finds its ground in *mediated* participation. Without mediation, there is no communion in the life and love of the Triune God. Also, if chapters 2, 3, and 4 argued for a *kath hypostasin* trinitarian soteriology, chapter 5 explained Torrance's *kat' ousian* trinitarian soteriology, and argued that the origin and goal of humanity's salvation is in strict accordance with the nature of God as a communion of love (p). Humanity's *perichoretic* participation in the triune life and love, therefore, finds its basis in the perichoretic life and love of the Triune God himself. The chapter also underscored Torrance's soteriological trinitarianism and trinitarian soteriology, or the reciprocal inseparability of both knowledge of the Triune God's being in his act and act in his being. Knowledge of the Triune God has its *telos* not in "complete clarification or understanding of God, but the reaching of a *communion* with him."[9]

Chapter 5 not only summed up and interrelated the arguments of the preceding chapters, but also offered caveats about Torrance's trinitarian soteriology. It concluded that although Torrance holds that our communion with God is not only with his energies but with God's essence, he does not hold a cosmonistic or uniform communion. But the most important caveat is that, far from understanding participation in the triune communion as humanity's substantial metamorphosis or divinization, redeemed humanity actually communes with God as humanized humans and personalized persons. "The exaltation of human nature into the life of God," Torrance writes, "does not mean the disappearance of man or the swallowing up of human and creaturely being in the infinite ocean of divine Being, but rather that human nature, remaining creaturely and human, is yet exalted in Christ to share in God's life and glory."[10] Important

---

9. Torrance, *Theological Dialogue* 2: 63.

10. Torrance, *Space, Time, and Resurrection*, 135. Torrance also regards our communion with the Triune God as the rest at the end of human journey, "a rest in which we share with God His own self-refreshment and peace. It is a rest in which the inner and essential being of man is quickened and renewed through partaking of the very life of God, that is, of the inner resources of God's own Being. This does not mean that the individual human being, when he dies, gets swallowed up and lost in the vast measureless ocean of deity, but that without losing his individuality or his distinct identity, he reaches the consummation of his life in communion with God," in B47 Untitled sermon on Hebrews 4:9–16, 1.

Summary and Conclusions

and interrelated here again are the humanizing agency of the incarnate Son and the creative and sustaining office of the Holy Spirit.

Perhaps the main weakness of this book is its generally appreciative tone, and therefore it only offers rudimentary critiques of Torrance's position. As an overall evaluation, Torrance's theology is phenomenally coherent and his writings exude consistency in both thought and methodology, which explains his somewhat repetitive style of writing as well. The critiques presented in the book were more like detection of avenues that need further elucidation or correlation rather than pointing out inconsistencies. On the one hand, these critiques are only minor, and Torrance could easily be acquitted, because any theologian could not be really considered at fault for failing to elaborate all the issues involved in a particular theme. But on the other hand, it seems that Torrance may be guilty of purposively evading topics that might provide avenues of critiques for inconsistency in his theology. For instance, he did not develop Irenaeus's "two hands of the Father" because it might vindicate the sole *monarchia* of the Father. He also did not have a well-treated view of the kingly office of Christ in relation to the *Christus Victor* and the Pauline "life in the Spirit" because they might lead to discussions on human agency, and thus subvert his emphasis on the objective and finished work of Christ. As such, it can be said that Torrance's determination towards theological consistency is achieved at the expense of neglecting important theological aspects.

The book also avoided making critiques of Torrance's theology by imposing on him categories from different perspectives. But this is just proper, because this book is descriptive and analytical in nature, and was never intended to be comparative. The fallacy of approaching Torrance's theology from a specific perspective is also purposively evaded to desist from imposing and measuring Torrance in accordance with the biases of a particular theological tradition. Similarly, approaching Torrance from a supposed Archimedean point is just spurious. If these approaches are undertaken, there will be many critiques of Torrance's position, but only because of prejudiced preferences rather than because of an informed engagement. Ho's *A Critical Study on Torrance's Theology of Incarnation* is an example of this biased reading of Torrance, and so although the book offers many critiques, these critiques do not really have an overall cohesive theological ground other than approaching Torrance from several traditions that are in conflict with Torrance's views. This is why I call Ho's book a cornucopia of awkward theological critiques.

Finally, this book has at least two strengths and contributions for wider Torrance studies. First, it is the first to offer an analysis of Torrance's *trinitarian* soteriology. It argues that communion *of* and *with* the Triune God constitutes the *origin* and *goal* of human salvation, and brings to focus Torrance's interrelated ideas of *mediated* participation and *perichoretic* participation in the triune life and love. Both are actually important in Torrance's view of humanity's sharing in the communion of love that God is, and they qualify each other. In summary, Torrance's soteriology is trinitarian because for him (1) the communion of God is the *origin* of human salvation, (2) the persons of the Triune God are the agents of mediation and reconciliation, and (3) communion with God is the *goal* of human salvation. Because of this three-fold consideration, how he understands each aspect, and how he sees their interrelation, Torrance's soteriology has a lot to offer Christian theology. Secondly, this book uniquely presents the interrelation of Torrance's scientific theology, evangelical theology, and trinitarian soteriology. It argues that Torrance's unique soteriological formulation is informed by *kat' ousian* and *kath hypostasin* principles. It also argues that Torrance's evangelical theology or understanding of the gospel guides both the *content* and *procedure* of his trinitarian soteriology.

Bibliography

Primary: Published Works

Torrance, Thomas F. "Alexandrian Theology." *Ekklesiastikos Pharos* 52 (1970) 185-89.
———. "Answer to God." *Biblical Theology* 2 (1951) 3-16.
———. "The Apocalypse Now." *Life and Work*, October 1988, 19-20.
———. *The Apocalypse Today: Sermons on Revelations*. London: James Clarke, 1960.
———. "The Atonement and the Oneness of the Church." *Scottish Journal of Theology* 7 (1954) 245-69.
———. *Atonement: The Person and Work of Christ*. Edited by Robert T. Walker. Milton Keynes, UK: Paternoster, 2009.
———. "The Atonement: The Singularity of Christ and the Finality of the Cross—The Atonement and the Moral Order." In *Universalism and the Doctrine of Hell*, edited by Nigel M. de S. Cameron, 225-56. Carlisle, UK: Paternoster, 1991.
———. "Babylon—Symbol of Worldly Power." *Life and Work*, December 1988, 16-17.
———, editor. *Belief in Science and in Christian Life: The Relevance of Michael Polanyi's Thought for Christian Faith and Life*. Edinburgh: Handsel, 1980.
———. "The Bible's Guidance on Baptism." *Life and Work*, September 1982, 16-17.
———. "The Biblical Conception of Faith." *The Expository Times* 68 (1957) 221-22.
———. *Calvin's Doctrine of Man*. Westport, CT: Greenwood, 1977.
———. "The Christian Apprehension of God the Father." In *Speaking the Christian God: The Holy Trinity and the Challenge of Feminism*, edited by Alvin F. Kimel, Jr., 120-43. Grand Rapids: Eerdmans, 1992.
———. *The Christian Doctrine of God: One Being Three Persons*. Edinburgh: T. & T. Clark, 1996.
———. *The Christian Frame of Mind*. Edinburgh: Handsel, 1985.
———. *Christian Theology and Scientific Culture*. Belfast: Christian Journals, 1980.
———. *Conflict and Agreement in the Church*, vol. 1, *Order and Disorder*. London: Lutterworth, 1959.
———. *Conflict and Agreement in the Church*, vol. 2, *The Ministry and the Sacraments of the Gospel*. London: Lutterworth, 1960.
———. "Concerning Amsterdam I. The Nature and Mission of the Church: A Discussion of Volumes I and II of the Preparatory Studies." *Scottish Journal of Theology* 2 (1949) 241-70.
———. "The Crisis of Community." *Life and Work*, December 1990, 16-17.
———. "Crisis in the Kirk." In *St. Andrews Rock: The State of the Church in Scotland*, edited by Steward Lamont, 13-23. London: Bellows, 1992.
———. "The Crisis of Morality." *Life and Work*, November 1990, 15-16.

Bibliography

———. "A 'Dark Whirlpool of Error' on the Scottish Identity." *Life and Work*, July 1982, 18–19.
———. "The Deposit of Faith." *Scottish Journal of Theology* 36 (1983) 1–28.
———. *Divine and Contingent Order*. Reprint. Edinburgh: T. & T. Clark, 1998.
———. *Divine Meaning: Studies in Patristic Hermeneutics*. Edinburgh: T. & T. Clark, 1995.
———. *The Doctrine of Grace in the Apostolic Fathers*. Reprint. Eugene, OR: Wipf & Stock, 1996.
———. *The Doctrine of Jesus Christ*. Reprint. Eugene, OR: Wipf & Stock, 2002.
———. "The Doctrine of the Virgin Birth." *Scottish Bulletin of Evangelical Theology* 12 (1994) 8–25.
———. "Ecumenism and Rome." *Scottish Journal of Theology* 37 (1984) 59–64.
———. "The Evangelical Significance of the Homoousion: Sermon on John 5:17." *Abba Salama* 5 (1974) 165–67.
———. "The First-Born of All Creation." *Life and Work*, December 1976, 12–14.
———. *God and Rationality*. Reprint. Edinburgh: T. & T. Clark, 1997.
———. "The Goodness and Dignity of Man in the Christian Tradition." *Modern Theology* 4 (1988) 309–22.
———. "The Gospel Depends on the Cross." *Life and Work*, November 1988, 20–21.
———. *The Ground and Grammar of Theology*. Charlottesville, VA: The University Press of Virginia, 1981.
———. "Hermeneutics According to F. D. E. Schleiermacher." *Scottish Journal of Theology* 21 (1968) 257–67.
———. "The Historical Jesus: From the Perspective of a Theologian." In *The New Testament Age: Essays in Honor of Bo Reicke*, vol. 2, edited by William C. Weinrich, 511–26. Macon, GA: Mercer University Press, 1984.
———. "History and Reformation." *Scottish Journal of Theology* 4 (1951) 279–91.
———. "Hugh Ross Mackintosh: Theologian of the Cross." *The Scottish Bulletin of Evangelical Theology* 5 (1987) 160–73.
———. "Immortality and Light." *Religious Studies* 17 (1981) 147–61.
———. "The Implications of Oikonomia for Knowledge and Speech of God in Early Christian Theology." In *Oikonomia: Heilsgeschichte als Thema der Theologie: Oscar Cullman zum 65 Geburstag Gewidmet*, edited by Felix Christ, 223–38. Hamburg: Reich, 1967.
———, editor. *The Incarnation: Ecumenical Studies in the Nicene-Constantinopolitan Creed AD 381*. Edinburgh: Handsel, 1981.
———. *Incarnation: The Person and Life of Christ*. Edited by Robert T. Walker. Milton Keynes, UK: Paternoster, 2008.
———. "Israel and the Incarnation." *Judaica* 13 (1957) 1–18.
———. "Jesus is God and Man in One Person." *Life and Work*, March 1986, 16–17.
———. *Juridical Law and Physical Law: Toward a Realist Foundation for Human Law*. Eugene, OR: Wipf & Stock, 1982.
———. "Karl Barth." *The Expository Times* 66 (1955) 205–9.
———. "Karl Barth: Appreciation and Tribute in Honour of his Seventieth Birthday." *The Expository Times* 67 (1956) 261–63.
———. *Karl Barth: Biblical and Evangelical Theologian*. Edinburgh: T. & T. Clark, 1990.
———. *Karl Barth: An Introduction to His Early Theology, 1910–1931*. London: SCM, 1962.

———. *The Kingdom and the Church: A Study in the Theology of the Reformation.* Reprint. Eugene, OR: Wipf & Stock, 1996.

———. "The Kirk's Crisis of Faith." *Life and Work*, October 1990, 15–16.

———. "The Light of the World." *Reformed Journal* 38 (December 1988) 9–12.

———. *The Mediation of Christ.* Rev. ed. Edinburgh: T. & T. Clark, 1992.

———. "*Phusikos Kai Theologikos Logos*, St Paul and Athenagoras at Athens." *Scottish Journal of Theology* 41 (1988) 11–26.

———. "The Place of Christology in Biblical and Dogmatic Theology." In *Essays in Christology for Karl Barth*, edited by T. H. L. Parker, 13–37. London: Lutterworth, 1956.

———. *Preaching Christ Today: The Gospel and Scientific Thinking.* Grand Rapids: Eerdmans, 1994.

———. "Predestination in Christ." *Evangelical Quarterly* 13 (1941) 108–41.

———. "The Pre-eminence of Christ." *The Expository Times* 89 (1977) 54–55.

———. "Proselyte Baptism." *New Testament Studies* 1 (1954) 150–54.

———. "Putting First Things First." *Presbyterian Survey*, October 1981, 10–12.

———. *Reality and Evangelical Theology.* Philadelphia: Westminster, 1982.

———. *Reality and Scientific Theology.* Edinburgh: Scottish Academic Press, 1986.

———. "The Reconciliation of Mind." *TSF Bulletin* 10 (1987) 4–7.

———. "Reformed Dogmatics, Not Dogmatism." *Theology* 70 (1967) 52–56.

———. "Revelation, Creation and Law." *The Heythrop Journal* 37 (1996) 273–83.

———. "A Right-about-Turn for the Kirk." *Life and Work*, April 1981, 20–21.

———. *The Royal Priesthood.* 2nd ed. Edinburgh: T. & T. Clark, 1993.

———. "Salvation is of the Jews." *The Evangelical Quarterly* 22 (1950) 164–73.

———. *The School of Faith.* London: Camelot, 1959.

———. *Scottish Theology: From John Knox to John McLeod Campbell.* Edinburgh: T. & T. Clark, 1996.

———. "A Serious Call for a Return to Devout and Holy Life." *Life and Work*, July 1979, 14–15.

———. "The Soul and Person in Theological Perspective." In *Religion, Reason and the Self: Essays in Honour of Hywel D. Lewis*, edited by Stewart R. Sutherland and T. A. Roberts, 103–18. Cardiff: University of Wales Press, 1989.

———. *Space, Time, and Incarnation.* Reprint. Edinburgh: T. & T. Clark, 1997.

———. *Space, Time, and Resurrection.* Grand Rapids: Eerdmans, 1976.

———. "The Substance of the Faith." *Life and Work*, November 1982, 16–17.

———. "The Substance of the Faith: A Clarification of the Concept in the Church of Scotland." *Scottish Journal of Theology* 36 (1983) 327–38.

———, editor. *Theological Dialogue between Orthodox and Reformed Churches.* 2 vols. Edinburgh: Scottish Academic Press, 1985 and 1993.

———. *Theological and Natural Science.* Reprint. Eugene, OR: Wipf & Stock, 2002.

———. "Theological Realism." In *The Philosophical Frontiers of Christian Theology: Essays Presented to D. M. MacKinnon*, edited by B. Hebblethwaite and S. Sutherland, 169–96. Cambridge: Cambridge University Press, 1982.

———. *Theological Science.* Oxford: Oxford University Press, 1969.

———. *Theology in Reconciliation: Essays Towards Evangelical and Catholic Unity in East and West.* Reprint. Eugene, OR: Wipf & Stock, 1997.

———. *Theology in Reconstruction.* Grand Rapids: Eerdmans, 1965.

———. "The Tide has Turned." *Life and Work*, March 1984, 14–15.

Bibliography

———. "The Transcendental Role of Wisdom in Science." In *Facets of Faith and Science*, vol. 1, *Historiography and Modes of Interaction*, edited by Jitse van der Meer, 131–49. Lanham, MD: University Press of America, 1996.

———. *Transformation & Convergence in the Frame of Knowledge*. Grand Rapids: Eerdmans, 1984.

———. *The Trinitarian Faith: The Evangelical Theology of the Ancient Catholic Church*. Edinburgh: T. & T. Clark, 1995.

———. *Trinitarian Perspectives: Toward Doctrinal Agreement*. Edinburgh: T. & T. Clark, 1994.

———. "Ultimate and Penultimate Beliefs in Science." In *Facets of Faith and Science*, vol. 1, *Historiography and Modes of Interaction*, edited by Jitse van der Meer, 151–76. Lanham, MD: University Press of America, 1996.

———. "The Uniqueness of Divine Revelation and the Authority of the Scriptures: The Creed Association Statement." *Scottish Bulletin of Evangelical Theology* 13 (1995) 97–101.

———. "Universalism or Election?" *Scottish Journal of Theology* 2 (1949) 310–18.

———. "The Way of Reunion: Issues Confronting the 1954 World Council of Churches—VI." *The Christian Century* 71, January-June 1954, 204–5.

———. *When Christ Comes and Comes Again*. Reprint. Eugene, OR: Wipf & Stock, 1996.

———. "Where is the Church of Scotland Going?" *Life and Work*, May 1989, 24–26.

———. "Where Do We Go from Lund?" *Scottish Journal of Theology* 6 (1953) 53–64.

———. "The Whole Universe Revolves Round Jesus Christ." *Life and Work*, April 1977, 12–14.

———. "Why Karl Barth Still Matters so Much." *Life and Work*, June 1986, 16.

———. "The Word of God and the Nature of Man." In *Reformation Old and New: Festschrift for Karl Barth*, edited by F. W. Camfield, 121–41. London: Lutterworth, 1947.

———. "The Word of God and the Response of Man." *Bijragen* 30 (1969) 172–83.

Primary: Unpublished Works

All of the unpublished works listed here are found in The Thomas F. Torrance Manuscript Collection. Special Collections, Princeton Theological Seminary Library. The list here is organized according to the Box Numbers they come from. Items in brackets indicate illegible or missing words.

Box 23 General Theology Lectures (Auburn Lectures, New College Lectures and other documents)

"Christian Doctrine of God"
"The Christian Doctrine of Revelation"
"Christ's View of God, and Ours"
"The Doctrine of God in Traditional Theology"
"Where is God?"

Bibliography

Box 36 Material collected for a proposed third volume of *Conflict and Agreement in the Church*

"From a Christocentric to a Trinitarian Ecumenism, Ecumenical Suicide or Christocentric Renewal"
"The Heart of the Matter, 'Down with Romantic Slush.'" Sermon preached at The Great St. Mary's Church. Cambridge, 14 November 1965.
"What is the Church?"

Box 38 Sermons, Lectures, and Addresses, in Scotland and Abroad

"Christ in the Centre of Mission." Sermon preached at Craiglockhart Parish Church (Centenary Celebration).
Communion Sermon. Whitekirk, 5 December 1993.
"Lessons on Isaiah 6:1-4 and Ephesians 2:8-16; John 14:1-20." n.p., n.d.
"No Other Name." Sermon on Numbers 6:22-27 and Acts 4:5-12. New Restalrig Church, Edinburgh, 9 February 1992.
"The Real Light." Sermon on John 1:9. University Sermon. Emmanuel Church, 15 November 1981.
"That in everything he might be preeminent." Sermon on Colossians 1:13. St. Giles, Edinburgh, 24 May 1977.
Untitled sermon preached at Beechgrove Church, Aberdeen, 2 November 1997.[1]
Untitled sermon on 1 Corinthians 2:1-5. n.p., n.d.
Untitled sermon on Isaiah 21:11-12. n.p., n.d.
Untitled sermon on John 1:6-9. n.p., n.d.[2]
Untitled sermon on John 5:17. Eton College, 27 November 1983.
Untitled sermon outline on Matthew 11:28-30.
"With God Is Terrible Majesty." Sermon on Job 37:22. n.p., n.d.

---

1. This sermon has similarity in content with B38 Untitled sermon at Penicuik, Midlothian, 5 September 1993; B38 Cluny Parish, Edinburgh, 17 October 1993; B38 Macdonald Memorial Church, Bellshill, 7 June 1998; B39 "'He that spared not his own Son,'" Cluny Church, 17 October 1993; "The Cross—a Window into the heart of the Father," First Presbyterian Church in Dillon, 2 February 1997.

2. This sermon has similarity in content with B38 Untitled sermon on 1 John 1:5, [_] 1973; B38 "I am the light of the World," sermon on John 8:12, Whitekirk, 31 August 1980; B38 "The Real Light," University sermon on John 1:9, Emmanuel Church, 15 November 1981; B38 Untitled sermon on John 1:34, Loretto, 4 November [_]; B39 "A Faith for Hard Times: The Living Light," n.p., 20 November 1977; B39 "Light: Its Theology and Physics," Lawnswood School, Leeds, 16 November 1981; B39 "Light," Moderatorial sermon while visiting Aberdeen Presbytery and University, Kings College Chapel, Aberdeen, 13 February 1977; B39 "Christ the Light of the World," Davidson College Presbyterian Church, 26 January 1997; B41 "Christ the Light of the World: with reference to James Clerk Maxwell," Parton Kirk, 11 June 1989; B41 "The Christian Faith and the Physics of Light, Eton College, Windsor, 26 January [_]; Washington, 27 February [_]; B45 Untitled sermon on 1 John 1:1-10; 2:1-11 (n.p., n.d.).

Bibliography

Box 39 Sermons, Lectures, and Addresses, in Scotland and Abroad

"At the ninth hour Jesus cried with a loud voice." Sermon on Mark 15:34. n.p., n.d.[3]
"The Centrality of Christ." Luke 22:31–32. n.p., n.d.
"Ecumenical Service—Kirk of the Greyfriars." Sermon on Acts 2:41–47, especially verse 42. Edinburgh, Trinity Sunday, 24 May 1970.
Untitled sermon on Exodus 20:1–4 and John 14:6, 9. Monkton Combe School Chapel, 3 November 1963.
Untitled sermon on Mark 2:5. Athelstaneford [and] Whitekirk, 12 August 1979.
Untitled sermon on 2 Corinthians 8:9. Beechgrove, 10 December 1967.
Untitled sermon on Matthew 5:23–24. n.p., 13 December 1973 and 8 September 1974.
Untitled sermon on Titus 3:4f. Baptism of Robyn Alison Meta Torrance. Hillswick, 31 March 1985.
"Violence in Society"[4]

Box 40 Sermons, Lectures, and Addresses, in Scotland and Abroad

"Aristotelianism and Calvinism in Scotland"
"Christian Protest and the Power of Evil." Fireside Chat with students, Eckerd College, March 1980.
"Implicit Faith"

Box 41 Lectures and Addresses in Scotland and Abroad

"Diaconate Service." Cluny Parish Church, Edinburgh, 23 November 1979.
"The Sanctification of the Temple." Sermon on Matthew 21:1–16. n.p., n.d.
"The Secularization of the Church"
"The Task of the Church in Britain in the Eighties"
Untitled sermon on 1 Corinthians 3:16. Beechgrove, 8 June 1975.
Untitled sermon on 1 Corinthians 1:22. Whitekirk, 6 September 1981.
Untitled sermon on Matthew 18:18–20. The Canongate Kirk, Edinburgh, 18 July 1978; Northmavine, Hillswick, Shetland, 24 January 1982.

Box 42, Folder "Sermons on Genesis"

"Creation." Sermon on Genesis 1:1. Alyth, 28 September 1941.
"Sin at the Door." Sermon on Genesis 4:7. Alyth, 1940.
"Lot and Daniel." Sermon on Genesis 13:12 and Daniel 6:10. Alyth, 9 February 1941.

---

3. See almost the same sermon B42 "My God, my God, Why hast thou forsaken me?" from Matthew 27:46, Braid Church, Edinburgh, 29 October 1967; and also found in Box 47.

4. Also preached at B41 IBA Lunch, Glasgow, 1 July 1976.

"Abram the Hebrew." Sermon on Genesis 14:13. Alyth, 1940.
"Oh that Ishmael might live before Thee." Sermon on Genesis 17:18. Alyth, 9 February 1941.
"For how shall I go up to my father, and the lad be not with me?" Sermon on Genesis 44:34. Alyth, Ascension Day, 1940.

Box 42, Folder "Sermons on Exodus"

"Knowledge of God." Sermon on Exodus 20:1, 3. Alyth, 9 March 1941.
"Second-hand Religion." Sermon on Exodus 20:19. Alyth, 1940; Beechgrove, December 1948.
"Aaron's Calf." Sermon on Exodus 32:1. Alyth, 1940, Blair[___], December 1940; Dun[___], December 1940; Pollok-Slagno, 2 May 1943.
"Moses wist not that the skin of His face shone while he talked with him." Sermon on Exodus 34:29. Alyth, 1940.

Box 42, Folder "Sermons on Leviticus"

"Harvest Thanksgiving." Sermon on Leviticus 26:10. Alyth, 1940.

Box 42, Folder "Sermons on Deuteronomy"

"Who is like unto thee, O people saved by the Lord?" Sermon on Deuteronomy 33:29. Alyth, 22 March 1942.

Box 42, Folder "Sermons on Judges"

"Samson." Sermon on Judges 16:20. Alyth, 1940.

Box 42, Folder "Sermons on 1 and 2 Samuel"

"Make us a King to judge us." Sermon on 1 Samuel 8:5. Alyth, 2 February 1940.
"Let him curse, for the Lord hath bidden him." Sermon on 2 Samuel 16:11. Alyth, 1941; Beechgrove, 2 May 1949.
"The Well at Bethlehem." Communion sermon on 2 Samuel 23:15f. Alyth, September 1940; Beechgrove, 10 April 1949; Pl[___] Edinburgh, 11 November 1951; L[___] tt[_], 24 November 1951.

Box 42, Folder "Sermons on 1 and 2 Kings"

"Naaman." Sermon on 1 Kings 5:10–12. Alyth, 1940.
"The unknown Prophet from Judah." Sermon on 1 Kings 13. Alyth, October 1940.
"Joash and Elisha." Sermon on 2 Kings 13:14–16. Alyth, 9 November 1941.

Bibliography

Box 42, Folder "Sermons on Esther"

"National Day of Prayer." Sermon on Esther 4:14. Alyth, 23 March 1941.

Box 42, Folder "Sermons on Job"

"Doth Job Fear God for nought?" Sermon on Job 1:9; 21:15. Alyth, 1940.

Box 42, Folder "Sermons on Psalms"

"What is Man?" Sermon on Psalm 8:4. Alyth, 1942.
"Prosperity of the Wicked." Sermon on Psalm 73:16–17. Alyth, 1940.
"Thanksgiving After Communion." Sermon on Psalm 116:12, 13. Alyth, June 1940.[5]
"O Lord, Thou hast searched me and known me." Sermon on Psalm 139:1. Alyth, 27 September 1941.
"Wonder in Christianity." Sermon on Psalm 139:14. Alyth, 9 March 1941.

Box 42, Folder "Sermons on Proverbs"

"There is a way that seems right unto a man." Sermon on Proverbs 14:12. Alyth, 27 September 1942.
"Foreign Missions." Sermon on Proverbs 24:11–12. Alyth, December 1940.

Box 43, Folder "Sermons on Ecclesiastes"

"Keep thy Foot." Sermon on Ecclesiastes 5:1. Alyth, 1940.

Box 43, Folder "Sermons on Isaiah"

"The Holiness of God." Sermon on Isaiah 6:3. Alyth, April 1941.
Untitled sermon on Isaiah 50:11. Alyth, 1940.
"The Messenger of Peace." Sermon on Isaiah 52:7. Alyth, Christmas, 1940.

Box 43, Folder "Sermons on Jeremiah"

Untitled sermon on Jeremiah 7:2. n.p., n.d.
"Cursed be the man that trusted in man." Sermon on Jeremiah 17:5. Alyth, 31 May 1942.

---

5. Same with "Thanksgiving after Communion," sermon on Hebrews 13:16, Alyth, 16 February 1941.

Box 43, Folder "Sermons on Ezekiel"

"The Little Sanctuary." Sermon on Ezekiel 11:16. Alyth, 1940.

Box 43, Folder "Sermons on Daniel"

"O man greatly beloved—be stronger." Sermon on Daniel 10:19. Alyth, 22 March 1942.

Box 43, Folder "Sermons on Matthew 1–9"

Untitled sermon on Matthew 1:18–25. Alyth, 20 December 1942; Beechgrove, Christmas, 1948; Athelstaneford and Whitekirk, 28 December 1975.
"The First Temptation of Jesus." Sermon on Matthew 4:1f. Alyth, 5 October 1941.
"The Second Temptation." Sermon on Matthew 4:5–7. Alyth, 5 October 1941.
"The Third Temptation." Sermon on Matthew 4:8–10. Alyth, 12 October 1941.
"Be ye therefore perfect." Sermon on Matthew 5:48. Alyth, 1 February 1942.
"The Hem of His Garment." Sermon on Matthew 9:20. Alyth, 19 January 1941; Beechgrove, 6 June 1948.

Box 43, Folder "Sermons on Matthew 10–19"

"The Fatherhood of God." Sermon on Matthew 11:27. Alyth, July 1941.
"Beware the leaven of the Sadducees." Sermon on Matthew 16:6. Alyth, 2 November 1941.
Untitled sermon on Matthew 16:24–25. Fettes College, Confirmation Service, 28 May 1978.
"Conversion." Sermon on Matthew 18:3. Alyth, 1941.
"The Lost Sheep." Sermon on Matthew 18:13 and Luke 15:14. Alyth, 1940; Beechgrove, 11 January 1948.

Box 44, Folder "Sermons on Matthew 20–28"

"Labourers in the Vineyard." Sermon on Matthew 20:16. Alyth, 1940; Beechgrove, 23 January 1949; Greentar[___], 23 September 1951.
"Following Christ in Service." Sermon on Matthew 20:28. Alyth, September 1940.
"Who is This?" Sermon on Matthew 21:10. Alyth, Palm Sunday, 29 March 1942.
"Palm Sunday." Sermon on Zechariah 9:9 and Matthew 21:10. Alyth, April 1941.
"Watchers at the Cross." Sermon on Matthew 27:36. Alyth, 1940.
Untitled Sermon on Matthew 28:19–20. Alyth, 21 September 1941.
Untitled Sermon on Matthew 28:19. Confirmation Service, n.p., n.d.

Box 44, Folder "Sermons on Mark"

"Christ: God or Not!" Sermon on Mark 3:21 and Matthew 26:65. Alyth, 1940; Beechgrove, 7 December 1949.

Bibliography

"Faith and Doubt." Sermon on Mark 9:24. Alyth, 23 March 1941.
"Moral Matrimony." Sermon on Mark 10:9. Alyth, 26 January 1941.
"Communion Sermon." Sermon on Mark 10:38. Alyth, June 1940; Blairgrove, May [_];
    Beechgrove, 18 January 1948.
Untitled sermon on Mark 13:33–37. Athelstaneford and Whitekirk, 4 January 1976.
"Why This Waste?" Sermon on Mark 14:4. Alyth, 1940.

Box 44, Folder "Sermons on Luke"

"What manner of child shall this be?" Baptism sermon on Luke 1:66. Alyth, 1940.
"What shall we do then?" Sermon on Luke 3:10. Alyth, 17 May 1942.
"The Story of Jairus." Sermon on Luke 8. Alyth, 19 January 1940.
"These Candidates for Discipleship." Sermon on Luke 9:57–62. Alyth, 3 August 1941;
    Beechgrove, 14 March 1948.
"The Pharisee and the Publican at Prayer." Sermon on Luke 18:10f. Alyth, 18 January
    1942.
"Then opened he their understanding." Sermon on Luke 24:45. Alyth, 5 April 1942;
    Beechgrove, 28 March 1948.
"Emmanuel." Easter Sermon on Luke 24:30f. Alyth, March 1940.

Box 44, Folder "Sermons on John 1–5"

"Behold the Lamb of God." Sermon on John 1:29. Edinburgh BBC Service, 28
    September 1952.
"The Fig Tree." Sermon on John 1:48. Alyth, 1940; Beechgrove, 11 January 1948.
Untitled sermon on John 3:1–21; Luke 10:25–37. n.p., n.d.
"He must increase, I must decrease." Sermon on John 3:30. Alyth, 2 February 1941.
"Search the Scriptures." Sermon on John 5:39. Alyth, September 1940.

Box 45, Folder "Sermons on John 11–15"

"I am the Way, the Truth and the Life." Sermon on John 14:6. n.p., n.d.[6]
"He who has seen me has seen the Father." Sermon on John 14:9. n.p., n.d.
"If a man die[s], shall he live again?" Sermon on John 14:14, 19. Alyth, 8 March 1942.
"The Peace of Christ." Sermon on John 14:27. Alyth, April 1940; C[___]sshill, May
    1940; Beechgrove, n.d.; Black[___], 9 September 1951; Old Hamstocks, 30
    September 1951.
"Greater love hath no man." Sermon on John 15:13 and 1 John 4:10. Alyth, September
    1942; Beechgrove, 21 March 1948.

---

6. Similar sermons are B45 "No man cometh unto the Father but by me," sermon on John 14:6, Alyth, 12 August 1945; "The Way, the Truth, and the Life," sermon on John 14:6, Alyth, 23 May 1943; Beechgrove, 7 August 1948.

Box 45, Folder "Sermons on Acts"

Untitled sermon on Acts 1:11. Beechgrove, 8 June 1975.
Untitled sermon on Acts 1:7 and Hebrews 13:8. Alyth, New Year, January 1941.
"Pentecost." Sermon on Acts 2:37–38, 39. Beechgrove, 5 June 1949.
"The Marks of the True Church." Sermon on Acts 2:42. Alyth, 30 November 1941.
"Jesus Christ our Saviour." Sermon on Acts 4:12. Alyth, 2 November 1947; Beechgrove, 1949.
Untitled sermon on Acts 5:3, 4. n.p., n.d.
"The Conversion of Saul." Sermon on Acts 9. Alyth, 17 January 1943.
"Paul and Silas at Philippi—Songs in Prison." Sermon on Acts 16:25. Alyth, 22 February 1942.
"The Philippian jailer." Sermon on Acts 16:30–31. Alyth, 22 February 1942.

Box 45, Folder "Sermons on Romans 1–7"

"The Epistle to the Romans." Sermon on Romans 1:16–18. Alyth, 13 December 1942.
"What is Faith?" Sermon on Romans 1:16–17. n.p., n.d.
"The Just Shall live by faith." Sermon on Romans 1:17. n.p., 24 January 1943; Beechgrove, 10 January 1949.
"Romans chapter 2." Alyth, 27 December 1942.
"Law and Grace." Sermon on Romans 3:19–20; 11:6. Alyth, 11 October 1942.
"Being justified freely by his grace." Sermon on Romans 3:24. Alyth, 25 November 1945.
"Justification." Sermon on Romans 3:24. Alyth, 24 January 1943.
"Reconciliation through the Person of Christ." Sermon on Romans 5. Alyth, 14 February 1943.
Untitled sermon on Romans 6:11. Alyth, 14 March 1943.
Untitled sermon on Romans 7. Alyth, 9 May 1943.

Box 46, Folder "Sermons on Romans 8–16"

"God commendeth his love toward us." Sermon on Romans 6:7–8. Alyth, 6 September 1942.
"The Spirit itself beareth witness with our spirit." Sermon on Romans 8:16. Alyth, 28 July 1946.
"Sacramental Prayer." Sermon on Romans 8:26–28. n.p., n.d.
"Put ye on the Lord Jesus Christ." Sermon on Romans 13:14. Alyth, December 1941.

Box 46, Folder "Sermons on 1 Corinthians"

"The Cross a stumbling block." Sermon on 1 Corinthians 1:23, 24. Alyth, December 1940; Beechgrove, 15 February 1948.
Untitled sermon on 1 Corinthians 2:2. Beechgrove, 18 October 1942; Alyth, 15 July 1945.
"Ye cannot drink the cup of the Lord and the cup of devils." Sermon on 1 Corinthians 10:20. Alyth, 15 February 1942.

Bibliography

"If Christ be not risen." Sermon on 1 Corinthians 15: 17, 18. Alyth, Easter April 1941.
"But now is Christ risen from the dead." Sermon on 1 Corinthians 15:20. Alyth, Easter April 1941.
"How are the dead raised up?" Sermon on 1 Corinthians 15:35. Beechgrove, 19 February 1950.

Box 46, Folder "Sermons on 2 Corinthians"

"Constraint of Love." Sermon on 2 Corinthians 5:14. Alyth, 1940.
Untitled Moderator's sermon on 2 Corinthians 5:18 during the National Service of Thanksgiving in Scotland on the occasion of the Silver Jubilee of Her Majesty the Queen. n.p., 17 May 1977.
"God in Christ reconciling the world." Sermon on 2 Corinthians 5:19. Alyth, Christmas 1940.
"The Poverty of Christ." Sermon on 2 Corinthians 8:9. Alyth, 1940.
"The Trinity." Sermon on 2 Corinthians 13:14. Alyth, November 1940; Beechgrove, 20 June 1949.
"The Communion of the Holy Spirit." Sermon on 2 Corinthians 13:14. Alyth, September 1940.

Box 46, Folder "Sermons on Galatians"

"He loves me and gave himself for me." Sermon on Galatians 2:20. Alyth, 10 January 1943; Beechgrove, 13 January 1948.
"O Foolish Galatians." Sermon on Galatians 3:1. n.p., 14 February 1948.
"Freedom from Bondage." Sermon on Galatians 3:3; 5:11. Alyth, 16 November 1941.
Untitled sermon on Galatians 3:26-29. n.p., 19 January 1969.
"Ye have known God, or rather are known of God." Sermon on Galatians 4:9. Alyth, 25 August 1945; Beechgrove, 14 December 1947; n.p., 26 December 1948.

Box 46, Folder "Sermons on Ephesians"

"Predestination in Christ." Sermon on Ephesians 1:4-6. Alyth, 15 September 1946.
"Ascension and Second Advent." Sermon on Ephesians 4:8-10. Alyth, 18 May 1947.
"A Disciplined Life." Sermon on Ephesians 4:11-15, 20-25. Beechgrove, January 1950.
Untitled sermon on Ephesians 4:20-24. Alyth, 10 March 1946.
Untitled sermon on Ephesians 4:26. Alyth, 10 November 1946; A[___], 1948.

Box 46, Folder "Sermons on Philippians"

Untitled sermon on Philippians 2:2-8. n.p., n.d.
"Incarnation." Sermon on Philippians 2:5-8. Alyth, December 1940.
"Work out your own salvation for." Sermon on Philippians 2:12f. Alyth, October 1940; Beechgrove, 18 September 1949.
"God's Arrows." Sermon on Philippians 3:8, 12-14. Alyth, 19 [_] 1942.

"The peace that passes understanding." Sermon on Philippians 4:7. Alyth, 12 January 1946; Beechgrove, 16 January 1949.

Box 47, Folder "Sermons on Colossians"

"Handwriting and Forgiveness." Sermon on Colossians 2:14. Alyth, 1940; Beechgrove, 28 December 1947.
"Your life is hid with Christ in God." Sermon on Colossians 3:3. Alyth, December 1940; Beechgrove, 4 January 1948.

Box 47, Folder "Sermons on 1 Thessalonians"

"Prayer without ceasing . . . despise not prophesying." Sermon on 1 Thessalonians 5:16-20. Alyth, 7 October 1945.

Box 47, Folder "Sermons on 1 and 2 Timothy"

"God's Faithfulness." Sermon on 2 Timothy 2:12f. Alyth, 1940.
"The Believer's sealing in Christ." Baptism sermon on 2 Timothy 2:19. Alyth, 27 January 1946; Beechgrove, 8 January 1950.

Box 47, Folder "Sermons on Hebrews"

"Christ tempted in all points like as we are." Sermon on Hebrews 2:8; 4:15. Alyth, 12 October 1941.
Untitled sermon on Hebrews 4:9-16. n.p., n.d.
"Leaving First Principles." Baptism sermon on Hebrews 6:1. Alyth, November 1940.
"Sure and Certain Hope." Sermon on Hebrews 6:17-20. Ar[____] Hall, NC, 7 October 1954.
"Christ the Priest of the Resurrection." Sermon on Hebrews 6:19-20. Beechgrove, 25 April 1954; St K[____] L[____], 13 June 1954.
"Such an high priest became us." Preparatory service sermon on Hebrew 7:26. Alyth, 19 October 1945.
"Without." Sermon on Hebrews 9:22; 11:6; 12:14. Alyth, 1940.
"Faith." Sermon on Hebrews 11:1. Alyth, 19 April 1942.
"Contradiction of Sinners." Sermon on Hebrews 12:3. Alyth, 1940.
"Esau's Birthright." Sermon on Hebrews 12:16f. Alyth, 1940.
"Jesus Christ the same yesterday, today and forever." Sermon on Hebrews 13:8. Beechgrove, 2 January 1949.

Box 47, Folder "Morning Service—Advent Series"

"What is God Like?—God in the Face of Jesus Christ." Advent Series 1/3. n.p., 6 December 1964.

Bibliography

"What is God Like?—God in Judgment." Advent Series 2/3. n.p., 9 December 1964.
"What is God Like?—God in Mercy." Advent Series 3/3. n.p., 20 December 1964.

Box 47, Folder "Sermons on 2 Peter"

"Time and Eternity." Sermon on 2 Peter 3:8. Alyth, 1940.

Box 47, Folder "Sermons on 1 John"

"Communion." Sermon on 1 John 1:1–3. Alyth, 16 February 1941.
"If we walk in the light." Sermon on 1 John 1:7. Alyth, 9 November 1941.
"Foreign Mission." Sermon on 1 John 2:2. Alyth, December 1940.
"Behold what manner of love." Sermon on 1 John 3:1. Alyth, 14 October 1945; Beechgrove, n.d.
"The Condemning Heart." Sermon on 1 John 3:20. Alyth, April 1940; Blair[___], May 1940; Edinburgh, October 1940; Beechgrove, 14 December 1947; Queen's [___], 6 June 1948; Bla[___], 4 May 1952; M[___] High Church, Edinburgh, 13 September 1952.
"Everyone that loveth is born of God." Sermon on 1 John 4:7-8. Alyth, 5 May 1946; Beechgrove, 11 September 1948.
"Herein is love." Sermon on 1 John 4:10. Glasgow University Hall, May 1943; St. Columba's, Oxford, 22 July 1945.

Box 47, Folder "Sermons on Revelation"

"The Message to the Church of Philadelphia." Sermon on Revelation 3:7, 8, 10, 16. Dedication of Elders, Alyth, 3 May 1947.
"Lion and the Lamb." Sermon on Revelation 5:5f. Alyth, 1940; Con[___]: St. Andrews, 1940; Blair[___]: St. Andrews, 1940.
"And there was no more sea." Sermon on Revelation 21:1. Alyth, 3 May 1942.

Box 47 Other Sermons

Untitled sermon on Romans 12:1. Preached upon the death of John Baillie. n.p., 1960.
"The Christ who came by water and blood." Communion sermon on 1 John 5:5-8. Alyth, 19 October 1941; Beechgrove, 11 April 1948.

Secondary Works: Published

Achtemeier, P. Mark. "The Truth of Tradition: Critical Realism in the Thought of Alasdair MacIntyre and T. F. Torrance." *Scottish Journal of Theology* 47 (1994) 355–74.
Allchin, A. M. *Participation in God: A Forgotten Strand in Anglican Tradition*. London: Darton, Longman and Todd, 1988.

Bibliography

Anderson, Ray S. "The Practical Theology of Thomas F. Torrance." *Participatio* 1 (2009) 49–65.
Anselm, *Cur Deus Homo*. Edinburgh: Grant, 1909.
Athanasius. *On the Incarnation*. Translated by Penelope Lawson. New York: MacMillan, 1981.
Awad, Najeeb G. "Between Subordination and Koinonia: Toward a New Reading of the Cappadocian Theology." *Modern Theology* 23 (2007) 181–204.
Baker, Matthew. "The Eternal 'Spirit of the Son': Barth, Florovsky and Torrance on the Filioque." *International Journal of Systematic Theology* 12 (2010) 382–403.
———. "The Place of St. Irenaeus of Lyons in Historical and Dogmatic Theology according to Thomas F. Torrance." *Participatio* 2 (2010) 5–43.
Barrett, C. K. "Shaliah and Apostle." In *New Testament Studies in Honour of David Daube*, edited by E. Bammel, C. K. Barrett, and W. D. Davies, 89–102. Oxford: Clarendon, 1978.
Barth, Karl. *Church Dogmatics* I/1. Translated by G. W. Bromiley. Edinburgh: T. & T. Clark, 1975.
———. *Evangelical Theology: An Introduction*. Translated by Grover Foley. Grand Rapids: Eerdmans, 1963.
Bauman, Michael. "Thomas F. Torrance." In *Roundtable: Discussions with European Theologians*, edited by Michael Bauman, 109–18. Grand Rapids: Baker, 1990.
Bevan, Andrew Maurice. "The Person of Christ and the Nature of Human Participation in the Theology of T. F. Torrance: A Post-Modern Realist Approach to Personhood." PhD thesis, University of London, 2002.
Billings, J. Todd. "John Milbank's Theology of the 'Gift' and Calvin's Theology of Grace: A Critical Comparison." *Modern Theology* 21 (2005) 87–105.
Bird, Michael F., and Michael R. Whitenton. "The Faithfulness of Jesus Christ in Hippolytus's *De Christo et AntiChristo*: Overlooked Patristic Evidence in the Πίστίς Χριϛτου Debate." *New Testament Studies* 55 (2009) 552–62.
Bloesch, Donald G. *God the Almighty: Power, Wisdom, Holiness, Love*. Carlisle, UK: Paternoster, 1995.
Bobrinskoy, Boris. "The Indwelling of the Spirit in Christ: Pneumatic Christology in the Cappadocian Fathers." *St. Vladimirs Theological Quarterly* 28 (1984) 48–65.
———. *The Mystery of the Trinity: Trinitarian Experience and Vision in the Biblical and Patristic Tradition*. Translated by Anthony P. Gythiel. Crestwood, NY: St. Vladimir's Seminary Press, 1999.
Boff, Leonardo. *Holy Trinity: Perfect Community*. Translated by Phillip Berryman. Maryknoll, NY: Orbis, 2000.
Bradshaw Timothy. "Karl Barth on the Trinity: A Family Resemblance." *Scottish Journal of Theology* 39 (1986) 145–64.
Bray, Gerald L. "Out of the Box: The Christian Experience of God in Trinity." In *God the Holy Trinity: Reflections on Christian Faith and Practice*, edited by Timothy George, 37–55. Grand Rapids: Baker Academic, 2006.
Buxton, Graham. *The Trinity, Creation, and Pastoral Ministry: Imaging the Perichoretic God*. Milton Keynes, UK: Paternoster, 2005.
Calvin, John. *Institutes of the Christian Religion*. Two volumes. Translated by Ford Lewis Battles. Edited by John T. McNeill. Philadelphia: Westminster, 1960.
Canlis, Julie. "Calvin, Osiander and Participation in God." *International Journal of Systematic Theology* 6 (2004) 169–84.

Bibliography

Cass, Peter. *Christ Condemned in the Flesh: Thomas F. Torrance's Doctrine of Soteriology and Its Ecumenical Significance*. Saarbrücken, Germany: VDM, 2009.

Clark, Kelly James. "Trinity or Tritheism." *Religious Studies* 32 (1996) 463–76.

Collins, Paul M. *Trinitarian Theology West and East: Karl Barth, the Cappadocian Fathers, and John Zizioulas*. Oxford: Oxford University Press, 2001.

Colyer, Elmer M. *How To Read T. F. Torrance: Understanding His Trinitarian and Scientific Theology*. Downers Grove, IL: InterVarsity, 2001.

———. *The Nature of Doctrine in T. F. Torrance's Theology*. Reprint. Eugene, OR: Wipf & Stock, 2001.

———, editor. *The Promise of Trinitarian Theology: Theologians in Dialogue with T. F. Torrance*. Lanham: Rowman and Littlefield, 2001.

———. "Thomas F. Torrance, 1913–." In *A New Handbook of Christian Theologians*, edited by Donald W. Musser and Joseph L. Price, 460–67. Nashville: Abingdon, 1996.

Congar, Yves. *I Believe in the Holy Spirit*, vol. 2, *Lord and Giver of Life*. Translated by David Smith. New York: Seabury, 1983.

Cooper, John W. *Panentheism: The Other God of the Philosophers from Plato to the Present*. Nottingham, UK: Apollos, 2007.

Cortez, Marc. "What Does it Mean to Call Barth a 'Christocentric' Theologian?" *Scottish Journal of Theology* 60 (2007) 127–43.

Crisp, Oliver. *Divinity and Humanity*. Cambridge: Cambridge University Press, 2007.

Crump, David. "Re-examining the Johannine Trinity: Perichoresis or Deification?" *Scottish Journal of Theology* 59 (2006) 395–412.

Cumin, Paul. "Looking for Personal Space in the Theology of John Zizioulas." *International Journal of Systematic Theology* 8 (2006) 356–70.

Davidson, Ivor J. "Pondering the Sinlessness of Jesus Christ: Moral Christologies and the Witness of the Scripture." *International Journal of Systematic Theology* 10 (2008) 372–98.

Davis, Stephen, Daniel Kendall, and Gerald O'Collins, editors. *The Trinity: An Interdisciplinary Symposium on the Trinity*. Oxford: Oxford University Press, 1999.

Dawson, Gerrit Scott, editor. *An Introduction to Torrance Theology: Discovering the Incarnate Saviour*. Edinburgh: T. & T. Clark, 2007.

———, and Jock Stein, editors. *A Passion for Christ: The Vision that Ignites Ministry*. Edinburgh: Handsel, 1999.

Dayton, Donald W. "Some Doubts about the Usefulness of the Category 'Evangelical.'" In *The Variety of American Evangelicalism*, edited by Donald W. Dayton and Robert K. Johnston, 245–51. Downers Grove, IL: InterVarsity, 1991.

Del Colle, Ralph. "'Person' and 'Being' in John Zizioulas's Trinitarian Theology: Conversations with Thomas Torrance and Thomas Aquinas." *Scottish Journal of Theology* 54 (2001) 70–86.

Dunn, James D. G. *Jesus and the Spirit*. London: SCM, 1975.

———. "Paul's Understanding of the Death of Jesus." In *Reconciliation and Hope: New Testament Essays on Atonement and Eschatology*, edited by R. Banks, 35–56. Grand Rapids: Eerdmans, 1974.

Feenstra, Ronald J., and Cornelius Plantinga, Jr., editors. *Trinity, Incarnation, and Atonement: Philosophical and Theological Essays*. Notre Dame: University of Notre Dame Press, 1989.

Fergusson, David. "Torrance as a Scottish Theologian." *Participatio* 2 (2010) 77–87.

Fiddes, Paul S. *Participating in God: A Pastoral Doctrine of the Trinity.* London: Darton, Longman and Todd, 2000.

———. "Salvation." In *The Oxford Handbook of Systematic Theology,* edited by John Webster, Kathryn Tanner, and Iain Torrance, 176–96. Oxford: Oxford University Press, 2007.

Flett, Eric. "Persons, Powers and Pluralities: Toward a Trinitarian Theology of Culture." PhD thesis, Kings College, London, 2004.

———. "Priests of Creation, Mediators of Order: The Human Person as a Cultural Being in Thomas F. Torrance's Theological Anthropology." *Scottish Journal of Theology* 58 (2005) 161–83.

Ford, David. Review of *The Trinitarian Faith,* by T. F. Torrance. *Scottish Journal of Theology* 43 (1990) 263–67.

Giles, Kevin. *Jesus and the Father: Modern Evangelicals Reinvent the Doctrine of the Trinity.* Grand Rapids: Zondervan, 2006.

Gill, Timothy Charles. "The Doctrine of Revelation in the Theology of Thomas F. Torrance." PhD thesis, University of Leeds, 2007.

Goulder, Michael, editor. *Incarnation and Myth: The Debate Continued.* Grand Rapids: Eerdmans, 1979.

Groppe, Elizabeth T. "Catherine Mowry LaCugna's Contribution to Trinitarian Theology." *Theological Studies* 63 (2002) 730–63.

Gunton, Colin E. *The Actuality of Atonement: A Study of Metaphor, Rationality, and the Christian Tradition.* Edinburgh: T. & T. Clark, 1988.

———. *Becoming and Being: The Doctrine of God in Charles Hartshorne and Karl Barth.* Oxford: SCM, 2001.

———. *Christ and Creation.* Carlisle, UK: Paternoster, 1992.

———, editor. *The Doctrine of Creation.* Edinburgh: T. & T. Clark, 1997.

———. *Father, Son, and Holy Spirit: Toward A Fully Trinitarian Theology.* London: T. & T. Clark, 2003.

———. *The Promise of Trinitarian Theology.* 2nd ed. Edinburgh: T. & T. Clark, 1997.

Habets, Myk. *Theosis in the Theology of Thomas Torrance.* Farnham, UK: Ashgate, 2009.

Hagner, Donald A. *Matthew 1–13.* Dallas: Word, 1993.

Hanby, Michael. *Augustine and Modernity.* London: Routledge, 2003.

Hankeys, Wayne. "Denys and Aquinas: Antimodern Cold and Postmodern Hot." In *Christian Origins: Theology, Rhetoric, and Community,* edited by Lewis Ayres and Gareth Jones, 139–84. London: Routledge, 1998.

Hanson, Richard P. C. *Studies in Christian Antiquity.* Edinburgh: T. & T. Clark, 1985.

———. *Search for the Christian Doctrine of God: The Arian Controversy 318–381.* Edinburgh: T. & T. Clark, 1988.

Hardy, Daniel W. "T. F. Torrance." In *The Modern Theologians,* 3rd ed., edited by Daniel F. Ford with Rachel Muers, 163–77. Oxford: Blackwell, 2005.

Harris, Harriet A. "Should We Say that Personhood is Relational?" *Scottish Journal of Theology* 51 (1998) 214–34.

Hart, Trevor A. "Humankind in Christ and Christ in Humankind: Salvation as Participation in our Substitute in the Theology of John Calvin." *Scottish Journal of Theology* 42 (1989) 67–84.

———. *Regarding Karl Barth: Essays Toward a Reading of His Theology.* Carlisle, UK: Paternoster, 1999.

Bibliography

———. "Sinlessness and Moral Responsibility: A Problem in Christology." *Scottish Journal of Theology* 48 (1995) 37–54.

———, and Daniel P. Thimell, editors. *Christ in Our Place: The Humanity of God in Christ for the Reconciliation of the World*. Exeter, UK: Paternoster, 1989.

Hays, Richard B. *The Faith of Jesus Christ: An Investigation of the Narrative Substructure of Galatians 3:1—4:11*. Reprint. Grand Rapids: Eerdmans, 2002.

Hector, Kevin W. "God's Triunity and Self-Determination: A Conversation with Karl Barth, Bruce McCormack, and Paul Molnar." *International Journal of Systematic Theology* 7 (2005) 246–61.

———. "The Mediation of Christ's Normative Spirit: A Constructive Reading of Schleiermacher's Pneumatology." *Modern Theology* 24 (2008) 1–22.

Heron, Alasdair I. C. "Calvin in the Theology of Thomas F. Torrance: Calvin's Doctrine of Man (1949)." *Participatio* 2 (2010) 44–63.

———. *A Century of Protestant Theology*. Reprint. Cambridge: Lutterworth, 1985.

———, editor. *The Forgotten Trinity 3: A Selection of Papers presented to the BCC Study Commission on Trinitarian Doctrine Today*. London: BCC/CCBI, 1991.

Hesselink, John I. "A Pilgrimage in the School of Faith: An Interview with T. F. Torrance." *Reformed Review* 38 (1984) 49–64.

Hick, John, editor. *The Myth of God Incarnate*. London: SCM, 1977.

Ho, Man Kei. *A Critical Study on T. F. Torrance's Theology of Incarnation*. Bern: Lang, 2008.

Holmes, Stephen. *Listening to the Past: The Place of Christian Tradition in Theology*. Carlisle, UK: Paternoster, 2002.

———. *The Wondrous Cross: Atonement and Penal Substitution in the Bible and History*. Milton Keynes, UK: Paternoster, 2007.

Hooker, Morna D. "ΠΙΣΤΙΣ ΧΡΙΣΤΟΥ." *New Testament Studies* 35 (1989) 321–42.

Hughes, Philip E. *The True Image: The Origin and Destiny of Man in Christ*. Grand Rapids: Eerdmans, 1989.

Hunsinger, George. "The Dimension of Depth: Thomas F. Torrance on the Sacraments of Baptism and the Lord's Supper." *Scottish Journal of Theology* 54 (2001) 155–76.

Jenson, Robert. *The Triune Identity: God according to the Gospel*. Philadelphia: Fortress, 1982.

Johnson, Elizabeth, and David M. Hay, editors. *Pauline Theology*, vol. 4, *Looking Back, Pressing On*. Atlanta: Scholars, 1997.

Jowers, Dennis W. "The Reproach of Modalism: A Difficulty for Karl Barth's Doctrine of the Trinity." *Scottish Journal of Theology* 56 (2003) 231–46.

Jüngel, Eberhard. *God's Being is in Becoming: The Trinitarian Being of God in the Theology of Karl Barth*. Translated by John Webster. Edinburgh: T. & T. Clark, 2001.

Kang, Phee Seng. "The Concept of the Vicarious Humanity of Christ in the Theology of Thomas F. Torrance." PhD thesis, University of Aberdeen, 1983.

———. "The Epistemological Significance of *Homoousion* in the Theology of Thomas F. Torrance." *Scottish Journal of Theology* 45 (1992) 341–66.

Kapic, Kelly M. "The Son's Assumption of a Human Nature: A Call to Clarity." *International Journal of Systematic Theology* 3 (2001) 154–66.

Kärkkäinen, Veli-Matti. *The Trinity: Global Perspectives*. Louisville, KY: Westminster John Knox, 2007.

Kelly, J. N. D. *Early Christian Creeds*. 3rd ed. London: Continuum, 2006.

———. *Early Christian Doctrines*. 5th ed. London: Continuum, 2006.

Kennedy, Kevin Nixon. *Union with Christ and the Extent of the Atonement in Calvin.* New York: Lang, 2002.

Kerr, Fergus. *After Aquinas: Versions of Thomism.* Malden, MA: Blackwell, 2002.

Kilby, Karen. "Perichoresis and Projection: Problems with Social Doctrines of the Trinity." *New Blackfriars* 81 (2000) 432–45.

Klinefelter, Donald S. "God and Rationality: A Critique of the Theology of Thomas F. Torrance." *Journal of Religion* 53 (1973) 117–35.

Kruger, C. Baxter. "The Doctrine of the Knowledge of God in the Theology of T. F. Torrance: Sharing in the Son's Communion with the Father in the Spirit." *Scottish Journal of Theology* 43 (1990) 366–89.

———. *The Great Dance.* Jackson, MS: Perichoresis, 2000.

———. "Participation in the Self-Knowledge of God: The Nature and Means of our Knowledge of God in the Theology of T. F. Torrance." PhD thesis, University of Aberdeen, 1989.

LaCugna, Catherine M. *God for Us: The Trinity and the Christian Life.* New York: HarperCollins, 1991.

———. "The Relational God: Aquinas and Beyond." *Theological Studies* 46 (1985) 647–63.

———. "The Trinity: Why It Takes Three Persons to Save One Soul." Interview by editors. *US Catholic* 58 (November 1993) 6–12.

Langford, Thomas A. "T. F. Torrance's *Theological Science*: A Reaction." *Scottish Journal of Theology* 25 (1972) 155–70.

Larsen, Timothy, and Daniel J. Treier, editors. *The Cambridge Companion to Evangelical Theology.* Cambridge: Cambridge University Press, 2007.

Lee, Kye Won. *Living in Union with Christ: The Practical Theology of Thomas F. Torrance.* New York: Lang, 2003.

Levering, Matthew. "Participation and Exegesis: Response to Catherine Pickstock." *Modern Theology* 21 (2005) 587–601.

Lull, Timothy F. "The Trinity in Recent Theological Literature." *Word and World* 2 (1982) 61–68.

Mackintosh, Hugh Ross. *The Doctrine of the Person of Jesus Christ.* Edinburgh: T. & T. Clark, 1913.

MacLeod, Donald. "The Atonement." In *Dictionary of Scottish Church History and Theology*, edited by Nigel M. de S. Cameron, 39–43. Edinburgh: T. & T. Clark, 1993.

———. *Jesus is Lord: Christology Yesterday and Today.* Fearn, UK: Christian Focus, 2000.

———. *The Person of Christ.* Downers Grove, IL: InterVarsity, 1998.

Marshall, Bruce D. "Trinity." In *Blackwell Companion to Modern Theology*, edited by Gareth Jones, 183–203. Oxford: Blackwell, 2004.

Marshall, I. Howard. *Aspects of the Atonement: Cross and Resurrection in the Reconciling of God and Humanity.* Milton Keynes, UK: Paternoster, 2007.

McCall, Tom. "Ronald Thiemann, Thomas Torrance, and Epistemological Doctrines of Revelation." *International Journal of Systematic Theology* 6 (2004) 148–68.

McCormack, Bruce L. "For Us and Our Salvation: Incarnation and Atonement in the Reformed Tradition." *Studies in Reformed Theology and History* 1 (1993) 1–38.

———. *Karl Barth's Critically Realistic Dialectical Theology: Its Genesis and Development 1909–1936.* Oxford: Clarendon, 1997.

Bibliography

McFarland, Ian A. "Fallen or Unfallen? Christ's Human Nature and the Ontology of Human Sinfulness." *International Journal of Systematic Theology* 10 (2008) 399–415.

McGrath, Alister E. *T. F. Torrance: An Intellectual Biography*. Edinburgh: T. & T. Clark, 1999.

———. "Thomas F. Torrance and the Search for a Viable Natural Theology: Some Personal Reflections." *Participatio* 1 (2009) 66–81.

McIlroy, David H. "Towards a Relational and Trinitarian Theology of Atonement." *Evangelical Quarterly* 80 (2008) 13–32.

McIntosh, Adam. "The Doctrine of Appropriation as an Interpretative Framework for Karl Barth's Pneumatology of the *Church Dogmatics*." *Pacifica* 20 (2007) 278–90.

McKinney, Richard W. A., editor. *Christ, Creation, and Culture: Studies in Honour of T. F. Torrance*. Edinburgh: T. & T. Clark, 1976.

Melissaris, Athanasios G. "The Challenge of Patristic Ontology in the Theology of Metropolitan John (Zizioulas) of Pergamon." *The Greek Orthodox Theological Review* 44 (1999) 467–90.

Micks, Marianne H. *Introduction to Theology*. New York: Seabury, 1983.

Milbank, John. *Theology and Social Theory: Beyond Secular Reason*. Oxford: Blackwell, 1990.

———, Catherine Pickstock, and Graham Ward, editors. *Radical Orthodoxy*. London: Routledge, 1999.

Minns, Denis. *Irenaeus*. London: Geoffrey Chapman, 1994.

Molnar, Paul D. "The Centrality of the Trinity in the Theology of Thomas F. Torrance." *Participatio* 1 (2009) 82–94.

———. "God's Self-Communication in Christ: A Comparison of Thomas F. Torrance and Karl Rahner." *Scottish Journal of Theology* 50 (1997) 288–320.

———. "Incarnation, Resurrection, and the Doctrine of the Trinity: A Comparison of Thomas F. Torrance and Roger Haight." *International Journal of Systematic Theology* 5 (2003) 147–67.

———. *Thomas F. Torrance: Theologian of the Trinity*. Farnham, UK: Ashgate, 2009.

———. "The Trinity, Election, and God's Ontological Freedom: A Response to Kevin W. Hector." *International Journal of Systematic Theology* 8 (2006) 294–306.

Moltmann, Jürgen. *History and the Triune God: Contributions to Trinitarian Theology*. Translated by John Bowden. London: SCM, 1991.

———. "Perichoresis: An Old Magic Word for a New Trinitarian Theology." In *Trinity, Community, and Power: Mapping Trajectories in Wesleyan Theology*, edited by M. Douglas Meeks, 111–25. Nashville: Kingswood, 2000.

———. *The Spirit of Life: A Universal Affirmation*. London: SCM, 1992.

Morrison, John Douglas. "Heidegger, Correspondence Truth, and the Realist Theology of T. F. Torrance." *Evangelical Quarterly* 69 (1997) 139–55.

———. *Knowledge of the Self-Revealing God in the Thought of Thomas Forsyth Torrance*. New York: Lang, 1997.

———. "Thomas F. Torrance's Critique of Evangelical Orthodoxy." *Evangelical Quarterly* 67 (1995) 53–69.

Mosser, Carl. "The Greatest Possible Blessing: Calvin and Deification." *Scottish Journal of Theology* 55 (2002) 36–57.

Muller, Richard A. "The Barth Legacy: New Athanasius or Origen Redivivus? A Response to T. F. Torrance." *Thomist* 54 (1990) 673–704.

Bibliography

Myers, Benjamin. "The Stratification of Knowledge in the Thought of T. F. Torrance." *Scottish Journal of Theology* 61 (2008) 1–15.

Neidhardt, Walter Jim. "Reflections on Remarks of David F. Siemens, Jr. Concerning the Theology/Science Integration of Thomas F. Torrance." *Perspectives on Science and Christian Faith* 43 (1991) 114–16.

———. "Thomas F. Torrance's Integration of Judeo-Christian Theology and Natural Science: Some Key Themes." *Perspectives on Science and Christian Faith* 41 (1989) 87–98.

Nelson, Richard D. "'He Offered Himself': Sacrifice in Hebrews." *Interpretations* 57 (2003) 251–65.

Newell, Roger. "Torrance, Thomas Forsyth (b. 1913)." In *The Dictionary of Historical Theology*, edited by Trevor A. Hart, 549–51. Grand Rapids: Eerdmans, 2000.

Newey, Edmund. "The Form of Reason: Participation in the Work of Richard Hooker, Benjamin Whichcote, Ralph Cudworth, and Jeremy Taylor." *Modern Theology* 18 (2002) 1–26.

Nimmo, Paul T. "Karl Barth and the *Concursus Dei*—A Chalcedonianism Too Far?" *International Journal of Systematic Theology* 9 (2007) 58–72.

Noble, Thomas A. "Paradox in Gregory Nazianzen's Doctrine of the Trinity." In *Studia Patristica* 27, edited by Elizabeth A. Livingstone, 94–99. Leuven: Peeters, 1993.

———. "Thomas Forsyth Torrance." In *Dictionary of Scottish Church History and Theology*, edited by Nigel M. de S. Cameron, 823–24. Edinburgh: T. & T. Clark, 1993.

O'Donovan, Joan E. "Man in the Image of God: The Disagreement between Barth and Brunner Reconsidered." *Scottish Journal of Theology* 39 (1986) 433–59.

Olson, Roger. *The SCM A-Z of Evangelical Theology*. London: SCM, 2005.

———, and Christopher A. Hall. *The Trinity*. Grand Rapids: Eerdmans, 2002.

Otto, Randall E. "The Use and Abuse of Perichoresis in Recent Theology." *Scottish Journal of Theology* 54 (2001) 366–84.

Palma, Robert J. "Thomas F. Torrance's Reformed Theology." *Reformed Review* 38 (1984) 2–46.

Pannenberg, Wolfhart. "The Christian Vision of God: Trinitarian Doctrine." *Asbury Theological Journal* 46 (1991) 27–36.

———. "Problems between Science and Theology in the Course of their Modern History." *Zygon* 41 (2006) 105–12.

———. *Systematic Theology*. Volume 1. Edited by Geoffrey Bromiley. Grand Rapids: Eerdmans, 1991.

Papanikolaou, Aristotle. "Divine Energies or Personhood: Vladimir Lossky and John Zizioulas on Conceiving the Transcendent and Immanent God." *Modern Theology* 19 (2003) 357–85.

———. "Is John Zizioulas an Existentialist in Disguise? Response to Lucian Turcescu." *Modern Theology* 20 (2004) 601–7.

Partee, Charles. "Calvin's Central Dogma Again." *The Sixteenth Century Journal* 18 (1987) 191–200.

Pickstock, Catherine. *After Writing: On the Liturgical Consummation of Philosophy*. Oxford: Blackwell, 1998.

Pinnock, Clark. *Flame of Love: A Theology of the Holy Spirit*. Downers Grove, IL: InterVarsity, 1996.

Bibliography

Plantinga, Cornelius, Jr. "Gregory of Nyssa and the Social Analogy of the Trinity." *The Thomist* 50 (1986) 325–52.

Powell, Samuel M. *Participating in God: Creation and Trinity*. Minneapolis: Fortress, 2003.

Rahner, Karl. "Anonymous Christians." In *Theological Investigations*, vol. 6, *Concerning Vatican Council I*, translated by Karl-H. and Boniface Kruger, 390–98. New York: Crossroad, 1982.

———. "The Concept of Existential Philosophy in Heidegger." Translated by Andrew Tallon. *Philosophy Today* 13 (1969) 126–37.

———. "The Concept of Mystery in Catholic Theology." In *Theological Investigations*, vol. 4, *More Recent Writings*, translated by Kevin Smith, 36–73. New York: Crossroad, 1982.

———. *Foundations of Christian Faith: An Introduction to the Idea of Christianity*. Translated by William V. Dych. New York: Crossroads, 1985.

———. *Spirit in the World*. Translated by William V. Dych. New York: Herder and Herder, 1968.

———. "The Spiritual Senses according to Origen." In *Theological Investigations*, vol. 16, *Experience of the Spirit: Source of Theology*, translated by David Morland, 81–103. New York: Crossroad, 1983.

———. "The Theology of Power." In *Theological Investigations*, vol. 4, *More Recent Writings*, translated by Kevin Smith, 391–409. New York: Crossroad, 1982.

———. *The Trinity*. Translated by Joseph Donceel. New York: Crossroad, 1974.

Rea, Michael C. "Relative Identity and the Doctrine of the Trinity." *Philosophia Christi* 5 (2003) 431–45.

Redman, R. R. "H. R. Mackintosh's Contribution to Christology and Soteriology in the Twentieth Century." *Scottish Journal of Theology* 41 (1988) 517–34.

———. "Mackintosh, Torrance, and Reformulation of Reformed Theology in Scotland." *Participatio* 2 (2010) 64–76.

———. "*Participatio Christi*: H. R. Mackintosh's Theology of the *Unio Mystica*." *Scottish Journal of Theology* 49 (1996) 201–22.

Robinson, J. A. T. "Universalism: Is it Heretical?" *Scottish Journal of Theology* 2 (1949) 139–55.

Sanders, Fred. "The Trinity." In *The Oxford Handbook of Systematic Theology*, edited by John Webster, Kathryn Tanner, and Iain Torrance, 35–53. Oxford: Oxford University Press, 2007.

Schubert, Frank D. "Thomas F. Torrance: The Case for a Theological Science." *Encounter* 45 (1984) 123–37.

Schwöbel, Christoph, editor. *Trinitarian Theology Today: Essays on Divine Act and Being*. Edinburgh: T. & T. Clark, 1995.

Seitz, Christopher, editor. *Nicene Christianity: The Future of a New Ecumenism*. Grand Rapids: Brazos, 2001.

Shin, Mun-Chul. "A Dialogical Trinitarian Pneumatology: A Critical Appraisal of Contemporary Discourse in Light of Torrance's Trinitarian Theology." PhD thesis, University of Aberdeen, 1997.

Siemens, David F. Jr. "Two Problems with Torrance." *Perspectives on Science and Christian Faith* 43 (1991) 112–13.

Skarsaune, Oskar. *Incarnation: Myth or Fact?* Translated by Trygve R. Skarsten. St. Louis, MO: Concordia, 1991.

Bibliography

Slater, Jonathan. "Salvation as Participation in the Humanity of the Mediator in Calvin's *Institutes of the Christian Religion:* A Reply to Carl Mosser." *Scottish Journal of Theology* 58 (2005) 39–58.

Smail, Thomas. *The Giving Gift: The Holy Spirit in Person*. Lima, OH: Renewal Academic, 2002.

Smith, Aaron T. "God's Self-specification: His Being is His Electing." *Scottish Journal of Theology* 62 (2009) 1–25.

Smith, James K. A. *Introducing Radical Orthodoxy: Mapping a Post-Secular Theology*. Grand Rapids: Baker Academic, 2004.

Stott, John. *The Cross of Christ*. Leicester, UK: InterVarsity, 1986.

Stubbs, David L. "The Shape of Soteriology and the *Pistis Christou* Debate." *Scottish Journal of Theology* 61 (2008) 137–57.

Tanner, Kathryn. "Trinity." In *Blackwell Companion to Political Theology*, edited by William T. Cavanaugh and Peter Scott, 319–47. Oxford: Blackwell, 2003.

Thiemann, Ronald. *Revelation and Theology*. Notre Dame, IN: University of Notre Dame Press, 1985.

Thompson, John. *Modern Trinitarian Perspectives*. Oxford: Oxford University Press, 1994.

Thorson, Walter R. "Scientific Objectivity and the Listening Attitude." In *Objective Knowledge: A Christian Perspective*, edited by Paul Helm, 59–83. Leicester, UK: InterVarsity, 1987.

Toon, Peter. *Justification and Sanctification*. London: Marshall Morgan and Scott, 1983.

———. *Our Triune God: A Biblical Portrayal of the Trinity*. Wheaton, IL: Victor, 1996.

———, and James Spiceland, editors. *One God in Trinity*. London: Bagster, 1980.

Torrance, Alan J. *Persons in Communion: Trinitarian Descriptions and Human Participation*. Edinburgh: T. & T. Clark, 1996.

Torrance, James B. "Calvin and Puritanism in England and Scotland: Some Basic Concepts in the Development of Federal Theology." In *Calvinus Reformator: His Contribution to Theology, Church, and Society*, 264–86. Institute for Reformational Studies. Potchefstrom University for Christian Higher Education, 1982.

———. "The Contribution of McLeod Campbell to Scottish Theology." *Scottish Journal of Theology* 26 (1973) 295–311.

———. "The Covenant Concept of Scottish Theology and Politics and its Legacy." *Scottish Journal of Theology* 34 (1981) 225–43.

———. "Covenant or Contract? A Study of the Theological Background of Worship in Seventeenth-Century Scotland." *Scottish Journal of Theology* 23 (1970) 51–76.

———. "The Incarnation and 'Limited Atonement.'" *Scottish Bulletin of Evangelical Theology* 2 (1984) 32–40.

———. *Worship, Community, and the Triune God of Grace*. Didsbury Lectures. Carlisle, UK: Paternoster, 1996.

Torrance, Thomas. *Expository Studies in St. John's Miracles*. London: James Clarke, n.d.

Treier, Daniel J., and David Lauber, editors. *Trinitarian Theology for the Church: Scripture, Community, Worship*. Downers Grove, IL: InterVarsity, 2009.

Turcescu, Lucian. "'Person' versus 'Individual', and Other Modern Misreadings of Gregory of Nyssa." *Modern Theology* 18 (2002) 527–39.

Turner, H. E. W. *The Patristic Doctrine of Redemption: A Study of the Development of Doctrine during the First Five Centuries*. London: Mowbray, 1952.

Bibliography

Vanhoozer, Kevin J., editor. *The Trinity in a Pluralistic Age: Theological Essays on Culture and Religion*. Grand Rapids: Eerdmans, 1997.

Vassiliadis, Petros. "Reconciliation as a Pneumatological Mission Paradigm: Some Preliminary Reflections by an Orthodox." *International Review of Mission* 94 (2009) 30–42.

Vickers, John. *Invocation and Assent: The Making and Remaking of Trinitarian Theology*. Grand Rapids: Eerdmans, 2008.

Volf, Miroslav. *After Our Likeness: The Church as the Image of the Trinity*. Grand Rapids: Eerdmans, 1998.

———. "'The Trinity is Our Social Program': The Doctrine of the Trinity and the Shape of Social Engagement." *Modern Theology* 14 (1998) 405–23.

Wanamaker, C. A. "Christ as Divine Agent in Paul." *Scottish Journal of Theology* 39 (1986) 517–28.

Webster, John, editor. *The Cambridge Companion to Karl Barth*. Cambridge: Cambridge University Press, 2006.

———. "Editorial: T. F. Torrance 1913–2007." *International Journal of Systematic Theology* 10 (2008) 369–71.

———. "The Holiness and Love of God." *Scottish Journal of Theology* 57 (2004) 249–68.

———. "Incarnation." In *The Cambridge Companion to the Modern Theology*, edited by Gareth Jones, 204–26. Oxford: Blackwell, 2004.

Weightman, Colin. *Theology in a Polanyian Universe: The Theology of Thomas Torrance*. New York: Lang, 1994.

Weis, John. "Calvin Versus Osiander on Justification." In *Calvin's Opponents*, edited by Richard C. Gamble, 353–69. New York: Garland, 1992.

Welch, Claude. *In This Name: The Doctrine of the Trinity in Contemporary Theology*. Eugene, OR: Wipf & Stock, 2005.

Whitenton, Michael R. "After ΠΙΣΤΙΣ ΧΡΙΣΤΟΥ: Neglected Evidence from the Apostolic Fathers." *Journal of Theological Studies* 61 (2010) 82–109.

Wigley, Stephen D. "Karl Barth on St. Anselm: The Influence of Anselm's 'Theological Scheme' on T. F. Torrance and Eberhard Jüngel." *Scottish Journal of Theology* 46 (1993) 79–97.

Wiles, M. F. "The Unassumed is the Unhealed." *Religious Studies* 4 (1968) 47–56.

Williams, Arthur. "The Trinity and Time." *Scottish Journal of Theology* 39 (1986) 65–80.

Wondra, Ellen K. "Participating Persons: Reciprocity and Asymmetry." *Anglican Theological Review* 86 (2004) 57–73.

Yeung, Hing Kau. "Being and Knowing: An Examination of T. F. Torrance's Christological Science." PhD thesis, University of London, 1993.

Young, Frances. *Sacrifice and the Death of Christ*. London: SPCK, 1975.

Zizioulas, John D. *Being as Communion: Studies in Personhood and the Church*. New York: St. Vladimir's Seminary Press, 1985.

———. *Lectures in Christian Dogmatics*. Edited by Douglas H. Knight. Edinburgh: T. & T. Clark, 2008.

General Index

Adam-Christ typology, 52–53, 56, 58, 68
adoption, 60, 71, 110–13, 183–84, 197, 209
Anselm, 2n6, 47n65, 62, 69n135
Apollinarianism, 37, 38, 67, 88, 181
apophatism, worshipful, 70, 116, 160, 162, 163, 210
Aristotle, 171, 176–77, 187
Arianism, 31, 32
Arius, 6, 32, 190
Aquinas, Thomas, 164, 176–77, 189, 196
Athanasius, 1, 5, 32, 34, 38, 40n36, 43, 44n51, 49, 54, 91, 92n36, 93, 94, 95, 101n66, 107n92, 117, 119, 121, 123–24, 145n133, 154, 161, 168n43, 170, 171, 184n109, 205
atonement
    doctrine of, ix, 47, 51, 53, 77, 105, 106, 183, 208
    extrinsicist, 35, 53, 79
    forensic, 23, 62, 79, 174
    incarnational, 49–51, 81n197, 137n97
    limited atonement, 23, 63n117, 69, 80, 104, 174, 208
    models/theories of, 52, 54, 61n111, 62n114, 63
    ontological, 53, 54n88, 61
    retrospective and prospective aspects of, 49n71, 53, 60–61
    Trinity and, 173–75
    vicarious, 38
atoning exchange, 68–71, 73, 114, 197, 208
atoning reconciliation, 30, 34, 52, 53
atoning sanctification, 136
Augustine, x, 41n43, 43, 45n57, 84n3, 118, 164, 168, 176, 177n81
Aulén, Gustaf, 62

Barth, Karl, 2, 5–6, 7, 9, 11, 15n58, 17–20, 26, 44n51, 50, 63n117, 75n164, 86n12, 107n92, 132, 145, 145n139, 161, 167, 191n136, 202, 206

Calvin, John, 6, 43, 49n71, 50–51, 68n132, 69, 71, 95n45, 100, 131, 133, 138–39, 142n120, 144, 146n139, 149n152, 179–82, 183
Calvinism, 81
    evangelical, 23
    federal, 23, 25, 52n81, 104, 173–74, 209
    scholastic, 52n81, 63, 104
    Synod of Dort, 69, 104
    Westminster, 53n86, 63n117
Campbell, John McLeod, 52n81, 63, 105, 144, 183–84
Cappadocians, 14n56, 43, 93–95, 159, 164, 166–67, 170n51
    Basil, 93, 94n40, 102n70, 117, 123, 129, 132, 167, 168n44, 169–70

General Index

Cappadocians (*cont.*)
  Gregory of Nazianzus, 40, 41,
    90, 93, 94n41, 117, 167, 170
  Gregory of Nyssa, 93, 94n40,
    122n29, 123, 170
Chalcedon, 12, 35, 37, 49
Christocentricism, xxi, 18–19,
    23, 43, 73, 75, 82, 84–85,
    87, 112n115, 115, 116, 130,
    148n147, 178n90
Christomonism, 82
Church
  body of Christ, 147–49, 152,
    154, 198, 202
  koinonia, 132–33, 148, 150–54,
    201n182, 210
  Trinity and, 198–202
Constantinople, 41, 107
Cyril of Alexandria, 43
Cyril of Jerusalem, 120

Descartes, René, 4n14, 6n22, 7
dogmatic/scientific theology, 2,
    4–15, 23, 24, 28, 139, 160,
    166n37, 206
dualism, 3, 4, 178, 190–91

Einstein, Albert, 3, 10, 11–14, 31,
    164
election, 57, 102–6, 146n139, 183
emanationism, 125, 176, 189
enhypostasia, 107, 120, 122, 124,
    146n139, 171, 186

Father, the Person of
  Arche, 93–95, 123, 167
  Monarchia, 93–95, 107, 123,
    124, 167, 213
  "two hands," 83, 107, 109–10

Gunton, Colin, 31, 69, 109, 121–22,
    129, 131n70, 135n85,
    149n151, 159, 162n21, 166,
    170n52, 189, 190n134, 192,
    199, 205, 207

Hart, Trevor, 42, 112, 180
Holy Spirit
  bond of love, 118, 125, 150
  Creator, 134–36
  filioque, 107, 123–24, 127,
    146n139, 192n145
  homoousios, 108, 117, 119,
    121–24, 126, 131, 154, 208
  Jesus Christ, and, 59, 126–33
  life in the, 137–39, 210–11, 213
  self-effacing, 120, 129–31, 140,
    148, 210

imago Dei, 50, 85, 100, 103, 110,
    137
imputation, doctrine of, 80–81
Irenaeus, 14n56, 49, 52, 53, 58,
    83, 106–7, 109, 137n97,
    148n146, 213

Jesus Christ
  anabasis and *katabasis*, 38–39,
    66, 71, 182, 206
  ascension, 51, 61, 63, 64–67, 76,
    77, 82, 88, 103, 129n57, 131,
    146n139, 182, 197, 208
  baptism, 59–61, 77, 127n52,
    152n161
  death, 39, 40, 50–51, 58, 60,
    61–64, 65, 67, 68–71, 78, 79,
    81n197, 88–89, 96, 101, 103,
    126n47, 131, 173–74, 208
  fallen humanity, 39–44, 53, 68,
    189
  homoousios, 13, 15, 31–38, 49,
    52n81, 84, 108, 117, 119
  hypostatic union, 15, 30, 46–47,
    49, 69, 72, 102, 141, 170,
    182–83, 185, 208, 210
  Immanuel, 32, 203
  obedience, 43, 52, 56, 68, 78, 79,
    88, 149
  parousia, 99, 169, 177, 192
  prokope, 58–59

240

General Index

Jesus Christ (*cont.*)
    resurrection, 51, 56, 61, 64–66, 75, 79, 80–81, 96, 101, 108, 126n47, 129n57, 152n161
    temptation, 30, 59–61, 127n52
    union with, 71–77, 78, 80, 87, 102, 113, 132–33, 150, 152, 156, 180, 182–83, 185
    virgin birth, 38, 51, 55–57, 64, 127n52
justification, 34n14, 48, 77–81, 181, 195

kata physin, 5–7, 15, 24, 91
kath hypostasin, xxi, 26, 30, 82, 96, 102, 125, 134, 148, 207, 208, 210, 212, 214
kat' ousian, 25, 207, 212, 214
kataphysic theology, xxii, 17, 24–26, 83, 84, 129, 206
kenosis, 42n44

LaCugna, Catherine, x, 159, 164, 168
Latin heresy, 53, 62
logic of grace, 9, 69, 157, 191, 203–4

Mackintosh, Hugh Ross, xix, 2, 64, 71, 101n66, 116n8
Maxwell, James Clerk, 10
Moltmann, Jürgen, 113n121, 122n30, 124, 162n22, 188, 189n127, 203
mythological thinking, 6, 32, 33n7

natural theology, 20, 44n51, 85, 115, 145n139, 176
Neo-Platonism, 176, 177, 179, 181, 189, 196
Nicea, 12, 32, 37, 49, 123
Noble, Thomas, 1, 12, 14n56, 94n41

onto-relations, 94, 116, 125, 166, 167, 190

Pannenberg, Wolfhart, 3n7, 122
panentheism, 135, 162n22, 177, 188, 189n127
participation theology, 80, 144, 176–82, 183, 186
penal substitution, 52n81, 63–64
perichoresis, 26, 82n200, 94, 124, 166–67, 170–71, 185–88
personhood, xi, 99n61, 166–67, 168–71, 200
pistis Christou, 78–79n186
Polanyi, Michael, 10, 11, 12, 144
predestination, 23, 80, 102–3, 104–5

Radical Orthodoxy, 177–79, 181, 189, 196, 197
Rahner, Karl, ix, x, 15n58, 99, 159, 160–61, 163, 164, 167, 178
regeneration, 126n47, 137, 152
revelation, x, 6, 7, 12–13, 17–19, 21, 27, 43, 44–46, 58, 81, 85–87, 91, 108–9, 116, 119–20, 130, 133, 140, 142n119, 143, 146, 154, 158, 161, 165, 172, 206, 209

sanctification, 39, 40, 40n36, 42n44, 45, 52, 56, 58, 68, 73, 74n163, 81, 89, 90, 126n47, 128, 129, 135, 137, 145, 149, 152, 183, 198, 202n184
Schleiermacher, Friedrich, 31, 116n6
Shaliach, 108–10, 127
stratification of knowledge, 11–15, 19, 21
Tertullian, 14n56, 164
theopoiesis, 196–98
theosis, xxi, 72, 111, 177, 179, 186, 193, 196–98

General Index

Trinity
  ad extra, 14, 20, 157, 160, 161, 162
  ad intra, 14, 15, 159–60, 161
  economic/evangelical, x, 13, 14, 20–21, 24, 67n127, 106, 119, 158–62, 193, 203
  immanent/ontological, x, 14, 15, 24, 34, 67n127, 119, 158–62, 163n26
  mia ousia, treis hypostaseis, 25, 202
triplex munus, 136, 139, 149n152
Torrance, Alan, 99n61, 143, 144, 167, 190n135
Torrance, James, 87–88, 106, 112–13

unio mystica, 71
universalism, 69–70, 75, 177, 208

worship, 12, 28–29, 74, 87–88, 144, 158, 185

Zizioulas, John, x–xi, 124, 129, 135n85, 166, 167, 169–70, 199

www.ingramcontent.com/pod-product-compliance
Lightning Source LLC
Chambersburg PA
CBHW050437240426
4366ICB000055B/2410